£9.95

₽X

Law

A Critical History

of

English Literature

VOLUME IV

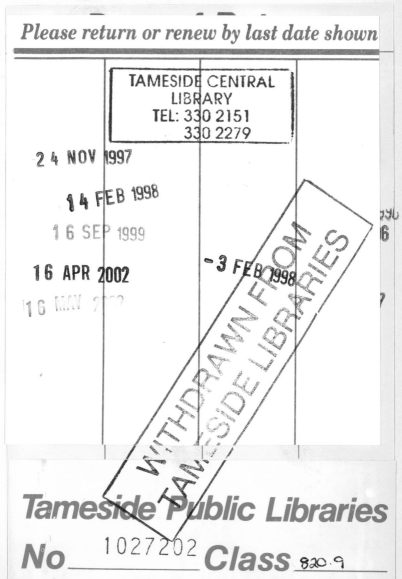

DAVID DAICHES

A Critical History

of

English Literature

SECOND EDITION

IN FOUR VOLUMES

VOLUME IV

LONDON · SECKER & WARBURG

First published in England 1960 by
Martin Secker & Warburg Limited
Michelin House, 81 Fulham Road, London SW3 6RB

Reprinted 1960, 1961, 1963, 1968

Copyright © 1960 by
THE RONALD PRESS COMPANY

Second edition 1969

Reprinted 1971, 1972, 1989, 1990

In this revised and enlarged edition the chapter on "Drama from 1700" has been considerably extended, and the epilogue to the first edition has been re-placed by two chapters on poetry and the novel in the twentieth century.

New matter Copyright © 1969
by David Daiches

ISBN 0 436 12107 7

Printed in Great Britain by
Richard Clay Ltd, Bungay, Suffolk

820·9

Contents

VOLUME IV

A C K O W L E D G E M E N T S

The publishers wish to thank the following for their permission to quote copyright material in this revised edition: J. M. Dent & Sons Ltd and the Trustees for the Copyrights of the late Dylan Thomas for three extracts from the *Collected Poems* of Dylan Thomas; Faber and Faber Ltd for extracts from the *Collected Poems* of Louis Mac-Neice, the *Collected Poems* of Edwin Muir, *The Sense of Movement* and *My Sad Captains* by Thom Gunn, *Lupercal* and *The Hawk in the Rain* by Ted Hughes; Mr M. B. Yeats and Macmillan & Co. for extracts from the *Collected Poems* of W. B. Yeats; Mr Robert Graves and Cassell & Co. for extracts from *Collected Poems 1959*.

A Critical History
of
English Literature

VOLUME IV

CHAPTER TWENTY-ONE

The Romantic Poets I: Blake, Wordsworth, and Coleridge

THE MIDDLE of the eighteenth century was (as earlier chapters have indicated) a period of transition and experiment in poetic styles and subjects, and it is interesting to see how the view of poetry as the refined and pleasing communication to educated ears of an aspect of civilized and generalized humanity seems to be abandoned in practice long before it is officially discarded by the critics. It would be a mistake, however, to diagnose all poets who show a stronger personal feeling or a passionate interest in the old and the odd and the unique as "pre-romantics" who point forward to a liberation of poetry which takes place in a violent poetic revolution at the end of the century. Shifts in the view of the nature and function of poetry proceed gradually and continuously, and the movement from the view that poetry is essentially "imitation" of human nature, in a general or ideal or deliberately synthesized or centralized or universalized sense, for the dual purpose of pleasing and edifying, and that the test of a work of literature is the degree to which it communicates its "imitation," with pleasure and edification, to its audience, to the view that poetry has for its major function the expression of the poet's emotion and that the relation of the poem to the poet is more significant than its relation to its audience—such a movement proceeds in a variety of ways throughout the century, and indeed one can sometimes see a mimetic and an expressive view of poetry held simultaneously, as in Dr. Johnson, who most strenuously urges that poetry should imitate human nature and also reproves Milton because "Lycidas" does not seem to be the overflow of genuine passion. The attitude of the self-styled Augustan age of Queen Anne was scarcely established as an attitude (and one which contained contradictory elements) before it began to be modified under the impact of a great variety of forces. The stability which English thought and society regained at the end of the seventeenth century could not in the nature of things be long maintained, and the unstable equilibrium of Queen Anne's period gave way to more complex and more obviously contradictory attitudes. Melancholy, interest in the uncivilized and the odd, a sense of change and of the impossibility of keeping static—some or all of these states of mind are seen quite early in the century; and by the time we arrive at Gray and Goldsmith and Cowper, the first and third of them are almost standard. The enclosing of village ground in the interest of big landowners and relatively large-scale farmers produced a change and unrest in the countryside (as Goldsmith's *Deserted Village* records), and the beginning of the Industrial Revolution toward the end of the century produced a very different view of the value of life in urban society from that found in the Queen Anne writers. Blake's "London" is written in another world altogether. Further, the strain of thought most clearly represented by Rousseau encouraged the notion that the conventions of civilization, far from being all that made a decent life possible, far from representing the refinement of a crude humanity into a gracious pattern of worthwhile living, represented intolerable restrictions on the individual personality and produced every kind of corruption and evil. This is in some degree the theme of Blake's *Songs of Experience* and the tenor of much of his thought, and Blake thus represents as complete an antithesis to the Augustan position of Lord Chesterfield as can be found. In this respect the poets of the full-fledged "Romantic Movement"—Wordsworth, Coleridge, Shelley, Keats, Byron—represented no advance on Blake, who had gone as far in that direction as it was possible to go. In many respects Blake is much further away from Dr. Johnson than Coleridge was, and Gray is in many senses of the word more "romantic" than Wordsworth. It does not help to label poets like Gray (still less, Blake) "pre-romantic," for that suggests that there was a single movement developing in a straight line and those who came later were more thoroughly in the movement than those who preceded them. In his view that poetry should use the real language of men, Wordsworth was closer to Dryden and Pope than to Gray—or to Coleridge. Wordsworth's "Tintern Abbey" has been called with some justice "the fine flower of eighteenth-century meditative poetry" in the tradition of the eighteenth-century poets Akenside and Thomson.

But having recognized all the difficulties in the way of describing the special qualities of the "romantic" poets, and the limited usefulness of the term "romantic," we have nevertheless to agree that the term has some justification in the light of poetic theory and practice, to realize that there *was* a significant shift in taste and attitude taking place throughout Europe in the latter part of the eighteenth century (however far back we might trace it in some of its aspects), and that this shift is reflected in literature. It is perhaps no great oversimplification to say that people of the earlier eighteenth century, in their gratitude for what civilization had achieved by way not only of making life agreeable but also of making men more amenable to regular observation, tended to think of the arts as a product of conventional urban society and of the function of literature as the representation of general aspects of human nature expressed in the language of that society and with all the resources of that society's traditional culture. One of the shifts in attitude that produced the new movement was the questioning of that very point. A generation that had survived the religious and civil disputes of the seventeenth century might well have accepted with relief and gratitude a norm of urbane moderation operating within strictly defined conventional limits, but a later generation, which had no memory of those disputes and no feeling of relief at having escaped from the perpetual conflicts between single-minded religious or political enthusiasts, came to feel a sense of constraint rather than a sense of freedom in the demands of urban gentility. They lifted their eyes from the gentlemanly limitations imposed on their horizon to contemplate with a certain fascination the world of Gothic superstition or heroic violence or primitive behavior of one sort or another. (It is worth noting that the Jacobite movement became a fertile source of literary inspiration in Scotland only *after* it had become a safely lost cause.) And of course the great paradox was that at the very core of eighteenth-century genteel culture lay two venerated works dealing with life in a very ungenteel society—the Bible and Homer. Sooner or later neoclassic culture would have had to come to terms with primitivism. Actually, it turned to investigate the "primitive" background of the Bible and Homer rather earlier than might have been expected—in Robert Lowth's *De Sacra Poesi Hebraeorum* (1753) and Robert Wood's *Essay on the Original Genius and Writings of Homer* (1769).

The extension of the horizon was social as well as chronological. Primitive and heroic societies became more and more objects of interest, and at the same time the life of men living outside the pale of urban gentility was coming to be regarded as legitimate, even as the most proper, subject matter for poetry. "Since it often happens that the most obvious phrases, and those which are used in ordinary conversation, become too familiar to the ear and contract a kind of meanness by passing through the mouths of the vulgar, a poet should take particular care to guard himself against idiomatic ways of speaking." So wrote Addison in 1712. By 1800, Wordsworth was writing: "Humble and rustic life was generally chosen, [as the subject of his poems] because, in that condition, the essential passions of the heart find a better soil in which they can attain their maturity, are less under restraint, and speak a plainer and more emphatic language; because in that condition of life our elementary feelings coexist in a state of greater simplicity, and, consequently, can be more accurately contemplated, and more forcibly communicated; . . ." Dryden and Pope had insisted that the language of poetry should be based on the conversation of gentlemen; Wordsworth held that it should be based on the conversation of peasants. Between the two views lay generations of gradual exaltation of the primitive (as opposed to the polished and highly civilized) as a state peculiarly favorable to poetry.

To look beyond the polished life of educated men in cities to wilder and cruder ways of living, to investigate ballads and folk poetry as representing something more genuinely poetic than modern literature (and Thomas Percy's *Reliques of Ancient English Poetry*, 1765, was only one of many eighteenth-century signposts in this direction, and not the clearest), to include as proper subject matter for serious poetry aspects of life which neoclassic critics would have considered "low" or "mean" ("men who do not wear fine clothes can feel deeply," said Wordsworth—a proposition Dr. Johnson would not have denied, but which he would have considered irrelevant to the production of poetry), and in general to hold that the conventions of contemporary civilization did not represent the only guarantee of valuable human behavior—we can at least say that these were attitudes which became increasingly common as the eighteenth century advanced. One might add to this list the desire to explore kinds of emotion and sensibility which someone like Lord Chesterfield would have carefully shunned as simply inviting trouble. The result of the application of these attitudes was that poetry which has come to be called "romantic" can exhibit either a calculated simplicity or an equally calculated exoticism. Coleridge, looking back many years later on the *Lyrical Ballads,* produced by Wordsworth and himself in 1798, explained that his own endeavor had been "directed to persons and characters supernatural, or at least romantic; yet so as to transfer from our inward nature a human interest and a semblance of truth sufficient to pro-

cure for these shadows of imagination that willing suspension of disbelief for the moment, which constitutes poetic faith." Wordsworth's task, Coleridge added, had been "to propose to himself as
his object, to give the charm of novelty to things of every day, and
to excite a feeling analogous to the supernatural, by awakening the
mind's attention to the lethargy of custom, and directing it to the
loveliness and the wonders of the world before us; . . ." Here we
see the poet's glance directed away from the world of social polite-
ness in two different directions—to the imaginative world of the supernatural, and to the everyday world of ordinary people outside
"society." Both poets were seeking a deeper reality than they considered any account of the urbane, conventional world of men and
manners could yield. (Not, of course, that the neoclassic writer
necessarily made the contemporary world of polite society his *subject matter;* but he addressed it as his audience.)

Thus the term "Romantic movement" has been used to cover such
different literary phenomena as the studied rustic realism of Wordsworth's *Michael*—whose most often quoted line is the impressive
matter-of-fact

And never lifted up a single stone,

and the deliberate indulgence of an exotic imagination that we find
on occasion in Coleridge and Keats and which reaches its sometimes
fantastic culmination in such a poet as Beddoes.

New political and social ideas helped to complicate the picture.
The French Revolution, the developing Industrial Revolution in
England which changed the physical appearance and the social
structure of the country, and new notions in psychology and metaphysics, all played their part. Wordsworth, enthusiastic about the
French Revolution when it first broke out, suspicious of "the increasing accumulation of men in cities," and eager to find the fundamental truths about man and the universe through a contemplation
of external nature, interested in the way in which "we associate ideas
in a state of excitement," showed the effect of these new ideas no less
than Shelley, who moved from the atheistic rationalism of William
Godwin to a passionate Platonic idealism. Byron, who combined an
antisocial irony with an equally antisocial self-pity, and Keats, who
understood what the individual life of the imagination could do for
a poet more clearly, perhaps, than any other English creative
writer, developed their own characteristic poetic themes, modes and
techniques—but they, too, like the early Wordsworth and like Shelley, were in some sense alienated from polite society; they rejected
the earlier eighteenth-century view that polite society was what

made man capable of civilized achievements, and explored areas of the imagination and the sensibility to which their readers had access only by reading and surrendering to their poems. Keats' "Eve of St. Agnes" distills the purest essence of passionate living in a society that is symbolically violent and magical, and his "La Belle Dame sans Merci" broods with strange beauty over the fact that we can love to despair what is nevertheless horrible: society as Pope or Prior saw it is wholly ignored in these poems. The poet is on his own, drawing nourishment from his solitary reading and imaginings. This means that each poem must create its own world and present it persuasively to the reader. In Keats' odes, as in Wordsworth's "Tintern Abbey," the mood and ideas of the poet are generated from a sensitive brooding over natural objects, and the poem becomes an organic unity wholly different in meaning and effect from any paraphrase or summary of its content.

It is thus to be expected that poets begin to consider a poem as an organic whole to be explained in terms of analogies from biology rather than as a craftsmanlike rendering of a previously discerned content to be discussed in mechanistic terms. Coleridge (drawing on recent German philosophy and criticism) was the first important English critic to emphasize and bring home the organic nature of form in art. Poetry which does not rest on a basis of social agreement, and one might almost add of social exclusiveness, becomes more and more concerned with the unique universe created by the individual poem, and discussions of "propriety" and "rules" become wholly irrelevant. The poem is referred back to the poet out of whose experience it is generated rather than forward to the audience whom it is designed to please or back to the nature it "imitates." What is "proper" is determined by the life generated by the specific poem, not by the attitudes of any social group to which it may be addressed. This view could not, of course, long survive, for after a period of unrest and poetic individualism, new norms arise and a new relation between the poet and his public develops: Tennyson was as much concerned with propriety as Pope, but it was a very different sort of propriety.

Whether the romantic poet moves out into the country with Wordsworth, or into a symbolic Middle Ages, as Keats sometimes did, or proceeds to have a passionate Platonic love affair with the universe such as we find in Shelley, he is illustrating in one way or another his isolation, his inability to draw nourishment from the conventional attitudes and culture patterns of a select society, his desire to escape from his lonelines not by normal human companionship but by discovering man in general through external nature.

In referring the poem back to the poet, we also associate it in a new way with the external world, which the poet's mind intuits and to which the poet's mind corresponds in a special way:

> No outcast he, bewildered and depressed:
> Along his infant veins are interfused
> The gravitation and the filial bond
> Of nature that connect him with the world.

The poet escapes from his fellows to find man through nature ("For I have learned /To look on nature, not as in the hour /Of thoughtless youth; but hearing often-times /The still, sad music of humanity"), and this is often the same thing as finding himself:

> There is a pleasure in the pathless woods,
> There is a rapture on the lonely shore,
> There is society where none intrudes,
> By the deep Sea, and music in its roar,
> I love not man the less but nature more,
> From these our interviews, in which I steal
> From all I may be, or have been before,
> To mingle with the Universe, and feel
> What I can ne'er express, yet cannot all conceal.

The voice of Byron here, for all its individuality, is also the voice of the romantic poet in his alienation from society.

William Blake (1757–1827) broke away deliberately and violently from the cultural pattern of his age and turned to the occult tradition (or traditions) in European thought—Jewish cabalistic ideas which had been floating about in certain Christian circles since the late fifteenth century, ideas from the Swedish visionary and religious thinker, Emanuel Swedenborg, from the German mystic Jakob Boehme, from the esoteric doctrine of Rosicrucianism, which had had adherents in England since Robert Fludd was initiated into the cult early in the seventeenth century, and from other mystical and magical ideas which, while far from the surface of eighteenth-century life and thought, nevertheless aroused increasing interest among some scholars and unorthodox thinkers as the century progressed. Blake himself was a visionary whose ideas often came to him in the form of clearly visualized encounters with angels, prophets, or other symbolic characters. Except for his first volume of poems, *Poetical Sketches*, Blake's poems and prophetic books were etched by himself on copper plates, with decorative designs. He was an engraver by profession, and his work as a poet and prophet was little known in his lifetime.

Blake's earliest poetry shows the influence of his reading of the lyrics of Shakespeare, of Spenser and Milton, of Thomas Chatterton and other eighteenth-century imitators of older styles. The Bible, *Ossian,* as well as the mystical writers already mentioned, also contributed to his style. *Poetical Sketches* (1783) has an Elizabethan freshness as well as some obvious signs of imitativeness. It is the lyric touch that impresses most in this volume:

> How sweet I roam'd from field to field,
>   And tasted all the summer's pride,
> 'Till I the prince of love beheld,
>   Who in the sunny beams did glide!

This is the first stanza of a poem entitled simply "Song," as are the following lines:

> My silks and fine array,
>   My smiles and languish'd air,
> By love are driv'n away;
>   And mournful lean Despair
> Brings me yew to deck my grave:
>   Such end true lovers have.

Sometimes the influence of specific Shakespearean lyrics is almost too obvious—"Memory, hither come, /And tune your merry notes," or "When silver snow decks Susan's clothes, /And jewel hangs at th' shepherd's nose"—and there are ballad imitations, Elizabethan dramatic fragments, an imitation of Spenser, meditations in a rhetorical prose which shows Ossianic influence, and invocations to each of the four seasons which show a rich pictorial sense and at times suggest Keats.

Songs of Innocence and *Songs of Experience,* etched between 1789 and 1794, "showing the two contrary states of the human soul," are more characteristic and more original. The freshness and purity of the lyrics of the former group, which deal with childhood as the symbol of an untarnished innocence which ought to be, but which in modern civilization cannot be, part of the adult response to the world, show a poetic imagination at once more direct and more visionary than that of the Elizabethan lyrists who influenced his earliest poetry. The introductory poem, "Piping down the valleys wild," "Nurse's Song," "Holy Thursday," the well-known "Little Lamb, who made thee?" have a childlike directness and a sense of controlled joy in the human and natural world that show none of the signs of a grownup writing for children or playing at being a child that so much deliberately simple poetry shows. There is an

intensity, a distilled quality about them which derives from the
prophetic and visionary Blake. The touch of moral primness in such
lines as:

> Tho' the morning was cold, Tom was happy and warm;
> So if all do their duty they need not fear harm

represents neither facile optimism nor smugness, but a half ironic,
half yearning vision of a world where, unlike this one, all men behave as Blake would have them behave. There is a biblical vision,
too, of the whole creation at peace:

> The sun descending in the west,
> The evening star does shine;
> The birds are silent in their nest,
> And I must seek for mine.
> The moon like a flower
> In heaven's high bower,
> With silent delight
> Sits and smiles on the night.
>
> Farewell, green fields and happy groves,
> Where flocks have took delight.
> Where lambs have nibbled, silent moves
> The feet of angels bright;
> Unseen they pour blessing
> And joy without ceasing,
> On each bud and blossom,
> And each sleeping bosom.
>
> They look in every thoughtless nest,
> Where birds are cover'd warm;
> They visit caves of every beast,
> To keep them all from harm.
> If they see any weeping
> That should have been sleeping,
> They pour sleep on their head,
> And sit down by their bed. . . .
>
> And there the lion's ruddy eyes
> Shall flow with tears of gold,
> And pitying the tender cries,
> And walking round the fold,
> Saying "Wrath, by his meekness,
> And by his health, sickness
> Is driven away
> From our immortal day.

"And now beside thee, bleating lamb,
I can lie down and sleep;
Or think on him who bore thy name,
Graze after thee and weep.
For, wash'd in life's river,
My bright mane for ever
Shall shine like the gold
As I guard o'er the fold."

The benedictory tone here is strengthened by the slow movement of the first four lines of each stanza and the rocking rhythm of the last four.

The sense of everything in its proper place, of peace and content, of order and spontaneity ruling together, rises from many of these poems:

When the voices of children are heard on the green
And laughing is heard on the hill,
My heart is at rest within my breast
And everything else is still.

"Then come home, my children, the sun is gone down
And the dews of night arise;
Come, come, leave off play, and let us away
Till the morning appears in the skies."

"No, no, let us play, for it is yet day
And we cannot go to sleep;
Besides, in the sky the little birds fly
And the hills are all cover'd with sheep."

"Well, well, go and play till the light fades away
And then go home to bed."
The little ones leaped and shouted and laugh'd
And all the hills echoed.

(Nurse's Song)

In *Songs of Innocence* all human desires are innocent; even discipline is innocent and makes for joy, as "Holy Thursday" shows:

'Twas on a Holy Thursday, their innocent faces clean,
The children walking two and two, in red and blue and green,
Grey-headed beadles walk'd before, with wands as white as snow,
Till into the high dome of Paul's they like Thames' waters flow.

O what a multitude they seem'd, these flowers of London town!
Seated in companies they sit with radiance all their own.
The hum of multitudes was there, but multitudes of lambs,
Thousands of little boys and girls raising their innocent hands.

Now like a mighty wind they raise to heaven the voice of song,
Or like harmonious thunderings the seats of Heaven among.
Beneath them sit the aged men, wise guardians of the poor;
Then cherish pity, lest you drive an angel from your door.

Here the conclusion makes explicit the moral, as happens more than once in these poems:

For Mercy has a human heart,
Pity a human face,
And love, the human form divine,
And Peace, the human dress. . . .

And all must love the human form,
In heathen, Turk, or Jew;
Where Mercy, Love, and Pity dwell
There God is dwelling too.

These are not versified moral platitudes, but profoundly held moral ideas springing directly from Blake's personal vision of the universe and rendered with lilting simplicity which reflects the primal nature of the subject.

"Without contraries is no progression," wrote Blake in *The Marriage of Heaven and Hell*, and his *Songs of Experience* do not simply represent the corruption of innocence by the immoral forces of society, but show the inevitable distortion and sadness which systematized empirical philosophy imposes on life, and through which the road to the ultimate wisdom lies. The true vision cannot come to the innocent, for innocence by its very nature is easily led astray, nor can it come to those who acquiesce in the distortions of experience; those distortions must be known and transcended. There is, that is to say, no road back to innocence, only a road forward through experience to a comprehensive vision. Nevertheless, *Songs of Experience* are clearly the product of disillusion, however temporary, and present an overwhelmingly sad picture of what man has made of man. "The Clod and the Pebble" sums up much of the collection:

"Love seeketh not itself to please,
Nor for itself hath any care,
But for another gives its ease,
And builds a Heaven in Hell's despair."

So sang a little clod of clay
Trodden with the cattle's feet,
But a pebble of the brook
Warbled out these metres meet:

"Love seeketh only self to please,
To bind another to its delight,
Joys in another's loss of ease,
And builds a Hell in Heaven's despite."

The picture now given of "Holy Thursday" is in striking contrast to that given in the poem of the same title in *Songs of Innocence*. The indictment is the stronger for the elemental simplicity of the language and the simple stanza form:

Is this a holy thing to see
In a rich and fruitful land,
Babes reduc'd to misery,
Fed with cold and usurous hand?

Is that trembling cry a song?
Can it be a song of joy?
And so many children poor?
It is a land of poverty!

The "Nurse's Song" of *Songs of Experience* is an even more direct counterpart to the poem of the same title in *Songs of Innocence*:

When the voices of children are heard on the green
And whisp'rings are in the dale,
The days of my youth rise fresh in my mind,
My face turns green and pale.

Then come home, my children, the sun is gone down,
And the dews of night arise;
Your spring and your day are wasted in play,
And your winter and night in disguise.

Blake's own ideas appear more strikingly in *Songs of Experience* than in the earlier poems; symbolic and visionary elements are more frequent, though the form is still simple and the images often still simple and familiar (as in "The Little Vagabond" and "The Chimney Sweeper"). The notion that spontaneity of the imagination and of the emotions has been killed by legalism and cold selfishness is expressed in many ways throughout these poems. In "The Human Abstract" Blake writes of Mercy and Pity in tones that savagely parody the kind of defense of things as they are which was so common in the eighteenth century (and which Dr. Johnson in a very different way also fiercely attacked):

Pity would be no more
If we did not make somebody poor;
And Mercy no more could be
If all were as happy as we.

> And mutual fear brings peace,
> Till the selfish loves increase:
> Then Cruelty knits a snare,
> And spreads his baits with care.

The fruit of deceit grows on a tree that springs from the analytic intellect:

> The Gods of the earth and sea
> Sought thro' Nature to find this Tree;
> But their search was all in vain:
> There grows one in the Human Brain.

Cruelty, hypocrisy, poverty, misuse of the intellect, distrust of the imagination, political and ecclesiastical institutions, frustration of desire, are associated evils which combine to corrupt and destroy:

> How the chimney-sweeper's cry
> Every black'ning Church appalls;
> And the hapless soldier's sigh
> Runs in blood down palace walls.
> But most thro' midnight streets I hear
> How the youthful harlot's curse
> Blasts the new-born infant's tear,
> And blights with plagues the marriage hearse.

And even more clearly:

> I went to the Garden of Love,
> And saw what I never had seen:
> A Chapel was built in the midst,
> Where I used to play on the green.
>
> And the gates of this Chapel were shut,
> And "Thou shalt not" writ over the door;
> So I turn'd to the Garden of Love
> That so many sweet flowers bore;
>
> And I saw it was filled with graves,
> And tomb-stones where flowers should be;
> And Priests in black gowns were walking their rounds,
> And binding with briars my joys and desires.

The change in rhythms in these last two lines provides a note both haunting and sinister.

The most striking poems in this collection are those where natural objects—flowers and animals—are used symbolically with visionary intensity. "Ah! Sunflower" with its slow movement and powerfully suggestive symbolism is a remarkable example of this:

> Ah, sun-flower! weary of time,
> Who countest the steps of the sun,
> Seeking after that sweet golden clime
> Where the traveller's journey is done:
>
> Where the youth pined away with desire,
> And the pale virgin shrouded in snow
> Arise from their graves, and aspire
> Where my sun-flower wishes to go.

The impact of this poem is powerful and immediate, and the theme (the search for redemption from frustrated desire, which destroys) clear enough even to the reader who has not worked out the symbolic pattern in any detail. The same can be said of "The Sick Rose":

> O Rose, thou art sick!
> The invisible worm
> That flies in the night,
> In the howling storm,
>
> Has found out thy bed
> Of crimson joy,
> And his dark secret love
> Does thy life destroy.

The most impressive—and by far the most well-known—of these poems is "The Tyger" (Blake's spelling is worth retaining, for it seems to emphasize the symbolic quality of the animal). The power and intensity of this short poem, achieved both by the imagery and by the way the beat of the line is handled at each point, are overwhelming, and again there is an immediate poetic meaning communicated even to those who cannot refer each image to its symbolic context. There is both beauty and terror in the elemental forces of nature. In that section of *The Marriage of Heaven and Hell* entitled "Proverbs of Hell" (and Hell for Blake was a deliberately perverse symbol of liberty and the spontaneous activity of genius), Blake wrote:

> The pride of the peacock is the glory of God.
> The lust of the goat is the bounty of God.
> The wrath of the lion is the wisdom of God.
> The nakedness of woman is the work of God. . . .
> The roaring of lions, the howling of wolves, the
> raging of the stormy sea, and the destructive sword,
> are portions of eternity, too great for the eye of man.

This provides a clue, if one were needed, to the meaning of the ambivalent symbol of the tiger.

Tyger! Tyger! burning bright
In the forests of the night
What immortal hand or eye
Could frame thy fearful symmetry?

In what distant deeps or skies
Burnt the fire of thine eyes?
On what wings dare he aspire?
What the hand dare seize the fire? . . .

When the stars threw down their spears,
And water'd heaven with their tears,
Did he smile his work to see?
Did he who made the Lamb make thee?

Tyger! Tyger! burning bright
In the forests of the night,
What immortal hand or eye
Dare frame thy fearful symmetry?

Later works of Blake can be used to explain the symbolism of the
stars throwing down their spears, but, as in Yeats' "Byzantium" which
can be explained with reference to Yeats' book *A Vision* but which
contains its own powerful meaning in immediate poetic terms,
the images have sufficient significance in their context to work effectively in the poem without reference to anything outside. Some
cosmic disaster associated with the creation, some divine miscar-
riage associated with divine creativity, is suggested here. Blake's
tiger is akin to the "rough beast" of Yeats' "The Second Coming"
in its combined suggestion of terror and wonder. The ultimate vision
of the universe is neither simple nor easy; and "the tygers of wrath
are wiser than the horses of instruction." The innocence of the lamb
is impossible in the world of experience, and the way to regeneration
lies past the tiger.

With *Tiriel* (written about 1789: it is impossible to give a date
of publication for these works of Blake for they were not published
in the regular way, and *Tiriel* was left in manuscript), Blake began
his series of works written in rhetorical free verse and using myths
and symbols of his own creation to embody his vision of the universe
and his doctrine of man. Though this kind of verse can achieve
remarkable force and eloquence, its great defect is monotony, and
few readers can read them at length without some degree of weariness:

And Har and Heva, like two children, sat beneath the oak:
Mnetha, now aged, waiting on them and brought them food and clothing;
But they were as the shadow of Har and as the years forgotten.

Playing with flowers and running after birds they spent the day,
And in the night like infants slept, delighted with infant dreams.

The same movement can be seen in *The Book of Thel* (etched in 1789):

> The eternal gates' terrific porter lifted the northern bar:
> Thel enter'd in and saw the secrets of the land unknown.
> She saw the couches of the dead, and where the fibrous roots
> Of every heart on earth infixes deep its restless twists:
> A land of sorrows and of tears where never smile was seen.

The French Revolution (1791) shows Blake's peculiar imaginative response to the events of his time, and the swinging rhetorical line is sometimes used here with great power:

> Troubled, leaning on Necker, descends the King to his
>   chamber of council; shady mountains
> In fear utter voices of thunder; the woods of France
>   embosom the sound;
> Clouds of wisdom prophetic reply, and roll over the
>   palace roof heavy.
> Forty men, each conversing with woes in the infinite
>   shadows of his soul,
> Like our ancient fathers in regions of twilight, walk,
>   gathering round the King;
> Again the loud voice of France cries to the morning; the
>   morning prophecies to its clouds.

In *Visions of the Daughters of Albion* (etched 1793), *America* (etched 1793), *Europe* (etched 1794), *Urizen* (etched 1794), *The Book of Ahania* and *The Song and Book of Los* (1795), *The Four Zoas* (first written 1795–97 and revised 1797–1804), *Milton* (1804–1808), and *Jerusalem* (1804–20), Blake presented his fully developed mythology in order to give his view of man and his destiny. Though the mythology is Blake's own and can be bewildering to the casual reader, it represents a clearly formulated system based on elements in long established mystical and symbolic tradition. Full appreciation of Blake's Prophetic Books is possible only to those who have worked out in detail his intricate system of myth and symbol; the less devoted reader can however respond to Blake's intense mythopoeic imagination, his unusual combination of the exotic and the everyday, and the beat and surge of his prophetic eloquence:

> But Los and Enitharmon delighted in the moony spaces of Eno,
> Nine times they liv'd among the forests, feeding on sweet fruits,
> And nine bright spaces wander'd, weaving mazes of delight,
> Snaring the wild goats for their milk, they eat the flesh of lambs:

> A male and female, naked and ruddy as the pride of summer.
>
> (The Four Zoas)

The lyric tone often rings out in the midst of rhetorical prophecy, as in the song at the anvil of the dancing males, caught "in the cruelties of the moral law," in *Milton*:

> "Ah weak and wide astray! Ah shut in narrow doleful form;
> Creeping in reptile flesh upon the bosom of the ground!
> The Eye of Man is a narrow orb, clos'd up and dark,
> Scarcely beholding the great light, conversing with the Void;
> The Ear a little shell, in small volutions shutting out
> All melodies and comprehending only Discord and Harmony;
> The Tongue a little moisture fills, a little food it cloys,
> A little sound it utters and its cries are faintly heard,
> Then brings forth Moral Virtue the cruel Virgin Babylon. . . ."

Biblical and Ossianic prose helped to mold the cadences of Blake's rhetorical speech, but the tone is always unmistakably Blake's:

> I behold London, a human awful wonder of God!
> He says: "Return, Albion, return! I give myself for thee.
> My streets are my Ideas of Imagination.
> Awake, Albion, awake! and let us awake up together.
> My houses are thoughts; my inhabitants, affections,
> The children of my thoughts walking within my blood-vessels,
> Shut from my nervous form which sleeps upon the verge of Beulah
> In dreams of darkness, while my vegetating blood in veiny pipes
> Rolls dreadful thro' the furnaces of Los and the mills of Satan.
> For Albion's sake and for Jerusalem thy Emanation
> I give myself, and these my brethren give themselves for Albion."

Though an understanding of the Prophetic Books depends on a knowledge of Blake's complicated mythological system, we can find in his prose aphorisms (a form of which he was a master), in various occasional writings, and in *The Marriage of Heaven and Hell*, sudden flashes that take us directly to the heart of his doctrine. "If it were not for the poetic or prophetic character, the philosophic and experimental would soon be at the ratio of all things, and stand still, unable to do other than repeat the same dull round over again." "He who sees the Infinite in all things, sees God. He who sees the Ratio only, sees himself only. Therefore God becomes as we are, that we may be as he is." "Those who restrain desire, do so because theirs is weak enough to be restrained; and the restrainer or reason usurps its place and governs the unwilling." "The reason Milton wrote in fetters when he wrote of Angels and God, and at liberty when of Devils and

Hell, is because he was a true Poet and of the Devil's party without knowing it." "For every thing that lives is holy." "In a wife I would desire /What in whores is always found— /The lineaments of gratified desire."

Blake was completely at odds with all the official doctrines of his time, theological, moral, political, and esthetic. His annotations to Sir Joshua Reynolds's *Discourses* show how bitterly opposed he was to the view that the function of the artist was to represent a generalized ideal based on selection, combination and idealization of particulars. When Reynolds writes that it would be absurd to understand poetic metaphors literally, or "to conclude that because painters sometimes represent poets writing from the dictates of a little winged boy or genius, that this same genius did really inform him what he was to write," Blake notes: "The ancients did not mean to impose when they affirmed their belief in vision and revelation. Plato was in earnest. Milton was in earnest. They believed that God did visit man really and truly, and not as Reynolds pretends. How very anxious Reynolds is to disprove and contemn spiritual perceptions." When Reynolds remarks that the "disposition to abstractions, to generalizing and classification, is the great glory of the human mind," Blake comments: "To generalize is to be an idiot. To particularize is the alone distinction of merit. General knowledges are those knowledges that idiots possess." And when Reynolds argues that "in the midst of the highest flights of fancy or imagination, reason ought to preside from first to last," Blake notes: "If this is true, it is a devilish foolish thing to be an artist." Blake's view of Reynolds is summed up in his introductory remark: "This man was hired to depress art."

Blake was not only a rebel; he was also a visionary for whom all knowledge came through the exercise of the imagination. As he noted on a descriptive catalogue of exhibitions of his paintings:

> The Last Judgment is not fable or allegory, but vision. Fable or allegory are a totally distinct and inferior kind of poetry. Vision or imagination is a representation of what eternally exists, really and unchangeably. Fable or allegory is formed by the daughters of Memory. Imagination is surrounded by the daughters of Inspiration, who in the aggregate are called Jerusalem. Fable is allegory, but what critics call the fable is vision itself. The Hebrew Bible and the Gospel of Jesus are not allegory, but eternal vision or imagination of all that exists.

The notes on this topic conclude with a passage which sums up his position vividly:

> "What," it will be questioned, "When the sun rises, do you not see a round disc of fire somewhat like a guinea?" O no, no, I see an innumerable company of the heavenly host crying, "Holy, Holy, Holy is the Lord God Almighty."

The message of Blake's Prophetic Books is not, however, simply that empirical reason and empirical science are enemies of true visionary understanding. Blake was no simpleton, and his fully developed system does not ignore the complexities and paradoxes of existence. In his myth reason is represented by Urizen, who created man, but in creating a necessarily limited creature out of the perfection and infinitude of God (who before the creation comprehended all) there must be a withdrawal or retraction of himself by God, and this can be achieved only by the limiting power of reason which produces the restricting dimensions of time and space and traps the spirit in the five senses. Urizen, who is associated with reason, law, all the restricting and limiting forces of society and the moral order, is necessary for the creation, but nevertheless must be fought against. At the other extreme is Los (imagination) and Luvah (passion). The Fall, which Urizen's act of creation made inevitable, can be undone by the reconciliation of Urizen with Los and Luvah, in order that complete and undivided man (Albion), who was divided into many at the Fall, may arise again. This resurrected and regenerated whole man is sometimes identified by Blake with Jesus Christ. Blake's use of Christian and Jewish imagery is not to be taken as a sign of his fundamental agreement with the orthodoxies of either religion; his association of Los with Satan is proof enough of that. Blake follows through his myths with massive particularization: he is not content with simple opposition of pairs of contraries, but complicates his story in order to follow the complexities of experience. Rebel though he was in so many ways, and in flat opposition to so much in the official thinking of his age, Blake also spoke for his age, rendering with his eccentric brilliance both its currents of political and social rebellion and the underground tradition of mystical and visionary ideas which had had a long history in European thought. His rhetorical utterance is sometimes wearisome and sometimes too dependent on a private mythopoeia to be readily intelligible, but his imaginative energy and his clear poetic eye are truly remarkable qualities, not easily paralleled in English poetry. However odd or willful he may sometimes appear, Blake remains one of the great—and fruitfully disturbing—figures of our literature.

Though Blake was a visionary influenced by Boehme, Swedenborg, William Law, and other prophetic and mystical thinkers as well as by some of the main underground currents of European mystical thought, he was also a man of his time who responded characteristically and sometimes violently to the main political and social events of his age, notably the French Revolution and the repressive policy which the British Government adopted in its fear of revolutionary activity at home, and the far-reaching changes in British social life which steadily developing industrialization was bringing in its wake. There runs through his work a strain of protest against tyranny and repression of all kinds and of plea for freedom both social, political, ecclesiastical, and intellectual. This strain is to be found, though in differing forms, in all the first generation of Romantic poets, at least in their youth. The French Revolution—or at least the idea of the French Revolution, and the *mystique* associated with it—was for a brief period one of the great stimulating forces on the English literary imagination. Without its impact neither Blake nor Wordsworth would have been the poets they were.

William Wordsworth (1770–1850) brought a completely new approach to the writing of English poetry. His objections to an over-stylized poetic diction, his attitude to Nature, his choice of simple incidents and humble people as subjects for his poetry—these well-known characteristics of his are but minor aspects of his revolutionary achievement. Poetry for him was primarily the record of a certain kind of state of mind, and the value of poetry for him lay in the value of the state of mind which the poem recorded. In his famous preface to the second edition of *Lyrical Ballads* (1800) Wordsworth proceeded to define poetry by first asking "What is a Poet?" A poet for Wordsworth was a man of unusual emotional vitality whose perceptions of his fellow men and of the world of external nature yielded intuitions of the relation of one to the other and of the psychological and moral truths underlying all existence. The process was not instantaneous; the high moments of perception yielded an emotion which on later recollection produced an awareness of its human and universal significance. The starting point was the poet's special kind of perception, which differed in degree rather than in kind from that of ordinary men, but of course this difference of degree was of prime importance; the end product was a record of the implications of the perception. No earlier English poet had held such a view, nor, in spite of Wordsworth's undoubted influence on later poetry, has any subsequent English poet held it in its purity. Wordsworth is thus unique in the history of English poetry.

But if Wordsworth was unique in his view of what constituted poetry, this is not to say that he was uninfluenced by the philosophical, social and political forces of his time. His views were in fact hammered out with reference to the impact cn him of the contemporary situation. The French Revolution and the social and political thought which preceded and followed from it; the eighteenth-century development of the psychological views implicit in

Locke's view of perception and knowledge; the rational and humanitarian principles of the Enlightenment; his own simple and democratic upbringing in the elemental countryside of the Lake District —these were all important factors in the development of his view of poetry. His walking tour in France and Switzerland in 1790, and his extended visit to France in 1792, had brought him into personal contact with the French Revolution and made him welcome the overthrow of corrupt and tyrannical institutions. His first poem of any length, *An Evening Walk* (1793), shows the influence of the French poets Rosset, Roucher, and Delille, who described the agricultural scene with antiaristocratic feeling, and of Saint Lambert, whose poem on the seasons (1769) emphasized the place of agriculture in the life of the nation; it also shows the influence of the eighteenth-century English topographical poem, with its meditative mood and moralizing digressions, and of eighteenth-century views of the picturesque. The verse form is the heroic couplet, for the most part end-stopped; the vocabulary is indistinguishable from that of any late-eighteenth-century minor poet. The scene is composite and idealized, though it is based on his native Lakes. *Descriptive Sketches*, also published in 1793, is another work written in a conventional mode of the day, though it bears more directly the influence of his French experience. It is a travel poem, dealing with his Alpine tour of 1790, but its main purpose is to show the free, simple, and happy life of the Swiss peasantry, who lived uncorrupted and independent in their mountain home. Wordsworth drew heavily on a translation and amplification of William Coxe's *Sketches of the Natural, Civil, and Political State of Switzerland* (1779) which had been made in clear but passionate French prose by Ramond de Carbonnières, and Ramond may be responsible for the greater vividness of Wordsworth's descriptive style. But *Descriptive Sketches*, written in heroic couplets, shows no real originality of conception or treatment. It took his unhappiness at seeing his own country proclaim war against France, his disillusion with the course taken by the French Revolution, his grasping at the rationalism and humanitarianism of William Godwin's *Political Justice* to find a compensating philosophy and his subsequent discovery that Godwin's rational scorn for the fundamental human relationships rendered his philosophy barren and unacceptable to enter a period of despair and confusion from which he was rescued by the influence of his sister Dorothy and by his friendship with Coleridge—it took all this to force him to take stock of his basic ideas and ambitions and in doing so work out a view of poetry which enabled him to develop fully his poetic genius.

It was a view which depended on the relation of the poet to the external world of man and nature; it depended, one might say, on perception. If perception failed, if the intermittent moments of awareness, the "spots of time" as he called them, failed to recur with some frequency, then poetry, which was built on recollection of such moments, would fail too, whatever the poet's technical resources. This is surely the explanation of the relatively early failure of Wordsworth's poetic gift and of its sporadic functioning even during his prime. It is true that he developed later a kind of poetry which was less dependent on the original moment, a poetry of moral rhetoric which is often (as in the best of the *Ecclesiastical Sonnets*) impressive; but the characteristic Wordsworthian poetry is different.

Lyrical Ballads were planned with Coleridge in 1797, when Wordsworth was living at Racedown with his sister. The volume appeared the following year, with four poems by Coleridge (including "The Ancient Mariner") and nineteen by Wordsworth. Wordsworth tried to explain what he was doing in a brief "Advertisement" (to be distinguished from the much more elaborate and famous Preface to the second edition) in which he declared that the materials of poetry can be found "in every subject which can interest the human mind" and explained that these poems were experiments written chiefly "to ascertain how far the language of conversation in the middle and lower classes of society is adapted to the purposes of poetic pleasure." He warned his readers that different people can mean different things by the word "poetry" and that his poems were probably not poems in the sense in which they were accustomed to use the word.

The question of poetic diction was really a red herring which has misled many since Wordsworth's day. The real point is that Wordsworth wanted a minimum of stylization because he was not working in any poetic tradition but kindling poetry from the naked experience, as it were. This is always a dangerous thing to do, for there is no conventional poetic effect (what Gerard Hopkins called "parnassian," the language of great poets when they are not working under plenary inspiration) to fall back on if the kindling does not take place. Wordsworth's task was not simply to describe the thing seen or the incident encountered or heard of, still less to render these things in a conventional poetic medium; he had to put it across with such naked force that the poet's feeling about it when he later reawoke the original perception, the poet's sense of its importance, became immediately clear to the reader. If he became simply didactic, pointing out in separate stanzas the meaning of what he had described or acting as a guide explaining the importance of what the reader was seeing, he ran the risk of separating the poet's mind from the external world. The whole point of poetry for Wordsworth was that the poet's mind and the external world came together in a special way. His poetry was intended to show that. He was thus liable to fall into one or other of two opposite faults. He failed when he told a story with a complete matter-of-fact bareness, so that the poet's sense of his relation to the events described does not come across; and when he talked *about* his sense of the significance of it all without embodying it in the narrative or the account of the situation. Success lay in walking the narrow path between didactic discursiveness and complete objectivity. Wordsworth was not a dramatic poet; his vein was what Keats called the "egotistical sublime"; he himself had to be implicated in everything he wrote, however apparently objective the narrative might be. His greatest poems are those where autobiography, perception, and narrative are woven seamlessly into one texture.

Lyrical Ballads has been taken generally to mark the true beginning of the Romantic Movement, and in so far as it contained Coleridge's "Ancient Mariner" it is indeed important in marking a significant development of the use of the supernatural in poetry. And in so far as simple diction and dealing with humble characters may be romantic, most of Wordsworth's poems in the collection may be so called. But Wordsworth's diction had little influence on the other romantic poets, either in theory or in practice; while his interest in the ballads, generally taken as a romantic characteristic, was quite different from the kind of interest shown by, say, Walter Scott, and in fact he rarely did well in the ballad form. The true ballad is above all things dramatic; it tells its story without any suggestion of the poet's sense of its significance conditioning it at every point. Wordsworth, whose task in his narrative poems was to tell a story with assumed objectivity while keeping his own sensibility before the reader continually, was really more at home in a more highly charged kind of verse. Something, of course, he learned from the ballads; the opening of "Goody Blake and Harry Gill," with its lively plunge into the very midst of the situation, seems to owe something to them; but in his best poetry he speaks in his own accents. In "The Thorn" he claimed to have put the narrative into the mouth of the retired captain of a small trading vessel, but we cannot take this very seriously, and in so far as the poem does seem to be spoken by such a character there is an unsatisfactory casualness in the narrative. "Simon Lee," again, is unsuccessful partly because the poet as observer and narrator and the poet as commentator are separate, and partly because Wordsworth's ear never seemed to have told him that certain double rhymes in English (" . . . the hall of Ivor," " . . . sole survivor") are, as W. S. Gilbert was to realize, irrepressibly comic. "The Idiot Boy" is a poem of strange power deriving from Wordsworth's ability to show the *interesting-ness* of this commonplace incident as he tells it. In the careful precision with which the actions are handled, in the clearly etched imagery and carefully chosen detail, the poet's humane curiosity shines through; the story is made to seem relevant, the characters to share something important with humanity.

"Tintern Abbey" is, of course, the star of the 1798 volume, and it shows how Wordsworth developed out of eighteenth-century meditative verse a richer and more personal idiom appropriate to a poetry which linked reflection to sensation in a new, organic way. The poem is important in giving one of the most succinct of Wordsworth's accounts of the development of his attitude to nature—moving from the animal pleasure of childhood through adolescent passion for the wild and gloomy to adult awareness of the relation of our perception of the natural world to our sense of the human and moral world—but its poetic interest lies in its brilliant combination of the lyric and the meditative, the exaltation of reminiscence into poetry through the proper handling of—to use Wordsworth's own phrase—"relationship and love." The visual scene, and emotion, the memories, the moral ideas, the benedictory attitude toward his sister, are bound up with one another with that special kind of Wordsworthian relevance that enabled him, in *The Prelude*, to write the only successful long autobiographical poem in the language.

In 1800 Wordsworth wrote the famous Preface in which he developed his view of the nature of the poetic process, the origin and purpose of poetry, and the language most suitable for it. He also explained exactly what he was trying to do in *Lyrical Ballads*:

The principal object, then, proposed in these Poems was to choose incidents and situations from common life, and to relate or describe them, throughout, as far as was possible, in a selection of language really used by men, and, at the same time, to throw over them a certain colouring of imagination, whereby ordinary things should be presented to the mind in an unusual aspect; and further, and above all, to make these incidents and situations interesting by tracing in them, truly though not ostentatiously, the primary laws of our nature: chiefly as far as regards the manner in which we associate ideas in a state of excitement.

The full significance of this description of his intention is made clear when he proceeds to define poetry by defining the poet:

. . . What is a Poet? To whom does he address himself? And what language is to be expected from him?—He is a man speaking to men: a man, it is true, endowed with more lively sensibility, more enthusiasm and tenderness, who has a greater knowledge of human nature, and a more comprehensive soul, than are supposed to be common among mankind; a man pleased with his own passions and volitions, and who rejoices more than other men in the spirit of life that is in him; delighting to contemplate similar volitions and passions as manifested in the goings-on of the Universe, and habitually impelled to create them where he does not find them. To these qualities he has added a disposition to be affected more than other men by absent things as if they were present; and ability of conjuring up in himself passions, which are indeed far from being the same as those produced by real events, yet (especially in those parts of the general sympathy which are pleasing and delightful) do more nearly resemble the passions produced by real events, than anything which, from the motions of their own minds merely, other men are accustomed to feel in themselves:— whence, and from practice, he has acquired a greater readiness and power in expressing what he thinks and feels, and especially those thoughts and feelings which, by his own choice, or from the structure of his own mind, arise in him without immediate external excitement.

The poet's record of his moments of perception and emotion necessarily give pleasure, a point on which Wordsworth insists: joy for him was a central principle of the universe and the recognition of the correspondences between the mind of man and external nature was bound to be a pleasurable experience. The poet "considers man and nature as essentially adapted to each other, and the mind of man as naturally the mirror of the fairest and most interesting properties of nature." The poet is "the rock of defence for human nature; an upholder and preserver, carrying everywhere with him relationship and love." "Relationship and love," like "joy," are key words and key concepts for Wordsworth. Nature, the individual, and human life in general are related; to see that relationship is to love one's fellows and to participate in the "joy in widest commonalty spread." As he wrote the same year as the Preface, in lines which he later prefaced to *The Excursion*:

> On Man, on Nature, and on Human Life,
> Musing in solitude, I oft perceive
> Fair trains of imagery before me rise,
> Accompanied by feelings of delight
> Pure, or with no unpleasing sadness mixed;
> And I am conscious of affecting thoughts
> And dear remembrances, whose presence soothes
> Or elevates the Mind, intent to weigh
> The good and evil of our mortal state.
> —To these emotions, whencesoe'er they come,
> Whether from breath of outward circumstance,
> Or from the Soul—an impulse to herself—
> I would give utterance in numerous verse.

This was the program, and in the subsequent, enlarged editions of *Lyrical Ballads* and in the poems of the 1807 volumes, he carried it out. His great creative period lasted for a relatively few years; after 1805, he turned more and more from a poetry based on moments of inspired perception to a rhetorical, moral poetry, often very effective in its way but lacking the characteristic Wordsworth touch. In the best poetry of his prime—in "Michael," in "Resolution and Independence," in the Lucy poems, in "The Old Cumberland Beggar" and elsewhere—he succeeds in giving moving cogency to the record of his experiences in an idiom of extraordinary freshness that combines quiet precision with poetic suggestiveness. Purity and power are the qualities of Wordsworth's most individual poems, and the power can be either of the massive, elemental kind that we find in "Michael" or something less obvious and made up of many cumulative touches of uncannily precise recording, where the clarity of perception or imagination gives the poem an atmosphere of almost trance-like lucidity; this latter quality can be found, in different ways, in the Lucy poems and in such poems as "The Idiot Boy" and "Peter Bell." And in such sonnets as that on Westminster Bridge, as well as in the poem on the daffodils and "The Solitary Reaper" and similar poems based on "emotion recollected in tranquillity," he shows to perfection his gift for giving poetic effect to the emotionally charged recall of luminous perception.

In the "Immortality Ode" Wordsworth gave his most complete account of the balance sheet of maturity as he saw it: in a poem whose very fabric is remembered perception giving way to reflection, he charts the course of the developing sensibility, much as he did in "Tintern Abbey" though in much greater detail. The naïve freshness of the child's awareness gives way to the more sober vision of the man; mediated by love, the child's perceptions in a strange world take on a meaning which, as he grows up, finally emerges as the recognition of profound human significance in nature. This poem is not—as is Coleridge's "Dejection Ode," in some ways so similar—a lament for the decline of poetic powers: it is a record of the profit and loss of growing up. The poet is only born when the child's bliss gives way to the man's more sober but more profound sensibility, which works through "relationship and love" rather than through mere animal sensation. The poem is thus one of Wordsworth's most central and illuminating works.

The poem in which Wordsworth could most fully and adequately exploit his gift for the "egotistical sublime" was *The Prelude*, that long autobiographical account of his own development. The first version—a truer and fresher though often more unequal account of the poet's development up to this time than the final form—was completed in 1805, but Wordsworth kept tinkering at it throughout the rest of his life, not only to improve crudities of expression but also to remove some of the more startling unorthodoxies of his earlier position. It was first published, in its final form, posthumously in 1850, having been originally intended as an early part of or a preliminary poem to *The Recluse,* "a philosophical poem containing views of Man, Nature, and Society . . . having for its principal subject the sensations and opinions of a poet living in retirement." *The Recluse* remained an unfulfilled ambition; only *The Excursion,* representing a small part of the total scheme, was written. But what *The Recluse* lost, *The Prelude* gained; the latter poem, drawing in characteristic Wordsworthian manner on reminiscence, rather than deriving from an abstract philosophical design, grew into a complete work in its own right, a remarkable and unique poetic autobiography. This kind of retrospective narrative poetry was particularly suited to Wordsworth's genius; when he tried narrative of any length without the personal element, the result, though interesting and sometimes impressive in its own way, was of a lower order of poetic achievement. "The White Doe of Rylstone," a narrative poem in seven cantos written in 1807, possesses imaginative vigor and shows the working of a moral imagination; but there are some lapses of style, and there is a sentimental rhetorical strain running through the poem, the moral meaning being achieved more through this means than in the manner to be found in Wordsworth at his most characteristic and greatest. The poem is by no means a failure, and some critics have considered it one of Wordsworth's greatest; but, while Wordsworthian in feeling, it is not truly Wordsworthian in treatment. Or at least it shows some of the poetic features of the later Wordsworth, the Wordsworth who achieved poetic success, when he did, in a tradition much closer to eighteenth-century rhetorical poetry than was his earlier work. One sees the transition, perhaps, in the "Ode to Duty," written in 1805 and first published in 1807, which both in theme and treatment shows Wordsworth moving away from his characteristic dependence on perception and its poetic consequences. In such later works as the *Ecclesiastical Sonnets,* written in 1821, we see the moral-rhetorical Wordsworth at his best; in "Mutability" and the sonnets on King's College Chapel, for example, he achieves a noble eloquence. But the earlier and greater Wordsworth was not content to be nobly eloquent; his best earlier poems combine the precise and the visionary in a wholly new kind of poetic activity. It was not because Wordsworth grew more and more conservative and respectable as he became older that his poetry thus changed in character; the earlier poetry was by its very nature the product of an unstable equilibrium, the balancing on a razor edge between triviality and mysticism, the exploitation in a special way of a rare kind of perceptiveness. No English poet depended more on inspiration than Wordsworth; he had no apparatus for writing his special kind of poetry when the grand primary inspiration failed. For him—as he makes clear in the famous Preface—poetry began as a state of mind, not as a feeling for words or a consciousness of craftsmanship. That helps to explain his greatness as well as his unevenness.

Wordsworth's range, even during the relatively few years of his prime, is greater than is often thought, and it is not simply a matter of his sometimes being ridiculously banal and sometimes being effectively simple. The opening of "The Idiot Boy," with its extraordinary clarity and immediacy, illustrates one kind of Wordsworthian effectiveness:

> 'Tis eight o'clock,—a clear March night,
> The moon is up,—the sky is blue,
> The owlet, in the moonlight air,
> Shouts from nobody knows where;
> He lengthens out his lonely shout,
> Halloo! Halloo! a long halloo!
>
> —Why bustle thus about your door,
> What means this bustle, Betty Foy?
> Why are you in this mighty fret?
> And why on horseback have you set
> Him whom you love, your Idiot Boy?

The uncompromising power with which Wordsworth renders the scene often brings him to the verge of the ludicrous, but he does not, in this poem, ever quite fall over; the power, the force, and purity of the realization of the action and its emotional reality, prevent that:

> And now that Johnny is just going,
> Though Betty's in a mighty flurry,
> She gently pats the pony's side,
> On which her Idiot Boy must ride,
> And seems no longer in a hurry.
>
> But when the pony moved his legs,
> Oh! then for the poor Idiot Boy!
> For joy he cannot hold the bridle,
> For joy his head and heels are idle,
> He's idle all for very joy.

Out of its context this may seem ridiculously jejune. But by the time
we reach this passage we have been forced to attend to the mother's
simple pride in her idiot son and the boy's pathetic pride in his being
sent on an errand on horseback by himself in such a way that when
the action is spelt out like this it seems appropriate and *real*. The
pony "moved his legs"; the boy is entranced by this sheer fact; and
the naked phrase emphasizes this. Similarly, when at the end of his
adventure all Johnny can tell of what happened to him "all this long
night" is that

> The cocks did crow to-whoo, to-whoo,
> And the sun did shine so cold!

we can recognize the ludicrous nature of the report while realizing
its elemental truth.

Wordsworth's most sustained effort in this style is "Peter Bell,"
the story of how an odd adventure with a faithful donkey and its
drowned master awoke in the heart of a coarse and insensitive
hawker some feeling for the sacredness of human emotions and their
relation to the natural world. The would-be humorous introduction
is hardly successful, but the tale itself is told with a stark particularization which achieves an almost trance-like clarity and compels the
reader into attention to the precise nature and meaning of the
strange things that befall Peter. The poem is both ordinary and
strange; both commonplace and fantastic. The combination can be
regarded as ludicrous, and sometimes it very nearly is—perhaps for
some readers it certainly is—but the quiet intentness with which the
whole action is realized redeems the poem and gives it its uncanny
fascination.

The style of "Michael" is very different, and its simplicity is of a
different kind. The opening has a persuasive colloquial movement
that Wordsworth often aims at but does not often succeed so fully
in attaining:

> If from the public way you turn your steps
> Up the tumultuous brook of Green-head Ghyll,
> You will suppose that with an upright path
> Your feet must struggle; in such bold ascent
> The pastoral mountains front you, face to face.
> But courage! for around the boisterous brook
> The mountains have all opened out themselves,
> And made a hidden valley of their own.
> No habitation can be seen; but they

> Who journey thither find themselves alone
> With a few sheep, with rocks and stones, and kites
> That overhead are sailing in the sky.
> It is in truth an utter solitude: . . .

As the story of the elderly rustic couple and their only child develops, the tone becomes more and more elemental and biblical—

> His days had not been passed in singleness.
> His Helpmate was a comely matron, old—
> Though younger than himself full twenty years.

The tone of grave personal meditation on the events the poet is recording is captured impressively in the verse paragraph following the account of the son's having gone to the bad and fled abroad:

> There is a comfort in the strength of love;
> 'Twill make a thing endurable, which else
> Would overset the brain, or break the heart:
> I have conversed with more than one who well
> Remember the old man, and what he was
> Years after he had heard this heavy news.
> His bodily frame had been from youth to age
> Of an unusual strength. Among the rocks
> He went, and still looked up to sun and cloud,
> And listened to the wind; and, as before,
> Performed all kinds of labour for his sheep,
> And for the land, his small inheritance.
> And to that hollow dell from time to time
> Did he repair, to build the fold of which
> His flock had need. 'Tis not forgotten yet
> The pity which was then in every heart
> For the old man—and 'tis believed by all
> That many and many a day he thither went,
> And never lifted up a single stone.

The rhythms of the blank verse here serve to give a simple gravity to the utterance, and the alternation between reflection, reminiscence and quietly controlled narrative of simple events helps to provide the poem's special kind of emotion. A somewhat similar effect is achieved in "The Old Cumberland Beggar," though here the moral is pressed more obviously.

In "Resolution and Independence" there is again a combination, often an alternation, of moral generalizations about life and narrative of the particular incident which prompted and illustrates the generalization. But here the use of the rhyme royal stanza enables Words-

worth to give a special shape to each significant moment in the
development of the moral situation:

> Such seemed this man, not all alive nor dead,
> Nor all asleep—in his extreme old age;
> His body was bent double, feet and head
> Coming together in life's pilgrimage;
> As if some dire constraint of pain, or rage
> Of sickness felt by him in times long past,
> A more than human weight upon his frame had cast.

The cliché "life's pilgrimage" is given a new, almost literal meaning
in this context. The significance of the old man's appearance to the
poet at that particular time and place, the paradoxical mood of
optimistic trust which the old man's way of life inspired in the poet,
and the sense of the old man's lack of awareness of the true significance of what he was telling, are conveyed by a deliberate juxtaposition of factual remarks and imaginative speculation, and the
sheer deliberateness with which Wordsworth sets these side by side
prevents the effect from becoming ludicrous, though it sometimes
almost becomes so, as the end of the following stanza shows:

> While he was talking thus, the lonely place,
> The old man's shape, and speech—all troubled me:
> In my mind's eye I seemed to see him pace
> About the weary moors continually,
> Wandering about alone and silently.
> While I these thoughts within myself pursued,
> He, having made a pause, the same discourse renewed.

The success of this poem, as of "Michael" and "The Old Cumberland
Beggar," lies in the air of quiet intentness which Wordsworth manages to throw over it: we sense the poet's moral feeling for his
subject by the way in which he sets about telling what happened.

"Tintern Abbey" is really a different sort of poem from any of
those just discussed. There is a confessional element here, with the
threads of the author's autobiography converging through his contemplation of a particular scene in the company of his sister, that
the others lack. This gives a pulse that throbs through the verse
suggesting control of an emotion which is only just under control,
only just mastered and understood:

>   If this
> Be but a vain belief, yet oh! how oft—
> In darkness and amid the many shapes
> Of joyless daylight; when the fretful stir

> Unprofitable, and the fever of the world,
> Have hung upon the beatings of my heart—
> How oft, in spirit, have I turned to thee,
> O sylvan Wye! thou wanderer thro' the woods,
> How often has my spirit turned to thee!

The tension here between welling emotion and formal verse rhythms, with interruptions and repetitions worked into the fabric of the verse, is most effective. We find the same thing in the benedictory conclusion addressed to his sister:

> Nor, perchance—
> If I should be where I no more can hear
> Thy voice, nor catch from thy wild eyes these gleams
> Of past existence—wilt thou then forget
> That on the banks of this delightful stream
> We stood together; and that I, so long
> A worshipper of Nature, hither came
> Unwearied in that service; rather say
> With warmer love—oh! with far deeper zeal
> Of holier love. Nor wilt thou then forget
> That after many wanderings, many years
> Of absence, these steep woods and lofty cliffs,
> And this green pastoral landscape, were to me
> More dear, both for themselves and for thy sake!

Different again in tone and style are those poems simply descriptive of experiences which moved Wordsworth at the time and which subsequently provided "emotion recollected in tranquillity." "I wandered lonely as a cloud" has a restrained eloquence, an almost rhetorical *élan*, with the pattern of rhyme and rhythm providing a relish and a sense of *Einfühlung:*

> Continuous as the stars that shine
> And twinkle on the milky way,
> They stretched in never-ending line
> Along the margin of a bay:
> Ten thousand saw I at a glance,
> Tossing their heads in sprightly dance.

"The Solitary Reaper" does something similar in a more subdued and melodious manner: here the verse movement enables the emotion to rise with the contemplation:

> Alone she cuts and binds the grain,
> And sings a melancholy strain;
> O listen! for the vale profound
> Is overflowing with the sound.

The alternation of short and long lines in the eight-line stanza is geared to the movement of the emotion to a degree unusual in Wordsworth.

There is yet another kind of Wordsworthian simplicity, related to some of those just discussed yet distinctive. It represents something he was often moving toward but rarely attained absolutely. This style is easier to illustrate than to describe:

> A slumber did my spirit seal;
>   I had no human fears:
> She seemed a thing that could not feel
>   The touch of earthly years.
>
> No motion has she now, no force;
>   She neither hears nor sees;
> Rolled round in earth's diurnal course,
>   With rocks, and stones, and trees.

The sheer purity of statement, in a style both natural and lapidary, is related to the mystical element in Wordsworth's faith. Here his mystical sense of the relation between life, death, and natural objects gives the poem its quiet intensity.

The Prelude has its barren and pedestrian patches, but Wordsworth is more successful than might have been expected in using blank verse here in order to give a sustained sense of emotional or moral excitement about his autobiography. A considerable amount of factual detail has to be carried along in the verse, and Wordsworth had no artful poetic devices for transforming these into material for richly varied poetic lines and paragraphs, as Milton had. The reader must be content to be carried on by "link" passages of wooden or meaninglessly artificial verse and diction to the next passage of liveliness and carefully wrought emotional rise and fall. Yet this is perhaps to give a wrong impression, for *The Prelude* is not a series of impressive passages (like the often quoted skating and stolen boat episodes) linked by tedious narrative. The reader is carried on, in spite of everything. The poem *moves*. It is Wordsworth's continuous interest in himself and in the meaning and moral implications of his own experiences and reactions that keeps it moving. His sustained fascination with the growth of his own mind and the general moral meaning of it all gives the poem its life, its movement, and its continuity.

Samuel Taylor Coleridge (1772–1834), who collaborated with Wordsworth in the *Lyrical Ballads* and whose association with Wordsworth was immensely profitable to both though it is not easy to determine precisely where the final balance of indebtedness lies, is a literary figure whose immense significance it is easier to agree on than it is to estimate precisely the value of each part of his uneven, often unfinished, remarkably various, ambitious, frustrated, yet in spite of everything quite astonishing literary output. He was both poet and critic, and even more than these, a seminal literary mind, whose speculations on the nature of the imagination and its capacity for reconciling opposites in art led to fruitful new ideas about the nature of art and of artistic form. He himself was anxious to present his view of poetry as part of a complete metaphysic, but the great work which was to set forth his grand system and show the relation of everything to everything else (a characteristic Coleridgean preoccupation, even an obsession) was, like so much else he planned, never written, though his *Biographia Literaria* (1817) does go part of the way toward the fulfillment of this task and owes its exasperating structure to Coleridge's continual urge to dash back to first principles before pursuing a particular argument any further. As a poet, he ranged from eighteenth-century meditative verse in the Cowper tradition and from odes in the manner of Gray and of Gray's disciple William Mason to the brilliant magical symbolic poetry of "The Ancient Mariner" and "Kubla Khan," which are "romantic" in a sense quite different from the romanticism of Wordsworth. Intermediate between the meditative and the magical are poems which, though in some ways still reminiscent of Cowper and sometimes exhibiting the Miltonizing of eighteenth-century meditative verse, show a more profound kind of reflection and a more exciting linking of the movement of thought to the almost startlingly precise visual image than the eighteenth-century meditators were capable of. The opening of "This lime-tree bower my prison," with its colloquial start, its tone of self-communion, its relish of the smallest details of natural scenery, shows one of Coleridge's poetic styles:

> Well, they are gone, and here must I remain,
> This lime-tree bower my prison! I have lost
> Beauties and feelings, such as would have been
> Most sweet to my remembrance even when age
> Had dimmed mine eyes to blindness! They, meanwhile,
> Friends, whom I never more may meet again,
> On springy heath, along the hill-top edge,
> Wander in gladness, and wind down, perchance,
> To that still roaring dell, of which I told
> The roaring dell, o'erwooded, narrow, deep,
> And only speckled by the mid-day sun;
> Where its slim trunk the ash from rock to rock
> Flings arching like a bridge;—that branchless ash,

> Unsunned and damp, whose few poor yellow leaves
> Ne'er tremble in the gale, yet tremble still,
> Fanned by the water-fall! and there my friends
> Behold the dark green file of long lank weeds,
> That all at once (a most fantastic sight!)
> Still nod and drip beneath the dripping edge
> Of the blue clay-stone.

The conclusion of this poem links observation with moral ideas in a way more reminiscent of the Wordsworth of "Tintern Abbey" than is usual with Coleridge:

> . . . Pale beneath the blaze
> Hung the transparent foliage; and I watch'd
> Some broad and sunny leaf, and lov'd to see
> The shadow of the leaf and stem above
> Dappling its sunshine! And that walnut-tree
> Was richly ting'd, and a deep radiance lay
> Full on the ancient ivy, which usurps
> Those fronting elms, and now, with blackest mass
> Makes their dark branches gleam a lighter hue
> Through the late twilight: and though now the bat
> Wheels silent by, and not a swallow twitters,
> Yet still the solitary humble-bee
> Sings in the bean-flower! Henceforth I shall know
> That Nature ne'er deserts the wise and pure;
> No plot so narrow, be but Nature there,
> No waste so vacant, but may well employ
> Each faculty of sense, and keep the heart
> Awake to Love and Beauty! and sometimes
> 'Tis well to be bereft of promis'd good,
> That we may lift the soul, and contemplate
> With lively joy the joys we cannot share. . . .

Coleridge's best meditative poetry—*sermoni propriora*, "more appropriate to conversation," as he quoted from Horace at the head of one of these poems—shows him pursuing a controlled association of ideas under the guidance of a dominating emotion and stimulated by visual images. "Frost at Midnight" is one of the finest examples of this. The poet is sitting in his cottage at night by the side of his baby in his cradle; the frost outside, the sleeping infant, the awareness of the village and its environment of "sea, and hill, and wood," the fire burning in the grate in front of him, all combine to lead him first to reflection on how thoughts and moods arise, then to a particular reminiscence of his school days, then to contrast his city childhood with that planned for his own child "By lakes and sandy shores, beneath the crags, /Of ancient mountain, and beneath the clouds," and finally to a benedictory hope for the child in the expression of which he returns to the frost outside with which the poem had begun. The opening sets the tone:

> The Frost performs its secret ministry,
> Unhelped by any wind. The owlet's cry
> Came loud—and hark, again! loud as before.
> The inmates of my cottage, all at rest,
> Have left me to that solitude, which suits
> Abstruser musings: save that at my side
> My cradled infant slumbers peacefully.
> 'Tis calm indeed! so calm, that it disturbs
> And vexes meditation with its strange
> And extreme silentness. Sea, hill, and wood,
> This populous village! Sea, and hill, and wood,
> With all the numberless goings-on of life,
> Inaudible as dreams! the thin blue flame
> Lies on my low-burnt fire, and quivers not;
> Only that film, which fluttered on the grate,
> Still flutters there, the sole unquiet thing.
> Methinks, its motion in this hush of nature
> Gives it dim sympathies with me who live,
> Making it a companionable form,
> Whose puny flaps and freaks the idling Spirit
> By its own moods interprets, every where
> Echo or mirror seeking of itself,
> And makes a toy of Thought.

This is Cowper with a dimension added. The thought is not merely cozy or self-indulgent, but exploratory, and related to "the numberless goings-on of life." The term "goings-on" was a favorite one of both Coleridge and Wordsworth, and reflects the interest each had (but each very much in his own way) in the relation between the individual mind and universe at large. The film on the grate, sign of a visitor's arrival in popular superstition, recalls how the sight of a similar film in his school days had led him to expect "townsman, or aunt, or sister more beloved." This section opens with a shift of movement:

> But O! how oft,
> How oft, at school, with most believing mind,
> Presageful, have I gazed upon the bars, . . .

In the section that follows, the movement shifts again:

> Dear Babe, that sleepest cradled by my side,
> Whose gentle breathings, heard in this deep calm,
> Fill up the interspersèd vacancies
> And momentary pauses of the thought! . . .

And the concluding verse paragraph brings the poem to rest in utter silence and peace:

> Therefore all seasons shall be sweet to thee,
> Whether the summer clothe the general earth
> With greenness, or the redbrest sit and sing
> Betwixt the tufts of snow on the bare branch
> Of mossy apple-tree, while the night thatch
> Smokes in the sun-thaw; whether the eave-drops fall
> Heard only in the trances of the blast,
> Or if the secret ministry of frost
> Shall hang them up in silent icicles,
> Quietly shining to the quiet Moon.

It is a perfectly modulated poem, the most successful of his poems in this style.

Like others of his generation, and like Wordsworth in particular, Coleridge began as a sentimental radical, influenced both by William Godwin and by the "associationist" psychologist David Hartley, enthusiastic about the French Revolution, disgusted by the oppressive policies of his own government, Utopian in his politics. He and Robert Southey, in despair at the prospects for the good society in England, planned a Utopian settlement in America, resolved to try "the experiment of perfectibility on the banks of the Susquehanna." Pantisocracy, as the plan was called, petered out, and the emigration never took place. Disillusionment with the course of the French Revolution, reflected in his poem "France: An Ode" (originally entitled "Recantation"), was one step on the road to a philosophical conservatism rooted in metaphysics and Christian orthodoxy which he spent much of his later life working out—as part of his vast unachieved total system. He had begun as a Unitarian, but later found the doctrine of the Trinity more consistent with his Hegel-like dialectic and more readily built into a view of reality in which unity in diversity and diversity in unity were key concepts. Nevertheless, in spite of his continuous interest in politics and religion, none of Coleridge's finest poetry is either political or religious, at least directly. "The Ancient Mariner," which he contributed to *Lyrical Ballads* and which he later revised to eliminate the crudely antique spellings as well as to improve in other ways, including the addition of the fascinating prose "argument," does not deal directly with any of his major interests at the time of composition. Drawing (as Livingstone Lowes' classic work has shown) on a great variety of reading, not of course always consciously, and stimulated by the revived interest in the ballads, he produced a haunting narrative poem of symbolic adventure in which the handling of visual detail, the selection and ordering of the incidents, the manipulation of the meter, the control and the deliberate varying of mood and tone, and the counterpointing between the familiar and the exotic, the factual and the magical, combine to produce an appeal so rich and powerful that any schematic analysis seems to mock rather than to explain the total meaning.

"The Ancient Mariner" opens with a ballad-like directness to introduce the Mariner himself—a figure who combines suggestions of Cain and of the Wandering Jew—buttonholing a wedding guest and keeping him from joining the wedding feast by the strange and gripping tale he tells. The Mariner's narrative begins with cheerfulness, sociability and normality:

> The ship was cheered, the harbour cleared,
> Merrily did we drop
> Below the kirk, below the hill,
> Below the lighthouse top.

But as the narrative proceeds the events become more strange and the tone both ominous and exciting:

> And now the storm-blast came, and he
> Was tyrannous and strong:
> He struck with his o'ertaking wings,
> And chased us south along.

> With sloping masts and dipping prow,
> As who pursued with yell and blow
> Still treads the shadow of his foe,
> And forward bends his head,
> The ship drove fast, loud roared the blast,
> And southward aye we fled.

> And now there came both mist and snow,
> And it grew wondrous cold:
> And ice, mast-high, came floating by,
> As green as emerald.

> And through the drifts the snowy clifts
> Did send a dismal sheen:
> Nor shapes of men nor beasts we ken—
> The ice was all between.

In this white and frozen atmosphere—where the ice is both dismal and beautiful, both rejected and desired, like the frozen world of art itself, the "cold pastoral" of Keats' "Ode on a Grecian Urn" and the marble floor of Yeats' "Byzantium"—the albatross appears and follows the ship, a bird of good omen.

> "God save thee, ancient Mariner!
> From the fiends, that plague thee thus!—
> Why look'st thou so?"—"With my cross-bow
> I shot the Albatross."

The Mariner's wanton shooting of the bird is of course the crisis of the action. This gratuitous act of destruction was a violation of a deep natural sanctity, and the rest of the poem shows how the curse fell and how it was at last if not completely cast off at least greatly mitigated. No summary or partial quotation can give any indication of the haunting richness of detail with which Coleridge develops the action from this point. The Mariner's shipmates, who take no moral responsibility for anything, at first blame him for having killed the bird "that made the breeze to blow," then, when the mist disappears and the sun rises no longer dim and red but gloriously golden and haloed, praise him for having killed the bird that brought the fog and mist. A sense of adventure and excitement rises as (in the words of the prose argument) "the ship enters the Pacific Ocean, and sails northward, even till it reaches the Line."

> The fair breeze blew, the white foam flew,
> The furrow followed free;
> We were the first that ever burst
> Into that silent sea.

But soon the wind drops, and the first part of the curse manifests itself:

> All in a hot and copper sky,
> The bloody Sun, at noon,
> Right up above the mast did stand,
> No bigger than the Moon.
>
> Day after day, day after day,
> We stuck, nor breath nor motion;
> As idle as a painted ship
> Upon a painted ocean.
>
> Water, water, everywhere,
> And all the boards did shrink;
> Water, water, everywhere,
> Nor any drop to drink.
>
> The very deep did rot: O Christ!
> That ever this should be!
> Yea, slimy things did crawl with legs
> Upon the slimy sea.

The Mariner's shipmates, speechless with thirst, looked their curses on the Mariner, and

> Instead of the cross, the Albatross
> About my neck was hung.

When at last a sail appears it is the Mariner who rouses his fellows by a strong effort of the will:

> I bit my arm, I sucked the blood,
> And cried, A sail! A sail!

But the ship brings only horror. It is a skeleton ship, and its crew consists only of "the Spectre-Woman and her Death-mate," Life-in-Death and Death, who have diced for the ship's crew. Life-in-Death has won the mariner.

> The sun's rim dips; the stars rush out:
> At one stride comes the dark;
> With far-heard whisper, o'er the sea,
> Off shot the spectre-bark.

By "the star-dogged moon" the crew die, one by one, cursing the Mariner with their last glances. At this point the wedding guest interrupts the narrative, expressing his fear that the Mariner too is a dead man; but he is reassured—the Mariner alone did not die. He was left in utter solitude on the empty sea:

> Alone, alone, all, all alone,
> Alone on a wide wide sea!
> And never a saint took pity on
> My soul in agony. . . .
>
> I looked upon the rotting sea,
> And drew my eyes away;
> I looked upon the rotting deck,
> And there the dead men lay. . . .
>
> I closed my lids, and kept them close,
> And the balls like pulses beat;
> For the sky and the sea, and the sea and the sky
> Lay like a load on my weary eye,
> And the dead were at my feet.

The Mariner remains in this desperate state for seven days and nights. Then comes a change:

> The moving Moon went up the sky,
> And no where did abide:
> Softly she was going up,
> And a star or two beside.

The suggestion of peace and coolness here is in sharp contrast to the images of heat and rot associated with the beating sun. In his prose gloss Coleridge expands his meaning here with a remarkable sentence: "In his loneliness and fixedness he yearneth towards the journeying moon, and the stars that still sojourn, yet still move onward; and everywhere the blue sky belongs to them, and is their appointed rest, and their native country and their own natural homes, which they enter unannounced, as lords that are certainly expected and yet there is a silent joy at their arrival." In the moonlight the Mariner watches the creatures of the deep, and suddenly finds himself blessing them:

> O happy living things! no tongue
> Their beauty might declare:
> A spring of love gushed from my heart,
> And I blessed them unaware:
> Sure my kind saint took pity on me,
> And I blessed them unaware.

At that moment he finds himself at last able to pray, and the albatross falls off his neck and drops "like lead into the sea."

The curse is removed, at least temporarily and partially, as a result of the Mariner's recognition of the beauty and happiness of the water snakes: he has recognized the oneness of creation and made some amends (even if he did so "unaware") for his wanton destruction of the albatross. The Mariner is able to sleep again: he dreams of rain, "And when I awoke, it rained." The ship's crew, whose bodies are now filled with angelic spirits, rise and man the ship. It is an eerie and wholly unnatural situation, with dead men working with the living Mariner, and the unnaturalness of it all is emphasized:

> The body of my brother's son
> Stood by me, knee to knee:
> The body and I pulled at one rope,
> But he said nought to me.

The release from the curse is clearly not complete, and other wonders are still in store for the Mariner. The ship moves on, and he hears supernatural music:

> And now 'twas like all instruments,
> Now like a lonely flute;
> And now it is an angel's song,
> That makes the heavens be mute.
>
> It ceased; yet still the sails made on
> A pleasant noise till noon,

> A noise like of a hidden brook
> In the leafy month of June,
> That to the sleeping woods all night
> Singeth a quiet tune.

These images of a familiar English nature contrast with the unnatural scene described a few stanzas before and emphasize the element of hope and regeneration in the Mariner's situation. The Mariner then hears two voices talking and learns from them that the Polar Spirit will require further vengeance for the killing of the albatross. Angelic power moves the ship northward faster than human life can bear, and while this rapid motion goes on the Mariner lies in a trance, from which he awakes to see again the curse in the stony eyes of the dead men, glittering in the moon. At last the ship, still supernaturally driven, reaches its home port.

> Oh! dream of joy! is this indeed
> The light-house top I see?
> Is this the hill? is this the kirk?
> Is this mine own countree?

The ship enters the harbor bay in the light of the moon. The angelic spirits leave the dead bodies and appear in their true form, a bright band of seraphs. At this point the pilot and his boy and the Hermit of the wood put out from shore to meet the boat. As they approach the ship, marvelling, there is a sudden rumble and "the ship went down like lead." The Mariner is taken ashore in the pilot's boat, and asks the Hermit to shrive him. He tells the Hermit his tale, "and ever and anon throughout his future life an agony constraineth him to travel from land to land" and tell his story and point the moral:

> He prayeth best, who loveth best
> All things both great and small;
> For the dear God who loveth us,
> He made and loveth all.

This may seem a preposterously sentimental and oversimplified moral to emerge from such a complex and powerful narrative; but it is the moral only when presented in the familiar context of routine activity in which the Mariner finds himself on his return. It is in a sense the measure of the cozy domesticity of this context—contrasting so sharply with everything that has gone before—that the moral should be put this way at this point. The total moral of the poem is of course much more complex. It is clear that the Mariner's killing of the albatross violated a fundamental principle in nature, and he had to pay for it. But there are other elements in the narrative too, and

whether or not one accepts the kind of schematic explanation of
the symbolism of the images that Robert Penn Warren has provided,
one cannot but see in the poem a richly suggestive exploration of the
nature and the claims of the imagination and indeed of the relation
of art to life. The poetic imagination is both warm, in its sympathy
with all creation, and ice-cold with the coldness of ecstasy—as he
put it in "Kubla Khan" it is

> A sunny pleasure-dome with caves of ice.

How far "The Ancient Mariner" can be said to be concerned with
the nature of the poetic imagination, or with the making of a work
of art, as in different ways Keats' "Grecian Urn" and Yeats' "Byzantium" are, is perhaps a matter of individual interpretation. The full
meaning of the poem escapes any schematic formulation. But "Kubla
Khan," with its pleasure-dome, its sacred river, its panting fountain,
its caves of ice, its ecstatic figure with flashing eyes and floating hair
who "on honey-dew hath fed, /And drunk the milk of Paradise," is
clearly about poetic creation. This record of an opium dream interrupted by a person from Porlock has traditionally been taken
to be a beautiful but chaotic fragment, in which images from
Coleridge's multifarious reading float about confusedly. But in fact
the images cohere perfectly. The opening description of the pleasure-
dome—

> In Xanadu did Kubla Khan
> A stately pleasure-dome decree:
> Where Alph, the sacred river, ran
> Through caverns measureless to man
> Down to a sunless sea—

shows that combination of pleasure and sacredness which for Coleridge as for Wordsworth was the sign of true art. The second stanza
explores the kinds of passionate and marvelous experience with
which poetry deals, goes on to suggest the way in which the creative
imagination operates, and ends with a hint of the vulnerability of
the pleasure-dome—"And 'mid this tumult Kubla heard from far
/Ancestral voices prophesying war!" The palace of art is always
under a threat from the violence of the external world.

The short third stanza brings together images of pleasure and of
the sacred river, and of coldness, of sun and of ice, which again
symbolize art or poetry:

> The shadow of the dome of pleasure
> Floated midway on the waves;

> Where was heard the mingled measure
> From the fountain and the caves.
> It was a miracle of rare device,
> A sunny pleasure-dome with caves of ice!

The final stanza recollects and describes a moment of poetic inspiration and expresses the wish that the poet could revive and prolong that moment so that he could build the palace of art and dwell there in continued poetic ecstasy:

> . . . Could I revive within me
> Her symphony and song,
>   To such a deep delight 'twould win me,
> That with music loud and long,
> I would build that dome in air,
> That sunny dome! those caves of ice!
> And all who heard should see them there,
> And all should cry, Beware! Beware!
> His flashing eyes, his floating hair!
> Weave a circle round him thrice,
> And close your eyes with holy dread,
> For he on honey-dew hath fed,
> And drunk the milk of Paradise.

The poem concludes, appropriately enough, with a picture of the poet (as seen by others) in his mood of poetic ecstasy.

"Kubla Khan" is the most perfect example of what might be called the purely magical strain in Coleridge's poetry. The third of the trilogy of poems generally associated with the Coleridgean form of romanticism ("the incidents and agents were to be, in part at least, supernatural; and the excellence aimed at was to consist in the interesting of the affections by the dramatic truth of such emotions, as would naturally accompany such situations, supposing them real") is "Christabel." But this poem is only a fragment, and though it shows some interesting metrical experiments and some intriguing deployment of "romantic" material, there is no clue as to how the story is to develop or how the different elements already introduced are to be brought into a unity, and the secondhand accounts that have come down of how Coleridge intended to continue the action are conflicting and unsatisfactory. It would seem that Humphrey House was right when he argued that in this poem Coleridge "was hampered by problems which belong to the psychological borderland where matters of religion overlap with matters of sex," and the conventions of the time would not allow of any adequate exploration of these matters in verse. This may well be the reason why Coleridge repeatedly tried to continue the poem and repeatedly failed. The inhibition lay in his age as well as in himself.

"Dejection: an Ode" suffers in the version generally available from a deliberate mutilation of the text which Coleridge wrought in order to avoid making public the precise nature of the situation (which involved his unhappy marriage and his love for Wordsworth's sister-in-law, Sara Hutchinson, to whom the poem was written) which prompted it. It is, nevertheless, even in the mutilated version, a remarkable poem, moving from a given situation described in a way reminiscent of his more conversational, meditative poems to a vivid account of the anguish with which he recognized the failure of his "shaping spirit of imagination," his loss of the sense of joy in Nature, of the inner exultation which alone could enable a poet to respond adequately to the natural world and see anything vital in it, to end with an eloquently expressed prayer that Sara may have what he has been deprived of. Wordsworth's "Immortality Ode" is also about loss, but it is about gain too, and the kind of gain which turns a heedless child, joyously responsive to Nature in an instinctive way, into a mature man who can find in Nature "thoughts that do often lie too deep for tears." The "Dejection Ode," in spite of its eloquent passages on joy, is an altogether more pessimistic poem. It has weight and passion, and the ode form, with its varying rhythms and stanza patterns, is brilliantly employed to convey the shifts from description of his present surroundings to retrospect, from speculation to sorrow and back to speculation, from elegy on his own failure of imagination to passionate prayer for the lady to whom the poem is addressed, from introspection to announcement, and other movements which give the poem power and vitality.

Coleridge's greatest fame in his lifetime was as a talker; in our own age he is generally most highly regarded as a critic. In spite of his never having completed his grand philosophical system, he did work out his theory of imagination and its implications for the art of poetry in considerable detail, notably in his *Biographia Literaria*. For Coleridge, the primary imagination is the great ordering principle, an agency which enables us both to discriminate and to order, to separate and to synthesize, and thus makes perception possible (for without it we should have only a collection of meaningless sense data). The secondary imagination is the conscious human use of this power. When we employ our primary imagination in the very act of perception we are not doing so with our conscious will but are exercising the basic faculty of our awareness of ourselves and the external world. The secondary imagination is more conscious and less elemental, but it does not differ in kind from the primary:

it projects and creates new harmonies of meaning. The employment of the secondary imagination is, in the larger sense, a poetic activity; a poem in the narrower sense is defined by Coleridge as "that species of composition, which is opposed to works of science, by proposing for its immediate object pleasure, not truth, and from all other species (having *this* object in common with it) it is discriminated by proposing to itself such delight from the *whole,* as is compatible with a distinct gratification from each component *part.*" One might, Coleridge points out, call anything in rhyme and meter a poem, but a *legitimate* poem is one "the parts of which mutually support and explain each other; all in their proportion harmonizing with, and supporting the purpose and known influences of metrical arrangement." A poem is always the work of a man employing the secondary imagination and so achieving "the balance or reconciliation of opposite or discordant qualities: of sameness, with difference; of the general, with the concrete; the idea, with the image; the individual, with the representative; the sense of novelty and freshness, with old and familiar objects; a more than usual state of emotion, with more than usual order; judgment ever awake and steady self-possession, with enthusiasm and feeling profound or vehement; and while it blends and harmonizes the natural and the artificial, still subordinates art to nature; the manner to the matter; and our admiration of the poet to our sympathy with the poetry."

The notion of organic unity within which apparent opposites are reconciled is common to Coleridge's view of poetry in the wider sense as any product of the secondary imagination and of a poem in the narrower sense of a special handling of language. "Nothing can permanently please which does not contain in itself the reason why it is so, and not otherwise," he remarked in discussing the place of rhyme and meter in a poem. Nothing that is "superadded" (in the word that Coleridge borrows from Wordsworth in argument against him), merely stuck on to give an optional extra pleasure, can really please in a poem: every one of its characteristics must *grow out* of its whole nature and be an integral part of it. This is related to Coleridge's distinction between imagination and fancy. The former is more fitted to achieve true unity of expression: "It dissolves, diffuses, dissipates, in order to recreate . . . It is essentially vital . . ." But fancy "has no other counters to play with but fixities and definites." Fancy constructs surface decorations out of new combinations of memories and perceptions, while the imagination "generates and produces a form of its own." The operation of the imagination can be compared to organic or biological growth and the forms it produces are organic forms, developing under its "shaping and modifying power" which is contrasted with "the aggregative and associative power" of the fancy. The imagination enables the poet to achieve a design which is described not in mechanistic but in biological terms, not a fitting together of a number of separable parts but a flowering forth of a central unity.

Coleridge's critical theories have proved influential in a variety of ways, especially in our own time, even though his interpreters often disagree widely with each other and find mutually incompatible positions in the master's work—that perhaps is a measure of the seminal quality of Coleridge's mind. His practical criticism, uneven as it is and proceeding by remarkable flashes of insight rather than through carefully worked out analyses, has proved equally influential and more readily comprehensible. His lectures on Shakespeare, delivered impromptu and existing only in transcriptions of the talks made as they were delivered, show some of his most mature critical thought. Earlier enthusiasts for Shakespeare had seen him as a natural genius whose lack of artistic sophistication was more than atoned for by intuitive understanding of human nature and an inspired poetic spontaneity. Coleridge (in spite of lapses into naïve moralizing) treated Shakespeare as a supreme artist, demonstrating his art with respect to the smallest details of imagery and action as well as by reference to the total organization of the plays. It is true that he had no interest in Shakespeare as a man of the theater, treating his plays as dramatic poems rather than strictly as plays and ignoring those aspects of them which derived from the technical knowledge of the experienced playwright of the Elizabethan stage rather than from the mind and art of the great poet; and in this he was followed by most of the important nineteenth-century critics of Shakespeare. But he did take Shakespeare's art seriously, and added a dimension to the criticism both of his poetic imagery and of his dramatic structure. His other miscellaneous prose, including the scattered observations on man, nature, and art which he entered in his various notebooks throughout his life, have recently come under ever-closer scrutiny, and the great modern edition of the notebooks by Professor Coburn has made public in an authentic text a mass of fascinating material which can only enhance the reputation of this versatile but disorganized genius. Illness, unhappiness, and periodical paralysis of the will combined to make much of Coleridge's work incomplete and his greatest literary ambitions unfulfilled; but what he did achieve was remarkable enough, both in itself and in its impact on the literary mind of England and America in later generations.

Robert Southey (1774–1843) was one of a trio with Wordsworth and Coleridge in the younger and more revolutionary days of them all, and was involved with Coleridge in the abortive Pantisocracy scheme. Influenced in his youth by revolutionary, rational, and sentimental currents of thought, he produced at first poems of humanitarian and egalitarian ardor, sometimes experimenting in dactylic and sapphic meters with no great skill. It was these poems that were parodied in the lively conservative periodical the *Anti-Jacobin* (1797–98), and some of these parodies (such as the verses by George Canning and J. H. Frere on the needy knife grinder) have outlived their originals. Disillusion with the course of the French Revolution led Southey eventually to an extreme Tory position in politics, but it was a romantic Toryism with something in common with the position Disraeli was to develop later in the century: he disapproved of political measures for increasing the franchise and advocated a regenerate and responsible ruling class that would promote education, humanitarian legislation, public works, and other measures to counteract the dehumanizing effects of the Industrial Revolution. He was a serious student of folklore, and the moderating of his earlier primitivism was as much the result of his growing knowledge of primitive societies as of his developing conservatism. His four epic poems—*Thalaba the Destroyer* (1801), *Madoc* (1805), *The Curse of Kehama* (1810), and *Roderick, the Last of the Goths* (1814)—dealing respectively with Mohammedan, Welsh *and* Aztec, Indian, and a combination of Christian, Gothic, and Moorish material, reflect his historical and anthropological curiosity, but their length and formlessness contributed to their rapidly falling into oblivion, though Coleridge, Scott, and Landor admired some of them. *Thalaba* is a wild tale in free, unrhymed stanzas, *Roderick* is in blank verse, the others are in varying verse forms with rhyme. But Southey's interest in the differing claims of different civilizations and the proper qualities of a hero is never sufficiently integrated into the fabric of the verse or the structure of the narrative, and though there are moments of picturesque wildness in these vast poems none can claim for a moment to be an effective epic.

His shorter and simpler poems, with their quiet humanitarian morality, are his most successful. The ballad-like simplicity of "The Battle of Blenheim" makes its point about the futility of military glory with quiet effectiveness, the repetition in the last line of the stanza of the phrase "famous victory" building up to an ironic climax at once shrewd and powerful. A poem such as "My Days among the Dead are Passed," written in the same stanza (ballad meter with an added octosyllabic couplet, a favorite of Wordsworth's also) lacks the irony of "The Battle of Blenheim" but shows that simple moral dignity which is one of Southey's most attractive qualities.

Southey was a professional writer, who took his profession with great seriousness and prepared himself for his writing by wide reading. His varied prose work includes a fair amount that has survived for the simple eloquence of the style and its quiet expository power. His *History of the Peninsula War* (1822–32) contains much skillfully deployed narrative, and the *Life of Nelson* (1813), for all its inaccuracies, has remained a minor classic of biography for the controlled power of the writing. The long, rambling work of his last years, *The Doctor*, is a miscellany of essays, jests, pedantries, and oddities centered on the reflections of a country doctor; it is remembered today only for the children's story which it includes—"The Three Bears." It is an irony of fate that this ambitious and dedicated writer of epics and histories should be remembered by one short poem and a nursery tale, but it is not altogether inappropriate, for these two works reflect the charm and the quiet assurance which, for all his prosiness and stuffiness, were an important part of Southey's character and the part that he retained from the romantic primitivism of his youth.

The Romantic Poets II:
Shelley, Keats, and Byron

WORDSWORTH LIVED to be old, respectable, and conservative, and younger and more ardent poets mourned his falling away from the revolutionary cause:

> Thou wert as a lone star, whose light did shine
>   On some frail bark in winter's midnight roar:
> Thou hast like to a rock-built refuge stood
> Above the blind and battling multitude:
> In honoured poverty thy voice did weave
>   Songs consecrate to truth and liberty,—
> Deserting these, thou leavest me to grieve,
> Thus having been, that thou shouldst cease to be.

So wrote Shelley in 1815, and Browning in "The Lost Leader" was to write something very similar thirty years later. Shelley's regrets were the more real and the more personal, for he was a true revolutionary poet in rebellion against the political, religious, and economic institutions of his country, influenced in his youth, as Wordsworth had been influenced in his, by the rationalist utopianism of Godwin's *Political Justice* and, though he was to change rapidly from a mechanistic determinism to a transcendentalist idealism, never abandoning his passionate hatred of the whole pattern that English politics assumed in panic attempts to forestall revolution at home. For this was an age of social misery and political repression: England immediately after the Napoleonic Wars came very near to revolution. Shelley died long before the tide of Victorian progress set in— even before the Reform Bill of 1832 heralded the changing of British politics. When he looked back to England from the "Paradise of exiles, Italy" (as he called it in his poem "Julian and Maddalo") it was to see

905

such things as the horrors of the "Peterloo Massacre" of 1819, where an open-air meeting of working men and women in Manchester, bearing banners inscribed with such mottoes as "Universal Suffrage," "No Corn Laws," and "Annual Parliaments" and advocating nothing more sinister than parliamentary reform, was attacked first by a local corps of volunteer cavalry and then by a body of the 15th Hussars, Waterloo veterans, with many casualties. As a result Shelley wrote "The Masque of Anarchy," one of his most powerful political poems:

> I met Murder on the way—
> He had a mask like Castlereagh—
> Very smooth he looked, yet grim;
> Seven blood-hounds followed him:
>
> All were fat; and well they might
> Be in admirable plight,
> For one by one, and two by two,
> He tossed them human hearts to chew
> Which from his wide cloak he drew . . .
>
> Last came Anarchy: he rode
> On a white horse, splashed with blood;
> He was pale even to the lips,
> Like Death in the Apocalypse . . .

The rhetorical ending is less impressive than the allegorical opening. The ill-paid or unemployed weavers and spinners of Lancashire, hard hit by the slump which followed the end of the war, passionately working and planning for parliamentary reform to which they pinned their hopes, are hardly recognizable as Shelley's "Men of England, heirs of Glory," who are exhorted to

> Rise like Lions after slumber
> In unvanquishable number—
> Shake your chains to earth like dew
> Which in sleep had fallen on you—
> Ye are many—they are few.

They were not asleep, but in those circumstances needed more of the fox than the lion. Nevertheless, the poet who addressed them was a revolutionary poet. In the same year as Peterloo he wrote his sonnet "England in 1819":

> An old, mad, blind, despised, and dying king,—
> Princes, the dregs of their dull race, who flow
> Through public scorn,—mud from a muddy spring,—
> Rulers who neither see, nor feel, nor know,

But leech-like to their fainting country cling,
Till they drop, blind in blood, without a blow,—
A people starved and stabbed in the untilled field,—
An army, which liberticide and prey
Makes as a two-edged sword to all who wield,—
Golden and sanguine laws which tempt and slay;
Religion Christless, Godless—a book sealed;
A Senate,—Time's worst statute unrepealed,—
Are graves, from which a glorious Phantom may
Burst, to illumine our tempestuous day.

Neither of these poems was published in Shelley's lifetime: revolutionary though he was, he was no poet of the people and wrote to satisfy his own idealistic passion.

Percy Bysshe Shelley (1792–1822) was of that second generation of Romantic poets that did not live to be old and respectable. In some respects he is the Romantic poet par excellence, his strange and brief life with its eccentric unworldliness, his moods of ecstasy and languor, his high mythopoeic imagination, his swooning idealism, combining to form a popular image of romanticism. From a disciple of Godwin whose youthful *Queen Mab* (written in 1812–13) tells of the corruption of man by institutions and his eventual regeneration with the defeat of Time and the dawning of the "morn of love" when "happiness /And science dawn, though late upon the earth," to a neo-Platonic theist moved by a passion which strangely combined a death-wish with a transcendental vision of a Utopia no longer worked out by reason and necessity but hardly won, after ages of accepted suffering, by the imagination and by love which the imagination strengthens, Shelley embraced many positions and spoke with many voices. Yet his voice is always recognizably his, whether in *Queen Mab* he talks of

dim forebodings of thy loveliness
Haunting the human heart

or in "Alastor" he writes

His wan eyes
Gaze on the empty scene as vacantly
As ocean's moon looks on the moon in heaven,

or in one of the incidental lyrics of *Prometheus Unbound* he exclaims

Lamp of Earth! where'er thou movest
Its dim shapes are clad with brightness,
And the souls of whom thou lovest
Walk upon the winds with lightness,

Till they fail, as I am failing,
Dizzy, lost, yet unbewailing!

or, in the same poem, talks of man

Nor yet exempt, though ruling them like slaves,
From chance, and death, and mutability,
The clogs of that which else might oversoar
The loftiest star of unascended heaven,
Pinnacled dim in the intense inane,

or talks of himself in "Epipsychidion" as

Wounded and weak and panting; . . .

or elsewhere manipulates his favorite images of sea, streams, ships, clouds, light, mountains, eagles, and serpents.

Though Shelley was expelled from Oxford as an atheist, he was never, even in his most rational Godwinian phase, a real atheist, and his idealistic, myth-making mind, haunted by Plato and indeed by Greek literature and civilization as a whole, soon led him from any simple belief in Utopian revolution to a more symbolic view of how good will eventually overcome evil. His poetry became less didactic, dwelling more on his favorite attitudes of mind for their own sake, exploring moods of mystery and languor and ecstasy, though never really giving up his "passion for reforming the world" and his high moral purpose. "Alastor, or the Spirit of Solitude" (1816) is a long poem in blank verse about "a youth of uncorrupted feelings and adventurous genius led forth by an imagination inflamed and purified by familiarity with all that is excellent and majestic, to the contemplation of the universe." But his "self-centred seclusion" leads to frustration; he attaches all his ideals to an imaginary being, for whom he seeks in vain. "Blasted by his disappointment, he descends to an untimely grave." It is a very Shelleyan theme, in its mixture of abstraction and passion, of mythopoeia and narcissism, of moralizing and emotional self-indulgence.

He lived, he died, he sung, in solitude,
Strangers have wept to hear his passionate notes,
And virgins, as unknown he passed, have pined
And wasted for fond love of his wild eyes.
The fire of those soft orbs has ceased to burn,
And Silence, too enamoured of that voice,
Locks its mute music in her rugged cell.

Words such as "pale," "wan," "dim," "pallid," "vacant," occur again
and again, even more frequently than the common "radiant," "azure,"
"dizzy." One can collect the phrases—"Now blackness veiled his dizzy
eyes," "His wan eyes /Gaze on the empty scene as vacantly," "Lost,
lost, for ever lost, /In the wide pathless desert of dim sleep," "the lone
Chorasmian shore," "And meet lone Death on the drear ocean's
waste," "In those flushed cheeks, bent eyes, and shadowy frame,"
"An image silent, cold, and motionless," "Upon those pallid lips /So
sweet even in their silence," "Encountering on some dizzy precipice,"
"O'er the fair front and radiant eyes of day," "And seemed with
their serene and azure smiles," "The passionate tumult of a clinging
hope"—they proclaim Shelley and no other poet. The appeal, it has
more than once been said, is to an adolescent ideal of poetry, to a
mood of tremulous, agonizing, rhapsodizing, yearning excitement,
and there is some truth in this. Yet this is not the whole truth. There
is a splendor of movement and a realization of visionary intensity
in the best of Shelley's poetry that move beyond the narcissism and
the mixture of rhetoric and self-pity which we find in "O world! O
life! O time!" or the beautiful but disorganized and melodramatic
elegy of "When the lamp is shattered." When his whole imagination is
involved and sustained, as it is for considerable stretches of *Prometheus Unbound* (1820), a richer and more satisfying poet emerges,
even if still a poet who operates in a realm of higher air than man as
we know him ever breathes.

Prometheus Unbound is a poetic drama in which Shelley develops
the Greek Prometheus myth in his own way so as to body forth in
symbolic terms the ultimate victory of love over hate and revenge.
In his preface Shelley announces that his poetic purpose "has hitherto
been simply to familiarize the highly refined imagination of the more
select classes of poetical readers with beautiful idealisms of moral
excellence; aware that until the mind can love, and admire, and
trust, and hope, and endure, reasoned principles of moral conduct
are seeds cast upon the highway of life which the unconscious pas-
senger tramples into dust, although they would bear the harvest of
his happiness." The lyrics sung by spirits and other characters
throughout the play show in their movement and imagery Shelley's
characteristic excitement:

> On the brink of the night and the morning
>   My coursers are wont to respire;
> But the Earth has just whispered a warning
>   That their flight must be swifter than fire:
>   They shall drink the hot speed of desire!

The cosmic setting provides scope for the idealized elemental imagery in which Shelley delighted:

> . . . A sphere, which is as many thousand spheres,
> Solid as crystal, yet through all its mass
> Flow, as through empty space, music and light:
> Ten thousand orbs involving and involved,
> Purple and azure, white, and green, and golden,
> Sphere within sphere; and every space between
> Peopled with unimaginable shapes,
> Such as ghosts dream dwell in the lampless deep,
> Yet each inter-transpicuous, and they whirl
> Over each other with a thousand motions,
> Upon a thousand sightless axles spinning, . . .

The stress is always on the elemental. "Man, oh, not men! a chain of linked thought, /Of love and might to be divided not" chants the Earth in triumph after Jupiter's overthrow and Prometheus' victory, and this preference for the generalized Man over individual men is part of Shelley's whole approach to his theme. Demogorgon's concluding announcement is full of abstractions:

> Gentleness, Virtue, Wisdom, and Endurance,
> These are the seals of that most firm assurance
> Which bars the pit over Destruction's strength; . . .

The final stanza is packed with personal moral feeling for all its generalizations:

> To suffer woes which Hope thinks infinite;
> To forgive wrongs darker than death or night;
> To defy Power, which seems omnipotent;
> To love, and bear; to hope, till Hope creates
> From its own wreck the thing it contemplates;
> Neither to change, nor falter, nor repent;
> This, like thy glory, Titan, is to be
> Good, great and joyous, beautiful and free;
> This is alone Life, Joy, Empire, and Victory.

Shelley was more successful in this kind of cosmic drama than in more limited themes. *The Cenci* (1819) a blank verse play about an innocent mother and stepdaughter who are driven frantic by the cruelty, violence, and incestuous lust of the father until in despair they conspire to murder him, is crudely melodramatic throughout, in spite of Shelley's attempt to present the story in such a way as to explore the human heart and project new moral insights. "Revenge, retaliation, atonement, are pernicious mistakes. If Beatrice had thought in this manner she would have been better and wiser; but she would never have been a tragic character," explains Shelley in his preface, and this sounds like a more interesting theory of tragedy than it turns out to be in practice. The varied echoes of Shakespeare do not help the play.

The symbolic abstractions of *The Witch of Atlas* (1820) may be in the great tradition of heterodox mysticism which modern scholars have found also in Blake and Yeats, but this does not prevent the poem, with its seventy-eight eight-line stanzas, from wearying through a lack of realization and immediacy. More appealing, in its preposterous way, is the dramatic satire *Swellfoot the Tyrant* (1820), which mingles Aristophanes, burlesque Sophocles, and the Punch and Judy show to mock George IV and Queen Caroline, in a setting reminiscent of George Orwell's *Animal Farm*. But that is not typical Shelley. The symbolic garden of "The Sensitive Plant" (1820), with its simply moving stanza and confident use of "archetypal images," is a happy rendering of a very Shelleyan theme. "Epipsychidion" (1821), in pentameter couplets, is the fullest of all Shelley's renderings of the theme of Platonic love; its combination of high Platonic idealism and self-pity hovers at times on the brink of the ridiculous, but never quite falls over:

> I never was attached to that great sect
> Whose doctrine is, that each one should select
> Out of the crowd, a mistress or a friend
> And all the rest, though fair and wise, commend
> To cold oblivion, . . .
>   Narrow
> The heart that loves, the brain that contemplates,
> The life that wears, the·spirit that creates
> One object, and one form, and builds thereby
> A sepulchre for its eternity.

Side by side with this defense of Platonic love (which must not be confined to one individual) is the note of self-pity:

> Then, as a hunted deer that could not flee,
> I turned upon my thoughts, and stood at bay,
> Wounded and weak and panting; . . .

The tone at times is almost preposterous. "The day is come, and thou wilt fly with me." "Emily, /A ship is floating in the harbour now, . . ." The sea over which the ship will sail is inevitably "azure." These are all symbolic images, but the note of personal coyness sometimes reduces their symbolic scope. And sooner or later the association of love and death, of passion and self-pity, is bound to recur:

> Woe is me!
> The wingéd words on which my soul would pierce
> Into the height of Love's rare Universe,
> Are chains of lead around its flight of fire—
> I pant, I sink, I tremble, I expire!

"Adonais" (1821), the well-known elegy on the death of Keats, profits from having to concentrate on another's death. Here Shelley marshals his neo-Platonic symbols with a splendid poetic energy, and even when, at the end, he must return to himself and his own unhappy condition he does so in such a way as to focus attention on Adonais, who has soared beyond this night:

> my spirit's bark is driven,
> Far from the shore, far from the trembling throng
> Whose sails were never to the tempest given;
> The massy earth and spheréd skies are riven!
> I am borne darkly, fearfully afar;
> Whilst, burning through the inmost veil of Heaven,
> The soul of Adonais, like a star,
> Beacons from the abode where the Eternal are.

Shelley's political and social hopes were increasingly associated with his transcendental view of the universe, and as a result his later works combine the contemporary and the mystical, even if the former is only obliquely referred to. *Hellas* (1822) is a lyric drama inspired by the possibilities of Greek revolt against Turkish domination; it does not fully come alive as a drama, however, and its great moments are lyrical outbursts such as the final chorus, one of the weightiest of Shelley's symbolic prophetic poems:

> The world's great age begins anew,
>   The golden years return,
> The earth doth like a snake renew
>   Her winter weeds outworn:
> Heaven smiles, and faiths and empires gleam,
> Like wrecks of a dissolving dream.

Shelley's final, unfinished long poem, *The Triumph of Life,* is a dream poem in *terza rima* with echoes of a number of Italian poets. It is a grim and powerful poem, for all its fragmentary nature and consequent obscurity, and the picture of all those who have been destroyed by worldliness following in Life's triumph (for it is a "triumph" in the Roman sense, and the Life that leads the captives represents not creative life but corrupting worldliness) suggests vividly the medieval Dance of Death. As the opening of "The Masque of Anarchy" showed, Shelley had a vein of grimness which he could exploit effectively when he was not vacillating between transcendental yearning and self-pity. It is not perhaps quite this quality of grimness, but a kindred quality of quietly ironic concentration which gives his sonnet "Ozymandias" such power; here again Shelley concentrates his imagery and achieves an intense realization of his subject in a way that his imagination, both soaring and narcissistic, all too rarely allowed him to do.

Of his more lyrical poems, the "Lines written among the Euganean Hills" (1818) shows Shelley's characteristic combination of the elegiac and the apocalyptic, though the octosyllabic couplets give the poem a quieter tone than that which is generally associated with this sort of theme in his work. The "Stanzas written in Dejection near Naples" (in 1818) shows the self-pitying note without the dizzy raptures:

> Yet now despair itself is mild,
> Even as the winds and waters are;
> I could lie down like a tired child,
> And weep away the life of care
> Which I have borne and yet must bear
> Till death like sleep might steal on me, . . .

The "Ode to the West Wind," in *terza rima*, has both the self-pitying and the apocalyptic note, the former almost uncomfortably naked:

> . . . Oh, lift me as a wave, a leaf, a cloud!
> I fall upon the thorns of life! I bleed!
>
> A heavy weight of hours has chained and bowed
> One too like thee: tameless, and swift, and proud.

But the poem ends on a note of exultation. A similar use of the pathetic fallacy is made in "To a Skylark" though here the stanza form of four lines of alternating rhyme and a long final line rhyming with the fourth gives a quite different kind of movement. "The Cloud" is a remarkable *tour de force*, using contemporary meteorological knowledge mythopoeically in rocking stanzas of varying length and arresting changes of tempo. These poems were published in 1820. Of those published in 1824, the song "Rarely, rarely, comest thou, Spirit of Delight," "To Night," "A Lament" ("O world! O life! O time!"), and "When the Lamp is Shattered" have for long represented Shelley's poetry to the general reader. In these poems he concentrates many of his characteristic attitudes with almost hysterical force. "To Night" is the most controlled, with its incantatory sadness. "When the Lamp is Shattered" begins in generalized sadness and ends in that strange despairing Shelleyan wildness:

> Its passions will rock thee
> As the storms rock the ravens on high;
> Bright reason will mock thee
> Like the sun from a wintry sky.
> From thy nest every rafter
> Will rot, and thine eagle home
> Leave thee naked to laughter,
> When leaves fall and cold winds come.

Modern critics have been hard put to it to trace the dialectic pattern of the imagery. Shelley's poems are not, however, constructed on a dialectical imagistic pattern. The images change with the turns of the mood, and each has its direct relation to the moment of emotion rather than to a total pattern woven by preceding and succeeding images.

The charge of adolescence cannot be completely dismissed in assessing Shelley's poetry. There is sometimes hysteria, self-pity, and emotional naïveté. But there is a power and conviction in his best work, a visionary integrity and a rhetorical force, that have their own high splendor. In the twentieth-century revolt against romanticism, or what was conceived to be romanticism, Shelley has suffered most, as was perhaps inevitable, as his kind of romantic poetry, with the suffering poet always the hero of his own poem, was the most vulnerable to the attack from the ironist and the champion of the metaphysical style. But it has been the shorter and more popular of Shelley's lyrics that have borne the brunt of this attack, and more elaborate works, such as *Prometheus Unbound* (which reflects many more aspects of Shelley's genius, including his metrical brilliance), have generally been ignored. Shelley can be strong and sweeping and resonant; he can also be languid and overtremulous. His intellectual powers were considerable and his human interests large. He grew up to a greater degree than many modern critics will admit. Yet it remains true that he is not a poet one can live with for any great length of time: one surfeits fairly soon. The lack of concrete realization in too many of his poems probably accounts for this.

The same passionate abstractions which we find in so much of Shelley's poetry is to be found in his *Defence of Poetry*, written in 1821 and published in 1840. This was first conceived as the defense of the value of poetry against the arguments brought against it by Thomas Love Peacock in *The Four Ages of Poetry* that poetry had outlived its usefulness and in an age of knowledge, reason, and enlightenment, appealed only to obscurantism and superstition. But as the work developed the polemic element disappeared and the essay emerged as a large theoretical statement of the nature and value of poetry, modeled in general style on Sidney's *Defence of Poesie*. It is a very Platonic argument: the central point is that the poet, through his use of the imagination, comes directly into contact with the world of Platonic ideas, and so with true reality (and does not simply imitate the reflections of those ideas, as Plato himself maintained). The achievement of a correspondence to the ideal order of things, Shelley argues, can be effected through any one of the arts or by lawmakers, politicians, and founders of religions. But language is the most effective servant of the imagination because the imagination itself produces it for its own needs. Harmony of utterance, achieved by the proper choice of words and the relation of sound to sense among the words, is part of the way in which the imagination achieves a correspondence with the ideal order. Another of Shelley's arguments in defense of poetry is that imagination is good because it enlarges sympathy, and as poetry strengthens the imagination it is therefore good. Shelley goes on to make a naïve identification of good art and good morals, which is quite untenable, and concludes with some ringing generalizations. "Poetry is the record of the best and happiest moments of the happiest and best minds." "Poets are the unacknowledged legislators of the world." There is some ingenious argument and some genuine (and very modern) awareness of the nature of language and of metaphor in the essay, but its tone is more important than its logic. This is the last of the great defenses of poetry done in the spirit of the Renaissance, with the added enthusiasm provided by Romantic neo-Platonism.

John Keats (1795–1821) is perhaps the greatest member of that group of second-generation Romantic poets who blossomed early and died young. He has worn better than Shelley because, for all the indulgent luxuriance of his imagery, he developed a self-discipline in both feelings and craftsmanship to which Shelley never attained. He is "Romantic" in his relish of sensation, his feeling for the Middle Ages, his Hellenism (very different from Shelley's), his conception of the role of the poet, but the synthesis he made of these elements was very much his own.

To some of his contemporaries, Keats appeared as a member of "the Cockney school of poetry," a disciple of Leigh Hunt, a dealer in self-indulgent and indelicate sentimentalities; and the notorious attacks on him in *Blackwood's* and the *Quarterly*, though inspired largely by Tory antipathy to Leigh Hunt's politics, were based on this assumption. Keats had, perhaps, something in common with Leigh Hunt, a minor poet with a freshness of sensibility and a mastery of fluid rhythms whose uncertainty of taste and lack of artistic control

(for he tended to confuse sensibility with art) kept him from developing major poetic stature; but he was certainly a member of no school.
Indeed, one of the most striking things about Keats is the independence with which he worked out his own poetic destiny, the austere
devotion with which he undertook his own artistic training. He
sought inspiration in the Middle Ages, sometimes as seen through
Spenser's idealizing eyes and sometimes more directly in the work
of Chaucer and Boccaccio; he believed, like Wordsworth, in the importance of sensation and its pleasures, but for him sensation included taste and touch and smell as well as sight and hearing, so that
in all his response to the physical world there is an impression of
testing things by the palate and of feeling their texture as well as the
Wordsworthian reactions to sight and sound. Sensation for Keats, as
for Wordsworth, was cognitive, it was a path to the knowledge of
reality, and the poet's duty was therefore to seek it and to render it
persuasively in words. This was a new view of the poet's task: Wordsworth never sought sensation, but accepted it with a "wise passive-
ness" when it came, and in any case his sensations were of the more
respectable senses, not those associated with sex or self-indulgence
or the repletion of infant feeding. In his earlier poems, where he was
simply exercising his ability to render sensations in words, Keats often
fell into a cloying abundance of imagery or a mawkishness of feeling;
yet even here there is a cunning in the use of the suggestive image
that points forward both to Tennyson and to the Pre-Raphaelites:

> For while I muse, the lance points slantingly
> Athwart the morning air; some lady sweet,
> Who cannot feel for cold her tender feet,
> From the worn top of some old battlement
> Hails it with tears, . . .

This is, of course, prentice stuff; "some lady sweet" and again the
indefinite "some old battlement" suggests an idle imagination picking
out the deliberately romantic from a dictionary of images, and this is
an artistic irresponsibility which Keats was soon to recognize and
abandon.

Keats' first long poem, *Endymion* (written in 1817 and published
the following year), is full of undisciplined luxuriance, of sensation
introduced for its own sake, so that the story—the Greek myth of
the shepherd of Mount Latmos who was loved by the Moon—is lost
in the abundance of contrived settings through which he takes his
hero: each setting being the excuse for the exercise of Keats' rich
descriptive power rather than playing an organic part in the development of the story or the enrichment of its meaning. Keats considered

the poem "a test, a trial of my Powers of Imagination and chiefly of my invention which is a rare thing indeed—by which I must make 4000 Lines of one bare circumstance." The "one bare circumstance" gets lost in the luxuriance of those 4000 lines. Keats asked: "Do not the Lovers of Poetry like to have a little Region to wander in where they may pick and choose, and in which the images are so numerous that many are forgotten and found new in a second Reading?" The answer to that question is simply that mature lovers of poetry do not ask for any such region; they do not consider a poem in that way at all. However rich in suggestive meanings a poem may be—and a great poem should of course be rich in this way—it should not be full of scattered or hidden images with the readers wandering about finding them like guests at a party game. Keats knew the faults of *Endymion* before he had finished it: in his preface he admitted that it was written in that dangerous stage between childhood and full manhood, in a period of adolescent mawkishness. But it was for him a necessary stage, and he felt a compulsion not only to write it but to publish it.

After *Endymion*, Keats matured with an almost feverish rapidity. How soon he knew or suspected that he had not long to live it is impossible to say, but the death from tuberculosis of his younger brother Tom and his own medical training must have warned him, even before the first coughing up of blood in February, 1820, that his own life was uncertain. That explains the sense of urgency we find continually in his letters: it is as though he compresses ten years of development into a few months in his desire to find his place among the great English poets before his death. Development we certainly find in *Isabella; or The Pot of Basil*, written immediately after revising *Endymion* for publication and published in 1820. Abandoning the rhymed couplet for *ottava rima*, he rendered this strange tale of love and death and devotion which he got from Boccaccio in an idiom deliberately primitive in feeling and coloring. There is a deliberate quaintness in the narrative style, of the kind that the Pre-Raphaelites were later to go in for; the emotion is not dwelt on but illustrated by carefully chosen images; everything is bathed in clear white light and the stylized primitivism—almost like figures in a tapestry—keeps the rather gruesome tale fresh and arresting. There is a ballad note in the poem, too, the concluding lament

O cruelty
To steal my Basil-pot away from me,

having something of the quality of a ballad refrain. The poem is a *tour de force*, a piece of craftsmanship which shows Keats giving objective poetic form to his response to this medieval Italian tale.

Hyperion, which followed, shows the influence of Milton in its relatively weighty and sonorous blank verse, a new style for Keats. As in *Endymion,* the theme is from Greek mythology, and again Keats endeavors to put profound allegorical meaning into the story. But though the verse has a certain grandeur, and an impressive musical and elegiac quality, and though some of the descriptive passages stand out as perfectly chiseled set pieces, the ultimate architectonic concept seems to be lacking and Keats was unable to keep the poem going. He left it unfinished, and later worked up a revised version (*The Fall of Hyperion*) where the style is less obviously Miltonic and a deliberately discursive and philosophic note is introduced; but this, too, he left unfinished, being unsatisfied with the results of Milton's influence on him ("English ought to be kept up," he said, feeling evidently that Milton's Latinized style was not for him) and believing that this was not the way to the union of thought and sensation to which he was moving in his final phase.

Both are remarkable poems, in which the story of the overthrow of the Titans by the new order of gods is treated both with imaginative particularization of setting and incident and with symbolic implications of the nature of poetry and the development of the poetic character. In the first version the poetic craftsmanship is devoted mainly to realizing the scene:

> Deep in the shady sadness of a vale
> Far sunken from the healthy breath of morn,
> Far from the fiery noon, and eve's one star,
> Sat gray-hair'd Saturn, quiet as a stone,
> Still as the silence round about his lair;
> Forest on forest hung about his head
> Like cloud on cloud. No stir of air was there,
> Not so much life as on a summer's day
> Robs not one light seed from the feather'd grass,
> But where the dead leaf fell, there did it rest. . . .

The revised version, which embodies many of the descriptive passages of the earlier version but with verbal changes directed toward a tightening up of the language and an avoidance of merely picturesque archaisms and sets the whole in a much richer context of reflection and experience, begins more discursively:

> Fanatics have their dreams, wherewith they weave
> A paradise for a sect; the savage too
> From forth the loftiest fashion of his sleep
> Guesses at Heaven; pity these have not
> Trac'd upon vellum or wild Indian leaf
> The shadows of melodious utterance.

But bare of laurel they live, dream, and die;
For Poesy alone can tell her dreams,
With the fine spell of words alone can save
Imagination from the sable chain
And dumb enchantment. Who alive can say,
"Thou art no Poet—may'st not tell thy dreams?"
Since every man whose soul is not a clod
Hath visions, and would speak, if he had loved,
And been well nurtured in his mother tongue.
Whether the dream now purpos'd to rehearse
Be poet's or fanatic's will be known
When this warm scribe my hand is in the grave.

In neither version is the relation between action, allegory, and symbol fully worked out in the texture of the verse and of the narrative; but since both are unfinished and the second a mere fragment it is impossible to pass final judgment on the structure.

The Eve of St. Agnes, written early in 1819, Keats' *annus mirabilis*, is not only Keats' greatest narrative poem (we can hardly judge the brilliantly begun but fragmentary *Eve of Saint Mark*) but the poem in which those aspects of his art which are conventionally called "romantic" are most perfectly illustrated. Written in Spenserian stanzas, it is not Spenserian in movement, though it has something of Spenser's use of color and imagery. The poem is a quintessential distillation of the medieval heroic concept of passion successfully braving chill danger. The handling of images of sensation are subordinated to the narrative with extraordinary effect, bringing out the contrast between the warm glories of sensation and the cold cruelties which threaten them. The deliberate confusion of the senses—warm colors challenging chill stone; "dainties" symbolizing sexual love; heraldic stained glass transforming the wintry moon—is part of the technique of the poem. Symbolic imagery is effectively used throughout: the storm outside, the heraldic forms and colors, the exotic list of dainties, and the central action itself, one of the great "archetypal" incidents of folklore, a young lover stealing away his bride from a hostile environment. The atmosphere is that of the Middle Ages, but a symbolic Middle Ages, where art, ritual, superstition, revelry, and luxury form a background against which nameless evil threatens perfect love. And at the end, it is all pushed back into the past—"And they are gone: aye, ages long ago. . . ."

The other products of Keats' brief maturity are equally remarkable. In the powerful short lyric, "La Belle Dame Sans Merci" he develops the folk theme of the beautiful but evil lady into an uncannily powerful expression of a sense of loss, mystery, and terror. And

in the great odes—surely too well known to require illustrative quotation—he explores the relation between pleasure and pain, happiness
and melancholy, imagination and reality, art and life, with brilliant
poetic force. The "Ode to a Nightingale" is generally admired for its
rich and slow-moving verse and for its expression of what are considered to be emotions proper to romantic poetry; but its true merits
are of a higher kind, deriving from its treatment of the nightingale's
song as a symbol of the timeless, of the escape from the world of
change and decay. Art and death are both escapes from time and
change, and the relation between art, death and life is the true theme
of the poem, as it is of the "Ode on a Grecian Urn," which considers
the arresting of life by art as both profit and loss—it represents the
escape from change and decay into eternity, but at the expense of
eternal unfulfillment: the "unravished bride" remains forever between the wedding ceremony and the bridal bed, as it were. The
theme of this poem is essentially the same as that of Yeats' "Byzantium." Both deal with the attempt to escape from

> All mere complexities,
> The fury and the mire of human veins

and the escape into the world of unchanging art is achieved at a certain price. In Yeats the wheel comes full circle, and the pulsing world
of human emotion—"that dolphin-torn, that gong-tormented sea"—
rushes in again at the end; in Keats' ode beauty and permanence remain with the figures on the urn, but they are after all only an "Attic
shape," an "attitude," a "brede of marble men and maidens" ("breed"
having become "brede," embroidery: they are eternal at the cost of
sacrificing their biological life), a "cold pastoral."

The "Ode to Autumn" stands apart: it is a brilliant rendering of a
scene and a season and a mood, the final perfection of English landscape poetry. The other odes, however, especially the "Nightingale"
and the "Grecian Urn," show Keats in his last and greatest phase finding a way of handling poetically his growing concern with the relation between art and life, beauty and reality. He treated the same
theme, less successfully, in his narrative poem Lamia, where an oversimplified, or perhaps merely confused, sense of the dichotomy between beauty and "cold philosophy" leaves the poem irritatingly un-
resolved, and has its effect, too, on the deployment of the narrative
and even the quality of the verse. A more mature poem than Endymion, it is on the whole a failure, though for very different reasons.

The Eve of St. Agnes, the odes, and a handful of sonnets represents
Keats' greatest and most mature work. They all show the disciplining
of sensation into symbolic meaning, and they show too that Attic

quality of luminous esthetic perception which Keats could achieve when he kept his sensibility under control. Indeed, though Keats was much influenced by medieval themes and by what he considered to be the atmosphere of the Middle Ages, it was ancient Greece that haunted his imagination most. He knew it mainly through Lemprière's Classical Dictionary, the Elgin Marbles, and Chapman's Homer, yet his instinctive understanding enabled him to use these inadequate approaches more effectively than many a better educated poet had used his sounder knowledge. It is probable that in the "Ode on a Grecian Urn" Keats had in mind illustrations of figures on some actual neo-Attic urns; but, if so, his profound feeling for earlier Attic art led him to describe the simpler decoration more appropriate to the earlier and greater period. Keats was the last great English poet to whom Greek mythology was a perpetual and living source not only of pleasure but of heightened awareness of the natural world.

Keats' reputation probably stands even higher than his poetry alone would have raised it because of the remarkable letters in which, with a completely unself-conscious earnestness (though with many flashes of humor), he sketched out to his correspondents his developing notions of poetry and his own aims as a poet. These letters are not only invaluable clues to our understanding of the working of Keats' genius; they are also important documents in the history of criticism and in particular of that branch of criticism which concerns the relation of art to sensation on the one hand and to thought and moral concern for one's fellow beings on the other. Wordsworth had given his view of this relationship in "Tintern Abbey," where he showed how he eventually learned to look on nature hearing "the still, sad music of humanity." Keats was concerned with this relationship all his life; he never solved his problem as neatly as Wordsworth; but then his kind of poetry depended less on his having found a personal solution. His great last poems are poetic statements of this problem and its significance rather than statements of its solution.

The disciplined sensuality of Keats' imagery looks back in some ways to Spenser and in others looks forward to Tennyson. Indeed, Keats, not Spenser, became for the later nineteenth century the "poet's poet," crushing the grapes of language on his palate and luxuriating in a magic world of dream and sorrow and sensation. This of course is a distorted view of Keats and does grave injustice to the true quality of the poems of his brief maturity; but it long remained the popular view—the view that saw the "Ode to the Nightingale" as the most poetical of all English poems because of its sensuously self-indulged melancholy. It is this quality that is still often taken as the popular criterion of romanticism; but we have seen how difficult

it is to accept any single definition of this term or to use it profitably
in critical or historical discourse. What Shelley and Keats had in
common is in many ways less interesting and less important than
what they did not have in common: a comparison between, say,
Shelley's "To a Skylark" and Keats' "Autumn" will reveal differences
in both attitude and technique of the most fundamental kind.

When we consider the third of the trio of second-generation Romantic poets, George Gordon, Lord Byron (1788–1824), the problem
of finding a common definition becomes even more complicated.
Byron, the melodramatic exploiter of his own emotions, the rhapso-
dist of Nature, the liberal idealist deploring political oppression, the
satanist deliberately reversing accepted moral attitudes, the patrician
observer contemplating history—we can find parallels to this Byron
(or rather, to these Byrons, for even here are multiple contradictions)
sometimes in Blake, sometimes in Shelley, sometimes even in Wordsworth and in Scott. Byron the ironist, the critic who wrote (in *Don
Juan*)

> Thou shalt believe in Milton, Dryden, Pope;
> Thou shalt not set up Wordsworth, Coleridge, Southey; . . .

the master of colloquial tone in verse, the inventor of a species of
discursive narrative poetry loose enough to contain an intermittent
ironic commentary on contemporary life and manners as well as on
himself, his fate, his taste, and prejudices, the wry hedonist who refuses to take himself or anybody else seriously—this Byron seems an
altogether different character, and one difficult to associate with the
Romantic movement as popularly understood. Modern criticism prefers the latter Byron, the author of *Don Juan* and *The Vision of
Judgment*, to the author of *The Bride of Abydos, Manfred*, or *Cain*,
or even of *Childe Harold's Pilgrimage*. Yet the histrionic, narcissistic,
attitudinizing Byron cannot simply be sliced off from the ironic
Byron and ignored; the two Byrons represent different sides of the
same medal, and to see the poet whole we must look at both sides.

Byron's first published collection, *Hours of Idleness* (1807), contains a number of indifferent lyrics dealing with love, regret, parting,
reminiscence, some fragments of translations from Latin and Greek
poetry, an imitation ballad, and other poems revealing a deliberately
worked up sensibility. He showed his fondness for the facile dactyllic
beat which he was to use somewhat indiscriminately in later lyrics—
"Away with your tissues of flimsy romance: /Those tissues of false-
hood which folly has wove!" "The roses of love glad the garden of
life. /Though nurtured with weeds dropping pestilent dew"; "When I
roved a young Highlander o'er the dark heath, /And climb'd thy steep

summit, oh Morven of snow." He uses this beat more effectively in a later poem, the well-known "Destruction of Sennacherib" (in *Hebrew Melodies*, 1815). *Hours of Idleness* also contains verses in heroic couplets, in octosyllabic couplets, and in a variety of stanza forms. *English Bards and Scotch Reviewers* (1809) is in quite a different vein: it is an attack on contemporary writers and critics who had annoyed him or with whom, sometimes for the most casual reasons, he felt annoyed, done in heroic couplets modeled on Pope's satirical verse but far less cunningly wrought and carried on by a negligent energy which later Byron was to learn to harness more effectively.

A life of self-conscious dissipation in England in 1809, was followed by a journey to Spain, Malta, Albania, and Greece which lasted almost two years and provided Byron not only with abundant new material for his poetry but also with an opportunity to build up the character of the sensitive and high-minded wanderer, exiled from a society which he despised yet suffering under his exile—a character which he was later to develop much further, as the characteristic Byronic hero (and also, of course, a self-portrait), after the collapse of his marriage and attendant scandals had driven him into permanent exile abroad, in 1816. The travels of 1809–11 bore fruit in the first two cantos of *Childe Harold's Pilgrimage*, 1812. The hero's travels follow Byron's, and Childe Harold himself, for all Byron's disclaimers, is a projection of the poet, a sensitive, disillusioned, generous-minded character, prone to rhapsodize over history and to exhort degenerate nations to arise and recover their lost glory. He is also the disenchanted libertine—

> For he through Sin's long labyrinth had run,
> Nor made atonement when he did amiss,
> Had sigh'd to many though he loved but one,
> And that loved one, alas! could ne'er be his—

racked by "disappointed passion," who has been alone and unloved in the midst of the wildest revelry. The description of the places visited, interspersed with moral, political, historical, and exhibitionist reflections and with lyrical interludes and apostrophes done in a variety of stanzas, is carried on in the Spenserian stanza, not the most appropriate form for the characteristic Byronic mélange, but handled nevertheless with a surprising variety and at times with remarkable vigor. For all its gesturing and its cultivated moods, this first instalment of *Childe Harold* does possess energy and variety; some of the descriptive passages have a picturesque vividness, and the account of Albania, then a quite unknown country to Englishmen, is particularly wild and colorful. Byron was entranced by "The wild Albanian

kirtled to his knee, /With shawl-girt head and ornamented gun,"
and describes the life he leads with exalted gusto. This exaltation
can however prove fatal to Byron: while it can elevate his mock-
antique verse to a high descriptive style—

> On the smooth shore the night-fires brightly blazed.
> The feast was done, the red wine circling fast,
> And he that unawares had there ygazed
> With gaping wonderment had stared aghast;
> For ere night's midmost, stillest hour was past,
> The native revels of the troop began;
> Each Palikar his sabre from him cast,
> And bounding hand in hand, man link'd to man,
> Yelling their uncouth dirge, long daunced the kirtled clan—

it can also lead him, as in his attempt to reproduce the "uncouth
dirge," to gross absurdities:

> Oh! who is more brave than a dark Suliote,
> In his snowy camese and his shaggy capote? . . .

Canto II ends with the poet brooding—as he was to do again, more
than once—over the degenerate state of Greece:

> Yet are thy skies as blue, thy crags as wild;
> Sweet are thy groves, and verdant are thy fields,
> Thine olive ripe as when Minerva smiled,
> And still his honey'd wealth Hymettus yields;
> There the blithe bee his fragrant fortress builds,
> The freeborn wanderer of the mountain-air;
> Apollo still thy long, long summer gilds,
> Still in his beam Mendeli's marbles glare;
> Art, Glory, Freedom fail, but Nature still is fair.

Byron's phil-Hellenism is more political than Keats', more melodramatic and less centrally cultural than Matthew Arnold's; but it is
part of a mood that worked on the English imagination in a great
variety of ways throughout the nineteenth century.

Byron's travels also provided subjects for more lyrical treatment,
and he produced a number of short poems recalling experiences in
Greece and elsewhere which show fluency and musical movement—
"Maid of Athens, ere we part," "The Girl of Cadiz," and others. Emotional problems encountered between his return home and his final
departure into exile prompted further lyrics, some of them rather
crudely histrionic ("Remember thee! remember thee!" "I speak not, I
trace not, I breathe not thy name, /There is grief in the sound, there
is guilt in the fame"; "When coldness wraps this suffering clay") but

a few showing more quietness and control and so allowing the slow musical movement to gain its effect:

> She walks in beauty, like the night
>   Of cloudless climes and starry skies;
> And all that's best of dark and bright
>   Meet in her aspect and her eyes:
> Thus mellow'd to that tender light
>   Which heaven to gaudy day denies.

The charm of such lyrical poetry may be superficial, but it is nevertheless real. The same note can be heard in "Stanzas for Music" ("There be none of Beauty's daughters /With a magic like thee"), but the other Byron also speaks in these lyrics, as in the lines "Written after Swimming from Sestos to Abydos," where he boasts of having swum the Hellespont as Leander had done and concludes

> 'T were hard to say who fared the best:
>   Sad mortals! thus the gods still plague you!
> He lost his labour, I my jest;
>   For he was drown'd, and I've the ague.

But the most memorable of Byron's lyrics is a simple little poem of four short stanzas he wrote in Italy in 1817, remembering the refrain of an old Scottish song and suddenly facing the loss of his youth and of his emotional venturesomeness:

> So we'll go no more a-roving
>   So late into the night,
> Though the heart be still as loving,
>   And the moon be still as bright. . . .

In 1813, Byron published *The Giaour*, the first of his series of melodramatic verse tales which ousted Scott from his position as chief purveyor of romantic verse narrative. *The Bride of Abydos, a Turkish Tale* followed later in the same year, and *The Corsair* and *Lara* in 1814. These wildly melodramatic stories of heroism and passion in exotic settings, with lonely and moody heroes enmeshed in circumstances that involve both love and alienation and lead predictably to doom, are told in a variety of verse forms—the octosyllabic couplet predominating in the first two and the heroic couplet in the third, but all have interludes in other measures—and sweep on with that negligent energy so characteristic of Byron. Preposterous as they are, with their thumping theatricality and all too obvious projection of the "Byronic" character, their great contemporary popularity is understandable: the immense *brio* with which Byron carries it off, and the dangerous deeps of illicit passion, incest, morbid pride, and other

SHELLEY, KEATS, AND BYRON

moral heresies and ambiguities, which Byron skirts without really entering, made Scott's more conventional heroic scenes appear tame by comparison and produced a kind of excitement somewhat akin to that produced by the Gothic terror novel but more extreme because more concentrated and more dashing. *The Siege of Corinth* (1816) continued the series with a violent story of apostasy, love, and self-sacrifice set amid the violence of the Turkish siege of Corinth of 1715, and *Parisina,* in the same year, takes a story of incest and revenge from Gibbon and works it up with deliberate "Gothic" horror. *The Prisoner of Chillon* (1816) is a monologue in which the hero recounts with masochistic relish his terrible experiences in a long and cruel imprisonment for righteousness' sake:

> My hair is grey, but not with years,
>   Nor grew it white
>   In a single night,
> As men's have grown from sudden fears:
> My limbs are bow'd, though not with toil,
>   But rusted with a vile repose,
> For they have been a dungeon's spoil,
>   And mine has been the fate of those
> To whom the goodly earth and air
> Are bann'd, and barr'd—forbidden fare:
> But this was for my father's faith
> I suffer'd chains and courted death; . . .

The third canto of *Childe Harold* appeared in 1816, and the fourth in 1818. Here Byron drops the mask—quite openly in the fourth canto —and the character of Childe Harold gives way wholly to that of Byron, while at the same time the occasional archaisms of the earlier cantos are dropped and the poem gains in directness and flexibility. There is a curious coming together of art and life here, with life imitating art. Byron has been acting out his own melodramatic imaginings, becoming more and more the Byronic hero he had created: he is by this time a genuine outcast from society, at least from upper-class English society, and he has genuine reasons for remorse and self-questioning. The energy of these cantos is a fiercely egotistical energy, and though there are objective set pieces of rhetorical or descriptive virtuosity (such as the well-known and perhaps overrated account of the eve of Waterloo), the real life of the poem comes from Byron's exploitation and manipulation of his own moods. As the exile wanders by the field of Waterloo, the Ardennes, the Rhine, the Alps, the Swiss lakes and in the cities and landscape of Italy, musing on man and on nature, recalling local heroes and moments of history, the tone becomes more assured, the point of view with which he con-

templates the human and natural world becomes steadier. Toward
the end of Canto III he sums up his position:

> I have not loved the world, nor the world me,—
> But let us part fair foes; I do believe,
> Though I have found them not, that there may be
> Words which are things, hopes which will not deceive,
> And virtues which are merciful, nor weave
> Snares for the failing; I would also deem
> O'er others' griefs that some sincerely grieve;
> That two, or one, are almost what they seem,
> That goodness is no name, and happiness no dream.

In Canto IV the past and present of Italy moves him to new
heights of eloquence, and the Byronic pose merges into genuine emotion conveyed by a verse at once passionate and elegiac:

> In Venice Tasso's echoes are no more,
> And silent rows the songless gondolier;
> Her palaces are crumbling to the shore,
> And music meets not always now the ear:
> Those days are gone—but Beauty still is here.
> States fall, arts fade—but Nature doth not die,
> Nor yet forget how Venice once was dear,
> The pleasant place of all festivity,
> The revel of the earth, the masque of Italy.

The contemplation of Venice rouses him to special eloquence: he
devotes over twenty stanzas to an evocation, at once nostalgic and
comforting, of the city's past and a contemplation of its present.
"The spouseless Adriatic mourns her lord; . . ." This canto contains many set pieces, including the well-known picture of the
dying gladiator ("I see before me the Gladiator lie"), the praise
of loneliness in Nature ("There is a pleasure in the pathless
woods, /There is a rapture on the lonely shore") and the rather too
self-conscious apostrophe to the sea ("Roll on, thou deep and dark
blue Ocean—roll!"). It is in such passages that Byron's kinship with
the other Romantic poets can be most easily traced by those who
wish to emphasize this aspect of the poet. The latter cantos of *Childe
Harold* take the Romantic Byron as far as he can go; but he has still
to find a medium in which the whole man can speak—he does that
only in *Don Juan*.

Byron turned his hand to historical drama, but the four verse
tragedies he produced—two on Venetian themes, one on the Assyrian
king Sardanapalus, and one set in Germany during the Thirty Years'
War—are inorganic and artificial works, in which moments of per-

sonal passion and attempts at historical and psychological recon-
struction remain unreconciled. More interesting, though still of dubious poetic merit, are his dramatic poems *Manfred* (1817) and *Cain*
(described as a "mystery," 1821), the former dealing with remorse and
nameless guilt with a melodramatic *élan* reminiscent of his verse
tales, and the latter giving a deliberately perverse twist to the biblical
story, making Cain a rebel hero rather as Blake saw Milton's Satan.
It is a relief to turn from these almost hysterical works to the relaxed,
genially ironic *Beppo* (1817), the first fruits of his reading of the Italian Renaissance authors of burlesque epic, Luigi Pulci and Francesco
Berni. Byron took from these authors the *ottava rima* stanza and suggestions for a style of mock-heroic impudence. Beppo is a slight
thing, "a Venetian story" in 99 stanzas telling how a wife whose husband was presumed lost at sea took a lover in his absence, and how
agreeably everybody behaved on the husband's return. The texture of
the verse however marks a most important development in Byron's
discovery of himself; its counterpointing of the colloquial and formal,
its ease and gaiety, its variations of speed and tone, show how much
more congenial to Byron's technical skills in verse the eight-line
abababcc stanza is than the more elaborate Spenserian. This is
proved conclusively in that remarkable, long, unfinished poem, *Don
Juan* (1819–24), in which Byron found the voice in which he could
speak most authentically and a theme which brought the man and
the mask together.

Writing to Thomas Moore in September, 1818 (and Byron was a
brilliant correspondent, his letters possessing tremendous vigor and
sparkle), Byron wrote: "I have finished the first canto . . . of a poem
in the style and manner of *Beppo*, encouraged by the good success of
the same. It is called *Don Juan*, and is meant to be a little quietly
facetious upon every thing. But I doubt whether it is not—at least,
as far as it has yet gone—too free for these very modest days." But
the adventures of his young Spanish hero, which eventually extended
to sixteen cantos of over a hundred *ottava rima* stanzas each, turned
out to be a much more than a "quietly facetious" mock-epic. The
negligent picaresque form provided Byron with a mold into which
he could pour his medley of attitudes as ironist and idealist, as jester
and critic, as observer and sufferer, and though the light tone is preserved throughout, and comic rhymes, colloquialisms, and such devices as anticlimax and sudden deviation into flippancy are frequent,
something is woven as the poem proceeds that is more than a tapestry
of facetiae. The opening, telling of the young Juan's first amorous
adventure, is richly comic, and spiced with observations often comic
in form but often serious (at least obliquely) in intent:

Oh Plato! Plato! you have paved the way,
    With your confounded fantasies, to more
Immoral conduct by the fancied sway
    Your system feigns o'er the controlless core
Of human hearts, than all the long array
    Of poets and romancers:—You're a bore,
A charlatan, a coxcomb—and have been
At best, no better than a go-between. . . .

Man's a strange animal, and makes strange use
    Of his own nature, . . .

Man's a phenomenon, one knows not what,
    And wonderful beyond all wondrous measure;
'Tis pity though, in this sublime world, that
    Pleasure's a sin, and sometimes sin's a pleasure;
Few mortals know what end they would be at,
    But whether glory, power, or love, or treasure,
The path is through perplexing ways, and when
    The goal is gain'd, we die, you know—and then—

What then?—I do not know, no more do you—
    And so good night. . . .

In Cantos II to IV, Juan is shipwrecked in the Mediterranean and rescued by the beautiful and innocent Haidée, with whom he has a love affair described in tones of tremulous beauty that somehow Byron manages to contain within the larger mock-heroic tone. It is a remarkable feat. It is the innocence of the relationship that is stressed:

Alas! they were so young, so beautiful,
    So lonely, loving, helpless, and the hour
Was that in which the heart is always full,
    And, having o'er itself no further power,
Prompts deeds eternity cannot annul,
    But pays off moments in an endless shower
Of hell-fire—all prepared for people giving
Pleasure or pain to one another living.

This stanza illustrates how deftly Byron moves from the lyrical to the mocking. It is a movement that suited his personality much better than the pose of melodramatic diabolist he had so often adopted earlier. The idyll of Juan and Haidée ends abruptly with the return of Haidée's pirate father; Juan is sold into slavery and the following cantos find him in Constantinople, bought by the Sultana who vainly tries to seduce him (he is involved with another, to say nothing of his loyalty to Haidée's memory). He escapes from these entanglements and in Cantos VII and VIII joins the Russian siege of Ismail. This leads to his becoming the lover of Catherine the Great, who eventually sends him on a mission to England. Juan in England gives Byron the opportunity for a brilliantly satiric portrait of English society, and though this part of the poem (Cantos XI to XVI, where the poem breaks off abruptly with the hero being pursued by a determined duchess) is very loosely put together, it gives Byron's considered view of his country built up cumulatively by a large number of small strokes.

The hero himself is throughout the poem curiously passive, for all his dashing success in love. He does not so much act as he is acted on; even the love idyll of Cantos II and III is more Haidée's than his. He is not Byron himself, as Childe Harold was, but an almost allegorical figure of sexual man whose function is to respond to different environments and to give his creator the opportunity of describing those environments. There is some deliberate mischief in *Don Juan,* some simple fun, some working off of high spirits. But the total effect is that of a Weltanschauung: in his lively, sauntering, various way, Byron manages to produce a mock-epic which is at the same time a criticism of life. Sometimes one can trace grand traditional themes transposed into a wholly new key, as in his treatment of the medieval *ubi sunt* motif:

> Where is Napoleon the Grand? God knows:
>   Where little Castlereagh? the devil can tell:
> Where Grattan, Curran, Sheridan, all those
>   Who bound the bar or senate in their spell?
> Where is the unhappy Queen, with all her woes?
>   And where the Daughter, whom the Isles loved well?
> Where are those martyr'd saints the Five per Cents?
> And where—oh, where the devil are the Rents?

> Where's Brummel? Dish'd. Where's Long Pole Wellesley? Diddled.
>   Where's Whitbread? Romilly? Where's George the Third?
> Where is his will? (That's not so soon unriddled.)
>   And where is 'Fum' the Fourth, our 'royal bird'? . . .

> Where is Lord This? And where my Lady That?
>   The Honourable Mistresses and Misses?
> Some laid aside like an old Opera hat,
>   Married, unmarried, and remarried (this is
> An evolution oft performed of late).
>   Where are the Dublin shouts—and London hisses?
> Where are the Grenvilles? Turn'd as usual. Where
> My friends the Whigs? Exactly as they were.

Don Juan is comic and satiric, but like all true comic satire it is based, however indirectly, on a view of man and of society—a view neither profound nor consistent, but a real one, developed by Byron out of his own experience.

Byron's one brilliant success in a purely satiric style is *The Vision of Judgment* (1822), provoked by Southey's extravagant panegyric of George III, which had been accompanied by a preface attacking the "Satanic School." The satire is aimed equally at the late king and his panegyrist; both are enveloped in the same overpowering mockery. The attitude to the king is one of pitying contempt; "this old, blind, mad, helpless, weak, poor worm" comes up before Heaven's gate for judgment in a mood of stupid bewilderment. Various witnesses give evidence and are in the middle of inconclusive discussion when a devil appears bringing in Southey, who proceeds to drive everyone to desperation by reading his poetry. Saint Peter finally knocks the poet down and he falls back to earth "into his lake." In the confusion King George slips into Heaven,

> And when the tumult dwindled to a calm,
> I left him practising the hundredth psalm.

The stanza form is Byron's by now favorite *ottava rima*, used with the same colloquial flexibility he employs in *Beppo* and *Don Juan*. It is scarcely an exaggeration to say that his discovery of this verse form was the making of Byron as a poet. How great a poet is he is a question less easy to answer than it is with the other Romantic poets. His reputation on the European continent has long been of the very highest, but in England the contradiction between the poseur and the satirist, as well as that between the facile exploiter of emotion and the mock-heroic poet, has often led to critical doubt and confusion. There was something Augustan in the cast of Byron's poetic personality, and he might have done better as a poet of the reign of Queen Anne. He needed a tradition and emotional discipline more than most poets, and he lived at a time when neither was easily available. But he did in the end discover his own, and found a way of counterpointing egotism and self-mockery which no other Romantic poet discovered: it was a remarkable enough achievement.

Byron was the one important Romantic poet who defended the eighteenth-century poetic tradition against his own age. That tradition did not, of course, die suddenly. Thomas Campbell (1777–1844) produced moralizing heroic couplets in his *Pleasures of Hope* (1799: now remembered only for the line " 'Tis distance lends enchantment to the view") as well as a handful of rhetorical patriotic lyrics ("Ye Mariners of England," "The Battle of the Baltic") which could be called Romantic if by Romantic one means something written in freely moving stanzas and expressing strong feeling. Campbell's *Gertrude of Wyoming* (1809) is Romantic in another sense—it is an idyllic tale in Spenserian stanzas of that same region of the Pennsylvanian Susquehanna where Coleridge and Southey had planned to establish their pantisocratic Utopia; its pathos is as unreal as its local color. The best of Campbell's battle lyrics, "Hohenlinden," achieves its effect by the low and steady beat of its rhythms and its concentrated imagery. His more pretentious pieces, affecting the sublime, were consistently unsuccessful. Campbell was a poet who responded to a variety of movements and moods in his time without ever realizing his own severe limitations. His patriotism and optimistic idealism were curiously limited versions of states of mind which in the major Romantic poets were only a part of much richer modes of thinking and feeling.

The facile charm of Thomas Moore (1779–1852) is seen to best advantage in his *Irish Melodies* (1807–34), poems set to Irish airs and drawing on Irish memories and simple emotions of nostalgia, regret, and both amorous and patriotic devotion. As songs many of the poems in this and other volumes have retained their appeal ("Believe me, if all those endearing young charms"; "Oft in the stilly night"); at their best they show a controlled tenderness or artfully manipulated display of feeling that characterize the kind of "soft classic" that continues to live in popular esteem. Moore's attempt to cash in on the popularity of the heroic or exotic narrative verse of Scott and Byron produced his oriental poem *Lalla Rookh* (1817), which was immensely successful in its day; but this series of four linked verse romances narrated in varying verse forms lacks Scott's vigor and Byron's melodrama and emotional violence, and the result, while possessing a certain picturesque charm ("Who has not heard of the Vale of Cashmere, /With its roses the brightest that earth ever gave . . . ?"), is altogether too glib and tenuous.

A poet of altogether larger stature, if still a minor poet to the eye of the critical historian, is Walter Savage Landor (1775–1864). His epic *Gebir* (1798) is one of those exotic oriental stories which the age went in for. The blank verse shows a quiet control unusual in Romantic verse tales of this kind, but the story itself is thin, and one is left with the impression of a poet in search of a subject. His short lyrics are altogether finer: here the control, the lapidary touch, the quiet concentration, the suggestion of emotional distance, work brilliantly, and poems such as "Rose Aylmer," "Mother, I cannot mind my wheel," "Past ruined Ilion Helen lives," "On his Seventy-fifth Birthday," are in sharp contrast to the emotional narcissism of Shelley and the posturing of Byron. He shared these poets' love of Italy and their phil-Hellenism, but these sentiments in him were not the result of idealizing historical excitement or of fierce political liberalism; they were linked, rather, to humanist admiration for the achievement of Periclean Athens and a psychological curiosity about great men of the past. His *Hellenics* (1847) succeed to a surprising degree in capturing the spirit of Greek mythology, and other poems on Greek themes show his characteristic coolness and restraint in handling subjects which Shelley handled with more obvious personal involvement and Keats with more imagistic luxuriance. The same control is shown in his series of prose essays, *Imaginary Conversations* (1824–54), where he brings together characters from the past and manipulates their dialogue with subtle dexterity so as to suggest rather than display ironic or dramatic conflicts between different points of view or between different types of character and experience. Landor stood in some ways apart from his age, a lonely figure who nevertheless used many of the materials of Romantic poetry in his own restrained and artful manner. There is a purity and a strength in his best work which are worlds away from the emotional turmoil of so many of the minor writers of his time; yet he too was molded in some degree by the spirit of the age, and his feeling for the ancient classical world was far removed from that of Pope or Gibbon.

Leigh Hunt (1784–1859) is altogether more relaxed and journalistic both in his prose and in his verse. A liberal idealist much influenced by the reforming ideas current in his youth, he ran a number of liberal journals at different periods in his career, and suffered imprisonment for attacks on the government in his journal *The Examiner*. Hunt's association with Keats has already been discussed. His own narrative poem, *The Story of Rimini* (1816), pioneered in the use of a freer pentameter couplet than the eighteenth century had developed, but an ineradicable verbal sloppiness spoils the effect. His taste was oddly uncertain, and though he was attacked for vulgarity and indecency largely on political grounds, the fact remains that there was a streak both of vulgarity and of facility in his verse and in his personality. This was not inconsistent with a certain charm both of feeling and of expression, and some of his shorter poems show something of the engaging quality of his personality to which his friends bore repeated testimony. "The Poets," ("Were I to name, out of the times gone by, /The poets dearest to me, . . .") has a pleasing informality of movement; "To the Grasshopper and the Cricket" ("Green little vaulter in the sunny grass") has a sprightly charm; the hackneyed "Abou ben Adhem" shows something of Hunt's simple idealism in an

effectively unpretentious little moral story in supple verse; the ron-
deau "Jenny kissed me" benefits by the discipline of the form to
achieve an attractive compactness in expressing a mood in which
self-pity and gaiety march together. His critical essays reveal a
method depending largely on profuse quotation and a point of view
best summarized in his definition of poetry: "Poetry . . . is the utterance of a passion for truth, beauty, and power, embodying and
illustrating its conceptions by imagination and fancy, and modulating
its language on the principle of variety in uniformity. . . . Poetry is
a passion, because it seeks the deepest impressions; and because it
must undergo, in order to convey them." His practical criticism is
sometimes remarkably perceptive in its pointing to specific uses of
metaphor or other devices, even though he deliberately confounded
art and the artist and helped to popularize that assessment of poetry
in terms both of the poet's personality and the reader's emotional
response which modern criticism has so violently repudiated. "While
writing this paragraph, a hand-organ out-of-doors has been playing
one of the mournfullest and loveliest airs of Bellini—another genius
who died young," he writes toward the end of his essay on Keats
(1844), and this genial discursiveness is part of his method. "All flows
out of sincerity and passion," he says in the final paragraph of the
same essay. That was one of his criteria for great poetry, and represents what might be called the popular Romantic position. Undisciplined, often undressed, in his writing, Leigh Hunt for that very
reason reveals more about the way popular taste was changing in
the early nineteenth century than does the work of many better poets
and critics.

CHAPTER TWENTY-THREE

Familiar, Critical, and Miscellaneous Prose of the Early and Middle Nineteenth Century

THE AUTOBIOGRAPHICAL EXPLOITATION of personality manifests itself in a great variety of ways among writers of the late eighteenth and early nineteenth centuries; it is symptomatic of a significant change in the relation between the writer and society. The change is a complex one, and cannot be easily defined as resulting from the Rousseauistic tradition that saw society as enslaving and the free exercise of the uninhibited individual imagination as liberating. The "egotistical sublime" of Wordsworth is very different from the melodramatic and exhibitionist posturings of the early Byron, but both show a dependence on personality which is very different from anything to be found in Augustan literature. Pope in his satires assumed a *persona;* he was the poet and the representative of good writing; an offense against him was an offense against art—and an offense against art was an offense against him. This was egotism of a kind, just as Milton's intense identification of himself with the cause he supported was also fierce egotism of a kind. And the brooding meditative verse of the eighteenth century "graveyard school" represented egotism of yet a different kind. But the use of the poet's self in Wordsworth's *Prelude* represents a new use of egotism in literature, and so does the *persona* projected by Byron in *Childe Harold.* Perhaps it can be said that in the Romantic period the tendency was for the writer to draw on his own personality either as an illuminating case history or as a gesture of defiance or showmanship or "alienation," rather than to objectify it in terms of a cause or a system.

The growth of the familiar essay, with its highly personal, often whimsical, flaunting of the writer's tastes, prejudices, and idiosyncrasies, represents another aspect of the Romantic exploitation of personality. It is not unknown in earlier writing—one can find it, in varying ways and degrees, in the seventeenth century, in Sir Thomas Browne and, very differently, in Cowley's essays, and in the eighteenth century, again in different ways, in Sterne and in Cowper—but in the first half of the nineteenth century it reaches a new stage and becomes for the first time a literary norm of its own. That it should have become a norm of its own has not on the whole been fortunate for subsequent literature: the familiarity of the familiar essay has been stressed by generations of writers since Lamb, and nineteenth- and early twentieth-century English literature is overloaded with minor writers struggling with unsuccessful whimsy, one of the less happy literary spectacles. But Charles Lamb himself (1775–1834), the master and in some degree the founder of the genre, is a subtler and more interesting writer than his influence might lead one to suspect. He is not the cultivated gentleman of leisure relaxing in easy chat; the circumstances of his personal life were harsh and even tragic; he was in large measure self-educated; his views on life and letters were worked out with an almost desperate geniality in order to preserve and develop a relish for the color and individuality of experience which for him was the only alternative to despair. His sentimentality —seen at its strongest in such an early work as *A Tale of Rosamund Gray* (1798), a melodramatic story of a girl ruined by a villain—is largely a defense-mechanism, and in its more tempered form, as in his essay "Dream-Children," is artfully controlled. He rejected the rational and Utopian systems so popular in his youth, and cultivated a mixture of restrained hedonism and humane feeling which appears in his essays in his appreciation of certain physical pleasures, his zest for the picturesque and the oddly individual in human character, and his occasional almost fierce attacks on the lack of human kindness that can be covered by a formal social code ("Modern Gallantry").

Lamb was essentially a Londoner: though he had great sympathy with and admiration for the moral views of his friend Wordsworth, he had nothing of Wordsworth's feeling for Nature. There was nothing in him, either, of the "alienation" of Byron (whom he disliked): he was sociable, talkative, and dependent on friendship. His *Essays of Elia* (1820–23) and *Last Essays of Elia* (1833), artfully artless in their personal, conversational tone, show his interest in curious persons and places, his relish of the color and variety of London life and characters, his attitudinizing, his whimsical or humorous assuming of roles, his carefully manipulated sentimentality, his parading of

himself, his skill in breaking off into jest just before he has exasper-
ated the reader by his whimsies, sentimentalities, or cultivated oddness. His antiquarian interests manifest themselves also, as do his
interest in survivals from an earlier generation—places, people, and
things. Recollection and nostalgia play an important part in his essays. On other occasions he can use mock seriousness (as in his famous "Dissertation Upon Roast Pig") or mock categorization (as in
"The Two Races of Men") or draw on real or assumed autobiography
in order to make, obliquely and half-humorously, some serious moral
point ("Old China"). The writer's own character is always there,
flaunted before the reader, but it is carefully prepared and controlled
before it is exhibited.

Lamb's critical works show more enthusiasm than discrimination.
He delighted in the Elizabethans and Jacobeans, and his *Specimens
of English Dramatic Poets Who Lived about the Time of Shakespeare* (1808) was influential in creating a new and lively interest in
non-Shakespearean Elizabethan and Jacobean drama. In literature as
in life he liked oddities, and was enthusiastic over such writers as Sir
Thomas Browne and Robert Burton, whom he regarded as "characters." He was devoted to Shakespeare, but regarded his greatest plays
as books to be read rather than as plays to be acted ("On the Tragedies of Shakespeare, considered with reference to their fitness for stage
representation"). His critical principles were neither consistent nor
were they applied with any great subtlety. He could confuse antiquarian with literary value, or identify oddness with greatness. He
believed in strength, color, individuality, and outspokenness in literature: these ideals may be too vague to serve as a truly discriminating
tool for evaluation, but in applying them he was able to convey his
own excitement and enthusiasm. His criticism was thus personal and
(in this sense) Romantic.

The works for children which he produced together with his sister
Mary in an effort to provide something less crudely moralizing than
the children's literature of the period include the *Tales from Shakespeare* (1807) and *The Adventures of Ulysses* (1808). They are not as
far removed from the moralizing tales against which he protested as
he seems to have believed, and the *Tales from Shakespeare*, for all
their protracted reputation, succeed in emptying the plays of all real
significance and reducing them to the crudest sketching of surface
plot. Lamb shared with many writers of his generation a feeling for
childhood, but this was not enough to make him a great children's
writer. His essays remain his most characteristic and most important
work, the artfully contrived testimony of a laughing philosopher
whose criticism of life was developed as a way of survival.

William Hazlitt (1778–1830) is a more vigorous and less mannered essayist than Lamb, an independent spirit who maintained his radicalism throughout his life, long after all the other eminent men of letters who had rejoiced in their youth in the French Revolution had modified or repudiated their early political idealism. His political views brought savage reviews of his work from such critics as William Gifford of the *Quarterly Review,* who deliberately confounded personal and political with literary criticism of contemporaries, but Hazlitt found it as hard to keep on good terms with his friends as with his enemies throughout his troubled life. His philosophical sympathies were largely with the older Romantic poets, with Wordsworth and Coleridge, and he benefited from the expansion of literary sympathies and the release of emotional excitement for which both the older and the younger generation of Romantic poets were responsible; but he remained outside any literary party. His prose style combines ease and strength, colloquial without being self-consciously familiar or indulging in *"cant* or *slang* phrases" (as he put it in his essay "On Familiar Style"). Hazlitt's influence on the English essay has thus been healthier than Lamb's; R. L. Stevenson's aping of him did the later writer nothing but good.

The range of subjects in Hazlitt's essays is greater than in Lamb's; he could write on painting as well as literature, on a prize-fight, on natural landscape, on going a journey, on "coffee-house politicians," as well as on more formal topics such as Milton's sonnets, Sir Joshua Reynold's *Discourses,* and the fear of death. He shared Lamb's interest in oddities of character, but not Lamb's relish of oddity for its own sake. "I hate to be surfeited with anything, however sweet. I do not want to be always tied to the same question, as if there were no other in the world. I like a mind more catholic." The *persona* which he exhibited to the world was not carefully prefabricated, as in many respects Lamb's was: he wrote what he thought on life as on letters, the mood and subject varying between good-natured observation, rapt reminiscence, irascible complaint, vivid description, enthusiastic demonstration of literary quality, and many others. His celebrated "gusto" was real: he had a relish for experience and the literary skill to convey it.

As a literary critic he illustrates the popular view of the Romantic position in his catholicity of taste and his dislike of rules. "If you like correctness and smoothness of all things in the world, there they are for you in Pope. If you like other things better, such as strength and sublimity, you know where to go for them. . . . If we have a taste for some one precise style or manner, we may keep it to ourselves and let others have theirs. If we are more catholic in our notions and want variety of excellence and beauty, it is spread abroad for us to profusion in the variety of books and in the several growth of men's minds, fettered by no capricious or arbitrary rules." ("On Criticism.") He begins his essay "On Poetry in General" with the declaration: "The best general notion which I can give of poetry is that it is the natural impression of any object or event, by its vividness exciting an involuntary movement of imagination and passion, and producing, by sympathy, a certain modulation of the voice or sounds expressing it." In practical criticism, his aim was to convey to the reader a vivid sense of the total nature of the work under discussion as he himself was struck by it, to "reflect the colours, the light and shade, the soul and body of a work." Yet he was all for objectivity, and preferred Scott to Byron because Scott does not exhibit himself but is "servile to nature." "We confess, however much we may admire independence of feeling and erectness of spirit in general or practical questions, yet in works of genius we prefer him who bows to the authority of nature, who appeals to actual objects, to mouldering superstitions, to history, observation, and tradition, before him who only consults the pragmatical and restless workings of his own breast, and gives them out as oracles to the world." ("Lord Byron.") Yet Hazlitt often consulted "the pragmatical and restless workings of his own breast," and it is this that gives vividness and reality to so much of his writing. He was artful as a writer but not as a character; he never posed before his reader as the writer of the familiar essay is so often tempted to do. Sometimes his lack of poise can be painful: his *Liber Amoris* (1823) is a feverish picture of a frenzied and tortured love affair with a silly and vulgar girl, which won him no respect in his lifetime or afterward.

Hazlitt turned to literary journalism after an unsuccessful career first as a painter and then as a philosopher. His first collection of literary sketches, *The Round Table*, appeared in 1817. The same year he produced his *Characters of Shakespeare's Plays*, which showed him employing the method of discussing the persons in the plays as independent psychological characters—a method which flourished throughout the nineteenth century and culminated in A. C. Bradley. He shared with other Romantic critics his preference for Shakespeare in the closet to Shakespeare on the stage, and showed no interest in his theatrical skill. "We do not like to see our author's plays acted, and least of all, *Hamlet*." His characteristic energy and enthusiasm are exhibited in his three collections of lectures, *On the English Poets* (1818), *On the English Comic Writers* (1819), and *On the Dramatic Literature of the Age of Elizabeth* (1820). Of his general and critical essays, *Table Talk* appeared in 1821–22, *The Spirit of the Age* in 1825, and *The Plain Speaker* in 1826. The last title sums up much of his work: he was an embattled spirit throughout most of his life, and he was also (partly cause and partly effect of this) a plain speaker, who brought to the English essay a new kind of life and a new kind of commitment.

Thomas De Quincey (1785–1859) spun literature out of his own life and emotions with little of Lamb's cultivated oddity or of Hazlitt's boisterous energy. His was a temper both dreamy and exhibitionist, whose numerous essays—he lived by literary journalism—show a somewhat generalized idealism, a love of the picturesque, an ability at times to enter into the spirit of another writer by an intuitive emotional leap, so that his criticism alternates between the gushing and the penetrating, and a style whose calculated eloquence and moments of wanton splendor hover disconcertingly between the confessional, the grand, and the meretricious. His autobiographical *Confessions of An English Opium-Eater* (1821) tells the story of his early life, which was unusual enough, and goes on to recount the dreams, some magnificent and some terrifying, which were stimulated in him by his taking of opium, a habit he first indulged in when quite young in order to alleviate neuralgia and in which he persisted intermittently throughout his life. Parts of the book are deliberately sensational, and account for the horrified delight with which it was received and for its long continued popularity. His other autobiographical works (*Autobiography*, 1834–53, and *Suspiria De Profundis*, 1845) reveal his interest in his own psychology and show an attitude to the significance of dreams and an awareness of the different levels of consciousness that are surprisingly modern. His natural tendency to transcendental attitudes was strengthened by his reading of German metaphysics, but, though he prided himself on his pioneering work in introducing Kant to English readers, he had no very profound understanding of Kant's philosophy. The influence of Jean Paul Richter strengthened his interest in the inner life of the spirit and the importance of solitary reverie. "No man ever will unfold the capacities of his own intellect who does not at least checker his life with solitude." God reveals His truths not by perishable words "but by signs in heaven, by changes on earth, by pulses in secret rivers, heraldries painted on darkness, and hieroglyphics written on the tablets of the heart." His sense of the disturbing and revealing relation between the ordinary, quotidian events of experience and the violent, or grotesque, or strange, is communicated with considerable virtuosity in his essay "On the Knocking at the Gate in *Macbeth*" (1823) and, with a mocking philosophic humor, in "Murder Considered as one of the Fine Arts" (1827). His essay on "The Literature of Knowledge and the Literature of Power" draws a distinction between the kind of literature which "speaks to the *mere* discursive understanding" and that which "speaks ultimately, it may happen, to the higher understanding or reason, but always *through* affections of pleasure and sympathy." "What do you learn from *Paradise Lost?* Nothing at all. What do you learn from a cookery book? Something new . . . in every paragraph. But would you therefore put the wretched cookery book on a higher level of estimation than the divine poem? What you owe to Milton is not any knowledge, of which a million separate items are still but a million of advancing steps on the same earthly level; what you owe is *power*,—that is, exercise and expansion to your own latent capacity of sympathy with the infinite, where every pulse and each separate influx is a step upwards, a step ascending as upon a Jacob's ladder from earth to mysterious altitudes above the earth." This is worlds away from the mimetic theories of Dryden and Johnson, from the view that great literature presents "a just and lively image of human nature"; it looks forward to I. A. Richards' distinction between referential and emotive language.

De Quincey's essays include highly imaginative reconstructions of historical scenes or incidents (e.g., "Flight of a Tartar Tribe") and "dream fugues" based on a topic which in itself may be quite ordinary (e.g., "The English Mail-Coach"). His essay on Joan of Arc is pitched at a level of high rhetorical sentimentality which is less pleasing and less interesting to the modern reader than the shrewd and detailed character studies of Coleridge, Wordsworth, and Wordsworth's sister Dorothy in his *Reminiscences of the English Lake Poets* contributed to *Tait's Magazine* in the 1830's. In this magazine, and in *Blackwood's*, the *London Magazine,* and others, the bulk of De Quincey's work appeared. What remains most interesting in that work is De Quincey's development of the psychological inquiries of the Romantic poets, his concern with states of mind and levels of consciousness, though his search for spiritual heights in the depths of the subconscious may seem naïve in the age of Freud. His prose, which at its most impassioned used to be ranked with the poetic prose of the great seventeenth-century masters, too often lacks the real order of art; it easily degenerates into a mixture of the exclamatory and the pretentious. But at its best it has power and eloquence.

Landor's *Imaginary Conversations* have been mentioned in Chapter 22: this carefully contrived dramatic prose has none of the obvious display of personality we find in Lamb, Hazlitt, and De Quincey and which can be regarded as one of the characteristics of Romantic prose. Landor's prose is formal, sometimes even stilted, and he achieves his effect by the cumulative interplay of ideas expressed in successive set pieces. There is a note of aristocratic order even in Landor's presentation of republican ideas: it might be said that he sought a classical form through which to express a romantic Hellenism. He was like Byron in his combination of aristocratic feeling with a passion for political liberty, but unlike him in his conscious search for a formal discipline for the emotions and in the moral idealism which underlies the ranging of his historical imagination.

The novels of Thomas Love Peacock (1785–1866) are in large measure dramatic dialogues in which the intellectual foibles of his generation are presented and satirized. His books present a gallery of contemporary types, observed with humorous irony, sometimes to the point of farcical caricature. The hard-drinking Epicurean clergyman, the romantic young lady, the bluff squire, the transcendental philosopher (satire of Kant and Coleridge), the political pamphleteer, the optimistic believer in constant progress, and the pessimistic Malthusian, all make their appearance. There is satire of the universities, dormant and self-indulgent throughout the eighteenth century and the early years of the nineteenth, and of the Church, worldly and complacent and suspicious of any attempt at reform, as well as of all ideas which Peacock considered newfangled and ridiculous. *Headlong Hall* (1816) is a somewhat immature mixture of farce, parody, and caricaturing dialogue between types of character representing views that provoked or amused Peacock. *Melincourt* (1817) is both more fantastic and more personal in its attacks, and includes grossly distorted and positively malicious portraits of Coleridge (Mr. Mystic), Southey (Mr. Feathernest), and Wordsworth (Mr. Paperstamp). *Nightmare Abbey* (1818) is an altogether more finished performance, equally farcical in action and situation but with an ebullience of genially mocking wit that succeeds for the first time in creating a comic world of its own, yet a world with a recognizable relation to the real one at which Peacock was laughing. Scythrop, the Shelley-like romantic idealist; Mr. Toobad, "The Manichaean Millenarian"; the accommodating Rev. Mr. Larynx; the morbid and lachrymose Mr. Flosky who had in his youth hailed the French Revolution as "the promise of a day that was to banish war and slavery, and every form of vice and misery, from the face of the earth" and because this promise had not been fulfilled "drew a conclusion that worse than nothing was done; that the overthrow of the feudal fortresses of tyranny and superstition was the greatest calamity that had ever befallen mankind; and that their only hope now was to rake the rubbish together, and rebuild it without any of those loopholes by which the light had originally crept in";—these and other characters and caricatures are brought together in *Nightmare Abbey* and are involved in fantastic adventures, revealing conversations, and sustained drinking bouts. *The Misfortunes of Elphin* (1829) moves away from contemporary England to sixth-century Wales, and conveys its satire (mostly political) in the guise of a historical novel, but with the same exuberance and comic exaggeration he uses in his other novels. *Crotchet Castle* (1831) and *Gryll Grange* (1861) return to the contemporary scene and represent Peacock's most mature handling of the dialogue-novel for purposes of satire with an increasing movement toward individualization of character and away from mere comic caricature. *Maid Marian* (1822) stands apart from the rest of Peacock's novels: it is a retelling, with enormous gusto and a lively mixture of irony and romance, of the Robin Hood story, with the emphases placed rather differently than other narrators of this story have placed them.

Peacock was no mere reactionary who attacked all the new ideas of his day; he attacked crusted Toryism as vividly as the latest forms of romantic idealism, and indeed was more concerned to show up the absurdity to which complacency or exaggeration could lead holders of a given view than the absurdity of the view itself. He remained throughout the ironic observer, but one who *enjoyed* what he saw, who actively relished absurdity at the same time as he exposed or reproved it. His novels are punctuated by poems, the best of which have a swinging and rhythmic energy which captivates the ear.

The quarterly reviews of the early part of the nineteenth century— the *Edinburgh*, founded in 1802, the *Quarterly*, founded in 1809, and *Blackwood's Magazine*, founded in 1817—provided spirited literary discussion by some of the best critical minds of the time, and although political bias often colored literary opinion, the popular view of these periodicals as voicing angry destructive criticism by Tories of Whig writers and Whigs of Tory writers derives from a small minority of minor if spectacular articles. These reviews provided much of the best practical criticism of the period; and if they sometimes showed themselves insensitive to literary values which later generations have come to take for granted (as in attacks on the Lake poets in both the *Edinburgh* and the *Quarterly*) they were for the most part committed to the view that literature was not an optional cultural game but an integral part of civilization with a relation to life and an implication in moral ideas that were paramount. Further, they were read by a higher proportion of the population than any serious critical journal in the twentieth century. The *Edinburgh* and the *Quarterly* between them had a circulation of twenty thousand copies, and on an average each copy was read by at least five people. In 1824, philosophical radicalism found a voice in the *Westminster Review,* which was to play an important part in Victorian intellectual life.

Among the political journalists thrown up by the political and economic stresses of the age none was more individual and yet at the same time representative of a typical strain of English thought than William Cobbett (1762–1835), whose movement from Toryism to Radicalism was derived from the direct impact of events on his own thinking. In his robust empiricism he was worlds away from the theoretical idealism of William Godwin. Prejudiced, narrow-minded, and egotistic, Cobbett had nevertheless a lively and sympathetic understanding of the English agricultural scene (he began life as a farm laborer, son of a small farmer), and he presented his brand of agrarian democracy—traditional and patriarchal, yet strongly radical in its opposition to otiose privilege—in prose of splendid clarity and vigor. The sustained agricultural crisis through which England was passing—the inevitable result of the Industrial Revolution turning England from a self-supporting agricultural country to a manufacturing country which exported the products of her industries and bought much of her food abroad—lies behind Cobbett's thinking on agricultural affairs. His *Rural Rides* (1830) presents a picture of rural England of the time—the land and the people—in a manner that is both persuasive and committed.

Sydney Smith (1771–1845), one of the founders of the *Edinburgh Review* and its first editor, is remembered chiefly for the brilliant wit of his conversation, but he is notable too as a Whig reformer who put his wit at the service of a humane and moderate individualism. His *Peter Plymley's Letters* (1807–8), a plea for Catholic emancipation (Roman Catholics in England remained subject to certain political disabilities until 1829), is a generous and spirited attack on religious intolerance; its combination of ironic humor, shrewdness, liveliness, and a tone both sophisticated and goodhearted—which is shown also in his many articles in the *Edinburgh* attacking all kinds of irrational and uninformed prejudice—suggests the Enlightenment rather than nineteenth-century England. Smith can be said to have put the traditions of the Enlightenment at the service of early nineteenth-century moderate Whig reformism.

Thomas Babington Macaulay (1800–59: he was raised to the peerage as Lord Macaulay in 1857) represents a more significant movement of the Whig spirit as it developed under the influences of Adam Smith's economic doctrine of laissez faire, utilitarian philosophy, and middle-class Victorian liberalism. Macaulay could perhaps be called the first eminent Victorian among British writers; in his attitude to history, to economics, to government, to questions of morality and religion, and to civilization and its prospects in general, he represented with peculiar brilliance the characteristic position of bourgeois Victorian enlightenment. He looked back over English history and saw the Revolution of 1688 as on the one hand based on tradition and precedent and on the other as the guarantor of all future political progress and extension of freedom. For him, the Whig tradition, based on moderate middle-class opposition to all absolutism in Church and State, the identification of the prosperity of England with the material prosperity of its commercial and industrial elements, and an equation of the progress of civilization with increasing national wealth, was the only possible tradition for an Englishman of sense and humanity: it was, indeed, the only true English tradition. He was the great proponent of what has since come to be called the Whig interpretation of history. He was no radical, nor did he have the interest in theoretical ideas of government found among so many of the Romantic poets in their youth. He believed that the function of government was simply to protect persons and property and keep the stage clear for the operation of enlightened self-interest: "It is not by the intermeddling of Mr. Southey's idol, the omniscient and omnipotent State, but by the prudence and energy of the people, that England has hitherto been carried forward in civilisation; and it is to the same prudence and the same energy that we now look with comfort and good hope. Our rulers will best promote the improvement of the nation by strictly confining themselves to their own legitimate duties, by leaving capital to find its most lucrative course, commodities their fair price, industry and intelligence their natural reward, idleness and folly their natural punishment, by maintaining peace, by defending property, by diminishing the price of law, and by observing strict economy in every department of the State. Let the Government do this: the People will assuredly do the rest."

This quotation is from Macaulay's long review of Southey's *Colloquies* (1830), and this sparkling and brilliantly argued essay provides a principal clue to the foundations of Macaulay's thought. Southey had attacked the Industrial Revolution and all its works and looked back nostalgically to an earlier agricultural England. He had contrasted a picturesque country cottage with a city slum. Macaulay replies by citing facts and statistics, remarking reproachfully that "it is not from bills of mortality and statistical tables that Mr. Southey has learned his political creed. He cannot stoop to study the history of the system which he abuses, to strike the balance between the good and evil which it has produced, to compare district with district, or generation with generation." In picturesque rural communities poverty is rife and poor-rates are high, argues Macaulay, quoting the figures; in cities there is less real poverty and poor-rates are accordingly lower. Southey prefers "rose-bushes and poor-rates, rather than steam-engines and independence." Macaulay conducts his argument, characteristically, like a debater rather than like a philosopher: his style might be called the apotheosis of the debating style. He uses both logic and historical facts to demonstrate the absurdity of Southey's position. He pours scorn on Southey's paternalistic theory of government ("Mr. Southey might as well say that the duties of a shoemaker are paternal, and that it is an usurpation in any man not of the craft to say that his shoes are bad and to insist on having better") and demolishes his view that the numerous contemporary expressions of discontent argued that England was on the brink of a violent revolution by citing Archbishop Laud's report of the state of the Province of Canterbury which "represents the Church of England as in the highest and most palmy state" on the very eve of the Great Rebellion. His point is that it is only when all opposition views are suppressed by an authoritarian government that an explosive revolution is in danger of occurring. If Southey argues that the signs of discontent are stronger in England now than they were in France on the eve of the French Revolution, Macaulay replies triumphantly that that is precisely why there will be no revolution in England. "Does he not know that the danger of states is to be estimated, not by what breaks out of the public mind, but by what stays in it? Can he conceive anything more terrible than the situation of a government which rules without apprehension over a people of hypocrites, which is flattered by the press and cursed in the inner chambers, which exults in the attachment and obedience of its subjects, and knows not that those subjects are leagued against it in a free-masonry of hatred, . . . ?"

Macaulay's principal argument in this essay is the rapid material progress of England and the degree to which machinery has made and is continually making contributions to industry and to communications. His view of science is that held by Francis Bacon: its function is, in Bacon's phrase, "the relief of man's estate" rather than metaphysical insight into the nature of reality. Literature he regards as a pleasing decoration of the surface of life. Macaulay was enormously well-read, and he had a prodigious memory, so that he knew *Paradise Lost* and many other literary classics literally by heart; but he had no profound feeling for literature as the imaginative exploration of the paradoxes of experience. His literary criticism is often brilliant in expression but always essentially superficial. He is indeed in many respects the essential Philistine as Matthew Arnold was to define him; but a Philistine so gifted, so lively, and with such debating skill, that in regarding him we are in danger of seeing the

Philistine as including his opposite. The concluding paragraphs of his essay on Southey's *Colloquies*, with its equation of civilization with material progress, betrays very clearly the Philistine cloven hoof. It is a key passage for an understanding of the Victorian middle-class mind:

If we were to prophesy that in the year 1930 a population of fifty millions, better fed, clad, and lodged than the English of our time, will cover these islands, that Sussex and Huntingdonshire will be wealthier than the wealthiest parts of the West Riding of Yorkshire now are, that cultivation, rich as that of a flower-garden, will be carried up to the very tops of Ben Nevis and Helvellyn, that machines constructed on principles yet undiscovered will be in every house, that there will be no highways but railroads, no travelling but by steam, that our debt, vast as it seems to us, will appear to our great-grandchildren a trifling encumbrance, which might easily be paid off in a year or two, many people would think us insane. We prophesy nothing; but this we say: If any person had told the Parliament which met in perplexity and terror after the crash in 1720 that in 1830 the wealth of England would surpass all their wildest dreams, . . . that for one man of ten thousand pounds then living there would be five men of fifty thousand pounds, that London would be twice as large and twice as populous, and that nevertheless the rate of mortality would have diminished to one-half of what it then was, that the post-office would bring more into the exchequer than the excise and customs had brought in together under Charles the Second, that stage coaches would run from London to York in twenty-four hours, that men would be in the habit of sailing without wind . . . our ancestors would have given as much credit to the prediction as they gave to *Gulliver's Travels*. Yet the prediction would have been true; . . . On what principle is it then that, when we see nothing but improvement behind us, we are to expect nothing but deterioration before us?

Our own age is perhaps peculiarly sensitive to the weaknesses of Macaulay's position, though it is hardly an exaggeration today that it is a position still held, on both sides of the Atlantic, by what we now call conservative politicians and businessmen. But, with all the weaknesses admitted, Macaulay remains a figure of astonishing brilliance. His debater's style, with its sharp contrasts and deft balances and comparisons, its exaggerations and simplifications and its rhetorical black-and-white surface is, for all its obvious weaknesses, a noble prose style, always full of life and energy, never languid or merely exhibitionist or self-consciously sophisticated (like that of Lytton Strachey, in some respects the modern equivalent of Macaulay so far as style is concerned). It is a style admirably suited to Macaulay's temperament and to the tone and mood and purposes of his writing.

Macaulay's biographical and critical essays, often in the form of reviews which in his hands became extended and admirably organized treatments of the subject of the book under review, represent an important part of his literary output. His acute sense of history often led him to organize his subject in a historical manner, discussing Dr. Johnson, for example (in a review of Croker's edition of Boswell's *Life*) in the light of the economic and social position of the writer in the eighteenth century, and Milton in the context of the religious and social conflicts of the time. His optimistic belief in progress and his acceptance of the Glorious Revolution and the Industrial Revolution as the two keystones of England's greatness never led him to conscious falsification or distortion in his treatment of historical fact. His interpretations may sometimes be unsatisfactory, but his facts are generally accurate. He exaggerated, of course; exaggeration was one of his principal stylistic devices. The famous contrast between Boswell the stupid and drunken buffoon and Boswell the prince of biographers is overdone; but it is immensely effective, as is his less violent contrast between the wise Johnson and the foolish and prejudiced Johnson. His essays on Lord Clive and on Warren Hastings (which appeared, like so many of his essays, in the *Edinburgh Review*) show him mingling history and biography so as to illuminate both. The penultimate paragraph of the essay on Hastings shows Macaulay's characteristic kind of eloquence employed in balanced summing up:

With all his faults,—and they were neither few nor small,—only one cemetery was worthy to contain his remains. In that temple of silence and reconciliation where the enmities of twenty generations lie buried, in the Great Abbey which has during many ages afforded a quiet resting-place to those whose minds and bodies have been shattered by the contentions of the Great Hall, the dust of the illustrious accused should have mingled with the dust of his illustrious accusers. This was not to be. Yet the place of interment was not ill-chosen. Behind the chancel of the parish church of Daylesford, in earth which already held the bones of many chiefs of the house of Hastings, was laid the coffin of the greatest man who has ever borne that ancient and widely extended name. On that very spot, probably, fourscore years before, the little Warren, meanly clad and scantily fed, had played with the children of ploughmen. Even then his young mind had revolved plans which might be called romantic. Yet, however romantic, it is not likely that they had been so strange as the truth. Not only had the poor orphan retrieved the fallen fortunes of his line. Not only had he repurchased the old lands, and rebuilt the old dwelling. He had preserved and extended an empire. He had founded a policy. He had administered government and war with more than the capacity of Richelieu. He had patronised learning with the judicious liberality of Cosmo. He had been attacked by the most formidable combination of enemies that ever sought the destruction of a single victim; and over that combination, after a struggle of ten years, he had triumphed. He had at length gone down to the grave in the fulness of age, in peace, after so many troubles, in honour, after so much obloquy.

Macaulay's masterpiece was his unfinished *History of England from the Accession of James II* (5 volumes, 1848–61). His energetic and persuasive style, his adroit manipulation of illustrative facts, and artful alternation between generalization and detail, combine to make this one of the most readable of extended histories. The famous Chapter III is a picture of England in 1685—of England, that is, on the eve of a movement which was to lead to the modern world in which Macaulay so rejoiced. His graphic picture of English society, communications, culture, politics, of the whole community at work and play in town and country, gains power from the author's continual sense of how much better things are in his own day. "The town [London] did not, as now, fade by imperceptible degrees into the country. No long avenues of villas, embowered in lilacs and laburnums, extended from the great centre of wealth and civilization and far into the heart of Kent and Surrey. In the east, no part of the immense line of warehouses and artificial lakes which now spreads from the Tower to Blackwall had even been projected. . . ." Contrast is part of his descriptive technique, and Macaulay's use of it is bound up with his sense of the difference between past and present as well as his sense of the continuity of history. He had no profound philosophy of history; indeed, he was no philosopher; but he had an educator's—perhaps a showman's—sense of how to manipulate contrast and continuity in such a way as to maintain interest. At the end of his account of England at the accession of James II, he comes out into the open with his theory of progress, looking backward with satisfaction at the progress which had been made and forward with optimism. Not for Macaulay any romanticizing of medieval or Renaissance England. "It is now the fashion to place the golden age of England in times when noblemen were destitute of comforts the want of which would be intolerable to a modern footman, when farmers and shopkeepers breakfasted on loaves the very sight of which would raise a riot in a modern workhouse, . . . We too shall, in our turn, be outstripped, and in our turn be envied." Macaulay did not live to carry his history beyond the death of William III in 1702; it remains essentially an account of England in the late seventeenth century from the standpoint of a Victorian Whig who was also a scholar, a wit, and a rhetorician.

Macaulay's optimism was based in part on the spectacular achievements of British industry in the early and middle nineteenth century. The rapid growth of railways, the increasing use of machinery in factories, the tremendous rise in the production of iron and steel, the great expansion of industrial cities, and the spectacular increase in the wealth of the middle classes, constitute a familiar part of the story of Victorian England. That these massive changes brought with them equally massive new social problems was all too obvious to those who looked honestly at the condition of the English people. Macaulay, intoxicated by his vision of perpetual material progress, minimized these problems and, while conceding that many English people lived under harsh conditions, cheered himself and his readers by insisting that even so the poorest slum-dweller of his day was better off than the peasants of an earlier age or of contemporary Europe. Others looked with less complacency on the Victorian social scene. And indeed there was much to be disturbed about. Overcrowding, squalor, and lack of sanitation in city slums and the ruthless exploitation of labor (including women and children) by employers for whom working people were simply debit items on a budget to be reduced to the lowest practicable figure, produced a rift between what Disraeli was to call the "two nations"—the working classes, for whom leisure and the amenities of life were unknown, and the middle and upper classes —that was a strange comment on the growing national wealth. The "condition of England question" came more and more to haunt the consciences of humane and thoughtful people.

The Utopian or Godwinian approach to contemporary social problems, which was common at the end of the eighteenth century, gave way early in the nineteenth century to movements for agrarian reform. But once it was seen that industrialism had come to stay, and that neither Tom Paine's schemes of "agrarian justice" nor Cobbett's backward-looking reform movement nor the practice of smashing machinery would alter matters, a more practical outlook developed. The combination of agricultural depression and economic slump that followed the end of the Napoleonic wars brought misery to both urban and rural workers. Wages dropped, factories closed down, unemployment increased. The resultant widespread suffering gave an impetus to radical agitation. Demonstrations and riots took place, but these only encouraged the government in its policy of severe repression. The working class, completely unorganized, depended for help on middle-class radicals, who had none but the most constitutional aims in view. It was not until after 1820 that some kind of constructive working-class policy began to take shape. Hitherto despair had been the main motive, and an unreasoning desire to get rid of the machines and return to pre-industrial conditions the most obvious feature, in all agitation. But improving conditions brought better organization and a developing sense of responsibility. The working classes began to make themselves felt in journalism, acquiring a method of putting their case before the public. They supported the movement which resulted in the Reform Bill of 1832, unaware that parliamentary reform that gave the vote to the manufacturing middle classes meant putting Parliament directly under the control of the class which, having long achieved economic domination, could no longer be kept from political power—the very class whose laissez faire economic views and practices had brought about the social conditions against which the workers were protesting. The Chartist Movement, begun in the late 1830's and continuing intermittently for a decade, demanded universal male suffrage, vote by ballot, equal electoral districts, annual parliaments, payment of members of parliament, and the abolition of the property qualification for voters. The Reform Bill of 1867 finally extended the vote to most industrial workers, and that of 1884 extended it further to include virtually all adult males. The political maneuverings, arguments, and party alignments that lay behind and accompanied these developments cannot be gone into in a literary history; but an understanding of the Victorian "prophets"—Carlyle, Ruskin, Matthew Arnold, William Morris—depends to a considerable degree on an awareness of the general nature of the social problems and of the ideas that were being mooted as remedies for them.

After the Reform Bill of 1832, both Whigs and Tories accepted the middle-class franchise as the basis of parliamentary activity, and the country settled down to enjoy complete bourgeois domination. The Tories became Conservatives and the Whigs became Liberals. Victorian Liberalism had for its main purpose the freeing of the individual from undue government interference, in the firm belief that the free play of individualism always worked out for the best. In the economic sphere, this view had been systematically expressed by Adam Smith in his *Wealth of Nations*, but free trade as a national policy was not put into operation until the repeal of the Corn Laws by Peel in 1846. But Liberalism was responsible for much more than free trade. Jeremy Bentham and James Mill, whose thought lay behind much Liberal policy throughout a large part of the century, were the apostles of freedom in the political and religious as well as in the economic sphere. The individual must be allowed to think and (within wide limits) to act as he pleases, for only by the economic balancing of forces thus achieved can the "greatest good of the greatest number" be attained. Thus the abundant legislation removing restrictions and disabilities of all kinds—such as the emancipation of the Catholics, the abolition of university tests, the establishing of free trade, the granting to Jews the right to sit in Parliament—were all products of this attitude, whether the particular laws were passed by a Conservative or a Liberal Government.

There was an ugly side to Liberal individualism. Believing as it did in the untrammelled plays of economic forces, it extended the doctrine of noninterference to matters of social distress and industrial conditions. The Factory Acts, abolishing by degrees the iniquities of child labor and gross overworking, were passed under protest after individual philanthropists had brought the appalling conditions to the notice of the public in a way that could not be ignored. Social legislation of this kind—the Factory Acts of 1833 to 1878, the Mines Act of 1842 forbidding the employment of women and children underground, the acts of 1867 and 1873 concerning the employment of women and children in rough agricultural labor, the acts of 1834 and 1864 concerning boy chimney sweeps, even the Public Health Acts of 1871–75—was put through under pressure and in the face of strenuous opposition from the individualist and laissez faire point of view. Any interference with the rights of private property and the free operation of economic laws was strongly resisted. Thomas Malthus' *Essay on Population* (1798), originally written as a reply to the optimistic radicalism of Godwin, encouraged this attitude. Malthus maintained that, as population increased in geometrical proportion, the natural checks provided by misery, poverty, disease, and war were necessary to prevent overpopulation. He urged the danger of "coddling" the people by too generous social services, which would only increase breeding and counteract natural forces, and advocated also "moral restraint" in keeping down the population level. Thus the Poor Law Amendment Act of 1834 was motivated by a mixture of Benthamism and Malthusianism: it was Liberal and Benthamite in that, by stopping outdoor relief and herding the poor together in deliberately unattractive workhouses, it put a premium on self-reliance and independent labor, however ill-paid, and Malthusian in that it restricted relief to a minimum and recognized the folly of maintaining the poor with comfortable doles—it was argued that the principle of granting doles to the poor in proportion to the size of the family only encouraged the poor to have children and thus added to the danger of overpopulation.

These were some of the forces and the arguments at work in the middle of the nineteenth century. Others—religious, moral, and scientific—will be looked at in the following chapter. Reform movements were on the whole based on the view that the wider the suffrage was extended the better things would be, while utilitarian attempts to work out the greatest happiness of the greatest number could be assured of providing some sort of pragmatic test of the degree to which the people of England were achieving or had the possibility of achieving the good life. But many who looked at England during this period were not satisfied that the remedy for what was wrong could be found in either extending the suffrage (which Macaulay, too, frowned on) or in applying an arithmetical calculus of happiness. "It is not to die, or even to die of hunger, that makes a man wretched; many men have died; all men must die,—the last exit of us all is in a Fire-Chariot of Pain. But it is to live miserable we know not why; to work sore and yet gain nothing: to be heart-worn, weary, yet isolated, unrelated, girt-in with a cold universal Laissez-faire: . . . The notion that a man's liberty consists in giving his vote at election-hustings, and saying, 'Behold, now I too have my twenty-thousandth part of a Talker in our National Palaver; will not all the gods be good to me?'—is one of the pleasantest!"

This is the voice of Thomas Carlyle (1795–1881), a very different voice from Macaulay's. Carlyle, a poor Scot who became an English prophet by grafting German transcendentalism onto his native Calvinist feeling for stern moral judgment and hard work and developing a powerfully original rhetorical style for capturing the mind and emotions of his readers, criticized the Victorian Liberal tradition from a position far outside it. Poverty and skepticism harried him in his young manhood, and he was redeemed from the latter by his discovery of German romantic literature. His essays on Schiller, Novalis, Jean Paul Richter, and others show the explosive force of the impact on him of these writers; while his *Life of Schiller* (1823) and his translation of Goethe's *Wilhelm Meister* (1824) indicate how serious and sustained was his interest in both poets, especially the latter. In 1827, he brought out four volumes of *Specimens of German Romance*.

German transcendentalism was heady wine, and Carlyle's gloomy yet enthusiastic temperament was profoundly and permanently affected by it. A Scottish Calvinist destined for the Church of Scotland, but seduced into skepticism in his student days by reading eighteenth-century philosophers and historians and then shaken into a new faith—no longer Calvinist nor even specifically Christian, but strongly spiritual, ethical, and theistic—could hardly be expected to develop into either a utilitarian philosopher or a worshiper of Victorian progress. In his wild ejaculatory book *Sartor Resartus*, which disguises autobiography as the life and opinions of a German Professor of Things-in-General, he recalls the moment of his conversion (which took place in June, 1821) in terms which indicate something of the general tenor of his thought:

. . . The Everlasting No had said: "Behold, thou art fatherless, outcast, and the Universe is mine (the Devil's);" to which my whole ME now made answer: "*I* am not thine, but FREE, and forever hate thee!"

It is from this hour that I incline to date my Spiritual New-birth, or Baphometic Fire-baptism; perhaps I directly thereupon began to be a Man.

The repudiation of the Everlasting No led to the Everlasting Yea, which is "Love not Pleasure; love God." Carlyle's attack on happiness as an ideal and his insistence on work and duty shows both his distance from and his kinship to the Victorian middle-class ideal. "Foolish soul! What Act of Legislature was there that *thou* shouldst be Happy? A little while ago thou hadst no right to *be* at all. What if thou wert born and predestined not to be Happy but to be Unhappy! Art thou nothing other than a Vulture, then, that fliest through the Universe seeking after somewhat to *eat;* and shrieking dolefully because carrion enough is not given thee? Close thy *Byron;* open thy *Goethe.*" This is a strange transmutation of the Puritan belief in work. And the excited language of Carlyle's exhortations, with its exclamations, Teutonicisms, and echoes of biblical prophecy, produces a style wholly idiosyncratic and unmistakable:

> I too could now say to myself: Be no longer a Chaos, but a World, or even Worldkin. Produce! Produce! Were it but the pitifullest infinitesimal fraction of a Product, produce it, in God's name! 'Tis the utmost thou hast in thee: out with it, then. Up, up! Whatsoever thy hand findest to do, do it with thy whole might. Work work while it is called Today; for the Night cometh, wherein no man can work.

Sartor Resartus appeared in *Fraser's Magazine* in 1833 and 1834, but it was not until three years after it had appeared in book form in America and after Carlyle had already achieved fame with his *French Revolution* (1837) that a British publisher found the courage to bring out as a book this strange and violent work. The *French Revolution* is Carlyle's most sustained and brilliant work. His account of what for his generation was still the greatest and most decisive movement in modern history—taken from its beginnings to Napoleon's seizure of power in 1795—is done with an impressionist vividness, a violent projection of the reader into the midst of the events described, that marks a wholly new method of writing history. Carlyle did not write as a mere scholar or even as a mere historian, but as a moralist, as an interpreter and demonstrator of the way in which the logic of human affairs works itself out. When government becomes atrophied into mere formalities and conventions, when the political, ecclesiastical and social life of a nation is emptied of real content and is carried on by means of outward shows merely, and when the rulers of a nation become so absorbed in those shows that they have altogether lost the substance in pursuing the shadow, then the divine justice that governs the working of all laws is inevitably brought into operation to lead the rulers to self-destruction. But what is achieved after the violent overthrow of such a government and such a society depends on the character and purpose of the men who then take the stage. History is not an inevitable chain of cause and effect; men make their own destiny. Carlyle was fascinated with the leading figures in the French Revolution and painted them in arresting phrases in violent flashes of intuitive insight and imagination, so that even where later scholarship has proved him to be wrong he remains powerfully persuasive. For Carlyle, the failure of the French Revolution lay in the failure of individual Frenchmen to rise to the occasion and show the proper kind of leadership. To use the term that he was soon to make peculiarly his own, the Revolution failed for lack of heroes.

The main interest of *The French Revolution* is not, however, in the implied moral or psychological ideas, but in the highly individual style which Carlyle forged in order to implicate his readers in the impressions and emotions he was continually striving to communicate. He retains a remarkable control over his narrative, and the whole vast story pulses with energy—an energy which is not merely one of style but which communicates itself as bound up with Carlyle's view of the enormous forces at work in the world, his view of the whole cosmos as alive and engaged in a perpetual struggle against all that is negative and inimical to the grand principle of spiritual life. The jostling metaphors are not merely picturesque or even merely energetic: they insistently communicate his sense of the nature, the significance, the representative quality and the inner reality of the events he is describing. Dramatic projections of scenes and incidents, rhetorical outbursts, grimly or wildly humorous sallies addressed to the reader, ironic play with names, innumerable devices to set himself and his readers in the midst of what he is describing— all these combine to make a style at once compelling and exhausting, a style which brings into a single context, one might even say into a single texture, the external reality of history and the inward reality of Carlyle's personality.

Carlyle preached renunciation, work, and hero-worship. In his increasingly bitter opposition to all the characteristic elements in Victorian Liberal thought, his distrust of democracy and opposition to widening of the franchise, his hatred of utilitarianism and materialism and of the economic doctrine of laissez faire and his contempt for those who believed in salvation by machines, gadgets, increase of physical comforts, and for the whole Baconian view of "the relief of man's estate" which Macaulay so warmly embraced, he came more and more to pin his trust on the individual hero. His *Heroes and Hero-Worship* (1841) treats of the hero as "divinity" (the gods of

Norse mythology), as prophet (Mohammed), as poet (Dante and Shakespeare), as priest (Luther and Knox), as man of letters (Johnson, Rousseau, and Burns) and as "king" (Cromwell, Napoleon). Originally delivered as lectures, these essays have a more colloquial tone than his more formal work, but they still show, though a little more equably, that insistent, teasing, rubbing-the-reader's-nose-in-it style which is the mark of all that Carlyle writes. With such a varied selection of heroes it is obvious that Carlyle must have a conception of the hero large and flexible enough to enable him to use his portraits of poets, statesmen, and others as a means of putting forward some of his central doctrines. Consider, for example, the use he makes of the character of Robert Burns in the following passage:

Sceptical Dilettantism, the curse of these ages, a curse which will not last forever, does indeed in this the highest province of human things, as in all provinces, make sad work; and our reverence for great men, all crippled, blinded, paralytic as it is, comes out in poor plight, hardly recognisable. Men worship the shows of great men; the most disbelieve that there is any reality of great men to worship. The dreariest, fatalest faith; believing which, one would literally despair of human things. Nevertheless, look, for example, at Napoleon! A Corsican lieutenant of artillery; that is the show of *him:* yet is he not obeyed, *worshipped* after his sort, as all the Tiaraed and Diademed of the world put together could not be? High Duchesses, and ostlers of inns, gather round the Scottish rustic, Burns;—a strange feeling dwelling in each that they never heard a man like this; that, on the whole, this is the man! In the secret heart of these people it still dimly reveals itself, though there is no accredited way of uttering it at present, that this rustic, with his black brows and flashing sun-eyes, and strange words moving laughter and tears, is of a dignity far beyond all others, incommensurable with all others. Do we not feel it so? But now, were Dilettantism, Scepticism, Triviality, and all that sorrowful brood, cast-out of us,—as, by God's blessing, they shall one day be; were faith in the shows of things entirely swept-out, replaced by clear faith in the *things*, so that a man acted on the impulse of that only, and counted the other non-extant; what a new livelier feeling towards this Burns were it!

Carlyle is here using his conception of the hero to indicate his view of the nature of reality. We can see a similar process at work in his definition of poetry, achieved by a defining and redefining of the meaning of a word, an appeal to his readers to consider and reconsider its essential significance, which is a characteristic Carlylean touch (he often uses real or false etymologies for the same purpose):

Truly, if pressed to give a definition, one might say this as soon as anything else: If your delineation be authentically *musical*, musical not in word only but in heart and substance, in all the thoughts and utterances of it, in the whole conception of it, then it will be poetical; if not, not.—Musical: how much lies in that! A *musical* thought is one spoken by a mind that has penetrated into the inmost heart of the thing; detected the inmost mystery of it, namely the *melody* that lies hidden in it; the inward harmony of coherence which is its soul, whereby it exists, and has a right to be, here in this world. All inmost things, we may say, are melodious; naturally utter themselves in Song. The meaning of Song goes deep. Who is there that, in logical words, can express the effect music has on us? A kind of inarticulate unfathomable speech, which leads us to the edge of the Infinite, and lets us for moments gaze into that!

Here Carlyle imposes his own meaning on a word—a meaning which leads him to the core of a favorite doctrine—by his rhetorical method of playing with it and repeating it.

Past and Present (1843) shows how far Carlyle had gone in his repudiation of the spirit of contemporary England. "It is," he wrote to John Sterling, "a moral, political, historical, and a most questionable red-hot indignant thing, for my heart is sick to look at the things now going on in England." A medieval monastic community is used as a foil to expose all that he disliked—"dilettantism," "mammonism," hedonism, utilitarianism, materialism—in the civilization of his day. Against the "Greatest-Happiness Principle" he sets his stern doctrine of silence and work. ". . . properly speaking, all true Work is Religion: and whatsoever Religion is not Work may go and dwell among the Brahmins, Antinomians, Spinning Dervishes, or where it will; with me it shall have no harbour. Admirable was that of the old Monks, *'Laborare est Orare, Work is Worship.'* " Democracy is attacked and hero-worship extolled. "Democracy, which means despair of finding any Heroes to govern you, and contented putting-up with the want of them,—alas, thou too, *mein Lieber*, seest how close it is of kin to *Atheism*, and other sad *Isms*: he who discovers no God whatever, how shall he discover Heroes, the visible Temples of God? —Strange enough meanwhile it is, to observe with what thoughtlessness, here in our rigidly Conservative Country, men rush into Democracy with full cry."

An age that has seen the *Führerprinzip* in action is not likely to have any sympathy for Carlyle's doctrine of hero-worship, still less so when in the latter part of his career he came more and more to adulate the strong-arm man and seemed to regard the establishment and maintenance of power as itself the guarantee of the possession of all the other qualities he admired. His massive *Letters and Speeches of Oliver Cromwell* (1845) and his long, carefully constructed and cunningly presented biography of *Frederick the Great* (6 volumes, 1858–65) show him extracting moral meanings from history and psychology, in the latter volume with considerable rhetorical brilliance in the building up of the total moral pattern. *Latter-Day Pamphlets*

PROSE TO MID-NINETEENTH CENTURY

(1850) and *Shooting Niagara: and After* (1867) continue the attack on his favorite targets. *Shooting Niagara* is Carlyle's response to Disraeli's Reform Bill of 1867, which he saw as leading further away from the possibility of true hero-worship and nearer to democratic anarchy. He pleads for a true aristocracy, "an open belligerent company, capable at last of taking the biggest slave Nation by the beard, and saying to it, 'Enough, ye slaves, and servants of the mud gods; all this must cease!'" He distinguishes between the Speculative Hero and the Practical Hero, both of whom will war against the "cheap and nasty" products of Democracy. "Were there but Three Aristocrats of each sort in the whole of Britain, what beneficent unreported '*Parliaments*,'—actual human consultations and earnest deliberations, responsible to no '*Buncombe*,' disturbed by no Penny Editor! . . . By degrees, there would some beginnings of success and Cosmos be achieved upon this our unspeakable Chaos; by degrees, something of light, of prophetic twilight, would be shot across its unfathomable dark of horrors,—prophetic of victory, sure, though far away."

Carlyle's voice grew shriller as he grew older, and though it was always clear what he was against, his positive remedies were too often wrapped in a generalized prophetic murk. His deep moral earnestness and his rhetorical eloquence made a great impression in his day, even among those who did not fully understand or agree with him. John Stuart Mill and Dickens, Tennyson and Browning, as well as Ruskin, Arnold, and William Morris, came in varying degrees and at various times under his influence. He was the first of the great Victorian prophets; and it is worth noting, especially by those who like to think of the Victorian age as one of optimistic complacency, that all the great Victorian prophets spoke out *against* the spirit of their age. There is no doubt that thoughtful people even in the self-congratulatory atmosphere of the Great Exhibition of 1851 were, however vaguely, troubled in their consciences about some aspects of their civilization; and Carlyle spoke disturbingly if not always luminously to that troubled Victorian conscience.

John Stuart Mill (1806–73) had an altogether different sort of mind—lucid, humane, analytic—and his writings, while they possess no distinctive literary qualities, no rhetorical *élan* or imaginative power, are of importance as illustrating Victorian reforming thought at its most reasonable and most disinterested. Educated from infancy by his father, the utilitarian reformer James Mill, to be a learned and astute propagandist and explicator of those views on human welfare and on politics which he and Jeremy Bentham had developed together—views which represented an ingenious but curiously mechanical application of contemporary psychological notions to construct a theory of happiness and a political system based on the "greatest happiness" principle—he suddenly discovered, early in his twenty-first year, the barrenness of a purely analytic approach to the most profound human problems. In his posthumously published *Autobiography* (1873) he records the depressing and paralyzing effect of this discovery. "All those to whom I looked up, were of opinion that the pleasure of sympathy with human beings, and the feelings which made the good of others, and especially of mankind on a large scale, the object of existence, were the greatest and surest sources of happiness. Of the truth of this I was convinced, but to know that a feeling would make me happy if I had it, did not give me the feeling. My education, I thought, had failed to create these feelings in sufficient strength to resist the dissolving influence of analysis, while the whole course of my intellectual cultivation had made precocious and premature analysis the inveterate habit of my mind." It was the poetry of Wordsworth that was largely responsible for rescuing Mill from the dark night of the soul into which his sense of the barrenness of his intellectual activities had plunged him. The result was enlarged sympathies and the awareness of the inadequacy of any system which postulated the calculated pursuit of an arithmetically defined happiness as the proper end of individual or political activity. "If I am asked, what system of political philosophy I substituted for that which, as a philosophy, I had abandoned, I answer, No system: only a conviction that the true system was something much more complex and many-sided than I had previously had any idea of, and that its office was to supply, not a set of model institutions, but principles from which the institutions suitable to any given circumstances might be deduced. The influences of European . . . thought, and especially those of the reaction of the nineteenth century against the eighteenth, were now streaming in upon me. They came from various quarters: from the writings of Coleridge, . . . ; from what I had read of Goethe; from Carlyle's early reviews in the Edinburgh and Foreign Review, though for a long time I saw nothing in these (as my father saw nothing in them to the last) but insane rhapsody. . . . I looked forward . . . to a future which shall unite the best qualities of the critical with the best qualities of the organic periods; unchecked liberty of thought, unbounded freedom of individual action in all modes not hurtful to others; but also, convictions as to what is right and wrong, useful and pernicious, deeply engraven on the feelings by early education and general unanimity of sentiment, and so firmly grounded in reason and in the true exigencies of life, that they shall not, like all former and present creeds, religious, ethical, and political, require to be thrown off and replaced by others."

This deepening of Mill's thought never led him to transcendental-ism or mysticism, but enabled him to reconsider political and philo-sophical problems in such a way as to give the utilitarian approach by far its most persuasive and deeply thought out expression. His writings on political and philosophical subjects—*On Liberty*, 1859; *Thoughts on Parliamentary Reform*, 1859; *Representative Govern-ment*, 1861; *Utilitarianism*, 1863; *The Subjection of Women*, 1869; *Three Essays on Religion*, 1874—show an awareness of the com-plexity and variety of human experience and the differences in quality as well as quantity between different kinds of human happi-ness that are far removed from the confident and narrow logic of Benthamism. Though an inveterate individualist and a profound be-liever in freedom of speech and in the right and even the value of personal eccentricity, he recognized the limits of laissez faire and the necessity for a careful balance between freedom of individual action on the one hand and protective and beneficent governmental action on the other. If he was still more optimistic about the nature of man than the survivors of the age of concentration camps and gas cham-bers can allow themselves to be, he nevertheless formulated many of the principles which still underlie the thinking of humane and moder-ate reformers who believe that men can plan their progress to a bet-ter world without reliance on supernatural sanctions. He believed passionately in the equality of the sexes, and he believed with equal passion in education as the only proper foundation for an expanding democracy. His mind was essentially secular, and he was agnostic without being hostile to religion, in whose historical and psychologi-cal aspects he was much interested. Though in his later years friendly with Carlyle and influenced by him, he remained in cast of mind and basic ideas fundamentally antithetical to him, while to Carlyle, Mill remained "a logic-chopping engine." In general it can be said that Mill represented nineteenth-century secular wisdom in the form in which it was most easily assimilated by the twentieth century.

CHAPTER TWENTY-FOUR

Victorian Prose:
John Henry Newman
to William Morris

Carlyle and Mill represented in some degree the extremes between which Victorian thought moved, the former transcendental, idiosyncratic, authoritarian, the latter empirical, reasonable, democratic. Mill represents what might be called the eighteenth-century inheritance, Carlyle the Romantic inheritance. Yet they were not opposed in all respects: Mill was influenced by Carlyle as he was by Wordsworth and Coleridge. And Mill found almost as much to protest against in the civilization of his time as Carlyle did. A very different kind of protest came from a very different quarter. Mill, though fundamentally agnostic, conceded the possible utility of religion in implementing morality and the conceivable truth of the Christian claim that Christ (but as man, not as God) had "a special, express, and unique communication from God to lead mankind to truth and virtue." Carlyle, while rejecting Christian dogma, preached the Christian virtues of renunciation and self-discipline and a spiritual view of reality. A third force was provided by a powerful revival of Christianity in its ritual and dogmatic aspect. Against the rising tide of liberalism, humanism, and historical and psychological interpretation of religion, a group of churchmen began in the 1830's to set the values and ideals of "that primitive Christianity which was delivered for all time by the early teachers of the Church and which was registered and attested in the Anglican formularies and by the Anglican divines." The series of *Tracts for the Times,* written by this group between 1832 and 1841, began by reviving the concept of the Church of England as the English Catholic Church of the great seventeenth-century Anglican ecclesiastics, a genuine *via media* between the irresponsibilities of Protestant individualism and the abuses of Rome, truly traditional and apostolic and at one with Roman Catholicism in its dogmas and its sense of continuity with the past. The final tract, Newman's famous (or notorious) Tract 90, interpreted the Thirty-nine Articles of the Church of England as essentially Catholic, rather than as a Protestant formulation against Roman Catholicism as they were usually regarded, and this produced a sensation in Anglican quarters. The logic of the attack on a state church, on the watering down of early Christian doctrine, on the exaltation of the Bible and of individual judgment, was to lead inevitably back to dogma, to ecclesiastical tradition, to a concept of the Church as the guardian and also as the living symbol of spiritual truth. The Church of England in the eighteenth and early nineteenth centuries had been worldly and slothful. The Methodist movement had injected new life and energy, but that had eventually been deflected into the camp of Protestant dissent, and Protestant dissent, with its breeding of quarreling sects, its dependence on the "inner light" and its repudiation of continuity and tradition in spiritual matters, was for the Tractarians a canker at the very heart of Christianity. Liberal theology, the secularizing of the history of religion, the reduction of Christianity to a code of ethics for gentlemen—this trend, which represented to the Tractarians the real enemy, was not to be fought against by "the dissidence of dissent and the Protestantism of the Protestant religion" (as Matthew Arnold, quoting the professed aims of a Nonconformist newspaper, was scornfully to put it), but rather by a revival of the conception of "The Church Catholic and Apostolic, set up from the beginning," of which the Church of England "was but the local presence and the organ."

The words just quoted are those of John Henry Newman (1801–90), the greatest figure in the Oxford Movement (as this movement came to be called), who followed what appeared to him at least to be the logic of his position to embrace Roman Catholicism in 1845. Newman's conversion was really the end of the movement, which exerted its greatest influence in the middle and late 1830's when it was pleading for a more Catholic conception of Anglicanism. Neither the Church of England nor the dissenting sects were able, in the view of the Tractarians, to resist the corrupting secularism which they saw, as Carlyle saw, threatening all spiritual values. "The vital question," wrote Newman later, looking back on this period, "was how we were to keep the Church from being liberalized? There was such apathy on the subject in some quarters, such imbecile alarm in others; the true principles of Churchmanship seemed so radically decayed, and there was such distraction in the councils of the Clergy." Parliamentary reform, which meant more and more that the Church of England was dependent on a Parliament whose members were not necessarily Anglicans or even Christians (for, being a state church, the Church of England was subject to parliamentary legislation), posed a further challenge to those who valued the independence and apostolic nature of the English Church.

The lines of battle were drawn. On the one hand, there were liberal Christians like Thomas Arnold who fastened on the ethical significance of Christianity and minimized the importance of ritual, of "theological Articles of opinion," and "all this stuff about the True Church." On the other, there was Newman, the most persuasive and appealing of those for whom "the long history of the Church, the Lives of the Saints, and the reasonings, internal collisions, and decisions of the theological Schools" acted out and summed up the meaning of Christianity, for which theology and dogma provided the background for devotion. Newman repudiated equally Protestant individualism and bibliolatry, nineteenth-century liberal Christianity, and the eighteenth-century deistical argument from design. "After all man is *not* a reasoning animal; he is a seeing, feeling, contemplating, acting animal. . . . Life is not long enough for a religion of inferences; we shall never have done beginning, if we determine to begin with proof." One accepted Christian truth and ecclesiastical authority by faith, and faith was a matter of acting out and so making real the promptings of conscience. Between Thomas Arnold and Newman there were of course all varieties of religious opinion, including a fairly powerful group of High Church Anglicans who were affected by the Oxford Movement but did not follow Newman to Rome. Nor must it be forgotten that a very large number of middle-class Englishmen remained Protestant Dissenters—Methodists, Baptists, and members of less well-known sects—equally suspicious of the Established Church (especially in its "High" ritualistic forms), of Rome, and of liberal theology.

This phase of English religious history comes into the history of literature not only as part of the thought of many important men of letters but as part of the very fabric of the mind and art of at least one of the great Victorian writers—Newman himself. Newman's tracts, sermons, theological writings, and miscellaneous essays have their own interest, but his *Apologia pro Vita Sua* (1864) and his *Idea of a University* (1852) have a status as literature in their own right in virtue of their quiet luminosity of style and the personal and persuasive way in which (in his own phrase) he has "thought out into language." *The Idea of a University* discusses intellectual culture as something desirable apart from religious and moral culture and considers why and how it is so. Newman's view of the function of knowledge is, as might be expected, anti-Baconian. "That alone is liberal knowledge which stands on its own pretensions, which is independent of sequel, expects no complement, refuses to be *informed* (as it is called) by any end, or absorbed into any art, in order duly to present itself to our contemplation. . . . And in like manner the Baconian Philosophy, by using its physical sciences in the service of man, does thereby transfer them from the order of Liberal Pursuits to, I do not say the inferior, but the distinct class of the Useful. . . . I am prepared to maintain that there is a knowledge worth possessing for what it is, and not merely for what it does; . . ." Proper cultivation of the mind makes the gentleman, not the Christian; but it is a good thing for the Christian to be a gentleman also. "Liberal education makes not the Christian, not the Catholic, but the gentleman. It is well to be a gentleman, it is well to have a cultivated intellect, a delicate taste, a candid, equitable, dispassionate mind, a noble and courteous bearing in the conduct of life—these are the connatural qualities of a large knowledge; they are the objects of a University; . . . but still, I repeat, they are no guarantee for sanctity or even for conscientiousness; they may attach to the man of the world, to the profligate, to the heartless—pleasant, alas, and attractive as he shows when decked out in them." And again: "Surely it is very intelligible to say . . . that Liberal Education, viewed in itself, is simply the cultivation of the intellect as such, and its object is nothing more or less than intellectual excellence." Newman distinguishes between mere learning and the "perfection of the intellect," the latter and not the former being the object of university education. "That only is true enlargement of mind which is the power of viewing many things at once as one whole, of referring them severally to their true place in the universal system, of understanding their respective values, and determining their mutual dependence. . . . But the intellect which has been disciplined to the perfection of its powers, which knows, and thinks while it knows, which has learned to leaven the dense mass of facts and events with the elastic force of reason, such an intellect cannot be partial, cannot be exclusive, cannot be impetuous, cannot be at a loss, cannot but be patient, collected, and majestic, because it discerns the end in every beginning, the origin in every end, the law in every interruption, the limit in each delay; because it ever knows where it stands, and how its path lies from one point to another." Thus, for all his bitter opposition to secularism and humanism, Newman offered an ideal of secular university education, not indeed as something which could take the place of religious education and personal devotion, but as something which could make the Christian a fuller and a more interesting man. He does therefore have some common ground with liberal humanists—though not in his conception of life as a whole—and this perhaps is one reason why liberal humanists have so often found him appealing.

But there is more to it than that. Newman's way of arguing—exploring the definitions of words with gentle insistence so as to show the emptiness or absurdity or self-contradictoriness of his opponents' view, his combination of introspective honesty with quietly controlled irony, the perfectly modulated flow of his prose—puts him among those Victorian prophets and critics of their time who contributed new techniques to the literature of persuasion. Like Carlyle, he is less a philosopher than a rhetorician, and his rhetoric is often subtler than Carlyle's. The contemporary appeal of his personality is often communicated by the tone of his discourse even to those who disagree radically with his whole point of view. Matthew Arnold's famous reminiscence sums up this aspect of Newman (he is recalling Newman before he joined the Roman Catholic Church, when he was Vicar of St. Mary's, Oxford): "Who could resist the charm of that spiritual apparition, gliding in the dim afternoon light through the aisles of St. Mary's, rising into the pulpit, and then, in the most entrancing of voices, breaking the silence with words and thoughts which were a religious music—subtle, sweet, mournful?" This is the Newman who is part of the Romantic Movement, who belongs with the deepening of interest in the imagination shown in Wordsworth and Coleridge. Indeed, from one point of view the Oxford Movement as a whole was a romantic rebellion against the perfunctory unimaginative routine into which the Church of England had fallen.

Newman's *Apologia pro Vita Sua* was written in reply to an attack by Charles Kingsley on what seemed to him to be the wanton dishonesty of Newman's Roman Catholic propaganda. Kingsley, who had been influenced by the Christian Socialism of Frederick Denison Maurice, saw Christianity as a doctrine of social humanitarianism: "What is the use of preaching about heaven to hungry paupers?" he once asked. Newman's concern with the Church as an institution and with Catholic dogma seemed to him mischievous and irrelevant, and, because he totally failed to understand how a mind like Newman's worked, Kingsley could not help believing him intellectually dishonest. But Newman had the better of the argument: his defense is still read, while Kingsley's attack is forgotten. To defend himself by recounting with scrupulous care the story of his own opinions and their development was for Newman the only truly persuasive method; for truth to him was personal and *lived,* not abstract and inferred. He gives a persuasive picture of a personality pervaded from early childhood with a sense of the numinous, moving, not in a straight line but nevertheless, the reader feels, inevitably, toward the Roman Catholic faith. "I understood these passages [of Clement and Origen] to mean that the exterior world, physical and historical, was but the manifestation to our senses of realities greater than itself. Nature was a parable; Scripture was an allegory; pagan literature, philosophy, and mythology, properly understood, were but a preparation for the Gospel." This is a clue to all Newman's beliefs. For him religious faith came not from arguments or "evidences," but (as for the mature Coleridge) from emotional commitment to the reality of what imagination and conscience postulated. Newman was never fooled by the "argument from design" which had been demolished by Hume and was still urged by Anglicans and others. "The truth is that the system of Nature is just as much connected with Religion, where minds are not religious, as a watch or a steam-carriage. . . . What we seek is what concerns us, the traces of a Moral Governor; even religious minds cannot discern these in the physical sciences; astronomy witnesses divine power, and physics divine skill; and all of them divine beneficence: but which teaches of divine holiness, truth, justice, or mercy? Is that much of a Religion which is silent about duty, sin, and its remedies? Was there ever a Religion which was without the idea of an expiation?" Thus the neo-orthodoxy of the nineteenth century answers the rationalizing deism of the eighteenth.

The stern prophecies of Carlyle, the reasonable humanitarian reformism of Mill, the gently persuasive Catholicism of Newman—each represented in its own way an attack on Victorian middle-class complacency. Meanwhile, an attack was developing from a quite unexpected quarter. "It is not that men are ill fed, but that they have no pleasure in the work by which they make their bread, and therefore look to wealth as the only means of pleasure." There is a ring of Carlyle in this voice, which is that of John Ruskin (1819–1900); but Carlyle, while preaching the gospel of work, retained his inherited suspicion of pleasure, and Carlyle would not have made, as Ruskin did, *art* the key to his view of the ills of the modern world.

And now, reader, look round this English room of yours, about which you have been proud so often, because the work of it was so good and strong, and the ornaments of it so finished. Examine again all those accurate mouldings, and perfect polishings, and unerring adjustments of the seasoned wood and tempered steel. Many a time you have exulted over them, and thought how great England was, because her slightest work was done so thoroughly. Alas! if read rightly, these perfectnesses are a sign of slavery in our England a thousand times more bitter and more degrading than that of the scourged African, or helot Greek. Men may be beaten, chained, tormented, yoked like cattle, slaughtered like summer flies, and yet remain in one sense, and the best sense, free. But to smother their souls within them, to blight and hew into rotting pollards the suckling branches of their human intelligence, to make the flesh and skin which, after the worm's work on it, is to see God, into leathern thongs to yoke machinery with,—this it is to be slave-masters indeed; . . .

And, on the other hand, go forth again to gaze upon the old cathedral front, where you have smiled so often at the fantastic ignorance of the old sculptors: examine once more those ugly goblins, and formless monsters, and stern statues, anatomiless and rigid; but do not mock at them, for they are signs of the life and liberty of every workman who struck the stone; a freedom of thought, and rank in scale of being, such as no laws, no charters, no charities can secure; but which it must be the first aim of all Europe at this day to regain for her children.

Let me not be thought to speak wildly or extravagantly. It is verily this degradation of the operative into a machine which, more than any other evil of the times, is leading the mass of the nations everywhere into vain, incoherent, destructive struggling for a freedom of which they cannot explain the nature to themselves.

This is from Ruskin's *Stones of Venice* (three volumes, 1851–53). The chapter on the nature of Gothic architecture and art in the second volume shows Ruskin for the first time relating art to economics and to the functioning of society generally. Ruskin esteemed the Gothic because it gave free play to the individual workman. "You can teach a man to draw a straight line, and to cut one; to strike a curved line, and to carve it; and to copy and carve any number of given lines or forms, with admirable speed and perfect precision; and you find his work perfect of its kind: but if you ask him to think about any of those forms, to consider if he cannot find any better in his own head, he stops; his execution becomes hesitating; he thinks, and ten to one he thinks wrong; ten to one he makes a mistake in the first touch he gives to his work as a thinking being. But you have made a man of him for all that. He was only a machine before, an animated tool." And again: "You must either make a tool of the creature, or a man of him. You cannot make both." Ruskin saw the whole system of Victorian industry as enslaving, because it made machines of men, prevented them from operating as individual workmen:

We have much studied and much perfected, of late, the great civilized invention of the division of labour; only we give it a false name. It is not, truly speaking, the labour that is divided; but the men:—Divided into mere segments of men—broken into small fragments and crumbs of life; so that all the little piece of intelligence that is left in a man is not enough to make a pin, or a nail, but exhausts itself in making the point of a pin or the head of a nail. Now it is a good and desirable thing, truly, to make many pins in a day; but if we could only see with what crystal sand their points were polished,—sand of human soul, much to be magnified before it can be discerned for what it is,—we should think there might be some loss in it also. And the great cry that rises from all our manufacturing cities, louder than their furnace blast, is all in very deed for this,—that we manufacture everything there except men; we blanche cotton, and strengthen steel, and refine sugar, and shape pottery; but to brighten, to strengthen, to refine, or to form a single living spirit, never enters into our estimate of advantages. And all the evil to which that cry is urging our myriads can be met only in one way: not by teaching nor preaching, . . . It can be met only by a right understanding, on the part of all classes, of what kinds of labour are good for men, raising them, and making them happy; by a determined sacrifice of such convenience, or beauty, or cheapness as is to be got only by the degradation of the workman; and by equally determined demand for the products and results of healthy and ennobling labour.

Ruskin began as an art critic with the publication of five volumes of *Modern Painters* between 1843 and 1860. This grew out of his bitter resentment of attacks on Turner's paintings, and originally was to be simply a defense of Turner and an attack on his critics; but it developed into a comprehensive discussion of the principles of painting, especially landscape painting. From the beginning Ruskin was determined to find more in art than simply technical excellence combined with a poetical imagination (as Sir Joshua Reynolds distinguished the two qualities in the fifteenth of his *Discourses*). Representative ability in itself he saw simply as the ability to handle language, nor does the great painter simply add imagination; he must have what Ruskin called "ideas," by which he meant moral ideas. "Most pictures of the Dutch school . . . excepting always those of Rubens, Vandyke, and Rembrandt, are ostentatious exhibitions of the artist's power of speech, the clear and vigorous elocution of useless and senseless words; while the early efforts of Cimabue and Giotto are the burning messages of prophecy, delivered by the stammering lips of infants." This point of view leads him to extol Landseer's "The Old Shepherd's Chief Mourner" because of the "thoughts by which the picture is separated at once from hundreds of equal merit, as far as mere painting goes, by which it ranks as a work of high art, and stamps its author, not as the neat imitator of the texture of a skin, or the fold of a drapery, but as the Man of Mind." Ruskin is more eloquent and more convincing when he is dealing with landscape, and describing the ways in which the imagination can respond to the most subtle details of color and form in the natural world (and he had cultivated from childhood a remarkable eye for details of natural scenery), than in endeavoring to make a direct connection between art and morality. It is not that a connection between art and morality is absurd, but simply that Ruskin never really followed his own insights through, but, sometimes rather uneasily, insisted throughout his long career as a writer on seeing only a simple and direct connection between moral virtue and great art. "The art is greatest which conveys to the mind of the spectator, by any means whatsoever, the greatest number of the greatest ideas; and I call an idea great in proportion as it is received by a higher faculty of the mind, and as it more fully occupies and exalts the faculty by which it is received. . . . All our moral feelings are so inwoven with our intellectual powers, that we cannot affect the one without in some degree addressing the other; and in all high ideas of beauty, it is more than probable that much of the pleasure depends on delicate and untraceable perceptions of fitness, propriety, and relation, which are purely intellectual, and through which we arrive at our noblest ideas of what is commonly and rightly called 'intellectual beauty.'" In *The Stones of Venice* he explains the rise and virtue of the Gothic in terms of the moral virtue of the society that produced it, and attributes its decline to the disappearance of that virtue. And in later works he reiterated this point in many different ways. "Of all facts concerning art, that is the one most necessary to be known, that, while manufacture is the work of the hands only, art is the work of the whole spirit of man; and as that spirit is, so is the deed of it: and by whatever power of vice or virtue any art is produced, the same vice or virtue it reproduces and teaches. That which is born of evil begets evil; and that which is born of valour and honour, teaches valour and honour. All art is either infection or education. It *must* be one or other of these. . . . You cannot paint or sing yourselves into being good men; you must be good men before you can either paint or sing, and then the colour and sound will complete in you all that is best. . . . No noble nor right style was ever yet founded but out of a sincere heart."

This insistence on a direct connection between moral and artistic value leads to some obvious confusions and difficulties in Ruskin's arguments; we are today rather more aware of the limitations of Ruskin's thought here than his own age was. Nevertheless, it provided him with a weapon of attack on the Philistines of his time that could be used with splendid vigor. In his lecture, "Traffic," delivered at the Bradford Town Hall in 1864 (and subsequently published with others in *The Crown of Wild Olive*, 1866), Ruskin attacked the Philistines in their own stronghold with extraordinary gusto. They had asked him to talk about the new Exchange they were about to build, hoping he would give advice on the latest style, and he replied by explaining that a style of architecture grows out of a way of life and cannot be delivered by a visiting expert. The tone is a telling mixture of friendliness and bitter irony. "Now, pardon me for telling you frankly, you cannot have good architecture merely by asking people's advice on occasion. All good architecture is the expression of national life and character, and it is produced by a prevalent and eager national taste, or desire for beauty." Even though he illustrates his points by arguments that few modern critics could accept—that High Renaissance art is bad because based on luxury while Gothic is good because based on noble individual labor or that David Teniers' picture of the backgammon players is "entirely base and evil" because it is "an expression of delight in the prolonged contemplation of a vile thing"—his main point, that quality in art is related to quality in living and you cannot buy a luxury art to stick on top of your civilization and still have it good art, remains sound and is put with splendid force. "I notice that among all the new buildings which cover your once wild hills, churches and schools are mixed in due, that is to say in large proportion, with your mills and mansions; and I notice also that the churches and schools are almost always Gothic, and the mansions and mills are never Gothic. May I ask the meaning of this?" He goes on to point out that in medieval times the Gothic style was not used only for churches. "But now you live under one school of architecture and worship under another. What do you mean by doing this?" No question put to a Victorian middle-class audience could have been more salutary (to use one of Matthew Arnold's favorite adjectives). And nothing in the whole of this remarkable lecture is more impressive than Ruskin's retelling of the story of Jacob's dream set in a contemporary northern English landscape familiar to his audience, in such a way as to bring home to them the relation between religion and daily life and work.

Perhaps the crudest of Ruskin's many attempts to relate art and morality is to be found in his *Seven Lamps of Architecture* (1849), but even here there are passages of fine perceptiveness. *The Stones of Venice* develops the same ideas, but in a much richer context of specific art criticism and art history. In his later work Ruskin became more and more concerned with "the condition of England question" and carried on the Carlylean attack on laissez faire combined with his own view of work and art. His enemies were the machine, the worship of what he called the Goddess of Getting-on, the lack of all individual self-realization in work. As he told his Bradford audience: "If you can fix some conception of a true human state of life to be striven for—life, good for all men, as for yourselves; if you can determine some honest and simple order of existence; following those trodden ways of wisdom, which are pleasantness, and seeking her quiet and withdrawn paths, which are peace;—then, and so sanctifying wealth into 'commonwealth,' all your art, your literature, your daily labours, your domestic addiction, and citizen's duty, will join and increase, into one magnificent harmony. You will know then how to build, well enough; you will build with stone well, but with flesh better; temples not made with hands, but riveted of hearts; and that kind of marble, crimson-veined, is indeed eternal." One of the most eloquent of all his statements about the meaning of life and the relation of beauty and dignity in daily living to all that is worthwhile in art and morality, is to be found in the third of the lectures included in the volume *Sesame and Lilies* (1865). His last works are sometimes confused, and overelaborated with a vague and cloudy rhetoric.

Ruskin's fight against laissez faire and against the dominance of the machine over the individual was also a fight against ugliness. He was one of the first English writers to express over and over again his horror at what industrialism had done to the face of England and to the living and working conditions of men and women. "The reckless luxury, the deforming mechanism, and the squalid misery of modern cities" are set against a vision not (as is sometimes charged) inspired by an idealized Middle Ages, though Ruskin did sometimes idealize the Middle Ages, but inspired by what he considered to be practicable as well as desirable in his own day, cities "with no festering and wretched suburb anywhere, but clean and busy street within, and the open country without, with a belt of beautiful garden and orchard round the walls, so that from any part of the city perfectly fresh air and grass, and the sight of far horizon, might be reachable in a few minutes' walk." In *Unto This Last* (1860–62), *Munera Pulveris* (1862–72), *The Crown of Wild Olive* (1866), and *Fors Clavigera* (1871–84), Ruskin preached his social and economic gospel, with varying degrees of coherence but often with magnificent eloquence, and even in his latest and too wordy style, with flashes of wit or irony or invective or visionary splendor that can light up whole pages. His influence on later thinkers and reformers led not only in the direction of a neomedieval concept of life, work, and the community but also toward more practical programs, such as that of Fabian Socialism and modern town-planning.

Ruskin's unfinished autobiography, *Praeterita,* appeared between 1885 and 1889; it throws much interesting light on an odd character, and it also directs us where to go in looking for the main influence on his style. This was the Authorized Version of the Bible, which he read assiduously throughout his childhood and of which he had to memorize large portions. The Bible has many styles, from the simple history of Samuel and Kings to the lyric eloquence of the Psalms, the rhetorical power of the Prophets, the direct narrative of the Gospels, and the concrete symbolism of Revelation, and the young Ruskin memorized samples of them all. Ruskin's style can be consciously poetic, with an accumulation of clauses in a periodic sentence ending with a calculated close, and it can achieve a lyric simplicity. It can offend by an excess of artfulness, and charm by a fine directness, and often succeeds in combining artfulness and simplicity. It is an eloquent style, aiming at persuasion, but it can also be carefully analytic, as in his earlier art criticism. He has his language most consistently and most effectively under control in the middle of his career; his earlier style can be too contrived and exhibitionist and his later too garrulous and even hysterical.

Ruskin took art as his guide to the deficiencies of contemporary civilization; Matthew Arnold (1822–88) took literature, and literature itself he took as the type of "culture." He looked round, as Ruskin did, on middle-class Victorian England and like Ruskin he deplored its ugliness, its unimaginative materialism, its lack of "sweetness and light." At the same time he believed that the English middle classes represented the hope of civilization, and he therefore set himself to educate them. Arnold was a humanist who devoted a large part of his life to demonstrating the central part that an adequate literary culture could and should play in society and (for him a closely related activity) to rescuing religion from the rationalist scoffers on the one hand and the rigid fundamentalists and dogmatists on the other by propounding a "liberal" Christianity based on a view of the Bible as poetry rather than as history or science, as "morality touched by emotion" rather than as an infallible book of rules. The connection between his view of poetry and his view of literature can be seen in the opening paragraph of the essay on poetry which he contributed as an introduction to Ward's *English Poets* (1880): "Our religion has materialised itself in the fact, in the supposed fact; it has attached its emotion to the fact, and now the fact is failing it. But for poetry the idea is everything; the rest is a world of illusion, of divine illusion. Poetry attaches its emotion to the idea; the idea *is* the fact. The strongest part of our religion today is its unconscious poetry." The truth of Christianity cannot be demonstrated by asserting the historicity of the Bible, which is increasingly in doubt; it rests on the degree to which the Bible, as poetry, can provide a moving revelation of the central moral realities of experience. But the converse also holds: if the Bible is great poetry, great poetry of any kind has a religious significance and is basic in civilization. "The future of poetry is immense, because in poetry, where it is worthy of its high destinies, our race, as time goes on, will find an ever surer and surer stay." If this is so, then we have a paramount responsibility to discover what is truly great poetry. "The best poetry is what we want; the best poetry will be found to have a power of forming, sustaining, and delighting us, as nothing else can." The literary critic is thus no dilettante or optional luxury in a civilization: he is, or ought to be, one of its mainstays, perhaps indeed its high priest. Further, the ability to criticize poetry properly is bound up with a sense of what is of worth in human society generally: the literary critic is concerned with culture and so with the whole contemporary scene.

At least two distinct trends can be discerned here. One is the trend that can be seen at its more fully developed stage in Walter Pater—the estheticizing of religion. Arnold did not intend to reduce religion to something which gives merely esthetic pleasure; he always insisted that religion was concerned with conduct, which was "three-fourths of life," and was not simply a rush of emotion; but the possibility of such a reduction was inherent in much of what he wrote on this subject. The second trend is the linking up of literary criticism with criticism of society. The way in which people respond to literature is intimately connected with the way they live and think and feel, and to achieve properly literary standards is to achieve also a proper way of life. In an age of almost universal literacy but not of universal liberal education, when society is divided into what Arnold called, in *Culture and Anarchy* (1869), Barbarians, Philistines, and Populace—i.e., aristocracy, middle class, and working class—the problem of achieving a proper critical response for literature was immense. The Barbarians have had their day; their gifts and graces relate only to outward culture; they may have "sweetness" but not "light," charm but not intelligence. (Arnold has none of Carlyle's feeling for the aristocratic hero.) The Populace lack powers of sympathy and of action, though they are improving. The Philistines, the great middle-class core of the nation, are both materialistic and puritanical, too "Hebraic" and too little "Hellenist," complacent about the virtues of free enterprise, wholly uncritical about their own narrowness and lack of taste and understanding. It is nevertheless the Philistines who must be saved, and who are capable of salvation. Arnold is thus the first of a long line of critics who castigate the middle classes for their own good, who fulminate against their lack of esthetic awareness and of truly humane values in the interests of literary and artistic health in the nation—and who connect that literary and artistic health with health in general. The line between Arnold's *Culture and Anarchy* and F. R. Leavis and Denys Thompson's *Culture and Environment* (1933) is a straight one. The nature of the reading public, the kind of education which makes the reading public what it is, and the whole complex modern problem that results from the splitting up of audiences into highbrow, middlebrow, and lowbrow, the problems of what F. R. Leavis has called (in a book in which Arnold's influence can be clearly traced) "mass civilization and minority culture"—all this as a proper object of inquiry for the literary critic is first to be found, if not always clearly articulated then at least implicit, in Arnold's social criticism.

Like Ruskin, Arnold is continually asking wherein the true greatness of a people consists. People claim that the greatness of England is based on its coal. Arnold replies: "Greatness is a spiritual condition worthy to excite love, interest, and admiration; and the outward proof of possessing greatness is that we excite love, interest, and admiration. If England were swallowed up by the sea tomorrow, which of the two, a hundred years hence, would most excite the love, interest, and admiration of mankind,—would most, therefore, show the evidences of having possessed greatness,—the England of the last twenty years, or the England of Elizabeth, of a time of splendid effort, but when our coal, and our industrial operations depending on coal, were very little developed?" Again and again he repeats that material prosperity is not the true criterion of national achievement:

The people who believe most that our greatness and welfare are proved by our being very rich, and who most give their lives and thoughts to becoming rich, are just the very people whom we call Philistines. Culture says: 'Consider these people, then, their way of life, their habits, their manners, the very tones of their voice; look at them attentively; observe the literature they read, the things which give them pleasure, the words which come forth from out their mouths, the thoughts which make the furniture of their minds; would any amount of wealth be worth having with the condition that one was to become just like these people by having it?' And thus culture begets a dissatisfaction which is of the highest possible value in stemming the common tide of men's thoughts in a wealthy and industrial community, and which saves the future, as one may hope, from being vulgarised, even if it cannot save the present.

Culture for Arnold included religion, and literature was the key to both. Further, culture could not be achieved by rampant individualism. Not only did Arnold oppose laissez faire; he also advocated certain kinds of centralization and state control, believing that an enlightened democracy required its education, for example, to be properly guided and supervised. "Perfection, as culture conceives it, is not possible while the individual remains isolated. The individual is required, under pain of being stunted and enfeebled in his own development if he disobeys, to carry others along with him in his march towards perfection, to be continually doing all he can to enlarge and increase the volume of the human stream sweeping thitherward." And he characteristically adds: "And here, once more, culture lays on us the same obligation as religion, which says, as Bishop Wilson has admirably put it, that 'to promote the kingdom of God is to increase and hasten one's own happiness.' "

Arnold makes a sharp distinction between religion as he understood it and the grim and narrow Puritanism of English Nonconformists. In *Culture and Anarchy* he quotes with scorn the motto of the dissenting newspaper, the *Nonconformist,* "The Dissidence of Dissent and the Protestantism of the Protestant religion" and comments: "There is sweetness and light, and an ideal of complete harmonious human perfection! One need not go to culture and poetry to find language to judge it. Religion, with its instinct for perfection, supplies language to judge it, language, too, which is in our mouths every day. . . . Men have got such a habit of giving to the language of religion a special application, of making it a mere jargon, that for the condemnation which religion itself passes on the shortcomings of their religious organisations they have no ear; . . . They can only be reached by the criticism which culture, like poetry, speaking a language not to be sophisticated, and resolutely testing these organisations by the ideal of a human perfection complete on all sides, applies to them." In one of his most biting passages, Arnold quotes the speech of the Liberal politician Mr. Roebuck: "Is not property safe? Is not every man able to say what he likes? Can you not walk from one end of England to the other in perfect security? . . . I pray that our unrivalled happiness may last." Arnold, in reply, looks at his daily paper and quotes: "A shocking child murder has just been committed at Nottingham. A girl named Wragg left the workhouse there on Saturday morning with her young illegitimate child. The child was soon afterwards found dead on Mapperly Hills, having been strangled. Wragg is in custody." He suggests that the only effective answer to Roebuck and his like is to reply to his songs of triumph by murmuring "Wragg is in custody." For Arnold, the squalor and cruelty of this incident, like the ugliness of the wretched girl's name, reflect the lack of humanity which is bound up with a lack of culture. Literary criticism is, in the last analysis, concerned with such things, for it is concerned with sweetness and light, with adequacy of living, with "the full perfection of our humanity," with "the best which has been thought and said in the world."

Culture and Anarchy is Arnold's central work as a critic of civilization; in later works, including *Friendship's Garland* (1871) and *Discourses in America* (1885), he elaborated and sometimes repeated its main ideas. His two most important works on religion, arguing for a liberal and "poetic" understanding of Christianity in order to save it from skeptic and fanatic alike, are *Literature and Dogma* (1873) and

God and the Bible (1875). The *Discourses in America* includes much discussion of education (in which Arnold, as an inspector of schools for thirty years, was professionally interested) and a defense of classical education against the claims of science. In America Arnold came up against a militant utilitarian materialism to an even greater extent than he had done in England, and in formulating his reply to its claims he uses arguments which every American defender of the liberal arts against purely vocational studies has drawn on ever since. Surprisingly, he shows himself optimistic about the long-term trend. ". . . the more that men's minds are cleared, the more the results of science are frankly accepted, the more that poetry and eloquence come to be received and studied as what in truth they really are—the criticism of life by gifted men, alive and active with extraordinary power at an unusual number of points;—so much the more will the value of humane letters, and of art also, which is an utterance having a like power with theirs, be felt and acknowledged, and their place in education be secured." If there is ever an ultimate choice between the humanities and the natural sciences, men will choose the former, for they "will call out their being at more points, will make them live more." He is even optimistic about the revived study of Greek in American colleges. And Greek for Arnold was a central humane subject. The Greeks were the greatest exemplars of "sweetness and light." From ancient Israel came "Hebraism," the stern insistence on rightness of conduct, and as conduct was three-fourths of life this was a necessary and a noble heritage. Hebraism is based on *strictness of conscience*. But one also needs, what Hellenism stands for, *spontaneity of consciousness*. And as the English middle classes have long been prone to an exclusive and excessive Hebraism, the way to their salvation lies through the counterbalance of Hellenism.

Arnold had a *mystique* about fifth-century Athens shared by many men of letters in his century; he saw it and its literature as the symbol and repository of *symmetria prisca*, ancient symmetry, the home of harmony, balance, beauty, joy:

Fit details strictly combined, in view of a large general result nobly conceived; that is just the beautiful *symmetria prisca* of the Greeks, and it is just where we English fail, where all our art fails. Striking ideas we have, and well executed details we have; but that high symmetry which, with satisfying and delightful effect, combines them, we seldom or never have. The glorious beauty of the Acropolis at Athens did not come from single fine things stuck about on that hill, a statue here, a gateway there;—no, it arose from all things being perfectly combined for a supreme total effect. What must not an Englishman feel about our deficiencies in this respect, as the sense for beauty, whereof this symmetry is an essential element, awakens and strengthens within him! What will not one day be his respect and desire for Greece and its *symmetria prisca*, when the scales drop from his eyes as he walks the London streets, and he sees such a lesson in meanness, as the Strand, for instance, in its true deformity! But here we are coming to our friend Mr. Ruskin's province, and I will not intrude on it, for he is its very sufficient guardian.

The image of fifth-century Athens and its art and literature was for Arnold what the idea of the medieval Gothic was to Ruskin: both used these ideas to castigate and improve their generation.

Arnold's literary criticism (*On Translating Homer*, 1861; *Essays in Criticism*, first series, 1865, second series, 1888, third series, 1910) is closely bound up with his view of culture and religion. If poetry is the central part of religion, if "without poetry our science will appear incomplete; and most of what now passes with us for religion and philosophy will be replaced by poetry," then, "if we conceive thus highly of the destinies of poetry, we must also set our standard for poetry high, since poetry, to be capable of fulfilling such high destinies, must be poetry of a high order of excellence." In his introduction to Ward's *English Poets* (reprinted as "The Study of Poetry" in the second series of *Essays in Criticism*) he endeavored to formulate his view of what constituted "the best poetry." "The best poetry will be found to have a power of forming, sustaining, and delighting us, as nothing else can." We must beware of judging by the historical estimate and seeing great intrinsic value in a work which is important chiefly for its pioneering or illustrative quality, and equally we must not allow ourselves to be misled by the personal estimate, judging the value of a work because of certain "personal affinities, likings, and circumstances" which may have nothing to do with its real worth. We must learn to see the object as in itself it really is; only thus will we be able to distinguish the true classic from the false. Arnold is fond of the term "classic"; it suggests his view of the centrality and sanity of great literature. But the "touchstone theory" which he recommends as a means of discovering what is truly classic is curiously vague. "Indeed there can be no more useful help for discovering what poetry belongs to the class of the truly excellent, and can therefore do us most good, than to have always in one's mind lines and expressions of the great masters, and to apply them as a touchstone to other poetry." So he quotes a few lines from Homer, Dante, Shakespeare, and Milton, and offers them as touchstones to the reader. Oddly enough, in spite of the fact that in his Preface to his 1853 volume of poems he had repudiated passive suffering as a theme for poetry, the majority of these passages are wistfully elegiac. In that Preface he had also attacked the modern method of judging a poem by single lines. "We have poems which seem to exist merely for the sake of single lines and passages; not for the sake of producing any total impression. We have critics who seem to direct their attention merely to detached expressions, to the language about the action, not to the action itself. I verily think that the majority of them do not in their hearts believe that there is such a thing as a total impression to be derived from a poem at all. . . ."

This points to a twofold contradiction at the center of Arnold's criticism, and in the last analysis they are perhaps part of a single contradiction. On the one hand his training in the classics and his admiration for classical form and balance led him to demand a poetry in which the organization of the action is central and "excellent." Excellent actions are those "which most powerfully appeal to the great primary human affections: to those elementary feelings which subsist permanently in the race, and which are independent of time." Suffering which "finds no vent in action" is not a proper poetic subject. On the other hand, his own sensibility led him to share the Victorian feeling that all poetry tends to elegy and that the most moving and memorable part of literature are lines expressing loss, nostalgia, and *lacrimae rerum*. Thus, while his head agreed with Aristotle on the importance of action and structure and rejected subjective sadness as a proper poetic theme, his heart led him to that elegiac mode which his own poetry—"Dover Beach," for example—rendered so well and which his age so frequently indulged in. Controlled self-pity is the theme of much of Arnold's poetry, as it is (not always controlled) of much of Tennyson's. So, in quoting his touchstone lines, Arnold in spite of himself favors the elegiac—quoting, for example, three short passages from the *Iliad* that are brimful of nostalgic melancholy and are quite uncharacteristic of Homer's general tone. This split between Arnold's head and his heart was responsible for his abandonment of poetry and concentrating on criticism: the poetry he really wanted to write was not the kind of poetry which his critical principles allowed him to admire.

Arnold was nevertheless a great critic, and a prophetic and influential one. His insistence on standards and his relating of the question of standards to the whole question of the way people live and think and feel, the total quality of civilization, have left permanent marks on modern criticism. His own criticism was sometimes marred by lack of precision, sometimes by naïve moralizing; his demand for "high seriousness" as a necessary quality in great poetry is neither sufficiently precise nor sufficiently perceptive in its view of the relation between art and morality; his dismissal of Shelley's circle—"What a set! What a world!"—is harmfully irrelevant to a consideration of his poetry and smacks more of the "personal" than of the "real" estimate; and it is not difficult to find other examples of the same sort of fault. His passionate idealization of what he regarded as the golden sanity of the ancient Greeks ("But I say, that in the sincere endeavour to learn and practise, amid the bewildering confusion of our times, what is sound and true in poetical art, I seemed to myself to find the only sure guidance, the only solid footing, among the ancients") may seem today uncritical and excessive. But he did see something of the way in which great literature gets at the roots of the human imagination; he saw its significance for the quality of a culture and was unremitting in searching out "the best" and in proclaiming, against the *ethos* of the great Victorian middle classes, that poet and critic alike are key figures in their society, whose "business is not to praise their age, but to afford the men who live in it the highest pleasure they are capable of feeling." Arnold is, in this and other respects, the first modern critic, the first to be concerned with the problems of literature in the world as we know it.

Arnold was a propagandist for culture, and in his propagandist books and essays he developed a style admirably suited to his purposes. He projects his own temper of sweet reasonableness by a variety of artful devices, and at the same time, by his ingenious use of pet terms and phrases deliberately repeated in different contexts, he can express irony, contempt, impatience, or schoolmasterly reproval. He is brilliant in his handling of personalities, succeeding in giving a tone of hectoring unreason to his opponents by the way he quotes them and the use he makes of his quotations. He can make his opponents appear ridiculous by gently but firmly repeating and repeating their remarks in a perfectly controlled context of ever-growing irony, until in the end even the courtesy with which he invariably treats them becomes a device for destroying them. He can build up the mood until even his thoroughly polite mentioning of the proper name of an opponent makes the man appear silly. He has nothing of Carlyle's prophetic violence or Ruskin's poetic eloquence; his quieter rhetoric has spoken more cogently to later generations.

Arnold's attempt to rescue Christianity from commitment to biblical fundamentalism—an attempt carried on in a variety of ways by many liberal theologians of the period—was made necessary by the impact on religious orthodoxy of German biblical criticism and of developments in geology and biology. "There is not a creed which is not shaken, not an accredited dogma which is not shown to be questionable, not a received tradition which does not threaten to dissolve," wrote Arnold in "The Study of Poetry." Protestantism, which based itself on the Bible, was more vulnerable to the new biblical scholarship than Catholicism, and the application of textual and historical criticism to the books of the Bible caused panic among many Protestant theologians, most of whom responded by insisting ever more shrilly on the divine inspiration and literal historical accuracy of the biblical text. Charles Hennell's *Inquiry Concerning the Origin of Christianity* (1838) was one of the first attempts in England to apply the results of new biblical scholarship to the study of Christian origins; its tremendous effect on young Marian Evans (George Eliot) is well known. Much more significant for the whole history of European religious thought was D. F. Strauss' *Life of Jesus* (1835) which George Eliot translated (1844–46); this was a far more detailed and comprehensive study than Hennell's, and in its combination of anti-miraculism, sympathetic psychological interpretation of the growth of religious ideas and attitudes, and belief in the profound truth of the symbolic core of Christianity while denying the literal truth of biblical story, it laid the foundations of a "modernist" Christianity of the kind Matthew Arnold, from his own special point of view, endeavored to construct. Meanwhile, Sir Charles Lyell's *Principles of Geology* (1830–33), *Elements of Geology* (1838), and *Geological Evidence of the Antiquity of Man* (1863) were having an even more disturbing effect, first in demonstrating the continuity of natural processes as demonstrated by the study of geology, secondly by adducing the compelling geological evidence for the earth's being much older and much more gradual in development than was compatible with a literal belief in the book of Genesis, and thirdly by showing that man must have lived on earth for a much longer period than biblical chronology would allow. Finally, the publication of *The Origin of Species* by Charles Darwin in 1859, putting forward with a mass of evidence his theory of natural selection and so relating man through evolutionary descent to the nonhuman animal world, and his *Descent of Man* (1871), dealing more particularly with the evolution of man and with sexual selection, outraged the orthodox and precipitated a debate that raged violently for many years. It is against this background that we must look at Arnold's attempts to save Christianity from fundamentalist and scientist alike by concentrating on its poetic significance, its meaning for spiritual experience, and leaving as, at the most, optional, literal belief in Old Testament chronology and New Testament miracles.

Darwin was not himself a skilled propagandist, though he could write with the charm that arises from absorbed interest in one's subject, as his early work, *The Voyage of the Beagle* (1839), an account of a voyage in southern latitudes to collect various specimens of plant and animal life, so clearly shows. He records in his informal autobiography the decay in middle life of his early taste for poetry, painting, and music. ("But now for many years I cannot endure to read a line of poetry: I have tried lately to read Shakespeare, and found it so intolerably dull that it nauseated me. I have also almost lost my taste for pictures or music.") He was, in his own phrase, a "philosophical naturalist," and spent the large part of his life quietly and methodically collecting and interpreting data. He left controversy for others. Fortunately he found a champion who was a brilliant controversialist as well as a man who combined scientific knowledge and enthusiasm with broad humanistic interests. This was Thomas Henry Huxley (1825–95), one of the great figures of Victorian controversy.

Huxley was not only a distinguished biologist and a great popularizer of science; he was also an essayist and man of letters, master of a prose style both cogent and elegant. He was no militant atheist, condemning all religion as superstition, nor was he the kind of narrow scientist who dismisses with contempt the claims of imagination and the arts. Like John Stuart Mill, he was influenced (though at an early stage in his life) by Carlyle; he was well-read in English and European literature and was a good linguist. He called himself an agnostic, because he recognized the limits beyond which the human mind could not go in explaining the ultimate mysteries of the universe. He stood for what might be called the new enlightenment, as distinguished from the eighteenth-century variety—an enlightenment based on the claims of "natural knowledge" and an understanding of what such knowledge can do for man, a hatred of obscurantism of all kinds, a belief in man's ability to control his own destiny provided that education and government do their business properly. In his championing of the Darwinian theory of evolution, he engaged for a large part of his life in continuous battle with ignorance and prejudice and with all those who believed that Darwin's theory, by breaking down the absolute barrier between man and the rest of the animal world, was inherently wicked and blasphemous. In the course of this battle he had to meet every kind of scorn, hatred, and misrepresentation. In published essays and in public debates with the most formidable antagonists of his time he demonstrated his confidence, his good humor, his mastery of all relevant facts, his power of marshaling argument, his compelling lucidity. In education, he pleaded for the sciences and opposed Arnold's insistence on the classics on the ground that even if taught as they should be taught the classics could not constitute a properly comprehensive study of man and the world, and that in any case most pupils never mastered the mechanics of classical knowledge sufficiently so as to be able to enjoy the literature properly. The ordinary schoolboy "finds Parnassus uncommonly steep, and there is no chance of his having time or inclination to look about him till he gets to the top. And nine times out of ten he does not get to the top." Education he defined as "the instruction of the intellect in the laws of Nature, under which name I include not merely things and their forces, but men and their ways; and the fashioning of the affections and of the will into an earnest and loving desire to move in harmony with those laws." Huxley's views on liberal education and the place of science in it is expressed forcibly in an address he gave to the South London Workingmen's College in 1868 and published in the same year in *Macmillan's Maga-zine,* and also in the title essay of *Science and Culture and Other Essays* (1881); these essays, together with Arnold's reply, first given as the Rede Lectures at Cambridge in 1880 and published in the *Nine-teenth Century* in 1882 (he also delivered this lecture in America and included it in his *American Discourses,* 1885), constitute an in-teresting and instructive clash of opinion between two great Vic-torians, each passionately interested in reforming English education. Mill's was the Victorian secular mind operating on philosophy and political theory; Huxley's, the Victorian secular mind working through a basic interest in the natural sciences; Arnold, the Victorian apostle of culture seeking for new techniques for bringing the re-ligious and literary heritage of the past into the modern world. All three were very much aware of the modernity of the modern world: Mill and Huxley looked forward with hope, while Arnold, though he sometimes appeared to do so, possessed a sensibility which, in spite of himself, remained rooted in nostalgia. In their differences as well as in their similarities (which are greater than might appear at first sight) they help to illuminate some of the finer reaches of the Victorian mind.

Meanwhile, Ruskin's approach to social and economic problems through art was being developed by William Morris (1834–96), who went much further than Ruskin in moving from a theory of art as "the expression of joy in labour" to active propaganda for Socialism. Like Ruskin, he hated industrialism and what it had done to the face of England and to the living conditions of the working people and the upper classes alike. He saw in medieval society and in the "small, white and clean" London which he imagined as having been the medieval city, something at least of the kind of life and art he pre-ferred to the Victorian variety. He admired Chaucer and medieval architecture and was interested in the conditions that produced them. He also admired old Icelandic literature, because the simple, vigorous life of the Norsemen, as reflected in the Sagas, attracted him, and he thought it had a valuable message for his own age. His translations and imitations of Norse poetry, produced at a period when his love of Icelandic life and art had for the time being completely conquered his medievalism, constitute some of the best literary work he ever did. But his practical interest in art and craftsmanship never slackened. In 1890, he founded the Kelmscott Press, designing his own fonts of type and ornaments, with which he printed his own works and medieval classics.

Morris' intense practical enthusiasm for art led him, as it had led Ruskin, to inquire into the function of art and the social conditions necessary for its healthy production. He came to see the progress of civilization from the Industrial Revolution onward—and in some respects from the Renaissance onward—as involving increasing mechanization of life and to believe that a radical reorganization of society was necessary if this debasement was not to continue. This led him to embark on a study of politics and economics from which he emerged a convinced Socialist, and, from 1883 until the end of his life, he gave his ardent support first to the Social Democratic Federation, then, from 1884 to 1890, to the Socialist League, and even in his last years to the Socialist cause by writing and lecturing. His combination of medievalism and Socialism is a paradox, but one characteristic of his age. He hated machines, and in his picture of a brave new world saw handicrafts restored to their rightful place and joy in work replacing the capitalist factory system. His *News from Nowhere* (1891), one of his most attractive pieces of prose writing, is a vision of England in the twenty-first century, an England devoid of railways and factories, with the large cities broken up into small towns, nature restored to its proper place in the English landscape, everybody beautiful, simple, and kind, with no private property and all labor done joyfully and voluntarily. It is a picture of a communist state very unlike anything that would arise to the mid-twentieth century imagination, and the whole work is in many respects naïve and even preposterous. Of course it is not meant as a political program or even as an accurate blueprint of the future, but simply as a projection of the sort of world in which he would be happiest. And it is not as politically naïve as its picture of a craftsman's Utopia might suggest, for it includes a detailed and fairly sophisticated account of the maneuvers and civil conflicts which brought this new world into being. *A Dream of John Ball* (1888) goes back to the time of the Peasants' Revolt of 1381, and gives an account of the activities and aspirations of the Peasants' Revolt: it has less of the quiet clarity of *News from Nowhere;* the deliberate archaisms of style are irritating; and the attempt to relate the medieval situation to the needs of his own time is rather strained. John Ball's sermon, which occupies an important place in the story, has however real eloquence in spite of the archaisms.

Morris's lectures and essays echo—but in his own idiom—many of the ideas of Ruskin. "To give people pleasure in the things they must perforce *use*, that is one great office of decoration; to give people pleasure in the things they must perforce *make*, that is the other use of it." This remark, from a lecture on "The Decorative Arts" delivered in 1877 and published in 1882 in *Hopes and Fears for Art*, is one of the many ideas developed by Morris from Ruskin's chapter on the Gothic in *The Stones of Venice*, a work to which Morris more than once paid tribute. In this lecture he not only preached the gospel of joy in work, and the relation of quality in art to the joy taken by the artist, but also attacked directly "that shortsighted, reckless brutality of squalor that so disgraces our intricate civilization." He has a fierce scorn for the behavior of the Victorian capitalist. "Is money to be gathered? Cut down the pleasant trees among the houses, pull down ancient and venerable buildings for the money that a few square yards of London dirt will fetch; blacken rivers, hide the sun and poison the air with smoke and worse, and it's nobody's business to see to it or mend it: that is all that modern commerce, the counting-house forgetful of the workshop, will do for us herein." As for science, it should turn its attention to reducing smoke and preventing river pollution by industrial waste. In other essays in the same volume, Morris returns to the attack on the ugliness of industrial England and the "enormous amount of pleasureless work" that the contemporary economic system forces on men. "Art made by the people for the people as a joy for the maker and the user" is only possible under a different order of society.

Morris' essays and lectures on art and economics have nothing of Carlyle's rhetorical violence or Ruskin's purple passages. His style is urgent, fairly colloquial, and sometimes rather formless. At its best it is simple and passionate. In the latter part of his life he moved in a much more actively political atmosphere than any other of the Victorian prophets had moved in, and his political ideas influenced a generation, notable among whom was George Bernard Shaw.

By the eighties of the nineteenth century the Liberal tradition in England ("the measureless power of Whiggery" as Morris called it) was becoming rather exhausted. The working classes, grown tremendously in influence and organization, were becoming a political force to be reckoned with, and, with a trade depression, an Irish problem, danger in India and muddle in South Africa, and growing unemployment at home, the powerlessness of the Liberals to provide any radical cure for discontents was becoming increasingly apparent. The prosperity of twenty years earlier had made it possible for Liberal governments to pursue a policy of slow reform combined with self-congratulation of the state of things as they were; but now they had little to offer. Attacks on free trade became common, and imperialist sentiment grew. But attacks on Liberalism from the right could find little support among the increasing number of rebellious intellectuals any more than among the members of the working class. The Socialist approach became increasingly popular.

Though the essence of Socialist doctrine had been proclaimed in 1848 in the *Communist Manifesto* of Marx and Engels, Socialism gained little in popularity in England during the next thirty years. British leaders of working-class movements had supported radicalism in a general sense, even Liberalism of the Continental brand, especially when it was combined with nationalism—witness the sympathy expressed by both the Chartists and the London Trades Council with Italian and Polish nationalism and the popularity in England of Mazzini and Garibaldi—but they had little or no connection with Socialist thought and Socialist organizations. The influence of Marx, the first volume of whose *Capital* did not appear until 1867, was slow in making itself felt. But gradually Socialism separated itself out from other ideologies, until by the end of the 1870's there was a certain amount of clearly defined Socialist activity on the Continent. In England, the International Working Men's Association, formed in London in 1864 largely under the influence of Marx, produced no immediate results in furthering Socialism; but, though it split up into different sections in the beginning of 1872, its rather checkered career had not been in vain, as the manifesto of the British Section in March, 1872, testifies. Trade-union leaders, who had long abandoned the revolutionary idealism of the Chartists, began to be attacked for their cooperation with the ruling classes. Different types of Socialist thought became increasingly vocal. By 1880, the turning point had been reached and Socialism began to move forward rapidly. On the Continent, the Socialist movement had reached a fair degree of consolidation after the reaction that had followed the failure of the Paris Commune of 1871; in England, three Labor candidates were successful at the general election of 1880. In the following year, as the result of the efforts of H. M. Hyndman, a Marxist propagandist though not viewed with much favor by Marx, the Democratic (later Social Democratic) Federation was founded. The investigation of Marxism by English intellectuals went on apace. In the course of the next ten years there was drawn into sympathy with

Socialism, if not wholehearted support, a number of important men of letters.

Morris joined the Democratic Federation in 1883, the year when Henry George came from America to lecture on Socialism in Ireland and England, and he threw himself vigorously into working for the movement with speeches, pamphlets, and poems. In 1884, seeking for a more active policy, Morris, with a number of others, left the Social Democratic Federation and founded the Socialist League. In 1894, in his essay "How I Became a Socialist," he gave his final definition of Socialism—"a condition of society in which there would be neither rich nor poor, neither master nor master's man, neither idle nor over-worked, neither brain-sick brain workers, nor heart-sick hand workers, in a word, in which all men would be living in equality of condition and would manage their affairs unwastefully, and with the full consciousness that harm to one would mean harm to all— the realisation at last of the meaning of the word COMMONWEALTH." In this essay too, he tries to answer a question which has troubled many modern critics of Morris: how he came to travel the road from Art to Socialism. Here are his last words on the subject:

> A last word or two. Perhaps some of our friends will say, what have we to do with these matters of history and art? We want by means of Social-Democracy to win a decent livelihood, we want in some sort to live, and that at once. Surely any one who professes to think that the question of art and cultivation must go before that of the knife and fork (and there are some who do propose that) does not understand what art means, or how that its roots must have a soil of a thriving and unanxious life. Yet it must be remembered that civilization has reduced the workman to such a skinny and pitiful existence, that he scarcely knows how to frame a desire for any life much better than that which he now endures perforce. It is the province of art to set the true ideal of a full and reasonable life before him, a life to which the perception and creation of beauty, the enjoyment of real pleasure that is, shall be felt to be as necessary to man as his daily bread, and that no man, and no set of men, can be deprived of this except by mere opposition, which should be resisted to the utmost.

Morris brought his medieval dreams and Pre-Raphaelite visions to the service of social and economic reform; but there were other late Victorians whose esthetic preoccupations led them away from contemporary society to brood over the inner meaning of art or attempt to distill the quintessence of esthetic experience in critical essays or in meditations over and reconstructions of an idealized past. Walter Pater (1839–94) brought his musically languorous prose style to bear on questions of art and experience, developing a view of the well-lived life as one that seizes on the shifting forms of experience at their moments of greatest intensity to savor them with deliberate relish. In his *Studies in the History of the Renaissance* (1873), he meditated with conscious artfulness over Renaissance art and life in an endeavor to illustrate and implement his view that "in aesthetic criticism the first step towards seeing one's object as it really is, is to know one's own impression as it really is, to discriminate it, to realise it distinctly." Pater's criticism was impressionist on principle. "What is this song or picture, this engaging personality presented in life or in a book, to *me*? What effect does it really produce on me? Does it give me pleasure? And if so, what sort or degree of pleasure? How is my nature modified by its presence, and under its influence?" He was aware of the limiting nature of individual experience. "Experience, already reduced to a swarm of impressions, is ringed round for each one of us by that thick wall of personality through which no real voice has ever pierced on its way to us, or from us to that which we can only conjecture to be without. Every one of those impressions is the impression of the individual in his isolation, each mind keeping as a solitary prisoner its own dream of a world." Thus in the conclusion of his *Renaissance* he admits the solipsistic nature of all discourse about art and goes on to draw his famous conclusion:

Every moment some form grows perfect in hand or face; some tone on the hills or the sea is choicer than the rest; some mood of passion or insight or intellectual excitement is irresistibly real and attractive for us,—for that moment only. Not the fruit of experience, but experience itself, is the end. A counted number of pulses only is given to us of a variegated, dramatic life. How may we see in them all that is to be seen in them by the finest senses? How shall we pass most swiftly from point to point, and be present always at the focus where the greatest number of vital forces unite in their purest energy?

To burn always with this hard, gemlike flame, to maintain this ecstasy, is success in life . . . While all melts under our feet, we may well catch at any exquisite passion, or any contribution to knowledge that seems by a lifted horizon to set the spirit free for a moment, or any stirring of the senses, strange dyes, strange colours, and curious odours, or work of the artist's hands, or the face of one's friend. Not to discriminate every moment some passionate attitude in those about us, and in the brilliancy of their gifts some tragic dividing of forces on their ways, is, on this short day of frost and sun, to sleep before evening . . .

This sounds like a philosophy of sensationalist hedonism, and it was taken to be so by many of Pater's disciples, including Oscar Wilde. But Pater himself became nervous of the effect of his doctrine and protested that he had been misunderstood. He omitted the Conclusion to the second edition of *The Renaissance*, but brought it back again in the third (1888) with a note explaining that it had been omitted in the second "as I conceived it might possibly mislead some of those young men into whose hands it might fall" but that he was now reprinting it "with some slight changes which bring it closer to my original meaning." He directed the reader to *Marius the Epicurean* for a fuller development of his thoughts on these matters.

Marius the Epicurean (1885) is hardly a novel in the accepted sense of the word: its subtitle is "His Sensations and Ideas," and it is the story, set in the second century A.D., of the development of the mind and sensibility of a young Roman lad from his first response to the appeal of the old Roman religion as it lingered on in country places to his final surrender to the appeal of the new Christian religion and his death while still a young man as a result of his association with Christian friends. Slow moving, interlarded with philosophical meditations and discussions, with Latin and Greek phrases woven at intervals into the elaborate English prose, inset Socratic dialogues, carefully wrought reconstructions of places and atmospheres, a retelling of the story of Cupid and Psyche, and continual echoes of late Roman lyric poetry (such as the *Pervigilium Veneris*) and of both pagan and early Christian liturgical literature, the book almost sinks under its own weight. If read as a novel it would indeed sink (as Dr. Johnson said of Richardson's *Clarissa*, if you read it for the story, "your patience would be so fretted you would hang yourself"), but it remains afloat as an extended exploration of the relation between art, religion, philosophy, and experience and how this relation can affect the sensibility. Marius' development is in a sense the presentation of alternatives that appealed to the author; each phase of the thought is explored with languorous intensity, Pater moving insensibly from Marius to himself and his own time:

But, without him there is a venerable system of sentiment and idea, widely extended in time and place, in a kind of impregnable possession of human life —a system, which, like some other great products of the conjoint efforts of human mind through many generations, is rich in the world's experience; so that, in attaching oneself to it, one lets in a great tide of that experience, and makes, as it were with a single step, a great experience of one's own, and with great consequent increase to one's sense of colour, variety, and relief, in the spectacle of men and things. The mere sense that one belongs to a system— an imperial system of organisation—has, in itself, the expanding power of a great experience; as some have felt who have been admitted from narrower sects into the communion of the catholic church; or as the old Roman citizen felt.

A wonderful order, actually in possession of human life!—grown inextricably through and through it; penetrating into its laws, its very language, its mere habits of decorum, in a thousand half-conscious ways; yet still felt to be, in part, an unfulfilled ideal; and, as such, awakening hope, and an aim, identical with the one only consistent aspiration of mankind! In the apprehension of that, just then, Marius seemed to have joined company once more with his own old self; . . .

The movement is from "him," to "one," back to "him." Marius' final perception, as he lies dying, is similarly presented as an insight both for hero and for author—and for reader: "Surely the aim of a true philosophy must lie, not in futile efforts towards the complete accommodation of man to the circumstances in which he chances to find himself, but in the maintenance of a kind of candid discontent, in the face of the very highest achievement; the unclouded and receptive soul quitting the world finally, with the same fresh wonder with which it had entered the world still unimpaired, and going on its blind way at last with the consciousness of some profound enigma in things, as but a pledge of something further to come."

Pater's criticism is best when exercised (as it most often is) on congenial subjects. The essays in *Appreciations* (1889) are prefixed by an essay on "Style" in which he develops his view of the artist as the transcriber "not of the world, not of mere fact, but of his sense of it." The lowliest form of literature seeks truth to fact, the highest seeks "truth as expression, that finest and most intimate form of truth, the *vraie vérité*." Complete union of form and content, as in music, is the ideal. "If music be the ideal of all art whatever, precisely because in music it is impossible to distinguish the form from the substance or matter, the subject from the expression, then, literature, by finding its specific excellence in the absolute correspondence of the term to its import, will be but fulfilling the condition of all artistic quality in things everywhere, of all good art." Pater concludes, somewhat surprisingly, by remarking that good art is not necessarily great art, for great art must also have something impressive in "the quality of the matter it informs or controls." It is on this, on "its compass, its variety, its alliance to great ends, or the depth of the note of revolt, or the largeness of hope in it, that the greatness of literary art depends." But the theme is not fully worked out. In his practical criticism, his concern is to lay his finger on the essential element in the mind or sensibility of the writer. Wordsworth, for example, "subdues man to the level of nature, and gives him thereby a certain breadth and coolness and solemnity." Coleridge he sees as "a true flower of the *ennuyé*." But he does not spend all his time trying to fit a writer into a single theory: his criticism is discursive, interspersed with biographical and general comments and with philosophical observations as when he breaks into his dis-

cussion of Coleridge to defend "the relative spirit" against the tendency "to turn ascertained truth into a dead letter" and to insist that
"the relative spirit, by its constant dwellings on the more fugitive
conditions or circumstances of things, breaking through a thousand
rough and brutal classifications, and giving elasticity to inflexible
principles, begets an intellectual *finesse* of which the ethical result
is a delicate and tender justice in the criticism of human life." We
must have no formula "less living and flexible than life itself." This
leads to criticism sometimes of remarkable perceptiveness, sometimes
merely impressionist or wrought up into a species of emotional
autobiography.

Pater's was not really an adventurous spirit; his life as a timid
Oxford recluse is not really in contrast with the boldness of his
hedonistic philosophy, because it was a philosophy concerned in the
last analysis only with the individual sensibility, never with the world
at large In this he was at the opposite pole from Ruskin and Morris.
The world for Pater existed to be absorbed into the refining and
refined (and isolated) sensibility. One of his most persuasive portraits
is largely a self-portrait, that of the young Florian Deleal in "The
Child in the House" (*Macmillan's Magazine,* 1878, reprinted in
Miscellaneous Studies, 1895). It is all very appealing in its richly
sensuous way, but a little cloying at last: "A touch of regret or desire
mingled all night with the remembered presence of the red flowers,
and their perfume in the darkness about him; and the longing for
some undivined, entire possession of them was the beginning of a
revelation to him, growing ever clearer, with the coming of the
gracious summer guise of fields and trees and persons in each succeeding year, of a certain, at times seemingly exclusive, predomi-
nance in his interests, of beautiful things, a kind of tyranny of the
senses over him." It is the recurrence of the Tennysonian and Arnoldian elegiac note that keeps preventing Pater's hard, gemlike flame
from remaining hard and gemlike. "A touch of regret or desire . . ."
For so many of the Victorians, regret and desire were almost inter-
changeable.

The Victorian age was also an age of historical scholarship and
historical writing. Carlyle used history for prophetic purposes, and
even Macaulay could hardly be said to have been interested in the
past for its own sake, though he may have thought that he was. Most
of the Victorian historians, especially those in the earlier part of the
period, wrote with some strong, and often admitted, passion or
prejudice. James Anthony Froude (1818–94) had a passionate interest
in the sixteenth century because he saw the climax of a whole phase

of civilization in the defeat of the Spanish Armada; he was a sound —though sometimes a careless—scholar of the period, but his *History of England from the Fall of Cardinal Wolsey to the Spanish Armada* (1856–70) is boisterously partisan in its championing of the Reformation and glorying in the defeat of Spain. The same spirit is seen in his *English Seamen in the Sixteenth Century* (1895). Froude writes history with verve and a fine attention to vivid detail. He believed that the historian should give the facts, not his own opinion of the facts; but he saw history as a great drama ("It is Nature's drama—not Shakespeare's—but a drama none the less"), and this inevitably meant portraying villains and heroes, high moments of destiny and acts of retribution and divine justice. "One lesson, and only one, history may be said to repeat with distinctness; that the world is built somehow on moral foundations; that, in the long run, it is well with the good; in the long run, it is ill with the wicked." Froude had a robust if not a profound mind; his *Short Studies in Great Subjects* (four volumes, 1867–83) reveal a vigorous, nondogmatic but opinionated Protestant curiosity about life and letters. His *Life of Carlyle* (1882, 1884) was attacked at the time as both indiscreet and inaccurate, but it remains a spirited work full of interest and vitality. Sir John R. Seeley's *Expansion of England* (1883) treats the development of the British Empire with an exuberance similar to Froude's in *English Seamen*. John Richard Green's *History of the English People* (four volumes, 1878–80) is important for its shifting of the emphasis from political and dynastic to social history. Something of Froude's vigorous patriotism, but directed toward a different area of English history, is to be seen in E. A. Freeman's *History of the Norman Conquest* (six volumes, 1881–82). Freeman was a passionate believer in the importance of the Germanic inheritance of the English people, and reflects a tendency in the Victorian period to minimize the Romance element in English literature and history and emphasize, in a somewhat romantic way, the Teutonic. More philosophical than any of these historians, and determined to track down the principles of historical causation in geographical environment and climate and the kinds of intelligence they foster, Henry Thomas Buckle produced in his *History of Civilisation in England* (1857–61) a work which claimed to handle history with a new kind of scientific understanding; but his brand of historical determinism is itself now only of historical interest. A similar rationalizing mind, and a more ambitious one, is that of W. E. H. Lecky, whose various works of intellectual and political history show a determination to bring every human phenomenon under the analytic gaze of positivist inquiry. But Buckle and Lecky did not set out to write literature; they considered themselves as philosophers or even scientists. Nor did the scholarly historical researchers—men like Bishop Stubbs who did so much pioneer work on the documents of English constitutional history, or the learned and indefatigable S. R. Gardiner who specialized in the seventeenth century, and many others—claim to be doing more than adding to knowledge about the past. As the century progressed, and in some degree under the influence of the German historian Leopold von Ranke, the ideal of English history became more and more the scientific and objective investigation of documents and study of facts. That trend was successfully opposed and in some degree reversed by G. M. Trevelyan, grandnephew of Macaulay, in the first three decades of the present century.

CHAPTER TWENTY-FIVE

The Victorian Poets

QUEEN VICTORIA CAME to the throne in 1837, and gave her name to the period which lasted until the end of the century. Poetry at the beginning of this period had been refreshed as well as sometimes muddied by two generations of Romantic innovation. The legacy which the Romantics handed on to the Victorians did not prove to be Wordsworth's simplicity or his autobiographical self-examination in quietly probing blank verse, nor was it in any conspicuous degree Shelley's mythopoeic excitement or Byron's alternation of dashing histrionics and a verse satire both colloquial and formal. But Keats' rich colors and the languid movement of his nightingale ode were taken over, as were eighteenth-century Gothic sensationalism and the desire to get behind the eighteenth century to Elizabethan and Jacobean models. The best known poem of George Darley (1795–1846), "It is not beauty I demand," was mistaken for a genuine seventeenth-century poem by F. T. Palgrave, editor of *The Golden Treasury*, and it is indeed suggestive of a Cavalier lyric in its imagery and movement:

> It is not beauty I demand,
>   A crystal brow, the moon's despair,
> Nor the snow's daughter, a white hand,
>   Nor mermaid's yellow pride of hair.
>
> Tell me not of your starry eyes,
>   Your lips that seem on roses fed,
> Your breasts where Cupid trembling lies,
>   Nor sleeps for kissing of his bed . . .

It is a little overdone, like so many nineteenth-century imitations of the Elizabethan and Jacobean, but it indicates an era habituated to seventeenth-century cadences. Darley was incapable of sustaining a theme or even of successfully sustaining a manner, and his longer works, *Sylvia* (1827) and *Nepenthe* (1836), are remembered only for the occasional song or lyrical passage, such as that beginning "O blest unfabled incense tree /That burns in glorious Araby" in *Nepenthe*.

A stranger and wilder poet, who sought to recapture something of the haunting violence of imagery of Jacobean dramatists such as Webster, was Thomas Lovell Beddoes (1803–49), who again is more successful in short lyrics and lyrical passages than in his complete tragedies. His drama *Death's Jest Book* (1850) contains many examples of his deliberately sensational imagery:

> Squats on a toad-stool under a tree
>   A bodiless childfull of life in the gloom
> Crying with frog voice, 'What shall I be?
> Poor unborn ghost, for my mother killed me
>   Scarcely alive in her wicked womb . . .'

The "Dirge for Wolfram," from the same drama, is more restrained in its imagery and shows the more brooding, plaintive side of Beddoes' poetic character, as well as illustrating his metrical facility (both he and Darley made interesting contributions to English metrics):

> If thou wilt ease thine heart
> Of love and all its smart,
>   Then sleep, dear, sleep;
> And not a sorrow
>   Hang any tear on your eyelashes;
>   Lie still and deep,
>   Sad soul, until the sea-wave washes
> The rim o' th' sun to-morrow,
>   In eastern sky.

Beddoes' morbid relish of the macabre can become wearisome; but he can also handle the macabre humorously (as in "Resurrection Song"). Madness fascinated him, and sometimes he handles it in a manner that is more suggestive of eighteenth-century Gothic than of Elizabethan or Jacobean:

> As mad sexton's bell, tolling
>   For earth's loveliest daughter
> Night's dumbness breaks rolling
>   Ghostily:
> So our boat breaks the water
>   Witchingly.

There is a suggestion of Shelley here, but Beddoes had none of Shelley's buoyant idealism. For Beddoes, poetry had above all to be *haunting*, and he often tried too deliberately to achieve this quality. Poets whose obvious desire is to make our flesh creep risk falling over into unconscious self-parody or sheer silliness. The necessity of being haunting comes together later in the century with the necessity of being plangent or evocative or misty, with unhappy effects on poetic imagery.

A simpler and purer inspiration is that of John Clare (1793–1864), the "Northamptonshire peasant poet," who was never able to achieve a proper status from which to exercise his talents and was deemed mad by his contemporaries for the last twenty years of his life (which he spent in an asylum). The quiet intensity of his observation in his descriptions of rural scenes, and the skill with which he organizes detail, combine to achieve a poetic utterance of remarkable power and control. His poetry is not Wordsworthian; he does not contemplate rural sights and sounds but, as a genuine countryman, speaks from among them with a calm lucidity that distills its own kind of meaning. He can move the reader by deploying simple objects and incidents in such a way as to suggest how eloquent of the human condition the sheer routine of daily affairs can be; he rejoiced in the *Dinglichkeit* of things and the reality of the trivial. Clare's voice is his own, his diction more eighteenth than nineteenth century in tone, in spite of the utter simplicity of his vocabulary (which sometimes includes dialect words). His poetry is Romantic in a sense, but it is also Classical in its. control and poise—as in "Signs of Winter," for example:

> The cat runs races with her tail. The dog
> Leaps o'er the orchard hedge and knarls the grass.
> The swine run round and grunt and play with straw,
> Snatching out hasty mouthfuls from the stack.
> Sudden upon the elmtree tops the crow
> Unceremonious visit pays and croaks,
> Then swoops away. From mossy barn the owl
> Bobs hasty out—wheels round and, scared as soon,
> As hastily retires. The ducks grow wild
> And from the muddy pond fly up and wheel
> A circle round the village and soon, tired,
> Plunge in the pond again. The maids in haste
> Snatch from the orchard hedge the mizzled clothes
> And laughing hurry in to keep them dry.

Clare remained outside the literary movements of his time. But if we turn to *Poems Chiefly Lyrical* published in 1830 by Alfred Tennyson (1809–92) we see what the Romantic Movement is going to bequeath to the Victorians:

> Where Claribel low-lieth
> 　The breezes pause and die,
> 　　Letting the rose-leaves fall:
> But the solemn oak-tree sigheth,
> 　Thick-leaved, ambrosial,
> 　With an ancient melody
> 　Of an inward agony,
> Where Claribel low-lieth.

Musical sadness amid fading roses; slow moving, vaguely suggestive, melancholy verse; images from nature used to evoke a generalized mood; the central situation itself left unspecified: this is the Tennyson of 1830 as it remains the essential Tennyson of 1889:

> What charm in words, a charm no words could give?
> O dying words, can Music make you live
> 　　　　　Far—far—away?

In the early volume we see again and again Nature conspiring to evoke the mood of loss and regret, and details of natural observation employed to suggest sad-sweet emotion:

> Heavily hangs the broad sunflower
> 　Over its grave i' the earth so chilly;
> Heavily hangs the hollyhock,
> Heavily hangs the tiger-lily.

Tennyson's objective is always to render a mood rather than to explore it. Consider, for example, the use he makes of objects in "Mariana":

> With blackest moss the flower-pots
> 　Were thickly crusted, one and all:
> The rusted nails fell from the knots
> 　That held the pear to the gable-wall.
> The broken sheds look'd sad and strange:
> 　Unlifted was the clinking latch;
> 　Weeded and worn the ancient thatch
> Upon the lonely moated grange.
> 　　She only said, 'My life is dreary,
> 　　　He cometh not,' she said;
> 　　She said, 'I am aweary, aweary,
> 　　　I would that I were dead!'

"The *broken* sheds look'd *sad* and *strange*"—the adjectives here as elsewhere are designed to give a sense of generalized loss or decay. The poem is in its way masterly: the steady building up of suggestions of loneliness, slow crumbling away, utter distance from an active busy world, is most effectively done. Tennyson started simply with the words from *Measure for Measure,* "Mariana in the moated grange," which he uses as epigraph, and then proceeds to weave his mood piece round them. It is a surrender to self-indulgent, melancholy musing; yet the artificer is always at work choosing and organizing the images:

> All day within the dreamy house,
>   The doors upon their hinges creak'd;
> The blue fly sang in the pane; the mouse
>   Behind the mouldering wainscot shriek'd . . .

As so often in Tennyson, the images move outward, to create a generalized mood, rather than inward, to build up a more complex meaning within the poem. The fly and the mouse in the stanza just quoted are symbols of domestic decay and nothing more.

The Victorian poets, like the Romantic poets, were more adventurous in stanza forms than the eighteenth century; Tennyson liked to use fairly elaborate stanzas in which he could swing his lines with the mood. The four shorter lines, operating as an almost incantatory refrain, in the "Mariana" stanza serve to gather up the implications of the imagery in the preceding lines and repeat, almost hypnotically, the suggestion of loss, regret, and weariness. The imagery is often Keatsian, but it is the Keats of magic casements and moonlight through stained glass throwing warm gules on Madeline's fair breast rather than the Keats of "To Autumn" (with its carefully *referred* imagery) or of "Hyperion." Tennyson sometimes copies Keats' heraldic use of color, but generally his use of color images is simply for the mood or atmosphere—as indeed are so many of his images. The opening of Part IV of "The Lady of Shalott" (first published in *Poems* of 1833 and later revised) is a good example:

> In the stormy east-wind straining
> The pale yellow woods were waning,
> The broad stream in his banks complaining,
> Heavily the low sky raining
>   Over tower'd Camelot; . . .

The two-syllable rhymes here ("Straining," "waning," "complaining") exist in order to provide a certain kind of dying fall; the meaning is incidental, and perhaps not always what the poet really wants—he stretches a point of meaning for the sake of the sound and for the generalized suggestion implicit in a particular combination of sound and evocation.

The two volumes which Tennyson published in 1842, show him establishing both his style and his reputation. The dominant tone is elegiac, and Tennyson's ability to modulate epic into elegy, revealed in "The Lotos-Eaters" (first published in 1832) and "Morte D'Arthur" among other poems, is particularly striking. "The Lotos-Eaters" begins with a heroic line: " 'Courage!' he said, and pointed toward the land." Within a few lines the tone is wholly different. Indeed, the theme of this poem is symbolic of a central aspect of Tennyson's genius; the heroic adventurers coming on the languid island and succumbing to a mood of sad-sweet dream represent, as it were, the fate of heroic themes when they enter Tennyson's poetic world.

> All round the coast the languid air did swoon,
> Breathing like one that hath a weary dream.
> Full-faced above the valley stood the moon;
> And like a downward smoke, the slender stream
> Along the cliff to fall and pause and fall did seem.

The use of natural images to achieve a dream landscape is again characteristic. The details are often well observed:

> A land of streams! some, like a downward smoke,
> Slow-dropping veils of thinnest lawn, did go;
> And some thro' wavering lights and shadows broke,
> Rolling a slumbrous sheet of foam below.
> They saw the gleaming river seaward flow
> From the inner land: far off, three mountain-tops,
> Three silent pinnacles of aged snow,
> Stood sunset-flush'd: . . .

There are Keatsian echoes ("Give us long rest or death, dark death, or dreamful ease"), but Tennyson's use of adjectives is more abandoned. He leans on the adjective to a greater degree than Keats does, using it to deflect attention from the central core of a noun's meaning and resolve all into a mood, a sense of elegy. His turning of Malory's stern story of Arthur's death into the muted melancholy of "Morte D'Arthur" is a technical achievement of a high order, even if the modulation of action into dream at last begins to pall by sheer excess. The heroic theme of "Ulysses," one of Tennyson's most controlled and perfectly wrought dramatic monologues, which presents the voice of the aged Ulysses planning a final voyage, is similarly presented in a context of musical sadness:

> Some work of noble note may yet be done,
> Not unbecoming men that strove with Gods.
> The lights begin to twinkle from the rocks:
> The long day wanes: the slow moon climbs: the deep
> Moans round with many voices . . .

The short lyric "Break, break, break" concentrates the Tennysonian elegiac mode at its simplest. The "cold gray stones" of the sea both symbolize and project the poet's mood. The poet is withdrawn, cut off from the outside world. The fisherman's boy and the sailor lad shout and sing at work or play, but their extrovert activities only emphasize the poet's sense of loneliness and loss. The world's work goes on: "And the stately ships go on /To their haven under the hill"; but the poet has no part in it; he is alone with his sorrow. This is a characteristic Victorian variation of the Romantic sense of isolation or alienation found so emphatically in Byron, and it is to reappear later in the century in still other guises. The poet cut off by private grief from a world at work recurs several times in Tennyson, never more effectively than in the concluding stanza of one of the sections of *In Memoriam:*

> He is not here; but far away
> The noise of life begins again,
> And ghastly thro' the drizzling rain
> On the bald streets breaks the blank day.

Tennyson's collection of 1842 reprinted many poems considerably revised from the 1833 volume. The revisions reveal the development of his craftmanship, the pruning of luxuriance, the elimination of mawkishness, the concentration of effect. But Tennyson was not content, even at this stage in his career—and still less later, when he allowed himself to be persuaded that he had a mission to be the Victorian poet-prophet—to confine himself to beautifully wrought musical moaning or cunning distillations of mood; he had things to say too. "The Palace of Art" is an allegory expressing the need of art to take account of ordinary life and humble people; but the elegant verse prattle in which Tennyson tells the allegorical tale is neither interesting enough in itself nor rich enough in intellectual content to amount to very much. He is better with such a poem as "Oenone," where he treats classical myth with considerable freedom to produce a dramatic monologue, rhetorical rather than singingly lyrical in tone, where cadence, phrase, and image (and certain carefully designed repetitions) combine to produce the characteristic Tennysonian sense of loss. The best of Tennyson's dramatic monologues in this elegiac vein, which was not published until 1860, though written much earlier, is "Tithonus," the lament of the mortal made immortal, but not free from age and decay, at the rash request of the dawn goddess who loved him. It is a theme calculated to bring out Tennyson's full powers of elegiac description and meditation; the slow-moving Vir-

gilian cadences convey most successfully that heavy autumnal sense
of perpetual loss which Tennyson so loved to indulge in:

> The woods decay, the woods decay and fall,
> The vapours weep their burthen to the ground,
> Man comes and tills the field and lies beneath,
> And after many a summer dies the swan . . .

Tennyson was a skilled metrist, and liked to experiment in unusual meters. He was not well advised, however, to succumb to the
swinging, fifteen-syllable couplets of "Locksley Hall" and its much
later sequel; this kind of advanced barrel-organ music does possess a
certain appeal, but it is neither subtle nor lasting. When a similar
beat is combined with a mawkish theme, as in "The May Queen," the
result is upsetting.

Tennyson's desire to choose topical and instructive subjects more
than once led him astray. *The Princess* (1847), which deals with the
higher education of women, is remembered today by Gilbert and
Sullivan's parody and by the incidental lyrics many of which were
added in 1850. In these lyrics Tennyson expresses his favorite elegiac
theme in a variety of meters and of contexts. The quietly singing lul-
laby, "Sweet and Low," the familiar modulation of heroic into melancholy in "The splendour falls on castle walls," the use of nature imagery to create a mood of loss and nostalgia in the unrhymed stanzas
of "Tears, Idle Tears," and the dissolving of passion in a glimmering
world of stars, sleeping flowers, and lake water that is suggested in
"Now sleeps the crimson petal"—these are some of the more successful experiments.

Like so many men of his time, Tennyson was a worrier. He worried
about God and Nature and man; about modern science and its effect
on belief; about Darwin and the significance of his theory of evolution; about the meaning of life. The death of his close friend Arthur
Henry Hallam in 1833 added an abiding sense of personal loss to his
basic worries, and the grief and the worries came together over the
years to produce slowly the series of linked lyrics he called *In Memoriam* (1850). Here Tennyson works his way through overwhelming
grief through worry to faith, but the progression is not genuine either
poetically or intellectually: at a certain point he simply stops worrying and proclaims a belief in a Love that is stronger than Death and
in "One God, one law, one element, /And one far-off divine event,
/To which the whole creation moves." The worrying stanzas of *In
Memoriam* are often interesting, but biographically rather than poetically. Tennyson worrying about a God who is careful of the type but
careless of the single life and about "Nature, red in tooth and claw,"

or stretching "lame hands of faith" toward a larger hope which may resolve these doubts and difficulties—this is a figure full of interest for those concerned with Victorian thought and the impact of Darwinism on the moral imagination. But *In Memoriam* lives as poetry (as we might expect) by its lyrics which distill personal mood. Many of these can be taken out of their context and read as individual poems. Nevertheless, though these are the finest single poems in the work, *In Memoriam* when read as a whole does impress and even move by its cumulative revelation of such a large tract of a man's emotional life; it has an integrity as autobiography that exceeds its integrity as poetry.

With the publication of *In Memoriam*, Tennyson's status as the poet of his age was assured; he was appointed Poet Laureate in the year of its publication, though he was not raised to the peerage until 1883. His sense of his mission to his age (continually urged by reviewers) inevitably grew, and produced large numbers of poems in which he was deflected from his natural bent to play the sage or the moralist. Yet he had the strength of purpose to produce *Maud* (1855), a "monodrama," a rapid and feverish record, in a series of lyrics, of a love affair blasted by a tragic accident. It is true that at the end the crushed hero rouses himself to proclaim his patriotic determination to fight in the Crimean War which he sees as a salutary stirring up of a slothful materialist nation; but this jingoistic coda has nothing to do with the monodrama as a whole. The speed and hothouse passion of the lyrics in *Maud* are impressive in spite of the almost morbid crowding of imagery. One can take a lyric like "Come into the garden, Maud" out of its context in the sequence and see it as frenzied and inorganic in its imagery and embarrassingly adolescent in emotion, but in its context it is surprisingly effective. Everything is hot and fevered. The rhythms swing and crash, passion grows exclamatory and anguished, natural images reflect or suggest the heavily scented atmosphere which surrounds the hero and his love. It is all a bit too much, a bit cloying. But it can be argued that this is what it is intended to be, and it took courage for Tennyson to do it.

Tennyson's verse dramas were no more successful than others of the age. His poem, "Dora," is an experiment in Wordsworthian blank verse narrative, which is mildly skillful but lacks the Wordsworthian tone of intimate exploration of meaning (though Wordsworth admired it). The much longer narrative poem, "Enoch Arden," tries to wring heroic significance out of a domestic situation treated with a moral feeling so "Victorian" (in the popular sense of the word) that all real life and complexity are lacking. The twelve books of the *Idylls of the King*, Tennyson's retelling of stories from Malory, represent his most sustained attempt to cast romantic material into a Victorian moral mold. Though he tells these stories in a blank verse of considerable technical accomplishment as in the movement of phrases, the control and variation of pauses, and the use of words with differing numbers of syllables—the attempt to be both evocative and moralistic, to simplify the moral meaning of the stories so that they could accommodate the nineteenth-century middle-class attitude to love and marriage while at the same time providing background poeticizing, is not on the whole successful.

Yet Tennyson keeps surprising us. That he was one of the most skillful metrists among English poets and could turn out fascinating exercises in odd rhythms is not perhaps as great a claim to poetic distinction as was once thought. But that he could write in 1868 such a poem as "Lucretius," the most daring and complex of his dramatic monologues, *is* a claim to distinction. And the same poet could write the rollicking narrative ballad, "The Revenge," and the two lively satirical dialect monologues, "Northern Farmer: Old Style," and "Northern Farmer: New Style." If he lacked complexity and, at times, emotional discipline, he could show himself master of the simple mood-lyric, a brilliant manipulator of language to the ear, and a conscientious craftsman who could work up a remarkably high polish to his work. Many of his best poems invite the reader to look through them to contemplate himself with self-pity, and this is not the function of the greatest poetry. But if Tennyson is not of the greatest English poets, he remains one of the most skillful and, within the area which he chose to cultivate, one of the most professionally competent.

The great achievement of Robert Browning (1812–89) was to break away from the post-Keatsian handling of sensory images and bring back a colloquial vigor to English poetry. Though not the great philosophical poet he was thought to be in the latter part of his own lifetime, Browning developed a remarkable ability to explore character argumentatively, as it were, to sound in his verse a note of robust individuality. He began under Shelley's influence as a poet of confessional excess, but his early work in this vein won no favor, and he soon turned to the mode in which he won his greatest successes. *Pauline*, published anonymously in 1833, is weakly feverish in autobiographical blank verse, and was deservedly ignored; *Paracelsus* (1835) is an inquiry into the nature of poetry in dramatic form but not really dramatic in style, still showing some crude Shelley influence; *Sordello* (1840), as unreadable today as its first audience found it, presents, like *Paracelsus,* the supposed views of a real historical character, but it again shows Browning discussing the nature and function of poetry. His blank-verse tragedy *Strafford* (1837) suffers, as all Victorian blank-verse tragedy does, from the shadow of Shakespeare; it is oddly exclamatory in style and the emotion is not adequately realized in the verse. *Pippa Passes* (1841) is the first work which shows something of the real Browning; it presents a number of dramatic situations on which the mill girl Pippa impinges as she walks singing past the various scenes, her singing having in each case a surprising effect on the action. The conception is interesting, and though there is no real dramatic movement (there almost never is in Browning) there are some effective moments of arrested drama when, in dialogue or soliloquy, characters and situations project themselves. But it is with *Dramatic Lyrics* (1842), *Dramatic Romances* (1845), *Men and Women* (1855), and *Dramatis Personae* (1864) that Browning fully develops his characteristic powers.

Tennyson used the form of the dramatic monologue in "Ulysses," "Tithonus," and a few other poems, but these are essentially mood pieces, while Browning's dramatic monologues are not written in order to build up an atmosphere of languid sorrow or quiet determination or heavy beauty, but to project with an almost quizzical violence a certain kind of personality, a certain temperament, a way of looking at life, even a moment of history realized in the self-revelation of a type. The method is not impressionistic or symbolic, nor is it really exploratory (T. S. Eliot's dramatic monologues are all three): these are set pieces in which a fully known character, seen in a clear light, is set sharply before the reader. The hints are never truly mysterious, even where the precise nature of an incident referred to may be left in doubt:

> Oh sir, she smiled, no doubt,
> Whene'er I passed her; but who passed without
> Much the same smile? This grew; I gave commands;
> Then all smiles stopped together.

These lines from "My Last Duchess" are very Browningesque both in movement (the poem uses decasyllabic couplets with a startlingly colloquial cadence) and in the abrupt hinting which they convey. The whole poem is but the visible part of the iceberg; but the submerged invisible part is not a matter of vague suggestiveness; it is both psychologically and historically defined. In many of these monologues the mingling of the colloquial and the unusual achieves an effect of grotesqueness that adds life and a kind of humor:

> Whew! We'll have our platter burnished,
> Laid with care on our own shelf!
> With a fire-new spoon we're furnished,

And a goblet for ourself,
Rinsed like something sacrificial
Ere 'tis fit to touch our chaps—
Marked with L. for our initial!
(He-he! There his lily snaps!)

These lines, from "Soliloquy of the Spanish Cloister," provide a fairly simple example; the following, from "Fra Lippo Lippi," show a more mature stage:

What's it all about?
To be passed over, despised? or dwelt upon,
Wondered at? oh, this last of course!—you say.
But why not do as well as say,—paint these
Just as they are, careless of what comes of it?
God's works—paint any one, and count it crime
To let a truth slip. Don't object, "His works
"Are here already; nature is complete:
"Suppose you reproduce her—(which you can't)
"There's no advantage! you must beat her, then."
For, don't you mark? we're made so that we love
First when we see them painted, things we have passed
Perhaps a hundred times nor cared to see;
And so they are better, painted—better to us,
Which is the same thing. Art was given for that;
God uses us to help each other so,
Lending our minds out. Have you noticed, now,
Your cullion's hanging face? A bit of chalk,
And trust me but you should, though! How much more,
If I drew higher things with the same truth!
That were to take the Prior's pulpit-place,
Interpret God to all of you! Oh, oh,
It makes me mad to see what men shall do
And we in our graves!

The cadences are not as colloquial as they sound; the exclamations and abbreviations which Browning employs are often artificial or archaic; but they give an effect of period and of individuality, suggesting that this is the authentic accent of this man at this historical moment in this place. (It is a device which Ezra Pound learned from Browning.) Double rhymes, almost but never wholly comic, sometimes help to achieve a similar effect. How much more individualized is Browning's "The Glove" (a reminiscence put into the mouth of the poet Ronsard) than Leigh Hunt's conventional treatment of the same theme: the double rhymes are essential for the setting and maintaining of the tone, from the opening

"Heigho," yawned one day King Francis,
"Distance all value enhances! . . ."

to the concluding

Venienti occurrite morbo!
With which moral I drop my theorbo.

This, of course, shows Browning merely amusing himself, but it is a
more profitable amusement for a poet than Tennyson's experiments
in Alcaics and hendecasyllabics.

Browning's interest in painting and music provided some of the
most effective subjects for his dramatic monologues, "Pictor Ignotus,"
"Fra Lippo Lippi," and "Andrea del Sarto," all dealing with painters,
are among his best, while "A Toccata of Galuppi's," "Master Hughes
of Saxe-Gotha," and "Abt Vogler" show him using composers (real
or imaginary) in order to project certain attitudes. The movement of
"A Toccata" is deliberately mechanical and regular; Browning uses
it adroitly in order to suggest both the period and the effect of the
music on the poet in evoking the period as a past moment in history:

"Dust and ashes!" So you creak it, and I want the heart to scold.
Dear dead women, with such hair, too—what's become of all the gold
Used to hang and brush their bosoms? I feel chilly and grown old.

Of course, the personalities and attitudes which Browning projects in
his dramatic monologues are not necessarily historically accurate;
often Browning uses a historical character as he uses an imaginary
one, in order to present an area of his own thought and feeling. The
flamboyant optimism of "Rabbi Ben Ezra" cannot be directly connected with the known views of Abraham Ibn Ezra. But sometimes
Browning makes a real effort of the historical imagination to endeavor to capture the essence of a period in a particular character.
The period which intrigued him most was the Renaissance, especially the late Renaissance in Italy, with its lush paganizing of a
nominally Christian civilization. "The Bishop Orders his Tomb at St.
Praxed's Church" was praised by Ruskin in his *Modern Painters* as
evoking the Renaissance spirit, "its worldliness, inconsistency, pride,
hypocrisy, ignorance of itself, love of art, of luxury, and of good
Latin," more adequately than Ruskin himself was able to do in thirty
pages of *The Stones of Venice*. The real poetic interest of this monologue, however, as of so many of Browning's more successful poems
of this kind, lies in the violence and vividness with which he renders
the impression of a personality caught unawares. Browning seeks for
the confessional moment, the crisis which forces out of a man the

whole truth about himself as he sees it, whereas in Tennyson's stately and well-modulated dramatic monologues we see a figure carefully posed in representative gestures. Browning aims continually at the effect of impromptu.

The more elaborate and pretentious of Browning's dramatic monologues tend to be the least successful. "Saul" moves in its latter part into a statement of Browning's own faith, and, though the guise remains dramatic, the dramatic immediacy is lost. But "Bishop Blougram's Apology" is maintained for over a thousand lines at a high level of virtuosity, and though the argument which the Bishop presents (and with which Browning is clearly in sympathy) is patently vulnerable, the sense of a man really baring the principles on which he has based his life is compellingly achieved. This Browning did again and again in his monologues; he did capture the accent of impromptu self-revelation, even when what was revealed turns out to be a favorite doctrine of the poet himself. Further, the metrical skill of these poems is considerable (Browning was in his way as artful a metrist as Tennyson), and in the most successful poems it is used in order to amplify and enrich the tone of the character who is speaking.

In *Men and Women* Browning devotes a large number of monologues to a presentation of aspects of the relation between men and women, and many, although far from all, of these are based on his own experience as lover and husband of Elizabeth Barrett. The best are those where a personal experience or intuition is twisted or refracted through a historical or other situation—as indeed all are intended to be, for Browning was scared away from direct confessional poetry once and for all by the reception (or lack of reception) of *Pauline*. The dramatic mode for Browning was not quite a mask, in the Yeatsian sense. It was often a way of making his own emotional experiences or the fruits of his imagination more amenable to poetic treatment. A poem like "A Grammarian's Funeral" expresses, through a projection (not directly dramatic this time) of the character of one of those heroic Renaissance scholars whose scrupulous and unwearied pursuit of the *minutiae* of classical learning helped to lay the foundations of modern classical scholarship, something of the essence of Renaissance Humanism; but it also expresses Browning's own view of the nature of heroism and the importance of continuous endeavor. Even the plausible rascals who present their justifications (for example, "Mr. Sludge the Medium") do not represent altogether a complete imaginative identification with a wholly alien character; there is an element of Bishop Blougram in most of Browning's deceivers, and there is more than an element of Browning in Bishop Blougram.

It is the gay or quizzical or impertinent Browning rather than the profound Browning who has survived. The lively (and ingenious) informality of "Waring," the sheer high spirits of "The Pied Piper of Hamelin," are read while the long philosophical poems of his old age are not. Nor is the long poem, once considered his masterpiece, *The Ring and the Book* (1868–69), read today except by experts. It is a considerable achievement, nonetheless, the story of the background of a criminal trial told in a series of long dramatic monologues. The trouble is, that this is no way to tell a story. There are some impressive parts (notably the Pope's concluding monologue), but a monologue to be effective must not go on and on, nor should it be bound up with other protracted monologues in a sequence that the reader has no dramatic reason for pursuing as a sequence. *The Ring and the Book* is a *tour de force*, and can be admired if not enjoyed as such. It is tainted with the garrulity that grew on Browning as he grew older and more successful.

As for Browning's "robust optimism," an attitude which also grew on him with age and success, it serves mainly to remind the literary historian that Browning, unlike Tennyson, made no real attempt to come to terms with his age. He brushed aside its doubts and problems, to contemplate intriguing Renaissance figures in Italy. His optimism was not Victorian: no other Victorian poet of any significance was optimistic. The typical Victorian literary man was either a prophet or a worrier or a doubter, and none of these are optimistic types. Browning married his poetess and carried her off to Italy, to return to England in later life, an admired widower, successful and content with his lot, believing in life and love and work and immortality. It was long before he achieved recognition, but the slowness of his rise to fame never embittered him either with England or with life in general. He had enormous vitality, which enabled him to lead his own life independently of much that was going on in Victorian England—something that Tennyson could not do. That vitality comes into his best poetry, where it goes together with a high degree of artistry and a gift for the colloquial and the immediate. Romantic though in many respects Browning was, he blew away some of the lilies and languors that the Romantic Movement had bequeathed to England. There were, however, other Victorian poets who were determined to bring them back.

Elizabeth Barrett Browning (1806–61) is known today chiefly for the romantic circumstances of her marriage with Robert Browning, but in her lifetime she was the more famous poet of the two. Her poetry has none of her husband's strength and verbal precision; it is highly emotional, sometimes embarrassingly personal in tone, and draws on conventional poetic images and diction. Yet it has individuality; that flamboyant emotional exhibitionism using a language sometimes rhetorical and stiffly formal ("Go from me. Yet I feel that I shall stand /Henceforward in thy shadow"), sometimes unpleasantly mawkish ("Open thine heart wide, /And fold within, the wet wings of thy dove"), sometimes feverishly romantic ("The fireflies and the nightingales /Throbbed each to either, flame and song"), is always recognizably its author's. Sometimes, as in "Grief" ("I tell you, hopeless grief is passionless"), she achieves an impressive formal discipline, but more often (as in "The Cry of the Children") when one of her poems is effective it is because of the affect of undisciplined and even awkward spontaneity of feeling breaking through. *Sonnets from the Portuguese*, recording her love for Browning, cannot be read through today without discomfort, though there are arresting moments. Other poems are read for their topical interest ("The Cry of the Children" is a protest against the employment of children in factories) or the slightly coy charm with which she treats figures from classical mythology ("What was he doing, the great god Pan, /Down in the reeds by the river?"). Mrs. Browning had a conventional Christian piety that was quite different from her husband's kind of religious optimism, but her religious poems are not successful in their efforts to fuse devotional and esthetic impulses ("God himself is the best Poet, /And the Real is His song"). She spoke for herself and in doing so represented her age more directly than the greater Victorian poets did; her popularity in her own day tells us a great deal about Victorian poetic taste.

The poetry of Matthew Arnold (1822–88) represented its age in a far profounder way. Here is the true voice of the sensitive Victorian intellectual brooding over inevitable loss of faith and the meaning of life. Nineteenth-century Hellenism, romantic interest in folk tale and legend, the preference for solitary meditation in evocative surroundings—these elements give something of its distinctive character to Arnold's poetry, but these elements he shared with other Victorian poets. His own note of controlled self-pity is quite distinct from Tennyson's. Arnold's first volume, *The Strayed Reveller and other Poems* (1849), includes "Mycerinus," the story of the just king who turned to reveling when he learned from the oracle that, in spite of his virtue, he was to die after six years; it ends, not in protest, but in that characteristic note of elegiac description of landscape which Arnold used so often and which is heard at its most sustained in the conclusion of "Sohrab and Rustum." Here it is a coda of only six lines, but it foreshadows much in Arnold's poetry:

So six long years he revell'd, night and day;
And when the mirth wax'd loudest, with dull sound
Sometimes from the grove's centre echoes came,
To tell his wondering people of their king;
In the still night, across the steaming flats,
Mix'd with the murmur of the moving Nile.

That still night haunts Arnold's poetry. We see it in the title poem of
The Strayed Reveller, breaking even into the midst of a symbolic
Circean revel:

Ah cool night-wind, tremulous stars!
Ah glimmering water,
Fitful earth-murmur,
Dreaming woods!

And we see it again and again in later poems:

In the deserted moon-blanch'd street
How lonely rings the echo of my feet!
Those windows, which I gaze at, frown;
Silent and white, unopening down,
Repellent as the world;—but see,
A break between the housetops shows
The moon! and, lost behind her, fading dim
Into the dewy dark obscurity
Down at the far horizon's rim,
Doth a whole tract of heaven disclose.

(A Summer Night)

And can this fragrant lawn
With its cool trees, and night,
And the sweet, tranquil Thames,
And moonshine, and the dew,
To thy rack'd heart and brain
Afford no balm?

(Philomela)

But the majestic river floated on,
Out of the mist and hum of that low land,
Into the frosty starlight, and there moved,
Rejoicing, through the hush'd Chorasmian waste,
Under the solitary moon; . . .
. . . till at last
The long'd-for dash of waves is heard, and wide
His luminous home of waters opens, bright
And tranquil, from whose floor the new-bathed stars
Emerge, and shine upon the Aral Sea.

(Sohrab and Rustum)

The opening of "Dover Beach" is perhaps the finest expression of
that symbolic scene of night quiet which provided the setting and
the emotional background of so much of Arnold's elegiac meditation:

>The sea is calm to-night.
>The tide is full, the moon lies fair
>Upon the straits;—on the French coast the light
>Gleams and is gone; the cliffs of England stand,
>Glimmering and vast, out in the tranquil bay.
>Come to the window, sweet is the night-air!
>Only, from the long line of spray
>Where the sea meets the moon-blanch'd land,
>Listen! you hear the grating roar
>Of pebbles which the waves draw back, and fling,
>At their return, up the high strand,
>Begin, and cease, and then again begin,
>With tremulous cadence slow, and bring
>The eternal note of sadness in.

Arnold's first volume was published anonymously and almost immediately withdrawn from circulation. His second, *Empedocles on Etna
and Other Poems,* appeared in 1852, but he did not reprint the long
title poem in *Poems* of 1853 because, as he explained in the preface
to the latter volume, situations "in which the suffering finds no vent
in action; in which a continuous state of mental distress is prolonged,
unrelieved by incident, hope, or resistance; in which there is everything to be endured, nothing to be done," are not fit subjects for
poetry. "What are the eternal objects of Poetry, among all nations
and at all times?" Arnold asked in his 1853 preface, and he replied:
"They are actions; human actions; possessing an inherent interest in
themselves, and which are to be communicated in an interesting
manner by the art of the Poet." But his poetic instinct was at odds
with his critical intelligence, and even where he chose "human actions" he surrounded them with his own mood of meditative elegy.
The end of *Empedocles*—

>The day in his hotness,
>The strife with the palm;
>The night in her silence,
>The stars in their calm—

brings us to that same silent night that we find at the end of "Sohrab
and Rustum" and which haunts all his attempts to deal with heroic
or active themes, such as *Balder Dead,* based on Norse mythology, or
Tristram and Iseult, a long poem wholly elegiac in tone:

The air of the December night
Steals coldly around the chamber bright,
Where those lifeless lovers be;
Swinging with it, in the light
Flaps the ghostlike tapestry.

This poem ends with Iseult of Brittany (Iseult of the White Hands, whom Tristram married, not Iseult of Ireland, whom he loved) telling her children, after her husband's death, the story of Merlin and Vivian, and Merlin's final imprisonment "in that dasied circle" by Vivian, "for she was passing weary of his love," everything fading away at last into a sense of weariness and loss. More effective as a narrative modulated into elegy is "The Forsaken Merman" of the 1849 volume, which ought to be sentimental, but which somehow is not, in spite of its pulling out all the emotional stops of which the story is capable. The merman's human wife leaves husband and children to go ashore and pray, to save her soul, and does not return as she promised:

Children dear, were we long alone?
'The sea grows stormy, the little ones moan;
Long prayers,' I said, 'in the world they say;
Come!' I said, and we rose through the surf in the bay.
We went up the beach, by the sandy down
Where the sea-stocks bloom, to the white-wall'd town;
Through the narrow paved streets, where all was still,
To the little grey church on the windy hill . . .
'Loud prays the priest; shut stands the door.'
Come away, children, call no more!
Come away, come down, call no more!

The "White-wall'd town" is the same as that which we see in the opening of "A Summer Night" and elsewhere in Arnold's poems; it is part of that landscape of elegy which was one of his main poetic properties. But it is not a property employed mechanically—at least, not in his better poems; it is his use of seashore imagery related to the daily affairs of men that helps to give the special haunting quality to "The Forsaken Merman" as it does to "Dover Beach." It is not unlike Tennyson's use of such imagery in "Break, Break, Break," but in Tennyson the self-pity is less controlled. Arnold is as great an exponent of what we have called the Victorian elegiac mode as Tennyson, and in "Sohrab and Rustum" he modulates epic into elegy (the poem is presented as a fragment of an epic, but its tone is wholly elegiac) in the same degree (though in a different manner) as Tennyson does in "Morte D'Arthur."

The conflict between Arnold's creative and critical faculties, together with his view that the main duty of a writer is to present in whatever medium he can as richly and luminously and broadly as possible his "criticism of life," contributed to his practically giving up poetry for critical prose. His *Poems, Second Series,* appeared in 1855, and *Merope,* his somewhat wooden attempt at a Greek tragedy, in 1858; after this, he published only one slim volume of poetry, *New Poems,* in 1867, and some twenty volumes of prose, between 1861 and 1888. His poetry remains in many ways the most appealing Victorian poetic voice. He gave moving expression to a modern malaise that is still very much with us, a sense of the isolation of the individual ("To Marguerite"), of "Wandering between two worlds, one dead, /The other powerless to be born" ("Stanzas from the Grande Chartreuse"), of the fears, hopes, and despairs of the thoughtful and sensitive man in a world of rapid change and increasing standardization.

> What is the course of the life
> Of mortal men on the earth?—
> Most men eddy about
> Here and there—eat and drink,
> Chatter and love and hate,
> Gather and squander, are raised
> Aloft, are hurl'd in the dust,
> Striving blindly, achieving
> Nothing; and then they die—
> Perish;—and no one asks
> Who or what they have been,
> More than he asks what waves,
> In the moonlit solitudes mild
> Of the midmost Ocean, have swell'd,
> Foam'd for a moment, and gone.

These lines are from "Rugby Chapel," Arnold's meditation on his father, Thomas Arnold, headmaster of Rugby (who had died fifteen years before). This poem is more rhetorical than Arnold's more characteristic elegies, and the unrhymed and flexible verse which he employs has an elegiac cadence of its own, particularly noticeable in the early part, with the typical scene-setting:

> Coldly, sadly descends
> The autumn-evening. The field
> Strewn with its dank yellow drifts
> Of wither'd leaves, and the elms,
> Fade into dimness apace,
> Silent;—hardly a shout
> From a few boys late at their play!

> The lights come out in the street,
> In the school-room windows; . . .

The use of nature imagery here, and the way it is set beside imagery from human activities and man-made objects and phenomena, evoke a moving suggestion not only of a particular time and place and not only of a quintessential English school scene, but also of the sadness that lies at the heart of men's working and playing against the revolving cycles of the seasons and the indifferent world of Nature.

Moonlight for Arnold does not go with roses and romance, but with melancholy, meditation, and sometimes even despair:

> But the same restless pacings to and fro,
> And the same vainly throbbing heart was there,
> And the same bright calm moon.

We see this, once again, in "Dover Beach," in which the Victorian problem of loss of faith is given its most memorable utterance: public values have disappeared, and all that is left are the private affections, the "little society" (as E. M. Forster was to call it) of love and friendship:

> Ah love, let us be true
> To one another! for the world, which seems
> To lie before us like a land of dreams,
> So various, so beautiful, so new,
> Hath really neither joy, nor love, nor light,
> Nor certitude, nor peace, nor help for pain;
> And we are here as on a darkling plain
> Swept with confused alarms of struggle and flight,
> Where ignorant armies clash by night.

The image of the ignorant armies clashing by night, is, significantly, an echo of Thucydides' description, in Book VII of his *History of the Peloponnesian War*, of the last disastrous battle between Athenians and Spartans in Sicily, fought at night in darkness and confusion, and marking virtually the end of Athenian chances. Periclean Athens remains Arnold's ideal of civilization.

Perhaps Arnold's two best-known poems are "The Scholar Gypsy" and "Thyrsis." The former, ostensibly about a seventeenth-century Oxford student who disappeared among the gypsies, is really about the poet himself and his generation; the scholar gypsy becomes a symbol in the light of which Arnold can develop his own position and state his own problems. Drawing on his knowledge of rustic scenes around Oxford, he produced a meditative pastoral poem whose language owes something to Theocritus but whose tone and emotional coloring are very Arnoldian. The fairly elaborate ten-line stanza helps to keep the movement of the poem slow and develop the note of introspection. At the end, in a daring and much discussed movement, Arnold moves right away from himself to etch a clear picture of Tyrian traders coming to Spain to avoid the livelier Greeks. Arnold may have intended a specific symbolism here; but the picture, with its calm assurance, is in line with many of Arnold's endings, and it serves (like the ending of "Sohrab and Rustum" and "Balder Dead") to sustain the mood of quiet gravity while removing any trace of melodramatic gesture and neutralizing the self-pity. More than once in his longer poems Arnold employs elaborate similes of this kind in order to achieve a mood of calm after feverish narration or introspection.

"Thyrsis," written to commemorate Arnold's friend Arthur Hugh Clough, who had died in 1861, is closely linked to "The Scholar Gypsy," though written many years after it. It has the same stanza form, the same general tone, it is set in the same Cumner country southwest of Oxford where Arnold and Clough had often walked together, and it contains actual references to "The Scholar Gypsy," a favorite poem of Clough's and one which seems to have contained some special symbolism known only to Arnold and his friend. Though the influence of the Greek pastoral poets is clearly discernible, the poem is steeped in that same deep feeling for the English countryside that we find in "The Scholar Gypsy," and, as with the earlier poem, the theme is really Arnold himself, his doubts and problems and introspective melancholy, developed indirectly in an elegiac context and (as so often in Arnold) in association with aspects of the English landscape which are most appropriate to the contemplative mood. Arnold, who spent so much of his life in dismal train journeys between one English provincial town and another in the course of his profession as inspector of schools, saw in the English countryside a genuine source of refreshment and regeneration. It was Wordsworth who taught him, though Wordsworth had not experienced the urban weariness which produced the need to turn from "the great town's harsh, heart-wearying roar" to the countryside for relief and comfort. Arnold's tribute to Wordsworth eloquently conveys what the older poet meant to the Victorians:

> He too upon a wintry clime
> Had fallen—on this iron time
> Of doubts, disputes, distractions, fears.
> He found us when the age had bound
> Our souls in its benumbing round;
> He spoke, and loosed our heart in tears.

He laid us as we lay at birth
On the cool flowery lap of earth. . . .
. . . where will Europe's latter hour
Again find Wordsworth's healing power?

(Memorial Verses)

It was as a healing power that Wordsworth was transmitted to the troubled Victorians. Arnold as a poet speaks with the voice of one who has been disturbed by Victorian doubts and problems, rendered permanently melancholy by a sense of tears at the heart of things, illuminated by a vision of ancient Athens, and cheered and comforted by the Wordsworthian vision of the relation between Man and Nature.

Arnold's friend Arthur Hugh Clough (1819–61) is perhaps the most perfect example among the poets of the Victorian intellectual seeking in vain for moral and metaphysical certainties. The account of Clough in Ward's *English Poets* begins: " 'We have a foreboding,' says Mr. Lowell in one of his essays, 'that Clough, imperfect as he was in many respects, and dying before he had subdued his sensitive temperament to the sterner requirements of his art, will be thought a hundred years hence to have been the truest expression in verse of the moral and intellectual tendencies, the doubt and struggle towards settled convictions, of the period in which he lived.' If doubt and struggle were the ruling tendencies of Clough's time, this lofty estimate may well be true; for in no writer of that day are they more vividly reflected. They are the very substance of his verse, they give it strength, they impose upon it the limitations from which it suffers." Lowell's estimate and Ward's endorsement of it have been revived and approved by modern criticism; but it is the historian of ideas rather than of literature who is most interested in Clough and who has been most responsible for the new interest in him. He was clearly a more interesting person than his poems reveal. The lyric of philosophic doubt can achieve at most a wry shrug at the universe:

It fortifies my soul to know
That, though I perish, Truth is so: . . .

Even his descriptive poems turn sooner or later to worry, as in his poem on Venice:

O, beautiful! and that seemed more profound,
This morning by the pillar when I saw
Under the great arcade, at the review,
And took, and held, and ordered on my brain
The faces, and the voices, and the whole mass
O' the motley facts of existence flowing by!

> O perfect, if 'twere all! But it is not; . . .
>   If the voice
> Ought to receive its echo from the soul,
> Wherefore this silence? If it *should* rouse my being,
> Why this reluctance?

We prefer him in his mood of frank cynicism:

> Thou shalt have one God only; who
> Would be at the expense of two?
> No graven images may be
> Worshipped, except the currency; . . .
> Thou shalt not kill; but needst not strive
> Officiously to keep alive: . . .

> (The Latest Decalogue)

It is significant that Clough did not publish this poem in his lifetime. But there were others, too, which first appeared in the posthumous volume of 1862, including the self-comforting "Say not, the struggle nought availeth," which seems to be a reply to the conclusion of Arnold's "Dover Beach," and the characteristic

> Where lies the land to which the ship would go?
> Far, far ahead, is all her seamen know.
> And where the land she travels from? Away,
> Far, far behind, is all that they can say.

Clough's lyrics of doubt and worry remain more interesting than their intrinsic poetic worth would warrant, for, though he never found a really adequate poetic form for his anxieties and uncertainties, he did speak out about his intellectual predicament to a degree that none of his contemporary poets did. His most original work, and by far the most lively and engaging of all his poems, is *The Bothie of Tober-na-Vuolich* (1848), his "Long Vacation pastoral," a sprightly narrative poem in hexameters set in the Scottish Highlands. This was his first volume, very much an Oxford work, with its university allusions and private university jokes, yet at the same time a far larger work in every sense than any of his later worrying poems. Precise and carefully realized description of natural scenery is combined with clear presentation of character and an action sometimes humorous, sometimes burlesque, sometimes simply moving, to make an appealing, if thoroughly odd, poem. As E. K. Brown has remarked, "It was reasonable to expect that the author of *The Bothie* might become a rival of Browning, endowed with a sharper awareness of contemporary realities and a greater power in projecting normal character." But he disappointed those expectations, and died at the early age of forty-two to be remembered principally as the subject of Arnold's "Thyrsis."

The poetry of meditation and worry, though it often drew on the Wordsworthian cadence and the Tennysonian languor, could not be expected to develop the vein of rich pictorial poetry that was implicit in the Keats-Tennyson tradition. This vein was developed by Rossetti and the Pre-Raphaelites, but in conjunction with other techniques and attitudes which make the whole situation complex and in some respects self-contradictory. The Pre-Raphaelite Brotherhood was originally a painters' movement, founded in 1848 by Dante Gabriel Rossetti (1828–82), Holman Hunt, John Everett Millais, William Michael Rossetti, and others, in revolt against the eighteenth-century academicism which still prevailed in official artistic quarters where the achievements of, for example, Blake, Turner, Constable, and Samuel Palmer, were ignored. The movement believed in simplicity and accuracy of detail, in freshness and directness and precision, and it looked to medieval art to find them. We thus get the paradox that the Pre-Raphaelites began both as realists and as medievalists. In actual practice, many of the Pre-Raphaelite painters chose literary subjects, showing themselves influenced by Keats and Tennyson just as the lesser Pre-Raphaelite poets reproduced so much of Keats and Tennyson. What was the relation between the demand for simplicity, the medievalism, and the Tennysonian pictorial languor?

Freshness and simplicity in the handling of detail went side by side with a deep sense of the significance of detail, the symbolic and sacramental meaning of objects, such as we find in the symbolism of medieval religion and painting. That was one link between the realistic and the medieval aspects of Pre-Raphaelitism. Further, the surface of Victorian life did not yield objects which seemed other than ludicrous or vulgar to the artists and poets of the time: trousers are notoriously intractable to the sculptor. Medieval artists used the fashions of their own day, but the Pre-Raphaelites, convinced with Ruskin of the ugliness of the Victorian surface, felt unable to use contemporary fashions (though Ruskin once admitted that theoretically this was desirable and "if it would not look well, the times are wrong and their modes must be altered"), and dressed their characters in "primitive" robes. One side of Pre-Raphaelite theory based the desire for naturalness and directness on the need for truth and the claims of science. But it was not really the interests of science that the Pre-Raphaelites were anxious to serve; the more interesting of them at least were concerned to give to *things* as well as to characters and situations the kind of symbolic reality they had to the medieval mind. In their desire to achieve this they were seduced by lilies and stars and roses to a vague neoromanticism which achieved the opposite of what they professed, but they were not always so led astray. The three lilies in the hand and the seven stars in the hair of Rossetti's Blessed Damozel might be mere literary properties, but

> Until her bosom must have made
> The bar she leaned on warm,

represents a new kind of bringing together of the spiritual and the almost embarrassingly physical, while the quiet detail of "My Sister's Sleep" gives meaning to objects in a more everyday context:

> Our mother rose from where she sat:
> Her needles, as she laid them down,
> Met lightly, and her silken gown
> Settled: no other noise than that.

Rossetti turned to poetry from painting, his mind nourished on Dante and the early Italian poets, his Italian heredity and background strongly felt. His first poems appeared in the short-lived Pre-Raphaelite periodical *The Germ* (1850), and others in the *Oxford and Cambridge Magazine* (1856) which printed also the early work of William Morris and others who in the early 1850's at Oxford banded together in a similar movement combining interest in medieval poetry, ecclesiastical history, and the work of Tennyson and Ruskin. His translations (in the original meters) of *The Early Italian Poets* appeared in 1861 and again in a new arrangement as *Dante and his Circle* in 1874. His first volume of original poems appeared in 1870; he published only one other new volume, *Ballads and Sonnets*, in 1881, the year before his death. It was Rossetti's early study of Dante which familiarized him with the symbolizing and sacramentalizing aspect of the medieval mind, and his own temperament also encouraged a tendency to identify the concretely physical with the permanently spiritual. This habit of mind was not one which came easily to the Victorians, with the result that Pre-Raphaelite influence in poetry apart from Rossetti's often led only to pseudomedieval attitudinizing, coy archaisms, and pictorial lushness. Rossetti has a strength and vibrancy in his imagery that these others lack. "The Blessed Damozel," in spite of an occasional false note, is a finely wrought poem in a mode that is not really either Keatsian or Swinburnian—nor truly Dantesque either, for that matter, for the disposition of the emotion is altogether too self-conscious. A poem such as "Love's Nocturne" is more Tennysonian in its languid dreaminess ("Master of the murmuring courts /Where the shapes of sleep convene!") and some of his ballad poems are too forced in their attempt to sound a medieval note. Occasionally he is wholly successful in his attempt to give an intensity of meaning to a situation described as strictly contemporary:

> Through the small room, with subtle sound
> Of flame, by vents the fireshine drove
> And reddened. In its dim alcove
> The mirror shed a clearness round.

It was to be expected that Rossetti should draw his images with a painter's eye, but in fact, though he employs considerable pictorial detail, it is the element of thought and even abstraction, the attempt to reduce everything to an idea or an essence, that is more characteristic of his poetry. Indeed, the chief fault of Rossetti's poetry is its reductiveness. It is this that makes his remarkable sonnet sequence, *The House of Life,* in the long run tedious: individual sonnets show power and passion, but the constant Platonizing, the constant equation of the physical with the vaguely spiritual, the constant turning of concrete natural objects into "an essence more environing /That wine's drained juice; a music ravishing /More than the passionate pulse of Philomel," end by reducing everything to a single note. It is true, as Watts-Dunton said, that Rossetti removed the asceticism from mysticism, and (with some exceptions) he did so without succumbing to mawkishness, and this was a considerable achievement, particularly in his age. But it is not the excess of sensuous imagery that disturbs us in his poetry; it is the way in which the sensuous is constantly dissipated into vague spirituality.

One can see this clearly in "Troy Town":

> Heavenborn Helen, Sparta's queen,
> *(O Troy Town!)*
> Had two breasts of heavenly sheen,
> The sun and moon of the heart's desire:
> All Love's lordship lay between.
> *(O Troy's down,*
> *Tall Troy's on fire!)*

Not only does the refrain have the effect of drawing the reader *away* from the actual fate of Troy into a purely incantatory spell, but even the particularizing of Helen's physical beauties reduces them to a symbolic pattern in which the sensuous as well as the sensual is wholly lost. Rossetti often tries too hard with his ballad refrains. The alternating refrains of "Eden Bower"—"Eden bower's in flower" and "And O the bower and the hour!"—with their constant iteration of the same "-ower" sound, not only rapidly lose all meaning but also lose any emotional effect other than annoyance. He does better with his late poem, *The King's Tragedy,* a long narrative in ballad meter which avoids the refrain and achieves a moving directness in its use of detail.

There was a touch of Browning in Rossetti. "A Last Confession," a dramatic monologue in which an Italian patriot confesses to a priest how he came to murder the girl he loved, has something of Browning's *bravura,* though its tone is less violent and its imagery makes greater use of symbolic objects than Browning ever did. "Jenny," a poem in almost two hundred octosyllabic couplets in which the poet addresses an exhausted and soon sleeping prostitute in her London lodging, is partly spoiled for modern taste by its unconscious but pervasive air of patronage and by the shirking of some of the main issues raised. But, in spite of this and in spite of some superficial and unrealized symbolism ("What, Jenny, are your lilies dead?") the poem has reality and power:

> Our learned London children know,
> Poor Jenny, all your pride and woe;
> Have seen your lifted silken skirt
> Advertise dainties through the dirt;
> Have seen your coach-wheels splash rebuke
> On virtue; and have learned your look
> When, wealth and health slipped past, you stare
> Along the streets alone, and there,
> Round the long park, across the bridge,
> The cold lamps at the pavement's edge
> Wind on together and apart,
> A fiery serpent for your heart.

Or in this description of the London dawn:

> And there's an early waggon drawn
> To market, and some sheep that jog
> Bleating before a barking dog;
> And the old streets come peering through
> Another night that London knew;
> And all as ghostlike as the lamps.

Rossetti's attempt to wed concrete particularization and tremulous symbolic meaning explains much that is characteristic in his poetry. In some respects it can be said that he tried to operate in a medieval mode in the Victorian world, and that he could only achieve limited success because of the context of his operations. Sometimes his pictorial mysticism led to mere archaism or mere verbal dissipation, but sometimes it succeeds splendidly, as it does in his imitation ballad, "Sister Helen," his most completely successful poem in the ballad style. The central situation—the rejected lover melting a waxen image of her false lover, thus causing his agony and death three days after his wedding to another—is projected indirectly, through the dialogue between the girl and her little brother, who reports the various emissaries from the dying husband pleading in vain for Helen to spare him. The refrain succeeds in increasing the tension and the horror, from the opening question, with its sinister implication, to the concluding despair.

> 'Why did you melt your waxen man,
>   Sister Helen?
> To-day is the third since you began.'
> 'The time was long, yet the time ran,
>   Little brother.'
>   (O Mother, Mary Mother,
> Three days to-day, between Hell and Heaven!)

The detail operates in the poem with tremendous effect, while the repetition of "Sister Helen" and "Little brother," even more than the concluding lines of each stanza, builds up the mood by emphasizing progressively the unnaturalness of this conversation between elder sister and younger brother. Rossetti remains an impressive, if in some respects a puzzling, poet, not to be explained altogether by reference to the Pre-Raphaelite Movement which he helped to found. He possessed an energy, even a savagery, that is very unlike anything we can find in the Pre-Raphaelite painters or in the other poets who contributed to *The Germ*. The line from Keats through Tennyson to Rossetti is a real one so far as the handling of certain kinds of pictorial imagery is concerned; but Rossetti's place at the end of that line is almost accidental: he had other sources of strength, though he could not always assimilate them to the other aspects of his art.

The poetry of Christina Rossetti (1830–94) has less complex sources than her brother's. Her religious imagination and her steady Anglican piety dominate her poetry as they did her life, limiting her interests and even inhibiting parts of her nature, yet, in her best work, giving precisely that combination of strength and simplicity without affectation or verbal posturing which the Pre-Raphaelites sought. There is nothing archaic or pseudomedieval in her use of symbol and allegory: she had the kind of religious sensibility that naturally sought expression in that way. Her lyrical poems show at times a quietly luminous clarity that almost—but never quite—suggests the religious poetry of the metaphysicals, George Herbert or, in a lesser degree, Henry Vaughan. Some of her poems for children have delicacy and charm, and the sprightly "Goblin Market" uses allegory with an unforced directness that is unusual in post-medieval English poetry. "The Prince's Progress," an allegorical narrative poem more serious in tone and more comprehensive in meaning, is somewhat more labored, but it possesses nevertheless something of the grace that characterizes her best poetry. But the shorter poems—"A Birthday," "When I am dead, my dearest," "Weary in Well-doing," "A Dirge"— are the most appealing. The series of sonnets, *Monna Innominata*, are of more biographical than poetic interest (Christina Rossetti rejected two offers of marriage on religious grounds, and the latter particularly left a permanent sense of loss); all except the final sonnet in the sequence have a certain thinness that is the most conspicuous fault of her weaker poetry. She published almost a dozen volumes of poetry, some purely devotional, and often her special gift of timeless clarity gives way to mere flatness. But at her best she could use simple rhythms and unpretentious imagery with a sharpness and a concentrated inwardness of meaning that achieve considerable power. Her temper was hardly Victorian, and she availed herself of few of the Victorian poet's professional tricks. She might have done better in the seventeenth century, when her strong religious feeling might have found itself less at odds with the world she lived in and less restrictive of the total personality.

William Morris (1834–96) began writing poetry as a Pre-Raphaelite, under Rossetti's influence. Poetry was only one of his many interests; architecture, painting, and most of all the "lesser arts" of decoration progressively took up his attention, and we have noted in discussing his prose in an earlier chapter the relation between his medievalism and his movement to socialism. *The Defence of Guinevere* (1858) is Pre-Raphaelite in manner and for the most part medieval in subject. The title poem, in *terza rima*, attempts to give precision and detail to a moment in the Arthurian stories, but in spite of the meticulous exactness of the imagery—

> But, knowing now that they would have her speak,
> She threw her wet hair backward from her brow,
> Her hand close to her mouth touching her cheek, . . .

the effects are dissipated in a central cloudiness. But Morris does not present his medieval world as a world of merely languorous beauty, and when he brings forward his sordid traitors and grim avengers he can produce, as in "The Haystack in the Floods," verse narrative of power and even horror. The octosyllabic couplets of "The Haystack" ring out much more effectively than the slower measures Morris often used. "Concerning Geffray Teste Noire," a story from Froissart, is told in more discursive style, with a certain amount of pseudome-

dieval colloquial idiom ("Your brother was slain there? I mind me
now /A right, good man-at-arms, God pardon him!"). And there are
ballad narratives with too self-conscious refrains, "Hah! hah! la belle
jaune giroflée" or "Ah! qu'elle est belle La Marguerite," and short
poems in a variety of stanzas presenting moments of chivalric hope or
love or disgrace: "Shameful Death" is one of the best of these latter.
It is all high spirited and often rather childish.

Morris' long narrative poems—*The Life and Death of Jason* (1867),
The Earthly Paradise (1868–70), *Sigurd the Volsung* (1876)—show
him trying a variety of poetic styles and following a variety of models.
He considered Chaucer his master in narrative verse; but he has not
Chaucer's discipline or irony. The eighteen books of *Jason* are too
long; what one remembers are some of the incidental songs, with their
delicate romantic feeling:

> I know a little garden close
> Set thick with lily and red rose,
> Where I would wander if I might
> From dewy dawn to dewy night,
> And have one with me wandering.

The cultivated naïveté of this sort of thing may sound a little coy
to modern ears, but it reflects—and captures—a genuine sensibility.
The dogged narrative often has a limpid movement, and there are
passages of quiet lucidity: Morris was always a competent workman,
even if he could give the impression of weaving a tapestry with one
hand while writing a poetic romance with the other: but the match of
the decasyllabic couplets, for all the incidental charms and beauties,
wearies at last. *The Earthly Paradise* is a collection of twenty-four
stories, some in heroic couplets, some in octosyllabic couplets, and
some in rhyme royal, set in a framework and introduced by a narrative prologue, "The Wanderers," in which the story is told of a group
of fourteenth-century "gentlemen and mariners of Norway" who,
after almost a lifetime of adventures by land and sea, come at last, as
old men, to an island where live the last survivors of ancient Greek
civilization. Thus the medieval Norse world and the ancient Greek
world come in contact with each other, and the two groups exchange
stories, half of them medieval and half of them Greek. The opening
of "The Wanderers" shows something of the impulse which led
Morris to choose such themes:

> Forget six counties overhung with smoke,
> Forget the snorting steam and piston stroke,
> Forget the spreading of the hideous town;
> Think rather of the pack-horse on the down,

> And dream of London, small, and white, and clean,
> The clear Thames bordered by its gardens green;
> Think, that below bridge the green lapping waves
> Smite some few keels that bear Levantine staves,
> Cut from the yew wood on the burnt-up hill,
> And pointed jars that Greek hands toiled to fill,
> And treasured scanty spice from some far sea,
> Florence gold cloth, and Ypres napery,
> And cloth of Bruges, and hogsheads of Guienne;
> While nigh the thronged wharf Geoffrey Chaucer's pen
> Moves over bills of lading—mid such times
> Shall dwell the hollow puppets of my rhymes.

Again, the tales themselves are on the whole prolix, the narrative bubbling on without adequate concentration; but the interspersed poems describing the different months of the year and providing an appropriate emotional situation for each are done with an almost Keatsian richness and beauty. In the introductory "Apology" to *The Earthly Paradise*, Morris describes himself as "the idle singer of an empty day," and in his epilogue he repeats that his intention has been simply to bring "fragrance of old days and deeds . . . back to folk weary." He wrote these poems to entertain and refresh.

Sigurd the Volsung is altogether sterner stuff. Here Morris was attempting to recapture the spirit of Norse saga, by which his imagination had been kindled. His travels in Iceland and his reading and translating of Old Norse and Anglo-Saxon literature gave him a vivid sense of the violent and gloomy world of these northern peoples. *Sigurd* tells a violent and gloomy story, drawing on the *Volsunga Saga*, both the Elder and the Younger *Eddas*, and the *Niebelungen-lied*. The verse form he uses is swinging couplets with lines of six beats, similar to the "Locksley Hall" meter but rougher and so less monotonous. Nevertheless, the strength of the verse suffers from archaisms and padding.

> Then the sword-folk rise round Gunnar, round the fetted and
>   bound they throng,
> As men in the bitter battle round the God-kin over-Strong.

The artifice is too obvious, the deliberate straining after an Anglo-Saxon vocabulary too blatant, for this kind of verse to be wholly successful. The verse form is as good a substitute for the Homeric hexameter or the Anglo-Saxon alliterative beat as can be devised in modern English, but the note of *pastiche* is rarely wholly absent:

> Then I taught them the craft of metals, and the sailing of the sea,
> And the taming of the horse-kind, and the yoke-beasts husbandry,

> And the building up of houses; and that race of men went by,
> And they said that Thor had taught them; and a smithying-carle was I.

This could never be mistaken for the real thing; it smacks of "Ye Olde Englyshe." Yet the vigor is undeniable, and the story does get itself told.

A considerable amount of Morris' later verse was inspired by his socialist faith. *The Pilgrims of Hope* (1885–86), a modern story of struggle in "the cause of the people," is told for the most part in the same verse form as *Sigurd;* but the verse is far from compelling and there seems no reason why the story should not have been told in prose. This poem and others appeared in *The Commonweal,* the organ of the Socialist League, which Morris founded and edited. *Chants for Socialists* (1885) include some spirited propaganda verse such as "All for the Cause" and "The March of the Workers." *Poems by the Way* (1891) reprinted many of the *Commonweal* poems and added others to make a varied volume with no new strain except perhaps "Iceland First Seen," which gives in its free rhythms a striking picture of Morris' first glimpse of the land of the Norsemen:

> Lo from our loitering ship
> a new land at last to be seen;
> on the east guard a weary wide lea,
> And black slope the hillsides above,
> striped adown with their desolate green: . . .

Pre-Raphaelite, medievalist, romantic storyteller, lover of the fierce Norse legends, socialist worker and fighter, and all the time craftsman and propagandist for the arts, Morris seems at first sight to be an inexplicable mixture. But the different strains in his life and work are not really difficult to sort out, or to relate to each other. He took to poetry almost casually, and it was never for long his main preoccupation. For him, craftsmanship, supreme in the Middle Ages, was the heritage and the guarantee of free men everywhere; poetry was a craft like any other, and he was prepared to weave words as he was prepared to weave carpets. There is something engaging in the careless confidence of Morris' approach to the arts. It is true that his poetry suffers from his casualness, but we never have the feeling that he failed through lack of discipline or of energy. We are left with the impression that the poetry of this versatile and indomitable craftsman was as good as he was capable of making it.

The diverse directions in which Pre-Raphaelites could lead is illustrated by Coventry Patmore (1823–96), who contributed to *The Germ* and went on to produce, in *The Angel in the House* (1854–56), a sequence of poems describing a modern courtship and marriage

with no attempt to archaize or to gloss over the manners and customs
—or the financial details—of contemporary Victorian life. The quiet
confidence with which Patmore marshals his quatrains, the steady—
one might almost say obstinate—charting of the course of upper-
middle-class love running smoothly to happy marriage, produce a
poem sequence of intermittent charm; there are languors and fatui-
ties, but there is also a restrained and precise recording of moods,
scenes, and situations that shows a new and successful kind of domestic poetry. To be fresh and natural was a Pre-Raphaelite ideal, and
The Angel in the House, for all its total lack of the medieval properties and of the symbolic objects which we associate with Pre-Raphaelitism, is Pre-Raphaelite in this sense. That the surface of Victorian
domestic and social life rendered in poetry was bound to appear
faintly comic not only to later eyes but to contemporary eyes is a
fact based on the psychology of our attitude to the familiar, and a
fact of which the Victorian poets were very conscious and which
they sometimes worried about. *The Angel in the House* may have
been laughed at, but it achieved great popularity in the years after
its publication, to be ousted at last only by the much headier wine
of Swinburne. Patmore was not, however, merely a poet of middle-
class emotion and felicity. He had a mystical streak, and in particular
an almost violent tendency to equate the humanly erotic and the
divinely spiritual—not in the medieval way nor yet quite in Rossetti's
way, but with a religious belligerence which is rarely successful
poetically. After his conversion to Roman Catholicism, his poetry
turned more and more toward this religious eroticism, which is
found in *The Unknown Eros* (1877) and other works. He attempts
sometimes the ecstasies of Crashaw, but his ardors are not poetically
realized in spite of metrical ingenuities and Pindaric structures; the
best of his later poems are descriptive of natural scenery or short
projections of a single emotional situation in a domestic context, as
in the well-known little lyric, "The Toys." Essentially, Patmore is not
a poet of ecstatic feeling or introspective subtlety; he is the poet of
genteel sensibility, which at his best he renders with moving conviction.

Patmore moved—or tried to—from gentility to ecstasy; James
Thomson (1834–82) from lower-middle-class hedonism to nihilistic
despair. Thomson's earlier poems, such as the sequences *Sunday at
Hampstead,* and *Sunday up the River* show a relish of the humbler
pleasures of life expressed in an unpretentious verse form and a
language which, while using something of the conventional poetic
vocabulary of the day, have an appealing brightness and a simplicity. Personal circumstance drove him to atheistic despair, and his ex-

pression of this in *The City of Dreadful Night* (1874), with its varied stanzas and verse forms, its tolling double rhymes, deliberate lethargic movement, and nightmare imagery, communicates with cumulative effectiveness a despair very different from the cultured elegy of Tennyson or Arnold. The concluding vision of "Melancolia" is one of the most memorable poetic visions of a sick despair in English. The later "Insomnia" achieves a similar mood more briefly and with more concentration.

Edward Fitzgerald's free poetic adaptation from the Persian, *Rúbaiyát of Omar Khayyam* (1859) puts an altogether more attractive face on pessimism. Thomson alternated between hedonism and despair; Fitzgerald expressed a hedonism grounded on skepticism in a long poem of carefully organized quatrains (the first, second, and fourth lines rhyming and the third unrhymed) in which a life of sensual pleasure is advocated with undertones of philosophic searching and echoes of gnomic wisdom. It is a remarkable texture of sadness and sensuality, of disillusionment and *carpe diem*. The poem moves with a slow music, the oriental names providing a slightly exotic flavor and at the same time helping to suggest the urbane sophistication of Ecclesiastes. A sense of the evanescence of life and the fleetness of the passions comes through all the advocacy of wine, women, and song, in an atmosphere of drugged and pleasing melancholy:

> Yet Ah, that Spring should vanish with the Rose!
> That Youth's sweet-scented manuscript should close!
> The Nightingale that in the branches sang,
> Ah whence, and whither flown again, who knows! . . .
>
> Ah Love! could you and I with Him conspire
> To grasp this sorry Scheme of Things entire,
> Would we not shatter it to bits—and then
> Remould it nearer to the Heart's Desire!
>
> Yon rising Moon that looks for us again—
> How oft hereafter will she wax and wane;
> How oft hereafter rising look for us
> Through this same Garden—and for *one* in vain!

It is a Tennysonian rose and garden and moonlight, but the oriental atmosphere, the sophisticated questioning of fate, the slow, incantatory march of the quatrains, give the poem a flavor of its own. Yet it is very Victorian both in mood and in poetic apparatus, and akin to the Victorian elegiac mode that we have discussed.

The poetry of George Meredith (1828–1909) reveals a more consciously modern intelligence, a development of the Darwinian theory of evolution into a pantheistic feeling for the mysteries and vitality of Nature, and a psychological curiosity about human relationships and human problems. His verbal sophistication took the form of elliptical phrasing and often also of unusual metrics, neither of which appear today as odd or as culpable as they once did but which nevertheless sometimes suggest a verbal and intellectual toughness that is more exhibitionist than real. *Modern Love* (1862), his series of fifty sixteen-line sonnets describing the break-up of a marriage, with a careful attention to emotional detail, is unequal, but contains some memorable poems, notably the forty-seventh—

> We saw the swallows gathering in the sky,
> And in the osier-isle we heard them noise.
> We had not to look back on summer joys,
> Or forward to a summer of bright dye: . . .
> Love, that had robbed us of immortal things,
> This little moment mercifully gave,
> Where I have seen across the twilight wave
> The swan sail with her young beneath her wings—

and the fiftieth, and there are passages elsewhere that have become almost proverbial, such as this from the forty-third:

> In tragic life, God wot,
> No villain need be! Passions spin the plot:
> We are betrayed by what is false within.

Meredith imitated a variety of poetic styles, and every now and again succeeded in achieving a strong and packed texture of metaphorical expression that is far removed from the generalized suggestiveness of the Tennysonian tradition. His *Poems and Lyrics of the Joy of Earth* (1883) contain some of his most interesting poems on the force and mystery of nature and illustrate his highly individual and imaginative use of the Darwinian position. "The Woods of Westermain" does not quite achieve full poetic realization of his vision of nature, but it has great emotional drive combined with more intellectual power than is generally found in Victorian poetry:

> On the throne Success usurps,
> You shall seat the joy you feel
> Where a race of water chirps,
> Twisting hues of flourished steel:
> Or where light is caught in hoop
> Up a clearing's leafy rise,
> Where the crossing deerherds troop
> Classic splendours, knightly dyes.

Or, where old-eyed oxen chew
Speculation with the cud,
Read their pool of vision through,
Back to hours when mind was mud;
Nigh the knot, which did untwine
Timelessly to drowsy suns;
Seeing Earth a drowsy spine,
Heaven a space for winging tons.
Farther, deeper, may you read,
Have you sight for things afield,
Where peeps she, the Nurse of seed,
Cloaked, but in the peep revealed; . . .

This is a different kind of thinking about nature and evolution from that which is found in Tennyson's *In Memoriam*. In other poems in the same volume, Meredith sought other ways of expressing similar views. The sonnet, "Lucifer in Starlight," is one of the most successful, and ends with a line that T. S. Eliot was later to make ironic use of:

Soaring through wider zones that pricked his scars
With memory of the old revolt from Awe,
He reached a middle height, and at the stars,
Which are the brain of heaven, he looked, and sank.
Around the ancient track marched, rank on rank,
The army of unalterable law.

Meredith was an ambitious, uncertain, and unequal poet. He aimed at a degree of dramatic compression, of complex and tightly knit allusiveness, that he often gave a show of achieving without fully realizing; but he did sometimes achieve these qualities memorably, and even when he was not wholly successful in achieving them he staked a claim in the Victorian rose garden for intellect and for economy of language.

Algernon Charles Swinburne (1837–1909) began to write poetry as a friend and admirer of Rossetti and the Pre-Raphaelites, but he soon developed his own style, making his own use of influences from Greek, Elizabethan, and Jacobean drama. His *Atalanta in Calydon* (1865) follows the form of Greek tragedy, and though it is not really Greek in spirit, its manipulation of pagan notions to achieve deliberate and exhibitionist skepticism with respect to conventional religious ideas does give something of a Euripidean flavor. The language is altogether more open-worked than it ever is in Greek tragedy, but the metrical skill and the splendor of passionate suggestiveness so characteristic of Swinburne's best verse help to disguise this from the casual reader. Though Swinburne is working under more self-discipline here than he uses in his later poetry, there is already in *Atalanta* that grandiloquent scattering of language which sounds as though it is saying more than it is:

> Rise up, shine, stretch thine hand out, with thy bow
> Touch the most dimmest height of trembling heaven,
> And burn and break the dark about thy ways,
> Shot through and through with arrows; let thine hair
> Lighten as flame above the flameless shell
> Which was the moon, and thine eyes fill the world
> And thy lips kindle with swift beams; let earth
> Laugh, and the long sea fiery from thy feet
> Through all the roar and ripple of streaming springs
> And foam in reddened flakes and flying flowers
> Shaken from hands and blown from lips of nymphs
> Whose hair or breast divides the wandering wave
> With salt close tresses cleaving lock to lock,
> All gold, or shuddering or unfurrowed snow;
> And all the winds about thee with their wings,
> And fountain-heads of all the watered world; . . .

The choruses, done in a variety of meters, show Swinburne experimenting in the intoxicated swing which was to be the mark of so much of his later poetry. The first chorus, "When the hounds of spring are on winter's traces," remains one of his most popular poems: its lilting neopagan suggestiveness retains its appeal even when it hovers on the brink of the absurd:

> For winter's rains and ruins are over,
>   And all the season of snows and sins;
> The days dividing lover and lover,
>   The light that loses, the night that wins;
> And time remembered is grief forgotten,
> And frosts are slain and flowers begotten,
> And in green underwood and cover
>   Blossom by blossom the spring begins . . .
> And Pan by noon and Bacchus by night,
>   Fleeter of foot than the fleet-foot kid,
> Follows with dancing and fills with delight
>   The Maenad and the Bassarid;
> And soft as lips that laugh and hide
> The laughing leaves of the trees divide,
> And screen from seeing and leave in sight
>   The god pursuing, the maiden hid.

This and other choruses aimed at suggesting a sensuality connected somehow both with the grand elemental forces of nature, the secret reality of sin, and the meaningless way the world is governed. "Pleasure, with pain for leaven; /Summer, with flowers that fell; /Remembrance fallen from heaven, /And madness risen from hell. . . ." It is Tennyson's rose garden overblown and darkened, inhabited by sensualists and by worn-out pagans.

We see this much more clearly in *Poems and Ballads* (1866), which so scandalized its first readers. Here the sensuality has definite sado-masochistic overtones, never spelt out clearly but deliberately left on a level of generalized suggestiveness, as in the wickedly hypnotic "Dolores":

> By the ravenous teeth that have smitten
> Through the kisses that blossom and bud,
> By the lips intertwisted and bitten
> Till the foam has a savour of blood,
> By the pulse as it rises and falters,
> By the hands as they slacken and strain,
> I adjure thee, respond from thine altars,
> Our Lady of Pain.

The extravagance is sometimes absurd, but sometimes the suggestiveness operates with remarkable force, as, for example, in "The Garden of Proserpine":

> Here, where the world is quiet;
> Here, where all trouble seems
> Dead winds' and spent waves' riot
> In doubtful dreams of dreams;
> I watch the green field growing
> For reaping folk and sowing,
> For harvest-time and mowing,
> A sleepy world of streams.

One can understand why the young men of Oxford marched through the streets chanting Swinburne's intoxicating rhythms. Their effect was hypnotic; at the same time they challenged to rebellion against all accepted ideas of religion and morality. "Hymn to Proserpine" gives the cultivated (but jaded) pagan view of the establishment of Christianity and the death of the old gods:

> Thou hast conquered, O pale Galilean; the world has grown
>   grey from thy breath;
> We have drunken of things Lethean, and fed on the fullness
>   of death.
> Laurel is green for a season, and love is sweet for a day;
> But love grows bitter with treason, and laurel outlives not May.

The conclusion invokes Proserpine as queen of death, not, as Tennyson saw her in "Demeter and Persephone," as symbol of a new religion of resurrection and love. Swinburne's lines are deliberately
provocative:

> Thou art more than the Gods who number the days of our
> temporal breath;
> For these give labour and slumber; but thou, Proserpina, death.
> Therefore now at thy feet I abide for a season in silence. I know
> I shall die as my fathers died, and sleep as they sleep; even so.
> For the glass of the years is brittle wherein we gaze for a span;
> A little soul for a little bears up this corpse which is man.
> So long I endure, no longer; and laugh not again, neither weep.
> For there is no God found stronger than death; and death is a
> sleep.

One of the longest and most successful poems in *Poems and Ballads*
is "The Triumph of Time," in which the sea imagery in particular
is employed with peculiar force and real emotional relevance: Swinburne's feeling for the sea was genuine and he could move himself
to strange transports by thought of "the great sweet mother." The
difference between Tennyson's sea imagery in "Break, break, break"
and that of Swinburne's stanzas on the sea in "The Triumph of
Time"—

> I shall sleep, and move with the moving ships,
> Change as the winds change, veer in the tide;
> My lips will feast on the foam of thy lips,
> I shall rise with thy rising, with thee subside; . . .

is symptomatic of what Swinburne makes of the Tennysonian tradition.

T. S. Eliot has claimed that Swinburne used language independently of the world to which it was intended to refer. "In Swinburne, for example, we see the word 'weary' flourishing . . . independent of the particular and actual weariness of flesh and spirit."
To live thus exclusively and consistently among words is, Eliot
claims, a characteristic of genius, but of a rather special kind of genius and obviously not the kind he really admires or would hold up
for imitation. There is some truth in this. But it would be a mistake
to consider the verbal devices of Swinburne as radically different in
kind from those of Tennyson or Rossetti or indeed from any other
significant Victorian poet except Hopkins. Like Tennyson, he was
trying to suggest an area of emotion, to use references to natural objects and imagined characters in order to build up a mood. The sad-
sweet mood which Tennyson so often sought to build up is rather

different from the roses and raptures of forbidden passion conjured up by Swinburne; but the conjuring in each case was done in an essentially similar way so far as the attitude to language is concerned.

Songs before Sunrise (1871) represented a turning away from these dangerous personal themes to celebrate and encourage the fighters for liberty and political independence in Europe (especially Italy). But, though he never loses his metrical ingenuity or his ability to create a great surge of language beating out a mass of suggestions and emotional invitations, there is nothing here as impressive as the best of *Poems and Ballads*. Some of the poems in this collection are on general philosophical themes; in "Hertha" he expresses a naturalism and a humanism not unlike the ideas expressed by Meredith some years later in "Earth and Man." But Swinburne is not a philosophical poet. His genius was for verbal seduction by rhythmic incantation and disturbingly suggestive imagery. Nothing could stem his stream of language, and he grew more diffuse as he grew older and more respectable. His verse plays, apart from *Atalanta*, have never been read to any extent, though they have their moments of Swinburnian splendor. And some of his later poems—for example, "A Forsaken Garden," "Neap-Tide"—show no loss in skill or power. He continued to write and publish until the year of his death. But his first volume of *Poems and Ballads* remains his most significant monument. If the function of poetry is to suggest rather than to explore, and to suggest by cadence and image, then Swinburne was truly a poet. He developed to an extreme a tendency that was implicit in the whole romantic tradition. But the poetry of exploration and discovery, which is the greatest kind of poetry, was not for him.

The poetry of Thomas Hardy (1840–1928) seems at first sight to belong more to the tradition of Browning or Meredith than to that of Swinburnian verbal excitement, and certainly there is nothing of Swinburne's intoxicated incantations nor indeed is there much trace of the Keats-Tennyson-Rossetti tradition of sensory images in the characteristic rough-hewn ironies of Hardy's shorter poems. Yet if Swinburne was seduced by mere language, it might be said that Hardy was often seduced by mere ideas. Richard Blackmur has pointed out that "the effect of the great liberating ideas of the nineteenth century upon Hardy's ideas was apparently restrictive and even imprisoning," and that the new scientific and philosophical discoveries and notions of the Victorian age worked in him so as to produce in many of his poems a confronting of experience with preconceived and even mechanical notions of irony, fate, coincidence, betrayal, determining the operations of love, memory, and death. Often the situation described in a poem is a trick one, given no new life and meaning by its poetic expression but merely set out, with either a masochistic or a spiteful satisfaction. His oddities of language, his use of dialect or archaic or technical or compound words, and his occasional unusual metrics and stanza forms, often combine to provide a sense of authenticity to his utterance, as though he had to speak in spite of his hoarse voice or his lack of linguistic resource; but his poetry only really comes alive when he is not content to describe a contrived situation or incident as an example of life's irony, but by restraint and indirection moves from illustration to illumination, letting the poem build up an area of suggestion and symbolic overtones that echo on long after the primary meaning has been communicated. When Hardy achieves this, when he has not, in Blackmur's phrase, "violated his sensibility with ideas" but finds a way to let his sensibility operate fully in language, he can produce some of the most impressive and moving as well as original lyrics of his time.

Something of the power and originality of Hardy's best poetry can be illustrated by the last four stanzas of "The Convergence of the Twain," his poem on the loss of the "Titanic":

> And as the smart ship grew
> In stature, grace, and hue,
> In shadowy silent distance grew the Iceberg too.
>
> Alien they seemed to be:
> No mortal eye could see
> The intimate welding of their later history,
>
> Or sign that they were bent
> By paths coincident
> Or being anon twin halves of one august event,
>
> Till the Spinner of the Years
> Said "Now!" And each one hears,
> And consummation comes, and jars two hemispheres.

The unusual stanza-form is justified by the way it works in the poem, giving a runic sense of doom to the whole. This is more impressive than such superficially appealing utterances of formulated pessimism as,

> Crass Casulty obstructs the sun and rain,
> And dicing Time for gladness casts a moan . . .
> These purblind Doomsters had as readily strown
> Blisses about my pilgrimage as pain.

Some of Hardy's best effects are achieved in the simple ballad stanza, such as "The Workbox," "She Hears the Storm," or the desperately simple "Paying Calls." More often his most fully realized poems seem to have carved out their own stanza form, as "The Walk":

> You did not walk with me
> Of late to the hill-top tree
>   By the gated ways,
>   As in earlier days;
>   You were weak and lame,
>   So you never came,
> And I went alone, and I did not mind,
> Not thinking of you as left behind.
>
>   I walked up there to-day
>   Just in the former way;
>   Surveyed around
>   The familiar ground
>   By myself again:
>   What difference, then?
>   Only that underlying sense
>   Of the look of a room on returning thence.

The colloquial rhythms, the apparent casualness, the absence of all verbal exhibitionism, combine to give a sense of the poet so absorbed into the experience he is describing that experience is completely realized in the texture of the verse, completely objectified and contained, so that it is now outside the poet wholly. Neither ideas on the one hand nor words on the other have dominated him; we have the feeling that the poet has found the perfect outward form for an inward state of mind. This is quite different from either Browning or Swinburne; indeed, it represents a use of language at the opposite extreme from the latter's. Hardy could use a more conventional Victorian poetic idiom, with lilting or soothing rhythms and "magical" language, as in the popular "When I set out for Lyonesse" shows; his verbal and metrical oddity was deliberate.

Between the poems of what might be called mechanical ironic coincidence and the restrained and haunting renderings of an experience fully realized in verse, there are more generalized poems, often in simple and conventional stanza forms, describing an illuminating incident, an attitude or a mood. "The Darkling Thrush" is of this kind; it lacks the immediacy of the latter kind but it has more conviction and vitality than the former. The poet leans on a coppice gate on a dull winter's day and suddenly hears the thrush break into lively song:

> So little cause for carolings
> Of such ecstatic sound

Was written on terrestrial things
    Afar or nigh around,
That I could think there trembled through
    His happy good-night air
Some blessed Hope, whereof he knew
    And I was unaware.

There is almost an air of album verse about this; it is very *pat;* and
Hardy has a considerable number like it. They have a certain charm
and persuasiveness, but they do not have the full Hardyesque individuality that we find in

We stood by a pond that winter day,
And the sun was white, as though chidden of God,
And a few leaves lay on the starving sod;
    —They had fallen from an ash, and were gray.

Your eyes on me were as eyes that rove
Over tedious riddles of years ago;
And some words played between us to and fro
    On which lost the more by our love.

                                                   (Neutral Tones)

Even such a simple poem as "Afterwards," limited to making a single
point, has the note of individual utterance:

When the Present has latched its postern behind my tremulous
                                                   stay,
    And the May month flaps its glad green leaves like wings,
Delicate-filmed as new-spun silk, will the neighbours say,
    "He was a man who used to notice such things"? . . .

But he is best of all when he resists all temptation to verbal elaboration or to pointing the ironic moral, and sets forth a situation with
grave and quiet precision, as in "She Hears the Storm":

There was a time in former years—
    When my roof-tree was his—
When I should have been distressed by fears
    At such a night as this!

I should have murmured anxiously,
    "The pricking rain strikes cold;
His road is bare of hedge or tree,
    And he is getting old."

But now the fitful chimney-roar,
    The drone of Thorncombe trees,
The Froom in flood upon the moor,
    The mud of Mellstock Leaze,

The candle slanting sooty wick'd,
The thuds upon the thatch,
The eaves-drops on the window flicked,
The clacking garden-hatch,

And what they mean to wayfarers,
I scarcely heed or mind;
He has won that storm-tight roof of hers
Which Earth grants all mankind.

Hardy's first published volume of verse was *Wessex Poems, and Other Verses* (1898), but this contained poems written very much earlier. After his last novel, *Jude the Obscure* (1896), and the outcry which followed it, Hardy turned entirely to poetry. His poetry is thus mostly written in the 1860's and 1870's and in the late 1890's and afterwards. Between 1903 and 1908 he published the three parts of his massive epic-drama of the Napoleonic Wars, *The Dynasts.* This vast work, with its hundred-and-thirty scenes, its mingling of historical episode and choric comments, with prose dialogues between ordinary people of the period and grand poetic panoramas of movements and significant incidents, dramatic moments of debate or decision rendered in swift colloquial verse, has survived largely as a quarry to be worked by those seeking to formulate Hardy's philosophy. The choric apparatus—the Spirit of the Years, the Spirit of the Pities, and others—builds up in a series of poetic statements what can be taken to be Hardy's view of an immanent will in the universe working toward consciousness and amelioration. The last chorus (of the Pities) expressed the hope

That the rages
Of the ages
Shall be cancelled and deliverance offered from the darts that were,
Consciousness the Will informing, till It fashion all things fair!

The Dynasts is not a great philosophical poem. It has memorable moments and some fine individual lyrics, but the ideas in it remain external, not realized in the texture of the drama. It remains interesting for students of Hardy's mind and a rich mine for anthologists, but nobody reads it as a whole. We turn with relief from this ambitious project to the moving simplicity of the poem on the First World War which he wrote in 1915:

Only a man harrowing clods
In a slow silent walk
With an old horse that stumbles and nods
Half asleep as they stalk.

> Only thin smoke without flame
>   From the heaps of couch-grass;
> Yet this will go onward the same
>   Though Dynasties pass.
>
> Yonder a maid and her wight
>   Come whispering by;
> War's annals will cloud into night
>   Ere their story die.

The poetry of A. E. Housman (1859–1936) is sometimes linked with that of Hardy on the grounds that each represents in his own way Victorian pessimism. There is indeed a superficial similarity between, say, this stanza of Hardy's

> I spoke to one and other of them
>   By mound and stone and tree
> Of things we had done ere days were dim,
>   But they spoke not to me,
>
> (Paying Calls)

and this of Housman's

> The wind and I, we both were there,
>   But neither long abode;
> Now through the friendless world we fare
>   And sigh upon the road.

Nevertheless, Housman's poetic procedure was radically different from Hardy's. Housman's aims at a combination of lilt and epigram, a classic simplicity and formality in the sound and shape of a poem, the strictly controlled catch in the throat:

> And since to look at things in bloom
> Fifty springs are little room,
> About the woodlands I will go
> To see the cherry hung with snow.

There is no deliberate colloquial roughness, no confident surrender to the meaning of objects, in Housman as there is in Hardy. When, in the sixty-three short poems of A *Shropshire Lad* (1896), Housman projects the character of the doomed young countryman—soldier, farmer, criminal, lover (his role changes)—and refers to him as "lad," as he so often does, it is not colloquial speech or a rustic dialect he is bringing into his verse, but a literary reminiscence. The note of proverbial rusticity—

> Up, lad: thews that lie and cumber
>   Sunlit pallets never thrive;

> Morns abed and daylight slumber
> Were not meant for man alive,

is not genuine, nor is it really meant to be: behind it lies the sophisti-cation of Greek and Latin lyric, the artfulness of Elizabethan song, the singing romantic irony of Heine. Housman's temptation is the melodramatic situation: the lad caught in some undefined trap to face the hangman at dawn, or betrayed and disillusioned in love, or bereft in youth of "golden friends" and "rose-lipt girls" to bear it out stoically or with hollow revelry. When he surrenders to the melo-dramatic pose and ekes it out with self-pity, the brave lilt of the lyrics becomes too histrionic, too obviously worked up; but when he withdraws and leaves the poem to speak for itself the result can be very fine:

> Lovers lying two and two
>   Ask not whom they sleep beside,
> And the bridegroom all night through
>   Never turns him to the bride.

Even here it might be asked whether the description of the dead as couples, as bride and bridegroom, is not too carefully posed: the dead are not (except on rare occasions) bride and groom, and to get extra ironic pathos out of the situation by treating them as though they are is, it might be alleged, mere trickery. But when trickery works it ceases to be trickery, and it often does work in Housman. The dialogue between the living and the dead beginning "Is my team ploughing" (it should be compared with Hardy's "Ah, are you dig-ging on my grave?") subdues the melodrama into a controlled but universal irony:

> Yes, lad, I lie easy,
>   I lie as lads would choose;
> I cheer a dead man's sweetheart,
>   Never ask me whose.

This is wholly successful, whereas the concluding stanza of the ninth poem is not:

> There sleeps in Shrewsbury jail to-night,
>   Or wakes, as may betide,
> A better lad, if things went right,
>   Than most that sleep outside.

Housman's greatest artistic achievement was to wring emotion out of controlled simplicities in verse form. Such a device as the adding of a fifth line to the common ballad stanza can achieve re-markable emotional effect, as it does in the poem "Bredon Hill,"

> In summertime on Bredon
>   The bells they sound so clear;
> Round both the shires they ring them
>   In steeples far and near,
>   A happy noise to hear.

The description of love and hope on Bredon is followed by an account, sufficiently brief and concentrated, of the girl's death and present funeral, with the final two lines of each stanza tolling through like a bell, until the end:

> The bells they sound on Bredon,
>   And still the steeples hum.
> "Come all to church, good people,"—
>   Oh, noisy bells, be dumb;
>   I hear you, I will come.

It is the repetitive effect—not the incremental repetition of the ballads, but a more sophisticated device—working through all seven stanzas that gives this poem its emotional impact. This effect is not always successful. In "The Lent Lily" the note is forced:

> Bring baskets now, and sally
>   Upon the spring's array,
> And bear from hill and valley
>   The daffodil away
>   That dies on Easter day.

The final line of the stanza is too obviously a trick.

The note of melodrama is even more obvious in *Last Poems* (1922), but again where the situation is posed adroitly enough the form and the cadence can get a chance to work and the poem can speak with the true Housman tone of combined elegy and irony:

> But men at whiles are sober
>   And think by fits and starts,
> And when they think, they fasten
>   Their hands upon their hearts.

The posthumous *More Poems* (1936) adds no new scope or strength. Housman was a poet of limited range and small output, whose deeply melancholy temperament and classical sense of form were combined with an oddly histrionic streak. It was the histrionic streak that so often threatened the integrity of his poetry: when he controlled it he could handle his few but elemental themes (the transience of life and especially of youth, the beauty and indifference

of Nature, the betrayals and ill chances that threaten love and friendship, the necessity of endurance) with memorable eloquence. Eloquence is the word, a haunting musical eloquence that contains
irony (consider, for example, the little poem, "Oh, when I was in
love with you") but echoes away at last in sheer melancholy—the
Tennysonian *lacrimae rerum* less generalized and dispersed, more
securely anchored in the context that distills it.

The Victorians cultivated many kinds of poetry—philosophical,
meditative, dramatic, patriotic, hortatory, picturesque, decorative,
exhibitionist, using themes derived from history, earlier literature,
mythology, personal emotion and circumstance, and nature, with
techniques which utilized a great variety of verse forms and exploited rhythmic effects and vowel music with considerable virtuosity. But the virtuosity tended to grow ever narrower, becoming the
mere refinement of traditional forms or the clever patterning of
rhymes and rhythms: it was rarely the technical response to a new
imaginative need, but rather a careful scraping of the barrel of a
poetic tradition. There were a few individual innovators, chief among
whom was Gerard Manley Hopkins; Hopkins' technical experiments
and new approach to poetic expression *were* the results of new
imaginative needs; but he was virtually unknown to his generation
and had no influence in the nineteenth century. In France the
symbolist movement, headed by Verlaine and Mallarmé, had well
before the end of the century developed a magical, incantatory kind
of poetry, with the meaning flowering obliquely out of mood and
imagery without being sustained by a recognizable intellectual
sequence, and this was in many respects a revolutionary movement,
breaking down traditional metrical and other forms, drawing on the
subconscious and on private association, and exploring kinds of
awareness that had never before been deliberately made the subject
of poetry. But as far as this movement affected English poetry in
the nineteenth century, it was only in the direction of encouraging
a more or less conventional dreamlike verse, which represented an
exaggeration of what after all had been an important side of Tennyson. In the twentieth century, however, the Symbolists had a more
revolutionary effect and their influence was absorbed in a more
radical manner.

The dream poetry of the *fin-de-siècle* poets—Ernest Dowson,
Lionel Johnson, Arthur Symons, and the other companions of the
young Yeats in the Rhymers' Club—stemmed from a rather vague
"art for art's sake" view of poetry. It had neither the emotional precision nor the formal inventiveness of the French Symbolists; it was

really in the Keats-Tennyson-Rossetti-Swinburne line (for one can trace such a line, though Keats' greatness does not lie in his beginning it and both Tennyson and Rossetti have their independent merits), the last romanticism, seeking in melancholy verbal suggestiveness, self-conscious hedonism, antibourgeois sensationalism, heady ritualism, histrionic world-weariness, or mere emotional debauchery, compensation for the drabness of ordinary life. The poetry these poets produced was occasionally arresting in mood or gesture, but on the whole its imagery was faded, its properties stagey. It was often a rather feverish acting out of their conception of the poet as an alienated man, lost and wantonly lost. Something of Byron and something of Pater lie behind this, though neither Byron nor Pater would have acknowledged it. It is a poetry bred out of literature, exhibiting more skill than energy and more pose than original rendering of experience, and if this be a definition of decadence, then it was a decadent poetry.

The one Victorian poet who made a radical attempt to reconsider the nature of poetic expression was Gerard Manley Hopkins (1844–89), whose poems were not published until 1918, long after his death, and whose influence on British and American poetry of the 1920's and 1930's was an important part of the poetic revolution of that period. Received into the Roman Catholic Church in 1866, to become subsequently a Jesuit priest and teacher, Hopkins was never a professional poet; but he gave to both the theory and practice of poetry an intense and dedicated concentration that is reflected in his letters to Robert Bridges and others. His poetic practice was in some essential respects the reverse of Tennyson's: instead of using imagery in order to achieve an expansion outward into a generalized mood, he used it so as to refer continuously and cumulatively back to the poem until a total structure of meaning was contained in the poem, a meaning that (to use his own term) "exploded" with immense force once it became known. "One of two kinds of clearness one should have," Hopkins once wrote to Bridges, "—whether the meaning to be felt without effort as fast as one reads or else, if dark at first reading, when once made out to *explode*." The explosion is the result of the total impact of the poem, so that sometimes we feel that Hopkins uses language so as deliberately to prevent the escape of premature meanings until the total expression has been achieved. "Obscurity I do and will try to avoid so far as is consistent with excellences higher than clearness at a first reading," he wrote in another letter.

Hopkins' endeavor was to achieve the unique and essential meaning of the experience he was embodying; "inscape," the individual and distinctive design, was for him the true reality and, as it were, personality of a poem. "No doubt my poetry errs on the side of oddness," he wrote Bridges, "but as air, melody, is what strikes me most of all in music and design in painting, so design, pattern or what I am in the habit of calling 'inscape' is what I above all aim at in poetry. Now it is the virtue of design, pattern or inscape to be distinctive and it is the vice of distinctiveness to become queer." He recognized the risk of becoming "queer," but it was a risk he had to take if he was to write real poetry at all.

One can see Hopkins' straining after both individuality and immediacy in the opening of "The Wreck of the Deutschland" (1875), his first fully mature poem:

> Thou mastering me
> God! giver of breath and bread;
> World's strand, sway of the sea;
> Lord of living and dead;
> Thou hast bound bones and veins in me, fastened me flesh,
> And after it almost unmade, what with dread,
> Thy doing: and dost thou touch me afresh?
> Over again I feel thy finger and find thee.

The normal English word order gives way to the order of emotional preference; the meter is not tapped out in regular feet but is in what Hopkins called "sprung rhythm," at the same time looser than conventional poetic meter and more closely geared to the emotional pattern of the line; the line lengths vary with the demands of the cumulatively developing meaning; and an almost Anglo-Saxon strength is given to the verse by the alliterative beat. Hopkins looked for new sources both of strength and individuality in English poetic speech. He was never content to rest in accepted poetic feeling. He charged older words with new meanings by the contexts in which he set them; he experimented with word combinations reminiscent of the Anglo-Saxon "kennings"; he restored their original meanings to dead metaphors thus providing a shock of surprise. Consider both the language and the rhythms of the opening lines of "The Starlight Night":

> Look at the stars! look, look up at the skies!
> O look at all the fire-folk sitting in the air!
> The Bright borough, the circle-citadels there!
> Down in dim woods the diamond delves! the elves'-eyes!

The exclamatory first line arrests and startles. The second seems to explain the note of astonishment by seeing the stars as a community of people (with "fire-folk," a "kenning"), and this idea is developed in the third line when the stars are "bright boroughs" and "circle-citadels." The fourth line, seeing the stars as digging into the woods, is a paradoxical reversal of the normal situation where men dig for diamonds—here the diamonds are digging, digging into the darkness of the woods to illuminate them: it is a mysterious process: they are "elves'-eyes." But the startling and arresting nature of this opening is not enough; the true meaning can only be seen if we follow the poem through. Then we realize that to see stars as people in boroughs is to see them as townsmen and merchants, concerned with diamonds and other precious and salable things, and that the beauty of the natural world "is all a purchase, all is a prize," to be bought and bid for. The poem concludes:

> Buy then! bid then!—What?—Prayer, patience, alms, vows.
> Look, look: a May-mess, like on orchard boughs!
> 　　Look! March-bloom, like on mealed-with-yellow sallows!
> These are indeed the barn; withindoors house
> The shocks. This piece-bright paling shuts the spouse
> 　　Christ home, Christ and his mother and all his hallows.

The shock treatment continues, but it is done by carefully working out the implications of the earlier imagery. You buy the beauty of the world with prayer, patience, alms. While you are hesitating the auctioneer, as it were, draws your attention to the beauty of the goods:

> Look, look: a May-mess, like on orchard boughs!

A mass of hawthorn, like pear blossom in an orchard. It is white, color of purity and innocence. "May" suggests Mary and "mess" suggests "mass," so there are Catholic devotional overtones in the imagery. And in the end the suggestion of protection and enclosure in "boroughs" and "circle-citadels" is carried on by the imagery: "These are indeed the barn; withindoors house /The shocks." The harvested sheaves are to be safely housed in the barn. But "shocks" also suggests the other and more familiar sense of the word—"the thousand natural shocks that flesh is heir to." By buying the beauty of nature with prayer, we learn to see God in nature and to possess both nature and God. Thus by "owning" nature we have a home for it—and for ourselves, protecting both "the shocks" of corn and ourselves from the shocks of life. At the conclusion Christ and his saints are brought into this communion of the sheltered and protected: it now becomes the communion of saints, and that, we now learn, is what "the fire-folk sitting in the air" really suggested. The poem, like so many in Hopkins, seeks to unite passionate appreciation and detailed awareness of the beauty of nature with a deep religious sense of God's presence and reality. It is done here by the structure of the imagery, and the poem cannot be seen for what it is until the whole of it has been allowed to live in the mind.

"Christ and his mother and all his hallows" shows Hopkins restoring an older word, "hallows," to its proper meaning, "saints." But giving it emphatic last place in the poem he forces us to linger on it and appreciate its meaning. Consider, too, such a device as the almost colloquial leaning on the word "indeed" in "These are indeed the barn." This is the preacher's tone, as he leans toward his congregation to emphasize and bring out the implications of what he has been discussing. The modulation of tone in this poem is remarkable, from the initial excitement to the calm, confident, secure feeling of the final line.

A full appreciation of Hopkins' technical brilliance requires a more careful analysis of individual poems than can be carried out in a historical discussion of this kind. One might take any one of at least a dozen poems and show the recharging of language, the vitalizing of rhythms, the counterpointing of colloquial and formal speech, the structuring of imagery into a complex totality of meaning. "God's Grandeur," another of his many poems dealing with nature and God, begins with urgency and excitement:

> The world is charged with the grandeur of God.
> It will flame out, like shining from shook foil;
> It gathers to a greatness, like the ooze of oil
> Crushed . . .

The first line is the organlike declaratory simplicity of a litany: indeed, it recalls the nineteenth Psalm: "The heavens declare the glory of God." The following "It will flame out" (with a strong beat on "will") adds the personal urgency, and the precise simile "like shining from shook foil" exacts a careful look at the world of objects. "I mean foil in the sense of leaf or tinsel," Hopkins explained to Bridges. "Shaken goldfoil gives off broad glares like sheet lightning and also, and this is true of nothing else, owing to its zigzag dints and creasings and network of small many cornered facets, a sort of fork lightning too."

Often Hopkins opens a poem with a winning simplicity, in the tone of a courteous stranger seeking our acquaintance. Then, as the imagery is built up, interrelationships of meaning are established, and in the end the meaning becomes both immensely rich and precisely pinpointed. We see such a process in his sonnet, "The Lantern out of Doors," which begins

> Sometimes a lantern moves along the night,
>   That interests our eyes. And who goes there?
>   I think; where from and bound, I wonder, where,
> With, all down darkness wide, his wading light?

The cunning word here is "interests." It appeals as an ordinary word used with a special kind of persuasiveness. At the same time (as the conclusion of the poem will show) it suggests quite another kind of "interest"—financial interest. Casual strangers, who interest us momentarily, are soon lost in the darkness; in life men pass and recede "till death or distance buys them quite." The sonnet concludes:

> Death or distance soon consumes them: wind
>   What most I may eye after, be in at the end
> I cannot, and out of sight is out of mind.
>
> Christ minds; Christ's interest, what to avow or amend
>   There, éyes them, heart wánts, care háunts, foot fóllows kínd,
> Their ránsom, théir rescue, ánd first, fást, last friénd.

Imagery of buying and consuming, lending at interest and ransoming, is deftly worked into the poem, and this grounding of devotional feeling in mundane human activities is a significant aspect of Hopkins' technique. He uses it continually. Similarly, he incorporates a simple proverb, "Out of sight is out of mind" into the texture of the sonnet without doing it any violence, but rather giving new strength and individuality to this unifying process, this tying up of human and divine, which is so often Hopkins' poetic aim.

Sometimes the complexity of the suggestions set up by the imagery, and the combination of almost breathless immediacy with interacting overtones of meaning that keep on reverberating almost too widely, produce a poem whose excitement and crowded implications can be recognized and even appreciated without being fully pinned down. Critics have long been debating the precise significance of the imagery in "The Windhover":

> I caught this morning morning's minion, king-
>   dom of daylight's dauphin, dapple-dawn-drawn Falcon, in his riding
>   Of the rolling level underneath him steady air, and striding
> High there, how he rung upon the rein of a wimpling wing
> In his ecstasy!

It is a powerful and remarkable poem, even if the fundamental "inscape," the basic insight in the light of which the imagery is tied together, remains open to question. It is a poem which achieves its effects by what one might call its secondary devices, while the great primary device remains a matter for controversy. That Hopkins can sometimes do this is a tribute to his technical brilliance. Sometimes he does not achieve even this, and in his desperate attempt to achieve a true "inscape," his refusal not to be led astray or have his experience defined or distorted by language, he can be led into confusion and spluttering. On the other hand, he can write with direct and moving simplicity—sometimes with a simplicity that accommodates a whole set of suggestive and teasing overtones, as in the charming "Pied Beauty," which swells out from the limpid

> Glory be to God for dappled things

to the final organ chord

> Praise him.

And "Spring and Fall: to a young child" has a lilting grace in its use of octosyllabic couplets that is seldom achieved in this verse form in English.

Perhaps the most impressive and the most profoundly moving of Hopkins' poems are his "terrible sonnets," where he expresses his experience of the dark night of the soul with extraordinary power.

> Not, I'll not, carrion comfort, Despair, not feast on thee;
> Not untwist—slack they may be—these last strands of man
> In me or, most weary, cry *I can no more*. I can;
> Can something, hope, wish day come, not choose not to be . . .

The most packed and powerful of all is the sonnet beginning "No worst, there is none," with its terrible sestet:

> O the mind, mind has mountains; cliffs of fall
> Frightful, sheer, no-man-fathomed. Hold them cheap
> May who ne'er hung there. Nor does long our small
> Durance deal with that steep or deep. Here! creep,
> Wretch, under a comfort serves in a whirlwind: all
> Life death doth end and each day dies with sleep.

Hopkins' "oddities"—his elisions, omission of relative pronouns, twisted word order, and so on—are part of his strength and individuality. They represent a calculated risk he took in his poetry: when they come off, they achieve an intensity of individualized expression that no other Victorian poet was capable of. His somewhat academic discussions of "sprung rhythm" are of less interest than his rhythmic practice, which is more like the beat of Anglo-Saxon verse than the more regular metrics of modern English poetry: provided the number of stresses was kept constant, the number of unstressed syllables did not matter. One of his greatest achievements was in refurbishing the poetic idiom. In a line like

> The Eurydice—it concerned thee, O Lord

or in the opening of "Hurrahing in Harvest"—

> Summer ends now; now, barbarous in beauty, the stooks arise
>   Around; up above, what wind-walks! what lovely behaviour
>   Of silk-sack clouds! . . .

he gives new meaning, new dignity and precision, to worn words such as "concerned," "lovely," "behaviour." But perhaps his greatest achievement was in breaking out of both the Victorian elegiac mode and of the Wordsworthian mode of nature poetry to achieve a fresh and original handling of personal sorrow and of feeling for nature. Put "No worst, there is none" beside "Break, break, break" or even "Dover Beach," or "God's Grandeur" or "Spring" beside "Tintern Abbey" and at once the originality of Hopkins emerges with astonishing clarity. He was neither in the Wordsworthian nor the Tennysonian tradition. The tradition that he did work in he really discovered for himself, out of his own reading and out of the needs of his own temperament and situation. His great poems are not more than a handful; but they are some of the most fully realized and perfectly rendered poems in English.

CHAPTER TWENTY - SIX

The Victorian Novel

THE NINETEENTH CENTURY was the great age of the English novel. This was partly because this essentially middle-class form of literary art was bound to flourish increasingly as the middle classes rose in power and importance, partly because of the steady increase of the reading public with the growth of lending libraries, the development of publishing in the modern sense, and other phenomena which accompanied this increase, and partly because the novel was the vehicle best equipped to present a picture of life lived in a given society against a stable background of social and moral values by people who were recognizably like the people encountered by readers, and this was the kind of picture of life the middle-class reader wanted to read about. The novel, like the medieval *fabliau,* is what Northrop Frye calls a "low mimetic" literary form. The purely escapist impulse to read about a high aristocratic world of ideal gallantry and beauty is as lacking in the typical Victorian novel-reader as the desire to see the fundamental problems of human experience projected imaginatively and symbolically through the presentation of "great" figures acting out their destiny on the grand scale. The Victorian novel-reader did want to be entertained, and in a sense he wanted to escape. But he wanted to be entertained with a minimum of literary convention, a minimum "esthetic distance." He wanted to be close to what he was reading about, to have as little suspension of disbelief as possible, to pretend, indeed, that literature was journalism, that fiction was history. Of course, the novelists fooled them—at least the great ones did. The ordinary reader may have had the illusion that what he was reading was a kind of journalism, a transcript of life as it was happening around him without the modifying effect of literary form and imagination. In fact, the great Victorian novelists often created complexes of symbolic meaning that reached far deeper than the superficial pattern of social action suggested to the casual reader; the novels of Dickens,

1049

for example, are full of symbolic images and situations suggesting such notions as the desperate isolation of the individual (the grotesque and the eccentric in Dickens' characters become almost the norm, suggesting that life is atomistic and irrational and that patterns of communication can never be real). But it has been left for modern criticism to investigate this aspect of Victorian fiction. The great majority of borrowers from Mudie's libraries and readers of serialized novels in magazines wanted to read about life as they thought they knew it. The impulse that makes modern television viewers so devoted to plays of ordinary life, dealing with people like themselves with whom they can identify themselves, but liberated by plot from the dullness of life as they actually live it—this impulse helped to create the English novel and to sustain it during its brilliant nineteenth-century career. That this indicates a gap between the demands of art and the expectations of its audience need not surprise us; such a gap is a commonplace in literary history. The best Victorian novels transcended the requirements of its audience and can be read by later generations for different and perhaps profounder reasons. But the same can be said of the best Elizabethan drama. The requirements and expectations of a given audience can help to explain the rise and flourishing of a given literary form, but cannot explain its true nature or value, except with reference to ephemeral works produced by hack writers merely to satisfy the contemporary demand.

With Charles Dickens (1812–70), journalism and melodrama are gathered into the novel to give it new life and a new and important place in middle-class entertainment. If he learned something from eighteenth-century novelists, especially Smollett, he learned even more from his own circumstances and observation, combining an extraordinary relish for the odd, the colorful, and the dramatic in urban life and in human character with a keen eye for the changes which the Industrial Revolution brought into England in his lifetime, an acute consciousness of his own lower-middle-class origin and the unhappy circumstances of his own childhood (which included his father's imprisonment for debt and his own much resented employment at a blacking factory as a youngster), and a sentimentally humanitarian attitude toward human problems. Beginning as little more than a comic journalist, he soon discovered his special gifts as a novelist, gifts which enabled him to present to his delighted readers stories set in his own day or the recent past in which the vitality of the characters, the enthusiastic savoring of their physical environment, the movement from comedy to pathos and from compassion to horror, and the sheer high spirits with which he rendered eccentrics, villains, unfortunates, hypocrites, social climbers, *nouveaux riches*, criminals, innocents, bureaucrats, exhibitionists, self-deceivers, roisterers, and confidence men, human oddities of all kinds each with his own physical and moral individuality and each involved in a rich pattern of interacting lives played out against social background whose sights and sounds and smells were rendered with a vivid particularity—in which all this is presented with an almost reckless profusion.

Dickens began with a great sense of life and little sense of form, capturing the individual oddity, the extravagant moment, with remarkable skill, and then marking time, as it were, until he could introduce another such oddity and another such moment. *Sketches by 'Boz'* (1836) is lively journalism merely, but with the *Pickwick Papers* (issued in monthly parts in 1836 and 1837) we can see him feeling his way from humorous journalism to something more. The full title is significant: *The Posthumous Papers of the Pickwick Club containing a Faithful Record of the Perambulations, Perils, Travels, Adventures and Sporting Transactions of the corresponding Members.* This reminds us not only that the *Pickwick Papers* were originally planned as a series of sketches to accompany a set of sporting prints, but also of the picaresque tradition in which Dickens began his career as a novelist. *Pickwick* began as burlesque, but soon moved into a more substantial kind of picaresque comedy, where the interest lies not only in particular absurd incidents but also, and more significantly, in the way in which given characters react to new kinds of environment. Each of the characters soon develops his own moral, physical, and emotional qualities, and the interest is kept up by showing how these qualities reveal themselves in new and unexpected situations. The simplicity, benevolence, and harmless egotism of Mr. Pickwick are placed in ever more testing circumstances, and the benign character who sets out in order to observe the world which he thinks he understands is faced again and again by situations which affront all his assumptions, threaten his status as benevolent observer, and lead him in the end, after the most violent experience of the indifference and intractability of the world of other people, to retirement and the closed circle of his friends, followers, and dependents, on whom he can confidently turn his benevolent observation. But the interest does not lie merely in our watching the behavior of Mr. Pickwick and his friends as they react to different environments: the characters themselves are drawn with lively humor, and the individual traits of Alfred Jingle or Sam Weller are pleasing and amusing in their own right. Further, in taking his characters through various parts of England, Dickens is able to give us a sense of the early nineteenth-century social scene, a feeling of English town and country just before the Industrial Revolution changed its face so startlingly, in the last phase of the great coaching days before the railways put an end forever to that phase of English life. Everybody in the book travels, and traveling means coaches and horses and—perhaps most of all—inns and innvards. Inns are focal points, where characters meet, ways cross, and different kinds of conviviality can be illustrated. Moreover throughout *Pickwick* there runs a steady vein of incidental satire—of electioneering methods, in the famous Eatanswill election, or political journalism, in the two Eatanswill editors; of lawyers and the law; of social convention, and innumerable other phases of English life, caricatured with rich comic effect through such characters as Mrs. Leo Hunter, Mr. Nupkins, Dodson and Fog, and so many more. Burlesque, caricature, satire, comedy, the presentation of the English scene, the panoramic view of life—these different aspects of the book are never fully drawn together; they do not always rise out of each other but exist side by side, so that *Pickwick* remains episodic, a bedside book to be taken up and put down at any point, a picaresque novel which stops simply because the author can think of no more to say.

If Dickens moved on to profounder and better organized works, he never left behind him the qualities he demonstrated in *Pickwick*. He never lost his touch for burlesque or for satirical comedy, his feeling for the eccentric, his sense of the inn as a symbolic as well as a literal crossing of the ways. And there is another quality in this book which points forward to the later Dickens. In the latter part, where Dickens brings Mr. Pickwick into the Fleet prison and turns him, perhaps unwittingly, from a comic figure to a saintly character presiding over a house of the wretched and persecuted, we get for the first time a glimpse of the tremendous well of sentimental compassion which Dickens was always able to draw on. How to reconcile this unphilosophic and sometimes almost hysterical view of human suffering with his great gifts as an ironist was always a major problem for Dickens, and the falling apart of *Pickwick* at the end—with the escape of its hero from any touch of the comic spirit and the unconvincing conversion of Mr. Jingle—is a symptom of a deep cleavage in the author's own mind and attitude which was again and again to threaten the integrity of his novels.

This was perhaps a Victorian dilemma; no other age has shown such strange combinations of the critical and the sentimental, though something of the sort can be seen among some of the Deists of the eighteenth century. A moral creed in the process of renouncing supernatural sanctions demands the most rigorous intellectual apparatus if it is not to be forced to ground itself in a naive sentimentality when dealing with the perennial problems of suffering and death. Dickens' intellectual apparatus was not of the strongest—he was in a way the most instinctive of all the great English novelists except Emily Brontë—and sentimentality was often his only way of handling difficult moral problems. This can be seen in *Nicholas Nickleby* (issued in monthly parts, 1838-39) where the solution to the problems of the hero and his family comes suddenly from the unmotivated benevolence of the Cheeryble brothers, two casually met characters. The novel is rich enough—though not nearly as rich as some others of Dickens' novels—in characters whose portrayal has that fierce individualizing quality that Dickens could achieve so well, from the savagely brilliant picture of Mr. and Mrs. Squeers and the whole atmosphere of Dotheboys Hall to Mr. and Mrs. Crummles and their theatrical environment, the Mantalinis, the Kenwigs, and such transient minor characters as Messrs. Gregsbury and Pugstyles. But Ralph Nickleby is a villain out of melodrama, and Nicholas himself is a conventionally virtuous young man whose real purpose in the novel is to come into contact with other and more interesting characters. The unfortunate Smike is a conventional exercise in the pathetic. Dickens, brilliant in his ability to present the facts of human behavior in all their richness and individuality, is so far incapable of illuminating its sources or motives, especially where the extremes of either malice or humility are concerned. The central vision of human fate in *Nicholas Nickleby*, if it exists at all, is weak and unconvincing, and certainly incapable of drawing together into a complex artistic whole the various scenes—so many of them magnificent in themselves—in the novel.

Oliver Twist (published serially, 1837–39) is the first of Dickens' novels to concentrate on specific social ills, but, as always with Dickens, the force of the indictment falls most heavily on the individuals who administer the attacked institution rather than on the institution as such. Oliver Twist, bandied between workhouse on the one hand, and benevolent protection on the other, with a third sinister alternative of forcible adoption into one of the criminal gangs of London, exists not so much to be saved as to illustrate the different kinds of environment into which innocence may fall. The book is full of nightmare symbols of loss, isolation, and incarceration. It is also a portrait gallery (done in Dickens' best style) together with a series of vividly etched pictures of physical locations and single incidents; it contains some great and memorable scenes, but the humanitarian feeling that informs the novel is not sufficient to give it adequate form: Oliver's salvation remains accidental, and comes only when (and because) Dickens has exhausted his ammunition.

Much of what was said of *Nicholas Nickleby* could be said of *The Old Curiosity Shop* (1840–41), powerful and brilliant though many of its episodes are: the death of Little Nell, which reduced to tears the populations of England and America, has become the standard example of Dickensian sentimentality, a sentimentality which expressed itself in an inflated, embarrassing style which it is difficult to believe could ever have caused intelligent readers anything but acute discomfort. *Barnaby Rudge* (1841) is a more controlled work, and a stranger one: in it Dickens first displays to the full his ability to discipline melodrama into a somber if not quite a tragic pattern and to relate individual eccentrics to a general atmosphere in which they seem somehow inevitable. But it was with *Martin Chuzzlewit* (1843–44) that Dickens first showed his real stature as a novelist, though, paradoxically enough, on its first appearance in the usual monthly parts there was a sharp drop in subscribers. It was still picaresque in structure, and was begun, like so many of Dickens' novels, without any clear idea of where he was going. The full title is even more facetious than the long titles he gave to *Pickwick* and *Nicholas Nickleby:* "The Life and Adventures of Martin Chuzzlewit, His Relatives, Friends, and Enemies. Comprising All His Wiles and His Ways, With an Historical Record of What he Did, and What He didn't; Showing, moreover, Who Inherited the Family Plate, Who came in For the Silver Spoons, and Who for the Wooden Ladles." The central theme revolves around Pecksniff, the superb hypocrite who never admits the truth of his own intentions even to himself, and the novel is a grimly ironical study of the effects of greed on character, and of the possibilities of self-knowledge as well as of real knowledge of others. For the first time Dickens has taken a moral situation rather than a group of picturesque characters and incidents as his starting point, and though his episodic technique, and the fact that he was feeling his way toward the plot as he wrote the book, led him to digress frequently and to introduce many scenes and characters who have no direct or even indirect relation to this theme, nevertheless the theme does remain central and the power of the novel derives from the pitiless humor with which Dickens pursues his investigation of the hypocrisies, pretensions, corruptions, and distortions to which men are liable if they gear their ambitions wholly to the material aspects of a civilization in which prestige derives from monetary wealth or in some other ways surrender their personalities to an idol. There are moments of rich comedy in the book—such as the scene where Mr. Pecksniff becomes drunk in Mrs. Todger's boarding house—but they derive from permutations and combinations of the factors out of which the moral meaning of the book is constructed—the relation between gentility and morality, between virtue and its appearance, between (in Yeatsian terms) a man's mask and his true self. Even the scenes in America, which Dickens put in on a sudden decision in the hope of increasing sales, and which have often been criticized as an excrescence, are related to this central concern, and the relation between appearance and reality, between moral pretensions and actual behavior, between true worth and public esteem, constitute the motivating force of the American incidents. Again, however, the positive moral base is flimsy and sentimental. Tom Pinch represents innocence, virtue, fidelity, in such a way as to make these virtues appear both unbelievable and fatuous, and though his relation with Pecksniff plays a significant part in the book by showing how vice can use virtue with virtue's innocent consent, his pastoral affection for his sister Ruth, done with that idealized eroticism with which Dickens describes equally fraternal and sexual love, is wholly unacceptable. Nevertheless, in spite of these and other faults, and in spite of (or perhaps because of) the fact that Dickens produced a different book from that which he apparently set out to write, *Martin Chuzzlewit* represents an important stage in Dickens' career in that it shows him taking a central moral situation as the focal point of the novel. This links him more clearly to the other Victorian novelists—Thackeray on the one hand and George Eliot on the other—than anything he had yet written could have done. In learning how to discipline his genius for caricature, comedy, and irony to a moral vision Dickens took his place among the Victorians as essentially one of them. Yet he never lost his individuality; his feeling for melodrama, for the *outré*, his sometimes irresponsible histrionic sense, and his unique and unquenchable vitality— these remained with him always to give the characteristic Dickensian flavor to all his work.

Dombey and Son (1846–48) joins richness of character and incident to unity of moral purpose with a new maturity, illustrating the drawing together by Dickens of his various gifts. By "moral purpose" is not, of course, meant a single didactic theme, but concentration on some central moral situation, often deriving (in Dickens) from the author's awareness of the tension between private affection and the apparent demands of a commercial civilization. In *David Copperfield* (1849–50), autobiography has been subdued into art with remarkable skill. The richness, flexibility, and strength of this novel give it a special place among Dickens' work. Here self-pity is sublimated into ironic observation, and as the novel follows the fortunes of its hero from idyllic infancy through the powerfully drawn Murd-

stone period to his aunt Trotwood's protection and thence on to manhood and love with their consequences in emotion and action, the
sense of life, individual and social, operating with all its complexity
and inevitability on the hero and his friends, emerges persuasively.
There are the inevitable Dickens sentimentalities—the fate of Little
Em'ly, David's relationship with Dora—but they pale beside the
strength and vitality of the whole. There is the clash of different
ways of life; different strata of society each with its own ideals of
gentility and worth come into conflict with each other, and in the
process Dickens explores once again the relationship between convention and reality, between public and private standards. *Bleak
House* (1852–53) shows the same kinds of strength as the two previous novels, together with an ingenuity of plot contrivance and
some touches of pure melodrama; but again it is the power of the individual scenes, the skillfully produced atmosphere, the concentration
on the tragic irony of human ambitions and professions through the
sheer accumulation of evidence, as it were, that make the novel.
Dickens' endings are often slick and unconvincing, though ingenious,
and show a contrivance of happy endings for favored characters on a
quite different level of probability from that which gives life to the
novel as a whole; but we accept this kind of convention because it
is superimposed lightly on the essential novel and does not seem
really to affect lt.

In *Hard Times* (1854) Dickens, always keenly aware of the social
situation around him, turned his attention to the morality of the
utilitarian industrialist and its affect on the possibilities of human
happiness. This novel is more of a simple fable than anything else
that the mature Dickens wrote, and the names of the characters
(Gradgrind, M'Choakumchild, Bounderby) sound like a comic Bun-
yan; but the force of the novel comes from its juxtaposition of apparent and real knowledge, of the mechanical and the imaginative, and
the moments of supreme irony—as when Cissy Jupe is forced to admit
ignorance of what a horse is because she cannot define it in strict
dictionary terms though she has lived and worked with horses all her
life—are much more than exercises in the grim or the bizarre or the
self-contradictory, but revelations of the tragic inadequacy of rational
schematizations to cope with the realities of human understanding
and imaginative awareness. In *Little Dorrit* (1855–57), *Great Expectations* (1860–61), and *Our Mutual Friend* (1864–65), Dickens
achieves that almost careless maturity that Shakespeare achieved in
his last plays; yet these novels are far from flawless, and the last of
them especially has at least the normal quota of sentimentalities and
frigidities. *Little Dorrit* presents with somber power, paradoxes of

fate and fortune while incidentally carrying the share of social propaganda (about prison conditions) which is an element in nearly all of the novels. *Great Expectations* explores, with more subtlety and more control than Dickens anywhere else displays, aspects of the relation between gentility and morality, and though it has its melodramatic moments (the Miss Haversham theme), there is no other of his novels where the characters and incidents are so perfectly subdued to the central moral vision. From the opening scene with Pip and the escaped convict—surely one of the most brilliant openings in English fiction—through the ambitions, expectations, and frustrations of the hero, the ironic vision never falters: Pip seeks to become a gentleman and to wash from his mouth forever the flavor of his early life, especially the encounter with the convict, while in fact it is the convict who has left him the money with which to pursue his genteel ambitions, for—supreme irony—the convict, too, conceives that there is no higher reward than the achievement of gentility. The great *anagnorisis*, the recognition by Pip of the convict as the true author of his fortunes, shows Dickens at the very height of his genius, and if the final working out of the action seems too full of complicated coincidences, this is no great matter, for the real story has by now been told and we are content with whatever ingenuities of explanation the author presents to us. *Our Mutual Friend* is the most consistent presentation in all Dickens' work of the effect of financial and social ambition on character; the meaning is achieved both on the literal level and through a complex symbolism. The character of Mr. Boffin, for example, heir to a dustman's fortune and both victim and *deus ex machina,* has many levels of significance, as has that of the sinister Wegg and the perfectly-named Veneerings. Meanness and generosity are set side by side in a thousand different forms; the Lammles, hoisted with their own petard and determined to get their own back on society; Mr. Twemlow, that almost Jamesian dweller on the borderland of high society; the complacent, bullying Podsnap with his pathetic daughter—these and many others are not only portraits in a brilliant portrait gallery but explorations and illuminations of the various ways in which fortune and character can be related. The heroine, Lizzie Hexham, poor but honest, though she appears in some magnificently rendered scenes, does not sustain adequately her role as a convincing character, and this is true of many of the upper-class "good" characters in the book: virtue combined with social position held no interest for Dickens, nor could he make the contented and virtuous poor interesting; he was more concerned with those realms where aspirations toward social position could affect moral behavior. So Our Mutual Friend himself is of no great interest, nor is Mr. Eugene Wrayburn, nor any of those characters who show pastoral or aristocratic or patriarchal virtue. Dickens had that large-ness of genius which enabled him to waste more of his energies in sentimentalities and melodramatics than most other writers had at their disposal altogether.

There was an element of the ingenious mystery writer in Dickens, which developed as a result of the example of Wilkie Collins; his last novel, unfinished, was *The Mystery of Edwin Drood* (1870), a high-powered thriller which still keeps critics guessing. And in *A Tale of Two Cities* (1859) he wrote an intense historical novel centered on the French Revolution. Both these works, though they display many of the characteristic Dickens strengths, were bypaths for him. Journalist, caricaturist, satirist from the beginning, he soon learned to subsume these gifts in a rendering of aspects of the social situation in terms of human foibles and weaknesses, the demands made by social conventions, and the relation between the social and economic fabric of society and the strengths and vulnerabilities of individuals. His vitality was enormous; he crowded his canvases with many more figures than the pattern of his story demanded out of sheer relish for the vagaries of human nature. If the weakness of his philosophical equipment prevented him from indicating any satisfactory moral base from which to contemplate the ultimate issues of human life, and thus led him into sentimentality and melodrama in order to cover up, as it were, this lack; if he was continually producing squibs and sketches and stories (such as "A Christmas Carol") where he pleased his contemporary readers by laying this kind of thing on with a trowel; and if his solution to social problems went no further than suggesting that people simply stopped behaving cruelly—let us remember that he did awaken the Victorian conscience on a great variety of subjects, from debtors' prisons to private schools, and that as a novelist he possessed a combination of gifts unknown among English novelists before or since. He had that joy in the varieties of human character that Chaucer and Shakespeare had, and to a degree shared by none but those; he had both a richness of pure comic in-vention and an extraordinary gift for irony and caricature; he had a pressing sense of the moral and social problems of his day and the genius to illuminate them through the presentation of character in action; and always and invariably he entertained. If Tennyson was the great prophet of the Victorian middle classes, Dickens was the great entertainer. Like Tennyson, he met his audience halfway; he accepted their preconceptions, cashed in on their emotional potentialities. Yet in doing so he exposed their shams and conventions and hypocrisies with almost frightening violence. The norm of his art remained bourgeois sentimental melodrama, but he transcended its limitations through the power and versatility of his genius.

William Makepeace Thackeray (1811–63) came to the writing of novels in something of the same casual way which led Dickens to fiction. More interested at first in drawing and painting than in writing, he came to literature through journalism and his early work consists of sketches, essays, satires, and much miscellaneous humorous and descriptive writing. From the beginning he had a keen eye for social pretension, for the disparity between professed and actual motives, for all the hypocrisies with which social man learns to cover up his true intentions. Some of his early work illustrates with preposterous melodramatic exaggeration the ironies of social success won at the expense of virtue, but where he was able to control his moral indignation and gaze with steady irony on the follies and villainies of the social scene, he produced some powerful satirical sketches. He was against affectation, Byronic attitudes, all those dregs of romanticism which came to be used for the purpose of putting a gloss on different kinds of villainy, and presented himself as a moral realist who looked at society as it really was and brought to the surface the hypocrisies, vanities, snobberies, and all-pervading selfishness which lay behind the charming masks of the socially successful. The life of the great seen through the pitiless eyes of a valet, the successes of an unscrupulous scoundrel narrated by himself in a tone of apparently innocent moral self-congratulation, exposures of snobs and double-dealers in every phase of society—these were characteristic achievements, and though the *Yellowplush Papers*, *The Luck of Barry Lyndon*, and *The Book of Snobs* are not much regarded today, together they provide a powerful record of Thackeray's main objections to man as a social animal. Further, such a work as *Barry Lyndon*, with its perfect capture of an eighteenth-century atmosphere and its maintenance throughout of a tone of complete innocence (adopted by the villain who tells the story), shows both a skill in historical *pastiche* and a gift for sustained irony. His preoccupation with snobs—a term which came to include every kind of defection from a simple ideal of openness and honesty which the demands of society produced—led him at times to a completely unrealistic appraisal of the nature of social life and the relation between personal and social morality, which came ill from one who considered himself a realist and exposer of the real truth about men; but it also provided him with a consistent point of view from which he could view the human scene in his more sustained and serious work.

Vanity Fair (which appeared in monthly parts in 1847 and 1848) shows the results of Thackeray's apprenticeship in satirical and mock-heroic writing, but its tone is less brittle and its subject more central than any of the lighter work which had preceded it. It is, from one point of view, a study of the way in which the demands of society operate on human character and vice versa; in this world the meek are not blessed, but are pushed to the wall, and wit, opportunism, and unscrupulousness form an unbeatable combination of qualities. Unbeatable, at least, until the final round, when somehow the rewards and punishments are readjusted and the simple prevail over the cunning after all. That there is a conflict here between Thackeray's conscious purpose and his deepest layers of understanding is generally realized; he wishes both to tell the whole truth about man in society *and* to be edifying. But if the truth is not edifying? Thackeray here gets himself into a difficulty similar to that which landed Dr. Johnson in one of his few contradictions in critical theory: Johnson knew (none better) that in this life the poor and virtuous are not happier than the rich and wicked and that what we call "poetic justice" rarely prevails, yet he demanded that literature should be at the same time true to life and a picture of life in which virtue was shown to be triumphant and vice punished. He both praised Shakespeare for being true to life and rebuked him for not allowing poetic justice to prevail often enough at the end of his plays. It might be said that nearly all the Victorian novelists were involved in this contradiction in some degree, but it is particularly flagrant in the case of Thackeray, for his role as the stripper off of the mask is the most deliberately cultivated. Becky Sharp, the real heroine of *Vanity Fair* for all her creator's protestations to the contrary, is born poor and of humble birth, and if she is to be successful on any worldly standard she must use her wits and play the cunning opportunist. Thackeray makes it perfectly clear that if she had been born in better circumstances she would have been a happy and virtuous wife and mother. His criticism of society becomes thus in effect a defense of its victim—for Becky is in a very real sense the victim of society. She plays her cards brilliantly, and makes a place for herself by her wit, vivacity, intelligence, and adaptability. Her flouting of conventional morality in favor of always giving the *appearance* of acting according to its dictates is the result of her scrupulously rendering to Caesar what is due to Caesar. We cannot but admire her liveliness and resourcefulness; she is the most gifted and the most interesting character in the book. Yet she is an adventuress, and she cannot be allowed to proceed unchecked to her triumph. So Thackeray contrives a brilliant scene in which she overreaches herself and falls out of good society—

yet how "good" that society is has already been made clear enough—and even goes further and brings out, as the novel proceeds, new and unpleasant traits in her character, such as her cruel indifference to her child, to make her fate seem more edifying. The picture of her in her decline contriving by successive maneuvers to keep herself going in one continental city after another is effectively done, and her repeated exposures are made to contribute to her deterioration very convincingly; but those exposures are themselves made by "snobs" on wholly unmoral grounds, and again Thackeray seems to be confused as between judge and criminal. And what of the virtuous characters? They cannot be conventionally successful people, for conventional success is itself suspect; so they must be simpletons like Amelia Sedley and Dobbin (though Dobbin becomes strangely more intelligent and full of character as the book proceeds and he is required as a hero). The fact is, that Thackeray has become so obsessed with the kinds of successful duplicity which unscrupulous intelligence can get away with that he almost becomes suspicious of intelligence itself. Wit and liveliness add up to opportunism and low cunning, and to be morally safe one must be almost stupid. There is something here very suggestive of the Victorian equation of innocence with ignorance in matters concerning the relation between the sexes—surely one of the most confused and dangerous positions ever taken up in the history of our culture.

It has been argued that Thackeray's profession of admiration for insipid virtue—not only in *Vanity Fair* but in such characters as Laura and Mrs. Pendennis in *Pendennis*—results from his carrying into the novels the emotions he felt in real life for the originals from whom those characters were drawn, and this may well be so. It is also true that Thackeray provides us with all the data, so that we may disagree with his verdict if we wish to: *we* know what is wrong with Amelia Sedley and Mrs. Pendennis even if Thackeray refuses to admit that anything is wrong. He rarely falsifies the facts; it is only his attitude to the facts that sometimes disconcerts us. And *Vanity Fair* remains a brilliant and powerful novel, full of a sense of the social passions at work: if the modern reader is irritated by Thackeray's intrusive moralizings he can easily skip those passages without in any way rending the fabric of the novel. For the novel lies in the succession of scenes which present the characters in action, in the sense of social context which comes through so vividly, the acid pictures of man as a social animal.

The effect of the plot as such, the degree to which the full meaning of the novel is achieved cumulatively by the order in which the events occur, is relatively slight in Thackeray. There was always the

element of picaresque in his writing, and his love for Fielding concentrated on that writer's spaciousness as well as his mock-heroic
skills (which he imitated often) rather than on the sense of epic proportion and contrivance that we find in *Tom Jones*. In *The History of
Pendennis* (1848–50) the plot becomes almost episodic, and the novel
might end, we feel, at almost any point. In taking a well-meaning and
intelligent young man through some of the emotional adventures and
predicaments of youth, Thackeray produces a *Bildungsroman* of a
kind common enough before and since; the value of the novel lies in
the vividness with which the significant moments are realized and
depicted and the balancing of various social types and attitudes
against each other as the story proceeds. Vanity Fair is here, too, and
the kinds of character and action that have most value in the market
place are sardonically examined, but the atmosphere on the whole is
more gentle than in the earlier novel and the contrasts between unscrupulous wit and insipid virtue less absolute. Major Pendennis is
worldly but far from contemptible, and Captain Costigan is a
rascal but an engaging one. There is a Dickensian touch about some
of the minor adventurers in the novel, as though Thackeray is allowing himself to contemplate men occasionally for their lively pictur-
esqueness rather than for their rating in his scale of snobs and hypocrites, but there is also a general slackness compared with *Vanity
Fair*, and there are moments in the latter half of the novel when the
reader gets a little wearied with it all. An episodic novel with some
magnificent scenes and moments—the picture of the young Pendennis in love with the Fotheringay, which opens the book, is one of the
most memorable things of its kind in the English novel—linked by
moralizing about virtue and society and temptation and so on but
not really organized into a fully integrated work of art, *Pendennis* is
a good example of how Thackeray so often tried but did not quite
succeed in reconciling his picaresque instincts with his desire to produce a well-plotted novel. Does he get across his vision of man in
society by a series of individual episodes, each of which is an independent example of the kind of thing he wants us to see, or is the
vision incomplete until the total story has unfolded itself? In *Vanity
Fair* one might almost claim the latter, but in *Pendennis*, as in *The
Newcomes* (1853–55) and *The Virginians* (1857–59), the former is
nearer the truth.

Thackeray's most perfectly integrated novel is *The History of
Henry Esmond, Esq.* (1852) where an eighteenth-century story is
told in an eighteenth-century style which has the merit, besides helping to capture the flavor of the period, of eliminating Thackeray's
garrulous interventions. The emphasis is once more on appearance

and reality—wherein resides *real* goodness in human character, amid all the attractive and unattractive disguises available for our superficial inspection?—but here the exposure of snobs and hypocrites and other aspects of social life is subordinated to the interest in character, the play of one character on another, the eventual uncovering of true motives and true moral quality. The novel is a remarkable piece of virtuosity, yet we feel that all of Thackeray's powers were not concerned in it and that the moral inconsistencies and personal interventions that are a feature of his other novels are somehow a part of his literary personality so that he cannot achieve full power without them.

It could be maintained that Thackeray never discovered the literary medium most fully congenial to his genius. His satirical powers, his moral preoccupations, his profound sense of the demands which social living makes on character, never seem to be working together in complete harmony. Perhaps the Victorian conventions were too much for him. In his preface to *Pendennis* he wrote: "Since the author of Tom Jones was buried, no writer of fiction among us has been permitted to depict to his utmost power a MAN. We must drape him, and give him a certain conventional simper. Society will not tolerate the Natural in our Art. . . . You will not hear—it is best to know it—what moves in the real world, what passes in society, in the clubs, colleges, mess-rooms—what is the life and talk of your sons." Yet he claims to have been more frank than was customary and to be "telling the truth in the main." In the confidential tone he adopts toward the reader—he described *Pendennis* as "a sort of confidential talk between writer and reader"—he is trying, perhaps, to achieve in attitude what he cannot wholly achieve in substance. However that may be, he strikes the modern reader as a novelist who was rather confused than helped by the moral climate of his day. With Dickens we cannot help feeling that here was a novelist for whom serial publication, for whom the great middle-class public with its taste for sensationalism combined with gentility, for whom indeed all the factors which operated in his day were grist to his mill. They drew out all that was strongest and most characteristic in his genius. But Thackeray was not so well equipped to make literary capital out of the limitations of the Victorian scene; there were elements in him of both Swift and Fielding, yet he was not allowed the freedom of either of those writers; so indignation became whittled down to moral disapproval and a deep sense of the great moral inconsistencies of life was weakened and softened to sentimentality. Matthew Arnold said of the poet Gray that "he never spoke out"; the phrase might more aptly be applied to Thackeray. Dickens took the teeming and confused life of his day and bodied it forth splendidly in fiction; George Eliot took the intellectual currents of her time and found a way of rendering them in the imaginative life of her novels; Thackeray, with a more fastidious talent than either, never quite found a way of coming to terms simultaneously with his age and with his art.

With the novel rapidly establishing itself as the dominant literary form, more and more different kinds of sensibility came to express themselves in it. The lonely individual genius as well as the writer who worked in the mainstream of Victorian thought was now likely to turn to fiction, and while the majority of novels produced during the Victorian age continued to handle the problems of man in society, and to deal with moral situations as they emerged in a specific social world with specific social and economic characteristics, there was also the occasional writer who turned to fiction to express those private passions and explore those realms of personal emotion which, in another age, would have been more likely to seek expression in lyrical poetry. This is especially true of the Brontës who, because of the fascination which the lonely life they shared in a bleak Yorkshire village has had for biographers, are generally considered together. Yet the Brontes are a unit to more than the biographical eye, for they shared an imaginative as well as a physical life. Only two of the four are of real literary importance: Charlotte (1816–55) and Emily (1818–48) would have been assured of fame quite apart from the interest aroused in their lives by Mrs. Gaskell's biography of the former; Anne, who shared the passionate introversion of her sisters, lacked their imaginative vitality, and her novels and poems are dull affairs; and the unfortunate Branwell, who in childhood had shared fully in the private dreamworlds which all four Brontes created continuously from a very early age, proved quite unable to come to terms with his imagination or his ambitions and is remembered only for his membership in that remarkable family.

The three sisters had started off, naturally enough, by publishing their poetry in a joint volume, in which the authors gave their names as Currer, Ellis, and Acton Bell. This anonymity—which was never officially broken in their lifetime—was not only the disguise which female writers of the period so often thought fit to assume in presenting themselves to the world as novelists; it was also part of their inwardness, their intense living to themselves, which in Emily's case was carried to almost fantastic lengths and produced that lonely power of the imagination that manifested itself so remarkably in her single novel and masterpiece *Wuthering Heights* (1847). Emily's poetry, which alone in the joint volume shows any distinction, draws on this same source: it draws on emotional situations created by an imagination of almost terrifying power and deriving nourishment from no obvious external events. Charlotte, sensitive, passionate, and sensuous by temperament, became involved in the external world more than Emily ever did and made some attempt to cast her fiction into a mold that at least bore some resemblance to that employed by more conventional novelists. *The Professor,* her first novel, though published after her death, is a muted version of passages in her own emotional history; *Jane Eyre* (1847)—her first published novel, and the work which brought her contemporary fame—shows her writing, with an almost melodramatic abandon, out of her own passions, dreams, and frustrations; parts of the book are practically straight autobiography, and other parts represent the kind of wish-fulfillment which few Victorian women had the courage or the power to translate into fiction. The book moves at high speed, and its emotional temperature never drops. There are elements of masochism as well as wish-fulfillment, and some scenes of stark melodrama, but they are all fused in the high temperature of the narrative so that they do not stand out as such. Normal conventions governing the relations between the sexes are not so much defied as simply ignored, so that when Jane Eyre and Mr. Rochester confront each other the fierce interplay of emotions has complete scope. The novel is sometimes preposterous, sometimes plain silly, but it is carried along from beginning to end through sheer power. Here is clearly a case of the imagination and the passions creating their own art form. *Shirley* (1849), Charlotte Brontë's next novel, is a dull thing in comparison, in spite of some admirable scenes; it draws on stories of antimachine riots which she had heard in her youth, and brings in many characters based on people in and about her own village of Haworth; but here the personal passion is interfused with much plodding contrivance, with the result that the true Brontë genius is not given much chance to emerge. *Villette* (1853), where she returned to her own emotional life, is based on her fierce and finally suppressed passion for her Brussels teacher, M. Héger; it is a kind of symbolic rendering of this chapter in her emotional history, with some incidents literally true, and it has the same feverish note that we find in *Jane Eyre,* with a less artificial resolution of the plot.

If Charlotte Brontë's novels are *sui generis,* to be judged on a standard which they themselves set up, the same is true, and in an even profounder sense, of Emily Brontë's *Wuthering Heights,* a work of stark grandeur in which a wholly nonmoral world of fierce symbolic action is localized quite precisely in the author's familiar Yorkshire—the bleak Yorkshire of the remoter moors—so that we have on the one hand the most careful realism in the description of physi-

cal objects and on the other a world of human relationships in which
the whole pattern of behavior is built on a purely imaginative conception of the nature and meaning of human emotional life and its
relation to action. The natural description is geared so cunningly to
the picture of human passions that it seems to render them convincing and even inevitable, and while he reads the reader is unconscious
of any gap between the realistic and imaginatively symbolic aspects
of the novel. The prose is firm and biting, and the action is deployed through the cunning interposition of intermediate narrators
in such a way as to emphasize at once the uniqueness and the power
of this strange and compelling series of events. There is nothing quite
like *Wuthering Heights* anywhere else in English literature. It is the
work of a woman who—whatever the psychological explanation—cut
herself off deliberately from normal human intercourse and lived
throughout her short life in a private world of imaginary passion.
Charlotte, too, lived in some degree in this way. But Charlotte made
an effort to come to terms with the world outside her; she allowed
herself to be hurt by it, and she sought comfort in it, and this con-
cession to a social world is reflected in the themes and structure of
her novels. Yet the strength of her work, like that of Emily's, derives
from the workings of a lonely imagination; there was little she could
learn from others. As for Emily, she could learn nothing at all from
others, and her one remarkable novel represents the one impressive
prose example in English of induced emotion creating its own "objective correlative" by the sheer force and conviction of its expression.

Before George Eliot (Marian Evans, 1819–80) the English novel
had been almost entirely the work of those whose primary purpose
was to entertain. Not that earlier novelists had lacked moral purpose;
Richardson "taught the passions to move at the command of virtue,"
and something similar might have been said of Goldsmith in his
Vicar of Wakefield. Of Thackeray's moral feeling we are never left
long in doubt and Dickens, too, worked within a clearly suggested
framework of values. Nevertheless, no English novelist from Defoe to
Thackeray could have been called a man of great philosophical
powers and unusual erudition; their presentation of the human scene
was never in any degree conditioned by the depth of their intellectual
penetration or the profundity of their moral speculations, still less by
the vastness of their learning. They were content to follow the
patterns of thought of their day and to handle ideas only obliquely
and symbolically. Their job was to construct stories—moving, edifying, entertaining, or something of all three—not to exhibit new ideas.
It was the poets, not the novelists, who in England traditionally

moved in the intellectual vanguard (though even the poets were rarely intellectual pioneers). From Fulke Greville to Wordsworth there had always been poets to present poetically new notions of man and the world; the novelists—to put the matter bluntly—were as a rule less well educated. George Eliot was the first English novelist to move in the vanguard of the thought and learning of her day, and in doing so added new scope and dignity to the English novel.

Neither profundity of thought nor quantity of learning is necessarily an asset to a novelist; there have been great novelists who lacked both, and there are scholars and philosophers who have written bad novels. But a powerful mind operating naturally through the medium of fiction does produce novels with merits all their own, and George Eliot, who had an eye for character, an ear for dialogue, and a clear sense of the social and economic conditions which govern men's daily living, as well as unusual intelligence and knowledge, can be said to have made the novel intellectually respectable without losing anything of its qualities of liveliness or entertainment. The sentimentality of Dickens and the intrusive moral platitudinizing—equally sentimental in its way—of Thackeray derive at bottom from a lack of intelligence. Unable to accept simple supernatural sanctions for morality, these writers found no alternative except a facile appeal to "feeling" and as a result were unable to cope convincingly with the really disturbing moral problems—the suffering or death of a good character, for example. George Eliot, who was both idealist and agnostic and derived both her idealism and her agnosticism from her own intellectual inquiries into moral and religious questions, had her own answer to these difficulties; she was too intelligent ever to try to solve a moral problem by mere sentimentality. One might quote again from F. W. H. Meyers' record of a conversation he had with George Eliot at Cambridge in 1873: ". . . she, stirred somewhat beyond her wont, and taking as her text the three words which have been used so often as the inspiring trumpet-calls of men—the words *God, Immortality, Duty*—pronounced, with terrible earnestness, how inconceivable was the *first*, how unbelievable the *second*, and yet how peremptory and absolute the *third*." This mixture of idealism and astringency, which may sound rather terrifying in straight philosophical discourse, can be a great source of strength when transmuted into terms of characters "doing and suffering" in a novel. It can enable irony and tenderness to coexist, as they do in *Adam Bede;* it can produce the kind of humor which manifests itself in the portrayal of the scatterbrained but not unsympathetic Mr. Brooke of *Middlemarch* and the relentless analysis of the dilemma and the deterioration of Dr. Lydgate in the same novel; it can make possible that impressive combination of censure and sympathy with which Gwendolyn Harleth is presented in *Daniel Deronda*. At the same time, that "terrible earnestness" can produce the unbelievable and oracular virtuousness of Daniel Deronda himself and of Felix Holt in the novel of that name, and is responsible, too, for the note of excessive idealization which occasionally obtrudes itself in even the best of her novels.

In all her fiction, George Eliot was concerned with moral problems of character, but she never abstracted her characters from their environment in order to illustrate their moral dilemmas. She was familiar with and responsive to the varied social contexts in which nineteenth-century men and women could live; she saw the relationship between town and country, between landed families living in an ever-diminishing feudal atmosphere and neighboring provincial towns where farmer and tradesman, banker and politician, jostled each other in a world of perpetually intersecting interests. She knew England, both town and country, metropolitan and provincial, agricultural, commercial, industrial, and professional, and she used her knowledge to make her characters move naturally in their daily occupations—something which Dickens was unable to do, for Dickens did not take the ordinary daily work of men seriously; lawyers, doctors, manufacturers, if they are seen at work at all in the novels of Dickens, are seen as engaged in quaint, preposterous, or outrageous occupations. Dickens, for all his immense sensitivity to sights and sounds and smells, to every aspect of a physical environment, could never think of man's business or professional labor as a significant daily activity, taking place normally in some particular environment, and having importance both for the character concerned and for the society of which that character was a part. Indeed, what English novelist before George Eliot took men's daily occupations seriously? From the *Canterbury Tales* onward, the English tradition was to show people on holiday and to refer to their trades or professions merely as background. But George Eliot's Dr. Lydgate is a doctor with real medical problems, and she reports his discussion of them accurately; we are told precisely the subject of Mr. Casaubon's research (in *Middlemarch*) and precisely wherein it is lacking; the agricultural activity of the Poysers in *Adam Bede* is presented fully and convincingly with a wealth of detail; and so throughout all the novels. Further, these pictures of men at work are intimately bound up with her presentation of character and of the moral problems of character. It is the relationships into which people are brought in the course of their daily activities that precipitate the changes and the crises out of which the ultimate moral meaning emerges. If Dr.

Lydgate had not been a medical man with specific views of medical research and progress the effect on his character of his marrying a flighty girl with no comprehension of his professional aims could not have been what it was; and so on.

Beginning with comparatively slight descriptions of men and manners, such as are found in *Scenes of Clerical Life* (1858), George Eliot soon proceeded to more complex kinds of fiction. *Adam Bede* (1859), her first full-dress novel, has an element of pastoral idealism in the character of the hero which recurs at intervals in George Eliot's work; but it is significant that this note is connected with the dignity of work, with the capacity to fit in usefully and happily to a social environment. Superficially, the plot of *Adam Bede* might be considered melodramatic, with its seduction of the pretty rustic maid by the squire and the subsequent excitement of infanticide and last minute reprieve from the gallows, but these violent elements take their place in the context of the novel with an extraordinary quietness, deriving partly from the author's sureness of psychological touch —the seducing squire, for example, is no villain of melodrama but a well-meaning if weak character presented throughout with a sympathetic understanding—and partly from her ability to anchor these events in the rhythm of daily life in the countryside. The whole novel has the air of a postlapsarian pastoral—no idealized story of shepherds and shepherdesses, but a story of virtue and vice confronting each other in a society where in the last analysis the dignity of labor and the simple virtues of faith and love can redeem life from squalor into peace and orderliness. True, the idealistic note is there, in the characters of Adam and of Dinah, and the marriage of these two at the end moves the story from the probable to the almost purely symbolic; but there is sufficient earthiness in the novel as a whole to remind us that we are not in the Garden of Eden, but in the modern world, after the Fall.

The Mill on the Floss (1860) is a more complex novel, but again one in which the moral problems of character are illustrated by the relation between one character and another, those relations in turn growing naturally out of the daily life and work of different members of a community. There is an autobiographical impulse in this novel (Maggie and Tom Tulliver are clearly projections in some degree of the young Marian Evans and her brother) which further complicates its pattern, giving it a pervasive emotion and sometimes an excessively high-pitched note so that at moments it reads like the work of a passionate and gifted adolescent. *Silas Marner* (1861), a simpler novel, much quieter in tone, is little more than a symbolic fable, though a brilliantly executed one. It has something of the tone of a fairy tale, with its story of the baby left at the door of the lonely weaver after his gold had been taken from him, and the change in his character and way of life which his rearing of the baby brings. This novel of redemption might be considered as an antitype to Hawthorne's *Scarlet Letter*, the latter being the story of the discovery of guilt and the former of the rediscovery of innocence. *Romola* (1863) and *Felix Holt* (1866) are of less interest than *Middlemarch* (1871–72), George Eliot's masterpiece, where the exploration of moral situations through the presentation of characters interacting on each other and belonging to intersecting social groups is achieved with a sustained brilliance. In a sense, the novel is one of moral discovery, each of the more important characters learning the truth about himself or herself as a result of what happens to him (and of course what happens to him is never arbitrary, but the result of a combination of character and fortune). The resolution of the novel—where the beautiful and idealistic Dorothea marries, as her second husband, the sensitive but somewhat dimly defined Will Ladislaw—is perhaps the least satisfactory thing about it; it seems to indicate a purely symbolic picture of feminine idealism married to a combination of all the masculine virtues, namely sensitivity, understanding, and a zeal for public welfare. But this ending is the least important part of the novel, whose richness of texture belies the simplicity of its conclusion.

There is a delicacy of psychological perception in George Eliot's handling of Dorothea's marriage to Mr. Casaubon which is quite beyond anything Dickens was capable of in this manner. The way in which Casaubon's intellectual deficiencies are gradually developed and made symbolic of his physical and emotional deficiencies, with the implication that Dorothea's discovery of what Casaubon lacks as a man is part of her own discovery of herself as a woman, marks a new kind of subtlety and complexity in the Victorian novel, while to make Dorothea's and the reader's disillusionment with Casaubon produce in both a kind of sympathy with him is to show an awareness of some of the paradoxes of human relationships that gives a new dimension to prose fiction. Similarly, the marriage of Lydgate and Rosamond is presented with a fineness of understanding that transcends simple moral judgment, Rosamond's fundamental selfishness and naïve belief that other people exist primarily to satisfy her wants being shown not merely as a moral fault to be censured but as part of an essential childishness that has, in spite of everything, an appeal of its own, which is closely related to the reason why Lydgate married her in the first place.

There are other features of *Middlemarch* which contribute to making it one of the very greatest of English novels. The different characters and different contexts of living in town and country are shown intersecting in their interests and activities in a way which is fruitfully symbolic not only of the relationship between the individual and society, but also of one part of society with another. Country squire, clergyman, farmer, agricultural laborer, banker, doctor, workers and idlers in town and country, are shown in the complex network of interrelationships which itself is a microcosm of man in the world. The characters presented are thus more than individuals brought in as examples, illustrations, psychological types, or caricatures; they are both real and symbolic, both highly individual portraits and organic parts of a carefully organized plot. Fred Vincy, the well-meaning but weak young man, is a brilliantly shrewd study of a recognizable type; the last days of Mr. Featherstone are drawn with grim and vivid particularization; the downfall of Mr. Bulstrode—and especially the scene between his wife and him after she has heard of his disgrace—is done with a degree of truth and imaginative understanding that is positively astonishing; and one could pick out other scenes and characters; but all these are elements in a grand design which weaves in and out of the novel and can be seen at last, when we view the novel as a whole from a certain distance, as paramount. The almost melodramatic apparatus George Eliot used to project certain important developments in the plot may strike the modern reader as somewhat forced, but it is not prominent enough to weaken the novel as a whole or to spoil the effect of life as it is lived, of provincial England at work, which is so important in the book.

Daniel Deronda (1876) contains some of George Eliot's most brilliant writing, but the novel seems to be conducted on two different levels of probability. As the story of Gwendolyn Harleth, the spoilt beauty who acquires moral character through suffering, the novel has psychological subtlety and moral power; but to find an adequate criterion on which the hollowness of Gwendolyn's world of empty social ambition is to be judged, George Eliot created Daniel Deronda, gentleman of mysterious birth who turns out to be the scion of a long line of Jewish sages and who eventually discovers it to be his destiny to reunite his ancient people in some new and unexplained way. Deronda is surrounded with dark figures of wisdom and beauty which make a strange (and deliberate) contrast to the social life of the fair English girls with their conventional families, and mediating between the worlds of Semitic profundity and English conventionality is the continental musician Klesmer. One has the feeling that George Eliot is reaching out in this her last novel to something more profound and universal than any novel based on the merely English social scene could achieve. She does not quite achieve it because her different groups of characters move on different levels and as a result the moments when they come into contact with each other are not rendered convincingly (with the exception of the great scene where Klesmer, summoned to Gwendolyn who wants him to tell her how to be an actress, tries to open her eyes to the true nature of the world of art). But with all its defects, *Daniel Deronda* remains a remarkable novel, and one which seems to be straining to burst the limits of Victorian fiction.

It must be remembered that George Eliot was one of the Victorian "sages" as well as a novelist, one of those who worried and thought and argued about religion, ethics, history, character, with all the concern felt by those most receptive to the many currents of new ideas flowing in on Victorian thought and most sensitive to their implications. A sage whose moral vision is most effectively communicated through realistic fiction is an unusual phenomenon—or at least was unusual at the time when George Eliot began to write. If it has become less unusual since, that is because George Eliot by her achievement in fiction permanently enlarged the scope of the novel.

More psychologically ambitious than George Eliot—indeed, than any of his English contemporaries and predecessors—George Meredith (1828–1909) never fully succeeded in giving his psychological and moral insights complete artistic realization in the novel form. Self-conscious, cumbersomely artful, not always successful in weaving together into a single complex pattern the points of view of characters and author, armed with an apparatus for observing life that often sticks out of the novels, Meredith is the most difficult of the Victorian novelists to come to critical terms with. In superficial theme he ranged over a great variety of subjects, from the oriental extravagances of *The Shaving of Shagpat* (1856) to the carefully ironic exposure of vanity in *The Egoist* (1879) and the portrayal of national struggle in *Vittoria* (1867), but his principal interests throughout his forty-year career as a novelist are in problems of self-awareness, the relation of character to ideas, varieties of vanity, the relation between natural and artificial factors in building up personality, and the character and behavior of women in a man's world. *The Ordeal of Richard Feverel* (1859) studies self-deception in the character of the hero's father, the conflict between system and instinct as well as between moral sense and desire in the character of the hero, in a context of sophisticated and ironic narrative which nevertheless lapses sometimes into sentimentality and sometimes into melodrama. The ironic tone, here and elsewhere in Meredith, seems to continually promise a greater wisdom than the total novel succeeds in communicating, though there are brilliant moments of witty description and of psychological diagnosis. *The Egoist* sets in motion a vast deal of machinery for probing and presenting the vanity and self-delusion of the hero, Sir Willoughby Patterne, especially in his relations with women; the comedy—constructed on principles that had been intellectually worked out beforehand—is deliberate and, as it were, conspiratorial, with author, reader, and selected intelligent characters looking down on the workings of the hero's egotism with ironic omniscience. In *Diana of the Crossways* (1885), *One of our Conquerors* (1891), *Lord Ormont and his Aminta* (1894), and *The Amazing Marriage* (1895), Meredith continued his investigation of egotism in particular relation to male weakness and female strength, developing his curiously thorny style of mixed objective and subjective presentation, throwing in his own observations directly or indirectly when the spirit moved him, continually and willfully showing his hand as manipulator, complicating the texture of the narrative with oddities of vocabulary or interrupting it with set pieces of natural description of an almost lyrical intensity.

Sometimes the Meredithian comedy vents itself in high-spirited and even farcically conceived characters and incidents (as in *Evan Harrington*, 1861, and *The Adventures of Harry Richmond*, 1871); there is a picaresque as well as a Peacockian streak in his fiction, especially in the earlier novels; and altogether he is a more versatile writer than his best known novels, *Richard Feverel* and *The Egoist*, would suggest. He was a feminist, who spoke out for full female emancipation, and his characters of women—Clara in *The Egoist*, Diana in *Diana of the Crossways*, Lucy (a very different type) in *Richard Feverel*, and many others—are drawn with strength and sympathy. But though one can pick out aspects of novels that delight and impress, and recognize a variety of skills employed in a variety of ways, one cannot help feeling that his genius was never properly focused: his achievement remains less great than his talents.

The novels of Thomas Hardy (1840–1928) also show some disparity between genius and achievement, but here the final achievement seems greater, not less, than a critical inspection of the talents at work would seem to warrant. Hardy's irony is not directed at human egotism or at the disparity between real and assumed worth, but at the very conditions of human existence. Setting his characters in that southern corner of England he named Wessex, a largely agricultural region steeped in history and slow to emerge from the older rhythm of rural life and labor into the modern industrial world, he saw them as elemental figures whose passions were doomed to run the course that the human condition set for them, figures who, contemplated against a background of immemorial and indifferent nature, of the recurring procession of the seasons, and of suggestive and mysterious relics of the human past—Roman remains, Stonehenge, or less tangible relics such as lingering folk customs and superstitions—acted out their generally tragic dramas with a dignity imposed on them by the simple fact of their having to endure the human lot. Hardy was neither a philosophical novelist nor a subtle psychologist; his view of man is neither wholly consistent nor in any degree profound. Nor was he a cunning artist who was able to work his insights so effectively into the form and texture of his narrative that the reader feels that he is here in the presence of the kind of illumination that only art can give. His prose has the air of being self-taught: it is often clumsy, sometimes pretentious, generally rough-hewn and unequal. Yet this very roughness gives a note of strenuous authenticity to much of his writing. The account of the night sky seen from a hill-top in Chapter Two of *Far From the Madding Crowd*, the pretentious description of Egdon Heath at the opening of *The Return of the Native*, and similar set pieces in other novels, gain their effect in spite of—indeed, because of—their awkwardness. We feel, as we often feel about the style of the American novelist William Faulkner, that it is precisely the author's amateur status as a novelist, his lack of professional slickness and obvious competence, that gives the writing weight and integrity. Hardy's vision of life was genuine, and he wrestled with it alone. The novels through which he tried to convey it sometimes break through into greatness despite technical faults, crudities of style and plot, and pseudophilosophical gestures, because the underlying rhythm is sound, and what Henry James called "the sense of felt life" is (though in a very un-Jamesian way) movingly present.

Under the Greenwood Tree (1872) is an idyllic tale of rustic life— "a rural painting of the Dutch school" was Hardy's subtitle—but the idyllic quality is not achieved by abstraction or even suppression. The rhythms of rural labor run through the book, and a sense of the grounding of these activities in immemorial custom that has flowed from generation to generation is strong throughout. Young love, with its vanities as well as its idealisms, is set against the movement of the generations, the certain and ever-present knowledge that what youth is age was and what age is youth will be. The passions and egotisms of the young lovers are rendered in a lively and engaging manner, but in a context which makes them emblematic of the human condition, so that the final happy ending is not, as it is in most romances, a promise of permanent felicity, but represents a decision of the author to stop *here*, at the symbolic moment of fulfillment, before subsuming the principal characters into the larger picture of the march of life; there are signs planted throughout the novel, or rather implicit in its very texture, that this couple are no exception to the human lot and that the pattern extends beyond what the author has chosen to show.

Under the Greenwood Tree is one of the slightest, though one of the most attractive, of Hardy's successful novels. *Far From the Madding Crowd* (1874) uses a wider canvas and takes a closer look at the nature and consequences of human emotions. There is still an idyllic element present, but misfortune, coincidence, and the intrusion into the pastoral scene of an element of sophisticated selfishness from the outside world combine to make this love story much more tangled and more violent in its light and shade. The love of Gabriel Oak— the very name suggests rustic steadiness and dependability—for the woman farmer Bathsheba Everdene begins as pastoral idyl; with the entry of the attractive and weakly self-indulgent Sergeant Troy the serpent enters this Eden; the self-destructive passion which Farmer Boldwood nourishes for Bathsheba further complicates and darkens the pattern; and though everything works out to a happy ending of sorts—Bathsheba marries Gabriel after her first and disastrous marriage to Troy—it is to a chastened and qualified happiness that they win through. Gabriel, whose fidelity and universal competence becomes almost wooden after a time, has nothing really to learn from experience; he exists in order to provide a haven for the chastened Bathsheba, who *does* learn from experience. It is not Eden, but the fallen world of limited possibilities clouded by memories of woe, into which the hero and heroine eventually emerge. The novel is not, however, memorable for its charting of the way expectation is chastened by experience, but rather for the moments of sudden insight into the way passion or vanity or desire works—such as the brilliant scene where Sergeant Troy fascinates Bathsheba with his swordplay —and the unexpected disciplining of melodrama into suggestions of tragedy.

The Return of the Native (1878) is a more ambitious work. Egdon Heath, sunk in history, representing both the indifferent world of nature and the stage on which human dramas have been enacted from time immemorial, sets the tone for this somber story of trapped human passions. Fulfillment for one is frustration for another; maternal love and pride is a mysterious and paradoxical combination of selfishness and self-sacrifice; characters are active or passive according to their natures, but actions never have their expected or intended consequences and the interweaving of passions produces strange patterns. The march of events, though continually instigated and affected by human will, is in the long run at the mercy of the impersonal logic of fact and coincidence. The dark violence of Eustacia Vye, the idealistic intelligence of Clym Yeobright, the will and affections of Mrs. Yeobright, the weakness of Wildeve, produce in their mutual interactions a tragic pattern which, seen against the background of the heath, the daily rural activities of the minor characters, and the sense of history that broods over the action, seems to reduce all life to a doom that is never final. Tragedies occur; hopes are crushed, expectations are cruelly disappointed; self-knowledge comes through sad or bitter experience; but life has been before and will go on. The notes of exaggeration and of melodrama that are occasionally sounded in the novel can be crude enough, but the novel as a whole is saved by its epic tone, its suggestion that here is a microcosm of human fate. Pretentious, unequal, often awkwardly handled, *The Return of the Native* has that combination of earthiness and visionary truth that is Hardy's most impressive quality. If it is not his best novel, it is one of his most characteristic and suggests how much he could achieve with his oddly flawed kind of writing.

The Mayor of Casterbridge (1886) shows a greater mastery of his material than can be found in any other of Hardy's mature novels. The course of action projected by Michael Henchard's original "selling" of his wife is determined in its later stages by a complex combination of factors, which as Hardy presents them constitute a searching symbolic map of the human condition. Nature, civilization, and human character work on each other continually. As so often in Hardy, the past lies half-visible behind the present:

> For a long time there was none, beyond the voice of a weak bird singing a trite old evening song that might doubtless have been heard on the hill at the same hour, and with the self-same trills, quavers, and breves, at any sunset of that season for centuries untold.

Nature does not change—or at least it has not changed, and characters like Michael Henchard regard Nature as something that can only be controlled by submitting to it. But the new spirit of science and industry that is abroad in the country eventually reaches even Casterbridge, a town which, Hardy emphasizes, is part of the surrounding countryside. "Thus Casterbridge was in most respects but the pole, focus, or nerve-knot of the surrounding country life; differing from the many manufacturing towns which are as foreign bodies set down, like boulders on a plain, in a green world with which they have nothing in common. Casterbridge lived by agriculture at one remove further from the fountain-head than the adjoining villages—no more." And again: "The farmer's boy could sit under his barley-mow and pitch a stone into the office-window of the town-clerk; reapers at work among the sheaves nodded to acquaintances standing on the pavement corner; the red-robed judge, when he condemned a sheep-stealer, pronounced sentence to the tune of Baa, that floated in at the window from the remainder of the flock browsing hard by; . . ." And in still another passage: "Casterbridge was the complement of the rural life around; not its urban opposite. Bees and butterflies in the corn-fields at the top of the town, who desired to get to the meads at the bottom, took no circuitous course, but flew straight down High Street without any apparent consciousness that they were traversing strange latitudes." Civilization here was seen in its simplest and most elemental forms, and man was still at the mercy of nature. "If anybody will tell me how to turn grown wheat into wholesome wheat, I'll take it back with pleasure," Henchard tells the complaining bakers who had bought his bad flour. "But it can't be done." But at that very moment the enterprising young Scotsman, Donald Farfrae, just arrived from the north, was in town with a scientific recipe for restoring bad grain. Man is not as dependent on nature as Henchard, with his instinctual temperament, imagines. Soon Farfrae is demonstrating his process to Henchard. Henchard is astonished:

"It's complete!—quite restored, or—well—nearly."
"Quite enough restored to make good seconds out of it," said the Scotchman. "To fetch it back entirely is impossible; Nature won't stand so much as that, but here you go a great way towards it."

There is a limit to man's control over nature, but it is not nearly so narrow as Henchard thinks. Later, when Henchard and Farfrae quarrel—and their quarrel is made to seem as inevitable as Henchard's initial liking for the younger man—Henchard makes contemptuous remarks about the new mechanical drill which Farfrae has imported. And Henchard's financial downfall is the result of the weather, and his desperate and superstitious attempts to predict it in order to know what the harvest would be like. Farfrae, however, uses the weather for his own purposes, and the same weather that ruins Henchard increases Farfrae's prosperity.

Henchard himself is almost a natural force, at the mercy of his instincts and emotions, lacking both in self-knowledge and in objective understanding of the external world. He can exert his will to almost any degree when pride or passion requires it; but he has no finesse, he remains a blunderer in life, and in the end the assault on his emotions by other characters and physical circumstances is too much for him. He has something of the willfulness of Oedipus and Lear, something of their dignity even in his weakness and in the manner of his self-destruction. The novel is not wholly Henchard's story. The other characters—Farfrae, Elizabeth-Jane, Lucetta—play significant parts in this tumultuous warfare between man and Nature, between man and man, and between man and his own passions. Each has his or her own place on the scale between instinct and reason, between Nature and civilization, between simplicity and sophistication. Lucetta's assumed sophistication is an important factor in the plot; ironically, it turns out not to be sophistication at all and she is destroyed by the naïve force of her own emotions. Henchard's shifting relationship with Elizabeth-Jane, whom he first believes to be his daughter, then learns she is not, then wishes she were and claims that she is, until at last he is found out and rejected, is presented with a profound and moving awareness of the ambiguities of paternal affection and the emotional vulnerability of the "strong" male. *The Mayor of Casterbridge* is genuine tragedy, and Hardy's most perfectly wrought work of fiction.

The Woodlanders (1887) is more artificially contrived, and depends on some rather creaking machinery for the movement of the plot, but here too Hardy brings into mutual contact different kinds of simplicity and sophistication in a context dominated by nature and her demands. Nature can be not only a symbol of man's environment with which he must at the same time continually wrestle and be fundamentally in tune; it also reveals the inadequacy of the way in which the world is governed:

On older trees still than these huge lobes of fungi grew like lungs. Here, as everywhere, the Unfulfilled Intention, which makes life what it is, was as obvious as it could be among the depraved crowds of a city slum. The leaf was deformed, the curve was crippled, the taper was interrupted; the lichen ate the vigour of the stalk, and the ivy slowly strangled to death the promising sapling.

But statements and formulations of this kind do not show Hardy's real strength, which lies in his working out of the action. Grace Melbury, torn between desire for sophistication and social position and affection for the simple and familiar, rejects Giles Winterbourne, the woodsman whom she really loves and who loves her, to marry the flashy doctor. She lives to repent her choice, and the doctor, too (somewhat unconvincingly), learns from experience and improves. Giles, planter of trees, has all the strength and dignity of the true country worker, the man who makes things grow. The symbolism is all rather obvious, and the novel lacks the richness of *The Mayor of Casterbridge*. But it contains some of Hardy's best writing, and if he wrings pathos rather than tragedy out of poor Marty's unfulfilled and undeclared love for Giles, this current in the novel does flow strong and deep, and makes possible the final paragraph, where Marty is at last alone with Giles, laying fresh flowers on his grave:

"Now, my own, own love," she whispered, "you are mine, and only mine; for she has forgot 'ee at last, although for her you died! But I—whenever I get up I'll think of 'ee, and whenever I lie down I'll think of 'ee again. Whenever I plant the young larches I'll think that none can plant as you planted; and whenever I split a gad, and whenever I turn the cider wring, I'll say none could do it like you. If ever I forget your name let me forget home and heaven! . . . But no, no, my love, I never can forget 'ee; for you was a good man, and did good things!"

Tess of the D'Urbervilles (1891) is generally regarded as Hardy's tragic masterpiece, and certainly it is his most ambitious tragic novel. This too is a story of innocence and sophistication, of man and nature, of history and its relation to the present, concentrated on the fate of a simple country girl whose parents' chance discovery of their descent from a once noble line sends her to seek the assistance of a degenerate supposed relative to whom she surrenders before parting from him in disgust. This part of the novel is not a simple seduction story: Tess is no paragon of chastity overborne by force or cunning, but a girl "simple, sensuous and passionate" who has never been able to come to terms with the world as she finds it and whose strong intelligence keeps her aware of the fact. She has her baby, and the baby eventually dies, and she goes to work as a dairymaid in an environment of agricultural richness and peace in which she finds at last a satisfying rhythm of life. Her courtship by Angel Clare, her final acceptance of him in spite of her murky past, and the coincidences which conspire to prevent her from confessing that past before the marriage, are described by Hardy with considerable awkwardness, and the further development of the story—Angel's horror at learning the truth at last, his symbolic sleepwalking with his terrified bride, his desertion of Tess who is forced back at last to live with the man who first "undid" her, her eventual discovery that this man deceived her in assuring her that Angel would never take her back and her murder of him in desperate hate and regret at what he has caused her to lose—all this is forced along with a certain grim relish. In spite of brilliantly perceptive moments, glimpses of character and bits of dialogue which are immediately illuminating, neither the motivation nor the actual course of the action is made really convincing. Angel Clare is a much worse character than Hardy seems to recognize, while the chain of circumstances that produce the murder with the inevitable hanging of Tess at the end of the novel seems altogether too contrived. The indomitable Angel Clare is left at the end with Tess's younger sister, "a spiritualized image of Tess," and they move on hand in hand: Angel is evidently determined not to be defeated by fate. But Tess is hanged; the black flag is raised, and Hardy comments, in the well-known sentence: "'Justice' was done, and the President of the Immortals, in Aeschylean phrase, had ended his sport with Tess." This suggestion that Tess was the deliberate victim of divine sadism is not really Hardy's view of how the world is governed, nor is it the view of life implicit in the novel. It is a piece of gratuitous savagery, and contributes to produce in the reader the feeling which *Tess* certainly does produce but which a true tragedy does not—a feeling of plain anger, of frustration and resentment. *Tess* is a remarkable novel containing some first-rate Hardy; but it is not, taken as a whole, a great tragedy.

The same can be said of *Jude the Obscure* (1896), Hardy's last and his most extraordinary novel. Jude, the poor country boy with visions of academic glory, escapes from his native village to Christminster after some dogged self-education in the classics, but he never achieves entry to the university and remains trapped between passion and intellect until his death. Before leaving his native region he had been tricked into marriage with a grossly sensual girl who had appealed to his own very real sensuality, and the account of the dreaming idealist caught fast in the snare of his own physical nature is one of the most powerful things in Hardy. Arabella, the girl he marries, goes off to Australia, but reappears later to reclaim her husband. Meanwhile, Jude meets in Oxford his emancipated intellectual cousin Sue Bridehead, and in developing their relationship Hardy probes some of the most puzzling paradoxes of love, sex, and character. Sue herself is a curiously frigid person; she marries a middle-aged schoolmaster, is carried off by Jude with whom she lives for years, takes charge of Arabella's little boy and produces children of her own. The son of Arabella and Jude, "Little Father Time," old and wrinkled even as a small boy, eventually hangs his stepbrother and stepsister as well as himself, leaving an announcement: "Done because we are too menny." Jude philosophizes about his late son's character: "The doctor says there are such boys springing up amongst us—boys of a sort unknown in the last generation—the outcome of new views of life. They seem to see all its terrors before they are old enough to have staying power to resist them. He says it is the beginning of the coming universal wish not to live." Sue, who had been a secularist, gets religion and rejoins her middle-aged schoolmaster out of a sense of duty, and Jude takes back Arabella and dies of it not very long afterward.

A novel which can surmount such monstrosities of plot must have a strange element of genius, and this *Jude the Obscure* does have. In his preface to the first edition, Hardy explained his intention somewhat defensively:

> For a novel addressed by a man to men and women of full age; which attempts to deal unaffectedly with the fret and fever, derision and disaster, that may press in the wake of the strongest passion known to humanity; to tell, without a mincing of words, of a deadly war waged between flesh and spirit; and to point the tragedy of unfulfilled aims, I am not aware that there is anything in the handling to which exception can be taken.

In the postscript to the preface, appended to the edition of 1912, Hardy remarked without saying whether he agreed or not that a German reviewer had seen Sue Bridehead as "the first delineation in fiction of the woman who was coming into notice in her thousands every year—the woman of the feminist movement—the slight, pale 'bachelor' girl—the intellectualized, emancipated bundle of nerves that modern conditions were producing, mainly in cities as yet." But obviously this is no serious clue to the novel's essential meaning. The conflict between flesh and spirit *is* a clue: it is a theme worked into the familiar Hardyesque theme of the relation between instinct and reason, simplicity and civilization, nature and artifice. Jude and Sue are trapped characters from the beginning—trapped by their own essential selves as well as by external circumstances. The novel is not really directed against the marriage laws nor against the refusal of Oxford colleges to admit rustics, though in his original preface Hardy talked as though these had been principal themes. It is about the inevitable frustrations of the human condition. But the nature of the inevitability is never made fully clear, the relation between circumstance and fate is not properly worked out, and the plot teems with suggestions of literal and symbolic meanings which do not seem to combine into any great central pattern of significance. The theme of the new generation, suggested by the doctor's remark about Little Father Time, is not integrated into the novel. Is Jude's fate the result purely of a given time, place, and situation, or is it the local and temporal manifestation of a human fate? In his 1912 postscript, Hardy called the novel "a tragedy, told for its own sake as a presentation of particulars containing a good deal that was universal, and not without a hope that certain cathartic, Aristotelian qualities might be found therein." One cannot help feeling, however, that the particular often gets in the way of the universal. Yet it is precisely the particularization, the touches of intense individualization in action and dialogue, that give life to the novel. It seems that Hardy had in *Jude the Obscure* more things to say than he could work into a unified artistic pattern or even than he could bear in mind at the same time.

Hardy remains a novelist of unusual power and integrity, who added an epic dimension to the familiar realism of the Victorian novel. His tragic vision of life was never adequately formulated and it could not always be counted on to work effectively through fictional material. But his deep sense of the conditions that constrict experience, his steady compassionate awareness of all the factors that limit and twist human aims, his striking always for the elemental in the life of a given time and place, helped to give an unsentimental largeness to his rendering of life that is like that of no other Victorian.

The novel in the nineteenth century rapidly became the maid-of-all-work of literature, and the most popular way of presenting an extended argument on social, political, or even religious questions was to cast it into novel form. Side by side with the novel as argumentative or illustrative fable, there flourished the novel as entertainment at many different levels of skill and seriousness. The line between art and entertainment is often difficult to draw and so is that between art and propaganda; many propagandist novels as well as many written merely as entertainment for the financial profit of the writer achieved a considerable degree of artistry. A complete account of nineteenth-century fiction, even if no more than a short paragraph were devoted to each author, would take up as much space as the whole of this history up to this point. A brief survey of some of the principal types, with some consideration of the more important practitioners of each, is all the literary historian can allow himself with so prolific a form if he is to preserve any sense of perspective.

One of the most solidly competent of the professional Victorian novelists who aimed to entertain by constructing stories grounded in the kind of life recognizable by his readers was Anthony Trollope (1815–82). By far his most popular novels are the Barsetshire series—*Barchester Towers* (1857), *Doctor Thorne* (1858), and four others—which deal with life and love in a small cathedral city, against a background of ecclesiastical politics and the hopes, fears, and intrigues of a society dominated by its clerical elements. Trollope had a keen sense of the relation between politics (whether ecclesiastical or general) to daily life. In *Phineas Finn* (1869), *The Prime Minister* (1876), and other novels in his parliamentary series, he exploited this with an air of studied realism which helps to make his readers feel thoroughly at home in the world he creates. He had an eye for character types and individual eccentricities, though no profound understanding of the complexities of human passion; he was thoroughly *knowledgeable* about England and the way it was run; he was capable of a restrained irony in handling the ethical problems involved in social and professional relationships. *Orley Farm* (1862), *The Claverings* (1867), *The Eustace Diamonds* (1873), *The Way We Live Now* (1875), and *Is He Popenjoy?* (1878) are others of his more than fifty novels. Without being a great novelist, Trollope had the imagination, the craftsmanship, and the knowledge of men and affairs to be able to construct a world substantial enough for the reader to retire to, and it is this quality in his novels that accounts for the cult of Trollope which began as a largely escapist movement during the Second World War and has grown steadily ever since.

A realist of a different kind was Charles Reade (1814–84), who combined documentary rendering of the contemporary social scene with moments of dramatic—sometimes melodramatic—vividness often with a view to exposing some evil or abuse, as in *It Is Never Too Late To Mend* (1856) and *Hard Cash* (1863), each of which is subtitled "A Matter of Fact Romance." By far his most popular work is his historical novel, *The Cloister and the Hearth* (1861), carefully prepared in its background of historical fact and with the foreground of emotion and action done with considerable vividness. Wilkie Collins (1824–89), who is best known as a father of the detective story with his ingeniously plotted novels of crime and discovery, *The Woman in White* (1860) and *The Moonstone* (1868), and whose intricate plot structures influenced the later Dickens, was also a documentary novelist of contemporary life who paid much attention to realistic detail and verisimilitude. With Mrs. Elizabeth Cleghorn Gaskell (1810–65) the novel of social description moves at a deeper level and with considerable fineness of psychological perception and humane feeling: *Mary Barton* (1848) and *North and South* (1855) deal with social problems of the day, examining the effects of industrialization and machinery on the lives of those involved and exploring the contrasts between agricultural and industrial England and their human implications. Her gentle mixture of humor, irony, and sentiment in her account of English village life in *Cranford*

(1853) is peculiarly English in its tone, which is both sly and benedictory. Her unfinished *Wives and Daughters* (1866) is the most
psychologically complex of her novels.

Charles Kingsley (1819–75) also used the novel as a means of
discussing "the condition of England question." In *Yeast* (1848) and
Alton Locke (1850) he presents with considerable emotional force
and strength of generous feeling the iniquities and injustices suffered by the British working classes in the age of Chartism. Kingsley's Christian Socialism was based on moral indignation and
humanitarian feeling, and these emotions dominate the two novels
and give them considerable appeal in spite of technical limitations
and artistic deficiencies. His historical novel, *Westward Ho* (1855),
is vigorously partisan and full of a sentimental buoyancy in its
treatment of Protestant Elizabethan heroes warring against Catholic
Spain: Kingsley made up in vigor what he lacked in subtlety.

Benjamin Disraeli (1804–81) tackled "the condition of England
question" in quite a different manner. His novels too are flamboyant,
but it is the flamboyancy of a grandiose political imagination in
which high idealism and exhibitionist dandyism are oddly combined. His Tory romanticism, his vision of a "Young England"
restored to an organic national wholeness and freed from the disinte-
grating effects of Whig economic individualism and lack of tradition, give a certain aristocratic tone to his political novels. *Coningsby*
(1844) and *Sybil* (1845)—the latter significantly subtitled "The Two
Nations," i.e., the rich and the poor—present his political and social
program for England, a conception of a society far from classless
but with the classes bound by mutual ties of loyalty, responsibility,
and tradition, a properly functioning aristocracy, a subordinated
but a loyal, protected, and happy peasantry. There is something of
Burke and something of Carlyle in this vision, but the air with which
it is presented is Disraeli's own. His other novels show either his
confident familiarity with aristocratic manners or his political and
historical imagination working on more fantastic schemes and
grandiose actions.

The historical novel, founded by Scott, had many practitioners in
the nineteenth century. Edward Bulwer-Lytton, Lord Lytton (1803–
73), like Disraeli both statesman and novelist, began under the influence of the Gothic novel with studies of injured outcasts (the
tradition of the Byronic hero is active here too), then, with *Pelham,
or The Adventures of a Gentleman* (1828), emerged as one of the
founders of the dandified novel of fashionable life, before settling
down as a historical novelist with *The Last Days of Pompeii* (1834),
Rienzi (1835), and *Harold, the Last of the Saxons* (1848). Bulwer-

Lytton, who was nothing if not versatile, turned at a still later period of his career to other varieties of fiction, both mysterious and fantastic (*The Haunted and the Haunters,* 1857, and others) and the realistic and domestic (*Kenelm Chillingly,* 1873). A versatile and talented novelist and a conscientious craftsman, without being anything more, Bulwer-Lytton responded to the varying tastes of his age so promptly that he remains an important figure for the student of literary taste and fashion. More single-minded historical novelists were William Harrison Ainsworth (1805–82), who developed a very respectable line of what Stevenson was to call "tushery" with over forty novels dealing with different periods of English history, and G. P. R. James (1801–60), who covered Europe as well as England within his sixty-five novels. Competently plotted intrigue, would-be period dialogue, and as much local color as could be conveniently brought in, was the recipe for the historical novel as practiced by these professionals.

A minor novelist who represents a characteristically English genre with remarkable spirit is R. S. Surtees (1803–64). This is the sporting novel, with its lively and humorous pictures of the way of life of the country gentry. *Jorrocks' Jaunts and Jollities* (1838), *Handley Cross* (1843), *Mr. Sponge's Sporting Tour* (1853), and *Ask Mamma* (1858), have a local, period, and class humor reminiscent sometimes of the early Dickens. Surtees is a rather special English taste; his appeal is not literary in the full sense; but he has always had his coterie of followers. It is perhaps not unfair to Charles Lever (1806–72) to put his breezy and lighthearted stories of Irish life—*The Confessions of Harry Lorrequer* (1839), *Charles O'Malley* (1841), and others—beside Surtees, even if some of his later work, such as *The O'Donoghue* (1845), represents a more serious attempt to project a phase of Irish history and society. The exploitation of Irish society by novelists in search of colorful or dramatic material represents a phase of Anglo-Irish literature that was later to give way to a more conscious and dedicated Irish national literary movement. But in the middle nineteenth century the "stage Irishman" was a popular literary figure, drawn with varying degrees of seriousness and concern. Samuel Lover (1797–1868) dealt with Irish types in his *Rory O'More* (1837) and *Handy Andy* (1842).

Regionalist in a different sense is R. D. Blackmore (1825–1900), whose Devonshire novels anchor the action in the local scene with loving particularity. *Lorna Doone* (1869) is historical as well as regional, a story of feuding and love set in the time of the Monmouth rebellion, done with a lyrical feeling and a powerful emotional rhythm that make it one of the most remarkable novels of its kind. It is overdone sometimes, yet it does come off. Of his four-teen other novels, *The Maid of Sker* (1872) and *Springhaven* (1887) show a similar gearing of human passion and natural description.

The eccentric egotism of George Borrow (1803–81), philologist, expert on gypsies, and wanderer, produced his original mixtures of fiction and autobiography, *Lavengro* (1851), *Romany Rye* (1857), and *Wild Wales* (1862), as well as his highly colored account of his adventures as an agent of the Bible Society in Spain, *The Bible in Spain* (1843). Brilliant, prejudiced, and highly unconventional, Bor-row exploited his own personality with an aggressiveness that both attracts and irritates. Books of travel were popular in the nineteenth century, as they had been in the eighteenth. A. W. Kinglake's *Eothen* (1844) is an agreeable account of a journey on horseback in the Near East, while Charles Doughty's *Travels in Arabia Deserta* (1888) is a curiously wrought narrative of his Arabian travels presented in a difficult style of picturesque archaism which is remarkably effective in rendering atmosphere and sense of significance: T. E. Lawrence's *Seven Pillars of Wisdom* was modeled on it. Doughty also wrote poetry in a similar invented style, often archaic in vocabulary and eccentric in word order: *The Dawn in Britain* (1906), with its epic tone and strenuously original handling of language is an impressive attempt to achieve singlehandedly an English epic style.

An altogether more simple-minded writer was Frederick Marryat (1792–1848), whose *Mr. Midshipman Easy* (1836), *Masterman Ready* (1841–42), and other adventure stories of the sea retained their popularity well into the twentieth century. Captain Marryat's books were straightforward, exciting, and at the same time thor-oughly moral, a favorite Victorian combination. Lewis Carroll (pen name of C. L. Dodgson, 1832–98) produced in *Alice's Adventures in Wonderland* (1865) and *Through the Looking-Glass* (1871) much more complex and sophisticated children's books, where below a surface of attractive and quaint adventure lay rich patterns of parody, irony, sentimentalism, and symbolic suggestiveness which can keep the most cunning modern analytic critic fully occupied. George Macdonald (1824–1905), novelist of Scottish provincial life anticipating if not belonging to the "kailyard school," wrote chil-dren's books colored with a mystical tenderness which has much ap-pealed to some modern critics; he was a moralist, a mythmaker, and a mystic of real originality. His children's books include *At the Back of the North Wind* (1871), *The Princess and the Goblin* (1872), and *The Princess and Curdie* (1883).

The naturalist W. H. Hudson (1841–1922) produced some re-markable accounts of the natural and animal world both in Argentina, where he was born, and in England. His view of that world was both patiently accurate and highly visionary. His novel *Green Mansions, A Romance of the Tropical Forest* (1904) is a South American fantasy showing these qualities with splendid power. Another naturalist, Richard Jefferies (1848–87), lacked Hudson's streak of fantasy but had a similar passion for the natural life of the countryside. The appealing descriptions of country life in *The Gamekeeper at Home* (1878), *Wood Magic* (1881), and other works, and the contemplative autobiographical strain that can be seen in other of his writings, notably *The Story of My Heart* (1883) with its characteristic gentle integrity, have an attractiveness beyond what might be warranted by the literary skill alone.

Various kinds of mystical and religious feeling found expression in the Victorian novel. J. H. Shorthouse's *John Inglesant* (1880), a historical novel dealing with English religious life in the mid-seventeenth century and giving a picture of the Little Gidding community in a gentle, pseudomystical tone which owes something both to the Tractarians and to the Pre-Raphaelites, is one of the most interesting of the many Victorian religious novels. William Hale White, in *The Autobiography of Mark Rutherford* (1881) and *Mark Rutherford's Deliverance* (1885) probes with persuasive psychological understanding the problems posed by religious doubt; they are perhaps the most distinguished examples of a peculiar Victorian form of fiction, the novel of religious worry, and show the hero moving through doubt to a compromise moral solution with the conviction that comes from genuine autobiography.

Samuel Butler (1835–1902) soon graduated from Victorian worry to full-scale attack on the whole Victorian *ethos* as he understood it. *Erewhon* (1872) is a satire on the Victorian concept of society, duty, morality, and religion through a witty portrayal of a Utopia which conveys the criticisms with the maximum amount of provocative irreverence. *The Way of All Flesh* (published posthumously in 1903) attacks the despotism of Victorian family life, the hypocrisy and cruelty of Victorian religion, and the cruelty as well as the inadequacy of Victorian education, to advocate, somewhat anticlimactically, a life of moneyed independence and lukewarm attachment to the establishment. It is a savage and powerful novel, though the power is somewhat reduced by the evolutionary view Butler intermittently takes when regarding his characters, a view which makes it impossible to blame anybody as the process works itself out. In the first part of the novel we see Theobald Pontifex suffering under the tyranny of a possessive and dominating father, but when he in turn becomes a father his own background has fitted him even

less for fatherhood than his father's had and he treats his own son
Ernest worse than his father had treated him. Victim becomes
villain, and in the process responsibility and free will seem almost
to disappear. But you cannot have satire without responsibility and
free will, so they are brought back again at intervals. Butler's
Lamarckian views on evolution influenced the organization of his
novel, but other pet ideas of his—such as his view of the importance
of money, which acts as *deus ex machina* in the novel—keep in-
tervening. In spite of lack of consistency and some confusion of
motive, *The Way of All Flesh* achieves tremendous satirical force,
and is more responsible than any other single book for the early
twentieth-century revolt against Victorianism. George Bernard Shaw
learned much from Butler, whose disciple in matters of religion and
evolution he remained all his life.

Of the professional purveyors of literary entertainment in the
latter part of the nineteenth century, Robert Louis Stevenson (1850–
94) was one of the most talented, with a real passion for the craft of
letters and an awareness of its technical demands that drew from
Henry James the remark: "It's a luxury, in this immoral age, to encounter some one who *does* write—who is really acquainted with
that lovely art." Beginning as a self-conscious essayist whose travel
books, *An Inland Voyage* (1878) and *Travels with a Donkey* (1879),
show him cultivating the neatly phrased observation and the carefully cadenced aside and whose shorter essays—whether they are
straightforward reminiscences of his youth, speculations and moralizings based on such reminiscences, or simply studies in the picturesque—show a carefully cultivated style utilized to give expression
to a dominating emotional rhythm, Stevenson went on to become a
novelist of considerable originality and power. *Treasure Island* (1883),
written as a boys' adventure story, is not only skillfully wrought,
with its breath-taking opening, its clearly etched incidents, its
magnificent movement, and its fine sense of *participation,* but also
embodies a carefully worked out moral pattern, and one which presents a dilemma rather than solves a problem. Heroic endeavor is
not automatically linked to obvious moral goodness; what we admire
is not always what we approve of; energy of personality belongs to
Long John Silver and not to any conventional hero; and the virtuous
are saved in the end almost contemptuously by luck and an irresponsible boy who does not quite know what he is doing. Thus even
in a boys' story Stevenson showed something of that interest in
moral ambiguities which he inherited from his Calvinist forebears
and retained from his own early Scottish education; it is an interest
that produced the powerful allegorical study of moral dichotomy,

Dr. Jekyll and Mr. Hyde (1886), as well as the fascinated presentation of the attractiveness of evil and the dogged dullness of virtue
that is found in the first and brilliant half of *The Master of Ballan-
trae* (1889). Stevenson's sense of moral ambiguity went side by side
with a deep feeling for Scottish landscape and history, and in *Kidnapped* (1886) he produced a novel of adventure both topographical
and historical, with the true function of both characters and action
the provision of an adequate "objective correlative" for the author's
feeling about Scottish country and about the clash between theatrical Jacobitism and prudent Whiggery in Scottish history. Its sequel,
entitled *David Balfour* in America and *Catriona* in Britain (1893),
shows a stronger autobiographical impulse at work, though indirectly and not always successfully. Stevenson's greatest novel was
unfinished at his death and remains a fragment—*Weir of Hermiston*,
set in eighteenth-century Scotland, partly in Edinburgh but chiefly
in the open moorland suggestive of the scenery of the Border
ballads. There is indeed a ballad note in this novel, whose texture
is essentially tragic, however Stevenson may have planned a more-
or-less happy ending. The conflict between the stern Scottish judge
and his sensitive and idealistic son is projected with poignant force,
and with a sympathy for both parties. The great dialogue between
the young man and his father, after the former has denounced the
hanging of a criminal whom his father had sentenced, shows a
Stevenson at last fully matured as a novelist of remarkable power
and insight. The manipulation of the Scots dialogue here—the father
speaks in Scots and the son in standard English, a deliberate device
which is most effective—is perhaps the most brilliant thing in the
novel. But *Weir of Hermiston* remains a fragment, an indication of
the rapid maturing of its somewhat puzzling and intriguing author,
an unfulfilled promise of what he could have done had he lived.

Nothing could be more different from Stevenson's romantic excitement than the pessimistic realism of George Gissing (1857–
1903), whose somber presentations of London poverty (in *Demos*,
1886, which tells of the rise and moral decline of a politician of
working-class origins, and in *The Nether World*, 1889) have been
compared with Dickens' pictures of poverty but which have about
them an air of philosophic resignation that is quite un-Dickensian,
though he claimed Dickens as his master. *New Grub Street* (1891)
has for hero a realistic novelist who has lost his inspiration, and
gives a picture of the marginal existence and fratricidal quarrels of
unsuccessful writers that reeks with the sour smell of poverty.
Gissing's realism sometimes gives the impression of being the result
of a frustrated idealism, and a sense of frustration runs through his

carefully rendered pictures of contemporary life. There are streaks of liveliness and even fantasy in Gissing, and his writings give evidence of more varied talents than he was ever able to bring to full artistic realization. *The Private Papers of Henry Ryecroft* (1903) shows his liveliness and charm as an essayist that one would rarely suspect from his novels.

George Moore (1852–1933) is one of the most unclassifiable of the novelists of his time. Beginning—as in some degree Gissing did—under the influence of French naturalism, he produced in *A Mummer's Wife* (1885) and *Esther Waters* (1894), pictures of lower- and middle-class English life done with a shrewd eye for character and a confident air of knowing how things really happen. Another side of Moore was represented by his championing of French impressionist painting, his "art for art's sake" point of view, and a pose of professional caddishness revealed in his boastful yet entertaining *Confessions of a Young Man* (1888) as well as in later autobiographical works. He became involved in the Irish literary movement (he was born in Ireland), and produced as a result a number of Irish stories, brought together in *The Untilled Field* (1903), and his novel *The Lake* (1905), the story of an Irish priest told with precision and sensitivity. Moore's progress from naturalism through estheticism to the strange synthesis of attitudes which produced his last work can be charted through a dozen novels, of which the most striking are *The Brook Kerith* (1916) and *Héloise and Abélard* (1921), which show his curiously elaborate and musical late style in which he presented his historical reconstructions of the later life of Christ and of the lives of the famous medieval pair. The texture of the narrative is so carefully wrought in these novels that everything—dialogue, action, description—is subdued to the same quiet verbal flow. It becomes wearisome when sustained through a whole long novel, yet it is an achievement of considerable virtuosity.

The apparent absurdity of moving from George Moore to his contemporary Rudyard Kipling (1865–1936) only shows the difficulty of arranging and classifying English fiction at this period. Moore was both naturalist and esthete; Kipling was neither, deriving his skills and his view of art far from the atmosphere of Paris studios, as a journalist in India observing the humors, the rituals, and the characteristic patterns of the life of the ordinary British soldier far from home helping to maintain an empire of which he had little real knowledge and in which he had no real interest. It is Kipling's misfortune—and in considerable measure his fault too—that his association with the imperialist view has damned him in the eyes of a later generation. His imperialism was not the romantic imperialism of

Disraeli, any more than his toryism was based on the organic view of tradition and society represented by Burke or the later Coleridge; it was in its way a schoolboy imperialism, deriving from a love of classes and orders and rituals and schoolmasterish views of duty and responsibility not thought out beyond the schoolboy level. But it was this very schoolboyishness that enabled Kipling to realize his special gifts as a writer of short stories and novels, to see the British soldier in India as dependent on his rituals and codes if he was not to be altogether lost in this strange civilization, to see the code of British sportsmanship as a kind of law of the jungle and the law of the jungle as a kind of British sportsmanship. The Darwinian survival of the fittest became in Kipling's simplified imperialist vision a perpetual struggle between the upholders of the law and the rest, a perpetual cricket match between decent people and outsiders (not necessarily identified with administrators and administered), where the latter had to be constantly watched to prevent any disobedience of the rules and punished if they did disobey. His stories of the British in India in *Plain Tales from the Hills* (1888) and other collections have a brilliance of outline because they all deal with a world on which Kipling had imposed his order; he always knew what he was dealing with, and even mysteries (for there are mysteries in his stories) are deliberate mysteries, indicating something that is going on in the headmaster's study while the schoolboys wait outside. The manipulation of the narrative, the actual putting together of the story, is often excellently done: Kipling's combination of a journalist's training and experience with his clear sense of the shape and pattern of things helps to account for this.

Later, when Kipling turned his attention to English life, his essential vision remained unchanged. It is all really in *The Jungle Book* (1894). The soldier, the engineer, the schoolboy, the fisherman—whatever a man is, he is involved in certain kinds of work, of responsibility, of ritual. Other codes and rituals may command wondering respect, as the Indian way of life does in *Kim* (1901), but that is ultimately because Kipling cannot really imagine the essential otherness of another way of life. The schoolroom (*Stalky and Co.*, 1899) and a fishing vessel (*Captains Courageous*, 1897) are equally adequate microcosms of the world and can illustrate equally the kind of education necessary to survive in the world. The vigor, the sense of local color, the projection of simple moral conflict and crisis, are all admirable in their way, and they all depend on the way Kipling looks at his world. Similarly, the real brilliance with which Kipling captures the very feel of Roman Britain in *Puck of Pook's Hill* (1906) results largely from Kipling's ability to see the Roman soldier as he saw the British private in India and to focus his view of empire through the character and attitude of the uncomprehending garrison, with their immediate needs and problems. Kipling in his novels and stories can be preposterously inadequate or narrow or offensive in his political and moral views; he was not a thinker, and never clarified to himself his own view of society, or morality, or even of empire; sometimes he wrote with a stridency that bordered on hysteria; but the same qualities that produced his faults also produced his virtues, and made him at his best the storyteller of an epoch, even of a phase of civilization.

Kipling had his moments of humility. The white man's burden imposed its obligations, and the "Recessional" he wrote for Queen Victoria's Diamond Jubilee in 1897 expresses, in the swelling organ tones of a full-bodied hymn, his awareness of the temptation to imperial pride posed by imperial obligation:

> God of our fathers, known of old,
>   Lord of our far-flung battle-line,
>   Beneath whose awful Hand we hold
>   Dominion over palm and pine—
>   Lord God of Hosts, be with us yet,
>   Lest we forget—lest we forget!

The rhythms of Methodist hymns run through much of Kipling's poetry, which often conveys with a fine rhythmic appropriateness the full measure of his perceptions of the nature of the relationships, duties, and moral patterns involved in life as he saw it. "Danny Deever," an account of the hanging of a delinquent soldier given indirectly through a dialogue between "Files-on-Parade" and the Colour Sergeant, has the dramatic quality of the ballads and a control of verse movement which admirably reinforces the emotional pattern: it is significant, and characteristic of Kipling, that the sense of the code being applied can coexist with a sense of compassion for its victim without any suggestion that the code is wrong or should not be brought into force in this instance. Sometimes Kipling's rhythms reflect the simplified ethic of the soldier or schoolboy for whom he speaks. "Fuzzy-Wuzzy" expresses patronizing admiration for the Sudanese soldiers whom the British had to fight; both the admiration and the patronage show a limited kind of imagination, but a more profound human probing is not required in this kind of verse: the fuzzy-wuzzies were worthy opponents in a good *Jungle-Book* kind of fight, so they are congratulated. A similar theme and technique can be seen in "Gunga Din" and in many other of his poems of Indian army life. "McAndrew's Hymn," in which a Scottish ship's engineer gives his reminiscences and his creed in fourteen-syllable rhymed couplets, shows how Kipling could use the dramatic monologue to express variants of his code; he did this too in "The Mary Gloster." The ritual element is strong in Kipling's poetry; there is often a suggestion of the schoolboy society keeping its end up with appropriate highfalutin ceremonial

> They sit at wine with the Maidens Nine and the
> Gods of the Elder Days.

His use of a kind of bastard cockney to indicate the common soldier's language ("Me that 'ave been what I've been—Me that 'ave gone where I've gone") can be irritating, for there is no real logic to this kind of convention. But he spoke out according to his vision, and annoyed Queen Victoria with "The Widow at Windsor," a poem which sums up much in his view of the British soldier, for it shows on the one hand the lonely queen sitting in distant Windsor Castle and on the other the "poor beggars in red" fighting her wars in distant parts without her awareness and without their understanding:

> We 'ave 'eard o' the Widow at Windsor,
>   It's safest to leave 'er alone:
> For 'er sentries we stand by the sea an' the land
>   Wherever the bugles are blown.
>   (Poor beggars!—an' don't we get blown!)
> Take 'old o' the Wings o' the Mornin',
>   An' flop round the earth till you're dead;
> But you won't get away from the tune that they play
>   To the bloomin' old rag over'ead.

The reference to the British flag as "the bloomin' old rag over'ead" is the pretended contempt which often accompanies the genuine belief in the code—again, a schoolboy attitude. It isn't the most obvious kind of drum-beating. And the blowing of the bugles has no immediate heroic overtones, suggesting instead only the wretched soldiers being jerked out of bed. But the bugles were blown all right, even if Kipling was one of the last to blow them.

CHAPTER TWENTY-SEVEN

Drama from the Beginning of the Eighteenth Century

As we have seen in Chapter 15, the Restoration dramatic mode persisted for some time after the political and social conditions that bred it had disappeared before gradually giving way to a more moral and more sentimental kind of drama. The charting of the course of eighteenth-century drama is a tedious business, for, with a few exceptions, it is a drama of very little literary interest or quality. Indeed, this can be said for the great bulk of English drama between Congreve and Shaw. The drama was never to recover the central position it held in the Elizabethan and Jacobean periods. The rise of the novel was partly responsible for this, as was the growing power of the theatrical manager, who decided what plays were to be accepted and, by putting on only what he thought could be relied on to appeal to popular taste, put the hack entertainer above the man of letters, thus eventually creating a damaging divorce between the theater and the creative literary minds of the age. Theatrical history after the seventeenth century has no necessary connection with literary history. True, the eighteenth century was an age of great actors and actresses, but their very acting skill had a blighting effect on the drama as literature, for they depended more and more on their virtuosity and less and less on the material with which they were provided, exploiting their abilities and personalities rather than the potentialities of the plays: it was the beginning, in a sense, of the star system, which has done so much harm in our own time. Several paradoxes resulted from this situation. Shakespeare was regularly performed and was immensely popular, but the Shakespearean repertoire of the eighteenth century was a theatrical ragbag of patched and "improved" plays and parts of plays which would horrify a modern producer. The reaction among serious critics was to lead them to see the true Shakespeare as a writer of closet plays, and the ignoring of Shakespeare's theatrical skills by men of letters went on through much of the nineteenth century. The dominance of the theater in the eighteenth century and the ignoring of the theatrical tradition in literary dramatic criticism in the nineteenth were equally harmful. It was all part of the divorce between art and entertainment which has been such a disturbing feature of modern culture. The dominance of the manager was part cause and part effect of the dominance of the audience; the audience dominated because a playwright was now dependent on the audience, rather than on aristocratic or royal patronage, for his success. The same can be said of the public for novels and other literature, but the effects here were not harmful in the same way, partly because the audience for literature was wider and more varied and at its best more intelligent than the audience for acted drama. There was a real drop in the intelligence of theater audiences in the eighteenth century, for reasons which are complex and not easily formulated.

Jeremy Collier's *Short View of the Immorality and Profaneness of the English Stage* (1698) was effective as an attack on the immorality of the drama because it coincided with a rising tide of bourgeois opinion. Restoration drama was written for a homogeneous audience of court wits who looked with equal contempt on London merchants and country squires. But the homogeneity of theatrical audiences was rapidly giving way to something much more mixed; the rising middle classes, who have featured so often in the preceding chapters, were buying their way into the squirearchy and the aristocracy, and the same situation which led Addison and Steele to write essays to provide a cultural surface for Londoners seeking to move with some assurance in society led to the theaters being filled by people who did not quite know whether to be titillated or shocked by the Restoration *ethos*. The drama reflected this uncertainty. Instead of the witty play between the sexes in which the conflicting claims of security, reputation, and sensual appetite were balanced against each other in a fundamentally amoral manner, we find indecency and innuendo in the first four acts being replaced by repentance and moral sententiousness in the fifth, which was a way of having one's cake and eating it. This transitional and hybrid kind of comedy soon gave way to a kind more thoroughly sentimental and moral. These terms can be variously defined, but in this context "sentimental" implies the mixing and even interrupting of action with frequent displays and expressions of pity and other emotions indicating a tender mind and a heart easily moved, while "moral" means the equally frequent expression of edifying generalization, sometimes self-congratulatory,

sometimes reproving, as well as a plot calculated to show virtue re-
warded and vice frustrated. It is easy to be condescending about the
influence of bourgeois morality on the drama, but we must remember that all great literature has a true moral pattern and the amoral-
ity of Restoration comedy, however brilliantly it might show, was
based on a shallow and cruel view of life on which no truly great
art could be founded. Our condescension is inevitable, however, because the morality in so many early eighteenth-century plays is laid
on so crudely and thickly and is not adequately realized in the texture of the work as a whole. Richard Steele, who made a genuine
and praiseworthy effort to replace the hollow moral world of Restoration drama by something with more humanity and decency, produced four comedies (including *The Tender Husband*, 1705, and
The Conscious Lovers, 1722) which are of interest because of the
determined belief in the essential goodness of the human heart
which they display, and the manner in which he manipulates the
action to illustrate this belief, but though there are moments of
tremulous emotion and intense pathos, as well as some lively dialogue and comic incidents, the plays are not true comedy in any
acceptable sense of the term; they have not the wit of Congreve, the
power of Ben Jonson, or the golden combination of humor and wonder we find in Shakespeare's "middle comedies"; they are of interest
as indications of a trend rather than as fully realized works of
dramatic art.

How strong the trend was, how deep-seated the popularity of
sentimental drama in the eighteenth century, and to what an extent
a strong moral and sentimental coloring with a plot contrived to reward the virtuous and punish the wicked would compensate in the
eyes of contemporaries for literary quality, can be seen in the plays
of Richard Cumberland, whose sentimental comedy *The West
Indian* (1771) was immensely popular and is still mentioned re-
spectfully by literary historians. The one good quality this play does
have is speed of action: events bowl along at a great pace. But the
dialogue, the situations, the characters, the plot, are all preposterous,
all simply slick manipulations of what had by long become stock
dramatic properties. The hero, a young man from the West Indies of
good heart but impulsive temperament (rather like Tom Jones), behaves with exaggerated and flamboyant generosity, gets himself involved in ridiculous misunderstandings with the other characters,
who are either all equally goodhearted or else thorough villains, and
in the end is proclaimed the long-concealed son of the goodhearted
merchant in whose house the play opens. The following extract from
Act V must serve as a sample of the dialogue:

Belcourt: Keep me no longer in suspense; my heart is softened for the affecting discovery, and nature fits me to receive his blessing.

Stockwell: I am your father.

Belcourt: My father! Do I live?

Stockwell: I am your father.

Belcourt: It is too much; my happiness o'erpowers me; to gain a friend and find a father is too much; I blush to think how little I deserve you. (*They embrace*)

Dudley: See, children, how many new relations spring from this night's unforeseen events, to endear us to each other.

Writers of this kind of comedy never achieved a proper kind of stylization. Their plays were set in contemporary society, but the dialogue employed neither the stylized wit of the Restoration dramatists nor a language that was able to sustain any colloquial tone beyond a few intermittent sentences. As soon as the characters got under way they began expressing themselves in long, sententious speeches which are not artificial enough for a purely formal style and not natural enough for the illusion of realism. And the dramatists' horror of what was "low" closed to them a major source of robustness and vigor. It is only after reading many plays of this kind that one can appreciate the comic iconoclasm of Goldsmith and Sheridan in comedies which, though they may appear sentimental enough to modern eyes, were in fact directed against the sentimental gentility in the drama of the time. They had been anticipated in this by occasional satirical comedies—George Colman's *Polly Honeycombe* (1760) for example—but Goldsmith's *The Good Natured Man* (1768) strikes more directly at some of the most popular devices of the contemporary dramatists, even though he has his own moments of high sentimentality and he never really mastered the problem of stylization: his dialogue is often as cumbersome as Cumberland's. In *She Stoops to Conquer* (1773), Goldsmith did very much better. Trivial though the plot is, and mechanical though the devices are which Goldsmith uses in order to project the humor (a young man thinks he is at an inn when he is really at a private house, and behaves accordingly, to the astonishment and indignation of his host), there is a rollicking ease about the play which had not been seen in English comedy for a long time. It is perhaps an indication of the poverty of eighteenth-century drama that this simple-minded comedy should enjoy the reputation it does, but it does possess genuine comic life. This is even truer of the comedies of Richard Brinsley Sheridan (1751–1816). In *The Rivals* (1775) we can see Sheridan working toward his comic ideal, and trace the Restoration and Jonsonian elements he drew on; it is a spirited play with some lively

Jonsonian humors and real comedy of character. Lydia Languish, the girl who is so soaked in romantic fiction that she will not marry unless she can elope under difficulties according to the best novels, is in the same ironic vein as Mark Twain's picture of Tom Sawyer's efforts to romanticize the escape of Jim in *Huckleberry Finn*; it is simpler and cruder, but it is dramatically achieved. And Mrs. Malaprop, though again a simple satiric conception, looks back, however faintly, to Shakespeare's middle comedies as well as forward to Dickens. *The School for Scandal* (1777) is Sheridan's masterpiece: it has a strong satirical note which is almost (but never quite) reminiscent of Jonson; but the wit is real, the character drawing vigorous and unsparing, the air of knowing the world as it is (something quite lacking in most eighteenth-century comedies) genuine and refreshing. And Sheridan has learned how to handle dialogue that has both naturalness and order. The brief "afterpiece," *The Critic* (1779), intended to be put on after a full-length play, is admirable satire of the vanities and fashions of playwrights and critics and tells us much about the run-of-the-mill eighteenth-century tragedy which nobody now reads.

It is by the parodies of it that eighteenth-century tragedy can be best looked at from the perspective of the twentieth century, for the parodies are at least readable, and in some cases extremely funny. Henry Fielding's *Tom Thumb the Great* (1730) is hilarious. By the time Fielding wrote, the moralizing, blank verse tragedy, generally conforming to the neoclassic "unities," on a theme from ancient or English history had become so standardized in manner and matter that it was clearly doomed as a dramatic form. Addison's *Cato* (1714) was the earliest successful play of this kind, a tragedy in end-stopped blank verse (mostly with "feminine" endings) with a minimum of action and a great deal of complacent speeches about his own virtue by Cato, and a perfunctory love interest hitched on to a play whose real motive is (in Johnson's well-known description) to provide "a succession of just sentiments in elegant language rather than a representation of natural affections, or of any state possible or probable in human life." The whole thing is utterly lifeless, and the blank verse adds no poetic dimension of any kind to the total pattern of meaning. This is how Cato talks:

> Then let us rise, my friends, and strive to fill
> This little interval, this pause of life
> (While yet our liberty and fates are doubtful),
> With resolution, friendship, Roman bravery,
> And all the virtues we can crowd into it;

That Heaven may say, it ought to be prolonged.
Fathers, farewell—the young Numidian prince
Comes forward, and expects to know our counsels.

When Juba, the "young Numidian prince," comes forward and hears Cato's resolution, he replies:

The resolution fits a Roman senate.
But, Cato, lend me for a while thy patience,
And condescend to hear a young man speak.
My father, when, some days before his death,
He ordered me to march for Utica
(Alas! I thought not then his death so near!)
Wept o'er me, pressed me in his aged arms. . . .

This is a fair sample of the wooden verse in which this lifeless play is written. One need not pursue this kind of tragedy through James Thomson's *Sophonisba* (1730) to Dr. Johnson's *Irene* (1749). The wonder is that the mode survived as long as it did.

Another kind of eighteenth-century tragedy aimed at pathos rather than at moralizing dignity, Nicholas Rowe's *The Fair Penitent*, 1703 (derived from Massinger's *The Fatal Dowry*), was a fountain-head here; his other tragedies (*Jane Shore*, 1714, *Lady Jane Grey*, 1715) wring pathetic scenes out of the predicaments of historical heroines. The verse is the same sort of emasculated Fletcher we saw in *Cato:*

No, though the royal Edward has undone me,
He was my king, my gracious master still;
He loved me too, though 'twas a guilty flame,
And fatal to my peace, yet still he loved me;
With fondness and with tenderness he doted
Dwelt in my eyes, and lived but in my smiles.

But Rowe's plays have a real emotional pattern, and the pathos, if only pathos, is achieved. The eighteenth-century domestic tragedy, developing a similar kind of pathos from the misfortunes of middle-class characters, is closely related to the kind of play written by Rowe, but the shift in class interest is of the first importance for the future of the drama, for it set the pattern for more than a century and a half of tragedy. This is the tribulations of ordinary people displayed in a prose drama in which the morality is emphasized by a simple division of characters into black and white and a perpetual uttering of moral platitudes by the good. George Lillo's *The London Merchant, or The History of George Barnwell* (1731) tells the story of a good apprentice seduced by a wicked woman into, first, robbery of

his master, and then, murder of his uncle. The merchant is the epit-
ome of virtue and integrity, as are his daughter Maria (who loves the
hapless George Barnwell) and his other apprentice Trueman—indeed, as is Barnwell himself, who is dominated and led astray by
Millwood, the thoroughly wicked and cunning she-devil. Barnwell
goes to the gallows repentant and sure of grace, after having vainly
tried to turn his gallows-mate Millwood to God. His last words are:
"Since peace and comfort are denied her here, may she find mercy
where she least expects it, and this be all her hell!" Thorowgood,
the good merchant, can only let justice take its course, advising his
errant apprentice: "Bear a little longer the pains that attend this
transitory life, and cease from pain for ever." His normal diction
is more orotund, as in his reproof to Barnwell for not turning up one
evening (he was in fact in Millwood's clutches): "Without a cause
assigned, or notice given, to absent yourself last night was a fault,
young man, and I came to chide you for it, but hope I am prevented.
This modest blush, the confusion so visible in your face, speak grief
and shame. When we have offended Heaven, it requires no more;
and shall man, who needs himself to be forgiven, be harder to ap-
pease? If my pardon or love be of moment to your peace, look up
secure of both." The real interest of the play lies in Barnwell's remorse and repentance. It is a sign of the general wretchedness of
English tragedy in the eighteenth and nineteenth centuries that *The
London Merchant* is still discussed with respect by historians of the
drama.

The eighteenth century was also the great age of pantomime and
of spectacular shows depending on ingenious and abundant use of
stage "machinery." The pantomime—developing as a result of converging strains from masque, mime, *commedia dell' arte,* and dance
—was often performed as an afterpiece, but eventually became a
full-blown and established form of its own; in the nineteenth century it became a peculiarly English institution. Italian opera was also
popular in England in the early eighteenth century, and it was as a
patriotic reaction against it that the ballad-opera developed, set to
native airs and written in English. The first and greatest of the bal-
lad-operas is John Gay's *The Beggars Opera* (1728), discussed in
Chapter 16. There were many imitations of Gay's successful ballad-
opera produced in the first half of the century; it eventually gave
way to the comic opera, where the music is specially composed instead of being taken from traditional airs. There were successful
comic operas in the 1760's, and Sheridan's *The Duenna* (1775), a
prose comedy with incidental songs composed by Thomas Linley,
enjoyed enormous success. Love and intrigue form the main interest

of late eighteenth- and early nineteenth-century comic opera; it was left to Gilbert and Sullivan to rejuvenate a by then much jaded form by turning it to satiric purposes.

The literary currents of the late eighteenth century affected the drama in various ways, but again the divorce between literature and the theater kept most serious "Romantic" drama off the stage, and again the lack of mutual influence between literature and the theater was harmful to both. Blank verse tragedy on high classical themes gave way as the eighteenth century progressed to a tragedy differing little in technique and moral sententiousness, but using more exotic themes and, like the domestic tragedy, stressing the pathetic. John Home's *Douglas* (1756) took its subject from the Scottish ballad "Gil Morrice," and Robert Jephson's *The Count of Narbonne* (1781) is derived from Horace Walpole's *Castle of Otranto*. Stress on the sensational and the pathetic, and the ability to arouse tears as the principal criterion of dramatic excellence ("the ladies in the audience were distinguished by their virtuous distress," one critic remarked), were not conducive to the development of a serious tragedy. Various kinds of rhetorical plays, some with Shakespearean or would-be Shakespearean echoes, and all endeavoring to exploit the emotional moment, were produced at the turn of the century, but few had any success on the stage.

What kept the theater going were melodrama and farce, the former (in the earlier part of the nineteenth century) often with Gothic trimmings and atmosphere. Distressed virtue, hardhearted villainy frustrating innocent love, the manipulation of the action so as to expose and punish the villain, often with the revelation of a concealed crime, and to bring hero and heroine together, all done in a standardized rhetorical speech, became a regular formula for melodrama, which soon moved from the Gothic to the domestic, so that the tradition of Lillo's *London Merchant* can still be traced. Early nineteenth-century farce is crude stuff, of no literary interest. Burlesque and extravaganza sometimes had rather more to offer; the latter, as developed by J. R. Planché, Robert Brough, and H. J. Byron, constituted the tradition taken over by W. S. Gilbert in the comic operas he wrote with Arthur Sullivan as composer. The tradition was to combine the supernatural, the gorgeous, and the satirical, to include burlesque and parody on the one hand and light fantasy on the other, while making lavish use of spectacle.

In the comedies of T. W. Robertson (*Society*, 1865, *Caste*, 1867, and others) there is a somewhat faint attempt to escape from the mechanical formulations and standarized sentimentalities of earlier nineteenth-century drama and cast an ironic eye on the social life of the time. But Robertson never really escaped from the conventions of his day; his ironies never cut deep, and they are compatible with an acceptance of all the Victorian moral and social commonplaces; but he did look at some contemporary social problems that other Victorian dramatists had wholly ignored. Put beside the domestic melodramas of Tom Taylor (*Still Waters Run Deep,* 1855), Robertson's plays represent an advance toward a more responsible and serious comedy. But there was no immediate response. The cloying sentimentalities of James Albery's *Two Roses* (1870) and the combination of melodrama and prettiness in the plays of Sydney Grundy as late as the 1890's show how strong the older tradition was.

With Henry Arthur Jones (1851–1929) and Arthur Wing Pinero (1855–1934), Victorian drama becomes more sophisticated, more technically accomplished, and concerned with moral problems more delicate and more contemporary than those dealt with in nineteenth-century melodrama. Both began in the older style, and worked their way out of it. Jones's *The Silver King* (1882) is in the sentimental melodramatic manner, brilliantly done in its way, almost the apotheosis of its kind; but *Breaking a Butterfly* (an adaptation of Ibsen's *A Doll's House*), *Saints and Sinner* (both produced in 1884), *The Crusaders* (1893), and *The Case of the Rebellious Susan* (1894) are "problem plays" dealing with some of the moral dilemmas of middle-class life. *The Case of the Rebellious Susan* was prefaced by an admonitory letter to Mrs. Grundy. Neatly constructed, with brisk dialogue and an air of knowingness, Jones's plays did not wholly escape from conventions of the melodramatic tradition, which are intermittently recognizable. Pinero's later plays concentrate on problems arising from the relations between the sexes in modern society: *The Second Mrs. Tanqueray* (1893) is his most serious effort, and the most "modern": it deals with the emerging dilemma of a "woman with a past," and forces the implications of attitudes to women's behavior in a man's world to a disturbing conclusion. But neither Jones nor Pinero were more than skillful theatrical practitioners who grew impatient with the mechanical patterns of drama as they found it and tried to provide novelty and depth by discussing problems of contemporary morality. They had the wit neither of Wilde nor of Shaw, nor did they have the literary imagination or the depth of moral and psychological understanding to be able to present a social problem as a tragic one.

The satirical wit, verbal dexterity, and keen eye for what was vulnerable in contemporary literary fashion, gave the comic operas of W. S. Gilbert (1836–1911) a brilliance and a vitality like nothing else on the Victorian stage. *H. M. S. Pinafore* (1878), *The Pirates of Penzance* (1880), *Patience* (1881), *The Mikado* (1885), and others are often thought of as delightful musical fantasies suitable for children, but in fact there is a comprehensiveness and a cruelty in Gilbert's destruction of the conventional romantic world by artful ridicule that strike at the heart of Victorian civilization. This may sound like a pretentious remark to make about a writer who was after all essentially an entertainer and who is generally regarded only as such; but a close look at his work reveals that behind the playfulness, the comic exaggeration, the absurd overemphasis of popular convention, there lies an almost nihilistic sense of the ridiculousness of human emotions and human dignity. It is unlikely that he was really aware of the implications he allowed into his own work, and there can be no doubt that Arthur Sullivan thought of his colleague's plays as no more than gay and amusing parodies with moments of lyrical feeling to be set in appropriate tuneful music. Sullivan's music, admirably tuneful though it is, and sometimes most amusingly parodying Italian opera, lacks a dimension we find in Gilbert's words.

The plays of Oscar Wilde have more surface brilliance and less genuine satiric undertone. Wilde belonged to the *fin de siècle* esthetic movement which believed in art less as an escape from than as a substitute for life: he acted out his estheticism in his own career, even to the extent of allowing his life to fall into a tragic pattern which he might easily have escaped, because he wanted to be hero in a trial scene and felt impelled to carry the play of his own life to its melodramatic conclusion. Wilde's estheticism was not essentially in conflict with Victorian melodrama; he wanted to subtilize it, just as he wanted to make sensationalism witty. The poets of the 'nineties who drank themselves to death or otherwise wore out their lives in suicidal poses were, like Wilde, acting out their esthetics. Though Gilbert, in satirizing the movement in *Patience,* was running together a number of different strains, including the Pre-Raphaelite, he was in essence right in presenting the behavior of the poet Bunthorne as a deliberate pose to shock and impress:

> Though the Philistines may jostle, you will rank as an
>   apostle in the high aesthetic band,
> If you walk down Piccadilly with a poppy or a lily
>   in your mediaeval hand.

That was in 1881; it was in the 1890's that the esthetic movement flourished most vigorously. Its members were out to shock, but also to demonstrate a way of life and a way of art (which were identical).

The *Yellow Book*, which ran from 1894 to 1897, was in some degree the organ of these sophisticated and exhibitionist young men, though it contained a great deal more dull realistic fiction and conventional work of one kind or another than is generally realized and contained nothing by Wilde.

Wilde's plays were not the direct product of those views of art and life which he expressed in his symbolic story *The Picture of Dorian Gray* (1891) or in his carefully wrought fairy tales. In his comedies he wrote for the theater and for success. He thus took formulas from Victorian farce and melodrama, but treated the dialogue with a polished wit which really removed the whole action into a never-never land of ultrasophisticated stylization. The stylization is the very *raison d'être* of Wilde's plays. The plots are ridiculous, sometimes degenerating into cheap farce. But the dialogue imposes the order of an ideal wit on the society it portrays. He achieves this most perfectly in *The Importance of Being Earnest* (1895), a play wrought entirely out of the studied wit of the dialogue, which projects the society of upper-class leisure as an English world so emptied of earthiness and genuine emotional, moral, or physical reality, that it is pure style, a world where action exists in order to make possible the appropriate conversation and where the appropriate conversation is a ballet-like exchange of epigrams. It is not a profound art, if an extremely clever one, and it is not an art that could have any real influence. The tradition of wit which Wilde bequeathed to the modern comedy of manners proved too tenuous as well as too self-sufficient to be usable by others.

Meanwhile, the influence of Henrik Ibsen had been making itself felt in English drama. The propagandizing and translating by William Archer and the enthusiasm of George Bernard Shaw (1856–1950) helped to spread the influence but also conditioned the way Ibsen was understood in England. Shaw's study of Ibsen, *The Quintessence of Ibsenism* (1891), presented the Norwegian dramatist as the exponent of a reforming naturalism with the emphasis on the prose "social plays," such as *A Doll's House* and *Ghosts*, and paying much less attention to the more poetic and symbolic plays. Such a view suited Shaw's own ideas of the function of the drama. Shaw saw the drama as a vehicle for presenting in entertaining and provocative form his views of the abuses and contradictions of the social order and his suggestions of the true way in which to view human experience and institutions. His object was to satirize, not the invented characters in the plays, but the audience. "I must warn my readers that my attacks are directed against themselves, not against my stage figures." In his desire to shock rather than to lull, to provoke rather than to amuse, Shaw put into his characters' mouths discussions in which his characteristic wit and love of paradox were given full play. A favorite device of his was to stand the popular view on its head, thus both outraging and titillating his audience. Yet in many respects Shaw took over the idea of the "well-made" play from his predecessors. He had been a dramatic critic for years before he became a dramatist, and his experience in the theater had familiarized him with all the popular tricks of the trade, which he adopted and exploited with considerable virtuosity. Ibsen's great contribution, as Shaw saw it, had been twofold: the presentation on the stage of life as it is really lived in contemporary society, and the introduction of the discussion into drama. His own plays incorporated both features.

Shaw regarded himself as primarily an antiromantic. The romantic view, he claimed, got in the way of people's seeing what really went on in the world, with the result that it made them accept the most appalling horrors in the name of edifying slogans and under the guarantee of social approval. The Swiss soldier in *Arms and the Man* (1894) behaved as Shaw maintained a soldier actually does behave, not as the conventions of Victorian melodrama would have a soldier behave: the play exhibited what Shaw called "natural morality" as against the "romantic morality" of those who objected to it. But Shaw was too clever to present his natural morality directly. He took the accepted pattern of Victorian melodrama or farce or drawing-room comedy and, at the most effective moment, inverted it, as it were, transposing the parts of the conventional hero and the conventional villain; and then, having done that and having led his audience to believe that this is a revolutionary or an iconoclastic play, he inverts it again, and shows that the conventional hero is, after all, a hero—but in a new sense. This double inversion is an immensely successful dramatic device, but it is more than that: it is part of Shaw's technique for making his audience look again and again at the particular situation he is presenting, until they have shed all illusions bred by either convention or by facile anticonventionality. The revolutionary hero of *Man and Superman* (1903) is built up into a conventional rebellious figure, then laughed at, then restored, in a different way, to his revolutionary status. The theme of this play is the way in which the Life Force works itself out in human affairs in order to improve the race—Shaw was a Lamarckian evolutionist influenced by Samuel Butler, believing that the Life Force cooperated with the individual will to achieve the further development of the human race. But he is least successful as a dramatist when dealing directly with such large themes. *Back to Methusaleh* (1921), which he considered his masterpiece, is pretentious and dull, showing a most undramatic desire to reduce all human life to disembodied speculation.

In his Preface to *Plays Pleasant* (1898), Shaw wrote: "I can no longer be satisfied with fictitious morals and fictitious good conduct shedding fictitious glory on robbery, starvation, disease, crime, drink, war, cruelty, cupidity, and all the other commonplaces of civilisation which drive men to the theatre to make foolish pretences that such things are progress, science, morals, religion, patriotism, imperial supremacy, national greatness and all the other names the newspapers call them. On the other hand, I see plenty of good in the world working itself out as fast as the idealists will allow it; and if they would only let it alone and learn to respect reality, which would include the beneficial exercise of respecting themselves, and incidentally, respecting me, we should all get along much better and faster." In the same preface, Shaw pleaded for a "genuinely scientific natural history." That is what Shaw considered his plays to present. In the Preface to *Major Barbara,* he called himself a "professor of natural psychology." In other words, like so many great innovators in English literature, his cry was "back to nature"—and he used the word "nature" in Pope's and Dr. Johnson's sense of human nature rather than in Wordsworth's sense. Thus there were no conventional heroes and villains in his plays; but neither is there any of the worried pity that we get in Galsworthy's humanitarian plays. Shaw was not concerned with the pity of it: he was concerned to diagnose sham and release vitality. All Shaw's heroes and heroines— Lady Cicely in *Captain Brassbound's Conversion,* Valentine in *You Never Can Tell,* Caesar in *Caesar and Cleopatra,* Candida, Major Barbara—stand in their own way for vitality. And often the real villain is not a character in the play, but the audience. For the audience, the average playgoer, represents that thoughtless, complacent, sentimental society which, for Shaw, was responsible for so much distortion of vision and so much evil and suffering. Readers of detective stories have sometimes wondered whether a detective story could ever be written where the murderer turns out to be the reader; Shaw comes near to that in making his audience the true villain of his drama.

This kind of plan succeeds best when it deals with a social problem or situation familiar to the audience or at least recognizable to them as the kind of situation which, in however modified a form, might well arise in their own society. For Shaw, like the great eighteenth-century moralists, believed that generalizations about the society you know best, your own contemporary society, are valid for men at all times, and thus he cheerfully assumed that he understood Caesar or Saint Joan on the basis of modern analogies. But he did not understand them, for he lacked historical imagination; and these characters became in his hands modern Shavian heroes rather than convincing historical characters.

Shaw had his own sentimentalisms and theatricalities, as the character of Eugene Marchbanks in *Candida* (1895) clearly shows. Further, though he brought a new kind of intelligence to the drama, he did not create—or attempt to create—a new dramatic idiom in which the total dramatic meaning could be fully expressed. His long and detailed stage directions, in which not only the actions of his characters but their states of mind, emotions, tones of voice, and intentions are fully described as though in a novel, confirm what is suggested by his criticisms of Shakespeare—that Shaw had no conception of the drama as a literary art form in which the total pattern of meaning is achieved cumulatively and completely by the language put into the mouths of the characters as they talk to and interact with each other. Detailed psychological stage directions put the burden of conveying meaning onto the actor and producer and help to perpetuate that very dominance of the drama by the theater that Shaw as a dramatic critic had so deplored. Shaw, by challenging the censorship, bringing ideas back to drama, and using plays as a vehicle for intellectual stimulation and provocation, rendered an immense service to the English theater. But his plays were not as new *as drama* as those early twentieth-century critics who talked about the "new drama" considered it to be. The Dutch-born drama critic Jacob Thomas Grein founded the Independent Theatre in 1891, and it was the Independent Theatre Society that first presented Shaw to the theater-going public, full of exuberance about the "new drama." This movement was much influenced by Ibsen and sought to make the drama a vehicle for responsible discussion of modern problems. This is not in itself a dramatic objective. Neither Shaw nor any other Ibsenite worked out an essentially new way of exploring reality dramatically. Shaw's comedy of ideas is full of life and fun; comedies like *Major Barbara* (1905), *Androcles and the Lion* (1913), and *Pygmalion* (1913) are entertaining as well as critical and stimulating; but all this comes from the sparkle of Shaw's mind, not from a fully realized dramatic projection of a complex vision of life. *Saint Joan* (1923) is in many ways a brilliant play; it is not a tragedy, but a comedy with one tragic scene, and the comedy lies in the way in which Shaw interprets his historical characters in the light of his own modern understanding and preoccupations. He never really comes to terms with the miraculous in this play: he uses it for comic effect and to implement his view that sainthood is merely inspired common sense, but, though this is amusing and even at first sight convincing, it begs too many questions to be ultimately satisfactory. Hens who have long ceased laying eggs and suddenly start to lay when Joan appears provide a splendid comic opening to the play; but if miracles are simply natural events presented in such a way as to inspire faith (as Shaw argues), then how *does* he explain the eggs, or the miraculous change of wind? A miracle cannot be at the same time both a funny stage trick and a profound religious fact. The fact is that Shaw remained an entertainer and a master of all the tricks of the entertainment trade, and his wit and intellectual brilliance were never fully absorbed into a dramatic form of appropriate depth and scope. This is not to say that Shaw was a great writer whose plays do not fit into any accepted category, but rather that he was a dramatist of immense talent and prodigious wit whose limited view of the nature of literary art prevented him from seeing the limitations of his own artistic imagination and so from seeking a dramatic form which could contain all he had to say about man absorbed wholly into the dramatic texture. This is perhaps as much as to say that the greatest drama must be poetic, for it needs the extra dimension of expression if it is to achieve its complex pattern of meaning without expository or discursive glosses by the author.

Shaw's stature is most easily seen if we set his plays beside those by his contemporaries. St. John E. C. Hankin (1860–1909) attempted to deal seriously with the problems of contemporary society, but his plays lack both wit and the sense of life. A more accomplished dramatist was Harley Granville-Barker (1877–1946), whose sensitive and perceptive work as critic and producer would seem to promise the subtlest kind of art in his own plays; but though a careful intelligence and a fine artistic sense are at work in *The Voysey Inheritance* (1905) and *The Madras House* (1910), they are too obviously contrived and lack the air of dramatic spontaneity.

How far technical theatrical skill could combine with a truly cunning exploitation of the sentimental tradition to achieve popularity in the age of Shaw is shown by James Matthew Barrie (1860–1937). Barrie was quite out of touch with the new literary movements of his time, but exploited with determination and professional assurance the emotions, whimsies, and sentimentalities implicit in the Scottish kailyard tradition and in so much Victorian and Edwardian middle-class feeling. He knew what he was doing; he wrought from the outside; as Edwin Muir has remarked, "his softness was really a kind of toughness, and the most deplorable fault of his work is not sensibility run to seed, but obduracy." *The Admirable Crichton*

(1902), *What Every Woman Knows* (1908), *Dear Brutus* (1917), and *Mary Rose* (1920) are masterpieces of theatrical journalism. They are quite different in intention from John Galsworthy's (1867–1933) humanitarian fables of social and moral worry; such plays as *Justice* (1910), *The Skin Game* (1920), and *Loyalties* (1922) command respect and sympathy for their technical competence and humane feeling, but these two qualities are not enough to make a great dramatist.

For the most part, the mixture of drawing-room comedy and morality play has continued to provide the ordinary fare of the British theater-goer. After Wilde and Shaw some degree of wit and some degree of serious concern with the problems of modern social life have become de rigueur, except, of course, for pure knockabout farce or detective plays. Intelligent and skillful dramatists who artfully tailor their stories to the requirements of the theater have not been lacking in the twentieth century: the tone can vary from sardonic irony to moral concern, the technique from straightforward use of realistically set scenes proceeding in chronological order to the use of flash backs, single symbolic settings, or even a bare stage. Formulas once accepted are repeated again and again with minor variations.

By far the most interesting development in dramatic literature in the first half of the twentieth century was the revival of poetic drama in the plays of W. B. Yeats (1865–1939) and T. S. Eliot (1888–1965). Yeats began by writing dreamy plays on Irish mythological themes, but from the beginning he showed a symbolic power in both action and imagery which suggested levels of meaning the drama had not sought after for a long time. The *Countess Cathleen* (1892), the story of the Irish countess who sold her soul to save her people, but reached Heaven after all, is languid in movement and has an oddly mixed vocabulary, but its meaning came across clearly enough for it to cause riots among Dublin audiences. Yeats' treatment of the Deirdre story (*Deirdre*, 1907), concentrates (unlike Synge's in *Deirdre of the Sorrows)* on the final moments with a heroic dignity which was part of his view of tragedy. His later plays are based on neo-Platonic and other mystic notions and symbols, and are highly stylized in a manner reminiscent of the Japanese no plays, by which Yeats was considerably influenced. *Calvary* (1920), *The Resurrection* (1931), *Purgatory* (1939), and *The Death of Cuchulain* (1939) are strangely impressive symbolic plays for the full understanding of which some knowledge of Yeats' symbolic system is necessary but which even without this have a haunting suggestiveness that leads not to mere dreaminess but to ironic contemplation of human psychology and history. The language combines the colloquial and the ritualistic, and it is out of the way the two work together that the irony is distilled. His prose play *The Words upon the Window-Pane* (1934) stands alone in both theme and treatment: it is a powerful evocation of a few key scenes in the life of Swift.

Yeats' dramatic career transcended the Irish literary movement out of which it grew in the same way as his career as a poet transcended its Irish context. But the Irish background, the Abbey Theatre, the national consciousness, and the view of Irish and Anglo-Irish history are all important for an understanding of how Yeats came to be the kind of dramatist he was. The Irish dramatic movement produced a number of humorous or sentimental quasi-realistic plays of modern Irish life. But it also produced, besides Yeats (whose later plays were not intended for the public theater), the plays of John Millington Synge (1871–1909), including *Riders to the Sea* (1904), *The Playboy of the Western World* (1907), and *Deirdre of the Sorrows* (1910). Synge turned to the speech and imagination of Irish country people to restore vitality to English drama. "On the stage," he wrote in his preface to the *Playboy,* "one must have reality, and one must have joy; and that is why the intellectual modern drama has failed, and people have grown sick of the false joy of the musical comedy, that has been given them in place of the rich joy found only in what is superb and wild in reality. In a good play every speech should be as fully flavoured as a nut or apple, and such speeches cannot be written by anyone who works among people who have shut their lips on poetry. In Ireland, for a few years more, we have a popular imagination that is fiery and magnificent, and tender; so that those of us who wish to write start with a chance that is not given to writers in places where the springtime of the local life has been forgotten, and the harvest is a memory only, and the straw has been turned into bricks." Synge deplored the debilitation of urban speech, and sought a vocabulary both poetic and real, both rich and natural. His own plays are not always successful in achieving this combination effectively, though the *Playboy* succeeds triumphantly as a comedy which is also a profound "criticism of life," while *Riders to the Sea* is a remarkable dramatic presentation of an elegiac situation redeemed from false pathos by the elemental dignity achieved by the language, and *Deirdre of the Sorrows,* in spite of its monotony of tone, is an experiment in a new kind of stylized, almost ritualistic, tragedy, that Yeats was to make much of.

Synge's poetic prose based on the speech rhythm of the Irish peasantry provided him with some of the resources of poetic drama.

The other significant dramatist of the Irish revival was a purely prose artist. Sean O'Casey (born 1884) used Irish material as Lady Gregory and Lennox Robinson and the other Irish national playwrights did, but in his best plays he used it with a sense of tragic irony, a violent species of humor, and a rich and highly flavored language that gave his work real dramatic stature. His best play is *Juno and the Paycock* (1925), which successfully welds tragic melodrama (based in part on the real violence of the civil war), humor of character, and irony of circumstance into an original and impressive unity. *The Plough and the Stars* (1926) is a symbolic documentary play, tragic in tone, presenting the pattern of Ireland's tragedy. In his later plays O'Casey's own passions and prejudices tend to come between him and the dramatic work he is trying to create, and when in addition he turns to expressionist techniques suggested by German dramatists and by the American Eugene O'Neill the result is generally unsuccessful. The verbal vitality and vivid humor of his earlier plays gave way in his later to conventionally "colorful" language and a rather mechanical verbal symbolism.

T. S. Eliot's poetic dramas represent an attempt to restore ritual to drama in quite a different way from Yeats'. *Murder in the Cathedral* (1935) remains the most successful of his plays because the ritualistic element is implicit in the situation; the chorus of women of Canterbury are the archbishop's congregation and the archbishop's central speech takes its place naturally as a sermon in an ecclesiastical context. But when Eliot moved away from the obviously ritualistic and tried to achieve overtones of myth and ritual in realistic plays of modern upper-class life, the clash of levels is dramatically disturbing. *The Family Reunion* (1939) is a most interesting attempt to render the theme of the Furies of Greek mythology and drama in contemporary terms. Eliot modulates the colloquial into the ritualistic and back again with impressive skill; the accents of conversation mingle or alternate with more formal kinds of utterance, choric or incantatory or stylized in one way or another, and the result is to build up a suggestive complex of meaning behind the overt action. But the attempt to deal with a religious-mythological theme in terms of the problems posed by family relationships in a modern country house is not altogether successful. Levels of meaning tend to get in each other's way instead of reinforcing or subtilizing each other. The hero's departure to expiate (in some unnamed way) his guilt is marked by his saying to his mother: "My address, mother, will be care of the bank in London until you hear from me," and this trivial precision about a detail of contemporary financial life tears the symbolic fabric of the action. In *The Cocktail*

Party (1950) and *The Confidential Clerk* (1954) Eliot makes an even more strenuous attempt to combine the socially amusing with an underlying Christian-cum-classical symbolism, but the two levels never really come together, or, when they do, the result is likely to be embarrassing, as in the behavior of Sir Henry Harcourt Reilly in *The Cocktail Party*. The verse in these plays is so chastened and filed away that it is hardly recognizable as verse at all in the theater; it shows how far verse can be brought toward conversational prose without actually falling over the edge—a remarkable balancing feat.

In the 1940's and early 1950's it looked as though the verse plays of Christopher Fry (born 1907) might establish a new mode of modern poetic drama. But the airy exuberance of Fry's imagery and the wit (half boisterous, half wistful) displayed in his handling of character and situation proved in the end to be more of a fashionable exhibitionism than a wholly successful confrontation of the problems involved in producing a drama that was both artistically effective and contemporary in feeling. *A Phoenix Too Frequent* (1946), *The Lady's Not for Burning* (1949), and *Venus Observed* (1950) impressed their first audiences by their linguistic exuberance and playfulness of imagination, but the language was inorganic and the imaginative playfulness too wilfully thrown about for the plays to have survived as serious literature.

Whether the plays of John Osborne (born 1929) will survive as serious literature it is impossible yet to say, but it can already be clearly said that the production of his *Look Back in Anger* by the Royal Court Theatre in 1956 marked the opening of an important new phase in twentieth-century English drama. The play itself—about a provincial graduate of humble social background married to a girl of an upper-class family and the mixture of self-pity and sadism with which he treats her—is confused in theme and uncertain in its emotional emphases, but it exploded on the English dramatic scene with enormous force because of the radically new kind of vitality in its dialogue and because its theme managed to touch on the raw some of the deepest anxieties and frustrations of Britain's new educated class. This class, young people who had grown up after the Second World War and were the beneficiaries of the Education Act of 1944 and of the welfare state brought into being by the Labour Government elected in 1945, consisted typically of sons and daughters (but mostly sons) of parents of limited education and fairly humble social position. They had gone to a "red-brick" university, not to Oxford and Cambridge, and the state had paid their way. But on leaving university to look for a place in the world they found that the prizes were still reserved for those who went through the traditional public school plus "Oxbridge" education, or at least that the values by which society was governed were those of a backward-looking "establishment" in which the raw product of, say, a provincial university in the Midlands felt awkward and out of place. They had expected a genuine meritocracy, with important places available for those with education, but found instead that the benefactions of the welfare state had fitted them to be misfits, self-conscious about their manners and background, and still—unless they were ruthlessly single-minded in their ambitions—far from the centres of power. Further, there was no special crusade to be worked up out of this situation. The heroic causes were all gone. The aftermath of the Second World War left a new generation curiously empty and puzzled. They partly envied those who had fought in the war (a very different situation from that which prevailed after the First World War) and partly resented them. They partly envied, too, those Labour pioneers who had worked for the setting up of a welfare state. That dream had come true. But it had brought deep disappointments and frustrations, of a kind not easily translatable into political programmes. And in certain quarters it brought a resentment, all the more intense for not being fully understood by those who felt it, of the older generation, of the "establishment" (a word which came to be increasingly used, in a disparaging sense), of the old aristocratic dream of high culture to which they were now supposed to have access.

The theme of the frustrated, anti-establishment young man in the provinces had already been treated, with a mixture of ironic comedy and high farce, by Kingsley Amis (essentially *homo unius libri*) in his novel *Lucky Jim* (1954). But where Amis is comic Osborne is savage. Jimmy Porter, the hero of *Look Back in Anger*, tortures his well-mannered and well-brought-up young wife partly because she comes from a social class which he resents, partly because he can find no proper outlets for his energy, partly in order to take out on her a host of half-understood resentments and grievances which are symbolized by his running a sweet-stall for a living (and he is a university graduate) and living in a "one-room flat in a large Midland town." The specification of the Midland town is significant. The problem diagnosed in this kind of literature is largely a provincial one, and the *outside* nature of the provincial town compared with London or with Oxford and Cambridge, at least as much as its drabness, constitutes its chief menace. This attitude toward the provinces is to be distinguished from older attempts in literature to depict the dullness or lack of opportunity of provincial centres. George Eliot, essentially a novelist of the English Midlands, never sees provincial England as frustrating because it is provincial; D. H. Lawrence shows the heart of provincial England as sounder than any superimposed tradition of gentility or than metropolitan sophistication; even Arnold Bennett's pottery towns, though they limit the horizons of its inhabitants, who have to leave if they want real adventure, are not presented as being outside the orbit of where all interesting and rewarding things are done. The flare-up of anger about the provincial boy who cannot accept the world that has been so benevolently prepared for him is essentially a mid-twentieth-century phenomenon. The mood changed in the next decade, when certain provincial cities (notably Liverpool) began to assert their own popular cultural idiom and provincial accents came to be cultivated by bright young people and by actors in television plays as a sign of being genuinely contemporary.

But Osborne caught the mood of the 1950's with uncanny accuracy: even the confusions in *Look Back in Anger* represented real confusions among real young people at the time. Self-pity is not admirable, and sadism (even when intermittently followed by sentimentality) is even less so, yet Osborne seems to hold Jimmy Porter up for our sympathetic understanding. Even those who are disturbed by the working out of attitudes in the play, however, can respond to the marvellous vigor of its dialogue. Osborne (like W. H. Auden before him, though in a different way) drew on the sharp rhythmic patter of the English music hall for the basic speed and toughness of his language: it is interesting that two of the characters in *Look Back in Anger* drop into music hall acts several times in the course of the play, and that Osborne's next play *The Entertainer* (1957) is actually about three generations of music hall entertainers and is concerned with the human problems that arise as the once popular and powerful art of the English music hall declines before more sophisticated modern forms of entertainment. The actual form of *The Entertainer* is that of a series of music hall acts.

"Look back" is an important part of Osborne's title: the frustration he presents is deeply bound up with nostalgia for a world his young characters never knew. "There aren't any good, brave causes left," says Jimmy Porter. "If the big bang does come, and we all get killed off, it won't be in aid of the old-fashioned, grand design. It'll just be for the Brave New-nothing-very-much-thank-you. About as pointless and inglorious as stepping in front of a bus." But the nostalgia coexists with anger at what the past has done. Of his wife's socially and politically successful brother Nigel, Jimmy remarks: "Somewhere at the back of [his] mind is the vague knowledge that he and his pals have been plundering and fooling everybody for generations." It is principally those who try to extend the habits of the older establishment generation to the present day that Jimmy hates; the aging representatives of the generation themselves are treated with respect and almost envy. "The old Edwardian brigade do make their brief little world look pretty tempting. All home-made cakes and croquet, bright ideas, bright uniforms. Always the same picture: high summer, the long days in the sun, slim volumes of verse, crisp linen, the smell of starch. What a romantic picture. Phoney too, of course. It must have rained sometimes. Still, even I regret it some-how, phoney or not. If you've no world of your own, it's rather plea-sant to regret the passing of someone else's." The look back here is to before the First World War. It was the high culture of the England that died in 1914 that still determined the values of the education Jimmy Porter (and for that matter Lucky Jim) had received in their provincial university: it is seen as irrelevant to their needs and as dishonestly venerated by the establishment.

Look Back in Anger is more important as a cultural phenomenon than as a work of literature in its own right. It spoke for a generation (the first generation, it might be added, to grow up in the shadow of the atom bomb) and in doing so brought a new vitality to English drama. The sharp, mocking, staccato language of Jimmy Porter re-vivified English dramatic dialogue. The same sort of dialogue is found in The Entertainer, a better though not so influential a play. Luther (1961) is a much more ambitious kind of play, a psychological exploration of Luther's personality and development moving in a larger symbolic atmosphere than the two other very English plays. The ear for dialogue is still prominent, but the harsh vigor of the language of the earlier plays has given way to something more con-trolled. Osborne's later plays A Patriot for Me (1965), Inadmissible Evidence (1965) and his adaptation from a play by Lope de Vega, A Bond Honoured (1966) show him experimenting, with varying degrees of success, with new kinds of technique, new kinds of dramatic situ-ation, new ways of counterpointing realistic and symbolic action. His restless, innovating mind, his feeling for spoken prose, and his highly theatrical craftsmanship are qualities which still, toward the end of the sixth decade of the twentieth century, promise well for English drama.

By the late 1950's an English dramatic renaissance was in full swing. The Birthday Party (1958), the first production of Harold Pinter (born 1930), revealed a talent very different from Osborne's. Influenced by the Franco-Rumanian dramatist Eugène Ionesco as well as by the French-writing Irish novelist and playwright Samuel Beckett, this play is a curious mixture of almost actionless naturalism with a disturbing but deliberately vague symbolism. The dialogue is deadpan, apparently aimless, for the most part aggressively colloquial, with pauses and repetitions giving the impression of a relentlessly slow build-up of cumulative meaning. This colloquial dialogue is, at certain points in the play, cut across by the rhetorical-sentimental speeches of one of the characters, Goldberg, with its oddly impressive mixture of establishment clichés and Anglo-Yiddish oratory. The action is minimal: Petey and Meg, an elderly couple, rent a room in their house in a seaside town to a rather shabby and run-down character, Stanley. Goldberg and his assistant McCann track Stanley down to this town, engage a room in the same house, insist on laying on a birthday party for him, and in the end, after a series of disturbing incidents which manage to spread a vague sense of terror over the whole action, dress the by now helpless and inarticulate (and for the first time properly shaved) Stanley in respectable middle-class clothes and take him off in a car for the "special treatment" they say he needs. The play may be symbolic of the forces of respectability lying in wait for the man who tries to opt out of the middle-class decencies, but there is a verbal (sometimes Joycean) wit and an imaginative buoyancy which transcend any such theme and give the whole play a puzzling air of being intended to mean more than it does. But dramatically it is remarkably successful and the dialogue, both colloquial and sinister, works with uncanny effect.

The Room and *The Dumb Waiter*, both written in 1957 but not produced until 1960, have this same combination of deadpan, aimless-seeming dialogue with ordinary incidents which gradually build up into a sense of something terrifying and symbolic of some deep dread at the heart of modern living. In the former play, the build-up from unremarkable speech and action in an ordinary, shabby environment into a sinister symbolic trap is done with considerable power; in the latter, the situation is strangely symbolic from the beginning, though the dialogue and the detail of the action remain insistently unspectacular. *The Caretaker* (1960) develops further what has by now become the familiar Pinter technique: this play of two brothers (one with a history of mental illness) and a tramp has the same relentless accumulation of detail until what at first seemed a mixture of the ordinary and the aimlessly odd turns out to be an increasingly disturbing symbolic presentation of some large but always deliberately distanced human theme. The tramp, who talks continually of going back to Sidcup where many years before he left his "papers," will never go back, if indeed he was ever there; the elder brother talks of building a shed he will never build, the younger of developing a number of building enterprises he will never develop. There is a strange inconsequential wit in both the language and the action; sometimes both brothers seem to be mental cases so that we cease for a while to have any expectations about their behavior and the play appears to be degenerating into a clueless puzzle; but somehow the detail of the dialogue and the trance-like precision of the action pull the play together in the end. One cannot help having the feeling that Pinter has succeeded in using the theatre brilliantly in order to play on his audience's nerves. For all their symbolic overtones, most of his plays lack a dimension, or perhaps lack a middle level between the surface realism and the background symbolism, that middle level of credible and moving significant human action that makes great drama immediately acceptable as memorable story while working at deeper levels to achieve further layers of meaning for the perceptive. But there is both theatrical and verbal brilliance at work in Pinter's plays, and one is left with great expectations.

The strength and variety of the dramatic renaissance of the 1950's and 1960's is seen by putting beside the work of Osborne and Pinter a third dramatist, very different from either. John Arden (born 1930) startled and puzzled the audience of the Royal Court Theatre in 1959 with his play *Sergeant Musgrave's Dance.* This story of a sergeant and three other regular soldiers, deserters all, coming to "a mining town in the north of England eighty years ago" with the skeleton of one of their dead comrades (who originally came from that town) in a box, in order somehow to reveal the cruelty and futility of war to the town's inhabitant's, is played out in an idiom which crosses rough soldiers' and miners' talk with folk-song and folk-ballad. "This is a realistic, but not a naturalistic play," wrote Arden in his introduction to the published text (1960), in asking for both scenery and costumes to be "in some sense stylized"; while the dialogue is mostly colloquial, the punctuating songs, with their over-tones of a tragic folk tradition, provide a sense of fatality and doom to accommodate the increasing grotesqueness of the action. The setting, a strike-bound mining town in a bitterly cold winter, provides a context of human desperation. The soldiers, who profess to have come on a recruiting drive, are welcomed by the civic authorities because it is hoped that they will both coerce some of the extremist elements among the miners into the army and also help restore order if rioting breaks out. At the end, with one of the soldiers already accidentally killed by one of his comrades, Sergeant Musgrave and his remaining two men confront the public in the market place. But instead of making a recruiting speech. Musgrave displays the skeleton of the dead soldier, denounces war, and attempts to turn his weapons on the civic dignitaries who are also present. His pacifist mission has turned sour, and led him to revel in the thought of mowing down the bosses. He ends in prison awaiting execution, together with Private Attercliffe, the soldier who had been responsible for killing the fourth of their number, and the play closes with Attercliffe singing a quasi-folk-song about a consumed apple whose seed will in the future "raise a flourishing tree of fruit." "They're going to hang us up a length higher nor most apple-trees grow, Sergeant. D'you reckon we can start an orchard?"

Like so many of the plays of this mid-century dramatic revival, *Sergeant Musgrave's Dance* is more impressive for its tone and technique than for the clarity of its theme. Arden was aware of this lack of clarity, and tried to explain matters in his introduction of 1960. "I have endeavoured to write about the violence that is so evident in the world, and to do so through a story that is partly one of wish-fulfilment. I think that many of us must have some time felt an over-powering urge to match some particularly outrageous piece of violence with an even greater and more outrageous retaliation. Musgrave tries to do this: and the fact that the sympathies of the play are clearly with him in his original horror, and then turn against him in his intended remedy, seems to have bewildered many people." The "moral" of the play, says Arden, is not nihilism but pacifism; yet because "complete pacifism is a very hard doctrine" and Arden himself tends to hit back when hit, he feels a certain uneasiness. "I do not care to preach too confidently what I am not sure I can practise." Thus Arden sees himself here as a man with a message, if an uncertain one. It is not the message, however, which makes the play interesting. Arden—and this is what gives him distinction as a dramatist—is continually seeking ways to probe the human dimensions of the situation he has chosen to develop. It is the tragic yet earthy imagination of the folk-singer and balladist that he turns to in order to find help in achieving this.

The folk element is even stronger in *Armstrong's Last Goodnight* (1964), a play about the early sixteenth-century Scottish Border chief, Johnny Armstrong, whose power and freebooting habits made him a danger to his sovereign and whose meeting with King James V in 1531, intended to be peaceable, ended in the King's sudden order for him to be hanged immediately. The hot-tempered king could not endure to see the pomp and pride of a man who was supposedly his subject. Later tradition suggested that there was an element of treachery in Armstrong's death, that he was lured to the meeting by false promises, but the earliest account does not suggest this. In ballad literature and in the Scottish imagination, however, Armstrong figures as a strong and proud Border chief who was enticed into a trap and killed. It is this version that Arden uses. Though he deliberately cultivates the ballad atmosphere, he rigorously avoids the romantic suggestions of the ballad version. The sub-title of the play is *An Exercise in Diplomacy*, and Arden presents the story as a complex case of *Realpolitik*, though he sets it against a background of human passions and ambitions in such a way as to make this very much more than a political play. The characters are partly historical —Armstrong himself, the poet, courtier and diplomat Sir David Lindsay, who master-minds the trap, and the young King—and others, including, as always with Arden, some powerfully delineated female characters, are wholly invented. The language, while not sixteenth-century Scots, retains many traditional Scottish forms and is cunningly contrived to give the impression of the living, spoken tongue of the period. Arden calls it "a sort of Babylonish dialect" modelled on "Arthur Miller's adaptation of early American speech in *The Crucible*." It is highly effective, at least to anyone with any knowledge of Scots, though it seems that many English theater-goers found it difficult. Verse plays a significant part in the play, characters breaking out into it to a greater degree than in *Sergeant Musgrave's Dance* to give an air of fatality, of courtliness, or simply to suggest the elemental nature of parts of the action. Some of the verse is in ballad-style, some in that of the "makars" of the early sixteenth century. Armstrong himself, who is effectively presented as normally inarticulate, with a speech impediment, so that he can only break out into eloquence under the stress of strong emotion, dies almost ritually, singing two stanzas of the Border ballad of Johnny Armstrong with his last breath. It is interesting (and perhaps relevant) that the first of these two stanzas was one which, according to Walter Scott's son-in-law and biographer, Scott "delighted to quote."

In *Armstrong's Last Goodnight* Arden was working toward a new kind of modern poetic drama, drawing its verbal strength partly from a vigorously handled prose suggestive of a particular time and place and partly from the ballad tradition. It is significant, perhaps, that its most effective performance was its first, at the Glasgow Citizens' Theatre, where Scottish actors, to whom the Armstrong story was part of their cultural background, did full justice to the Scots element in the dialogue. It was less successful when done in England later. This suggests that Arden demands more from his audience than most of his contemporary dramatists. He is also, in a sense, more literary: that is, he uses a sense of the past—the past of the language as well as past events—to give dimensions to his action. In many ways he is the most remarkable of the young dramatists of the 1960's.

Though the late 1950's and early 1960's saw a considerable number of interesting new plays and playwrights, including Robert Bolt (*A Man for All Seasons*, 1960, Brendan Behan (*The Quare Fellow*, 1956; *The Hostage*, 1959), and Shelagh Delaney (*A Taste of Honey*, 1958), the latter two of whom emerged from the lively experimental Theatre Workshop of Joan Littlewood, the only other playwright whose work has been central in the mid-century dramatic renaissance is Arnold Wesker (born 1932). Wesker is a left-wing moralist who has used the drama to say things about contemporary society. Yet he is not at all a naïve propagandist. His trilogy which began with *Chicken Soup with Barley* (1958) and went on through *Roots* (1959), to *I'm Talking about Jerusalem* (1960) takes us through some of the problems of English social and political life from 1936 to the late 1950's and documents with fine emotional precision some of the basic changes in mood among English left-wing idealists. The technique of these plays is conventional compared to that of Osborne or Pinter or Arden and the dénouement sometimes suggestive of left-wing political rhetoric of the 1930's: Beatie's self-discovery at the end of *Roots*, for example, stands out of the play like a harangue from the author. Yet Wesker does get the authentic quality of English working-class speech into drama in a way that had not been done before, and there is a quiet authenticity about his domestic scenes that combines the documentary with the sympathetic. *Chips with Everything* (1962) is a play about the English class system as it works in the Royal Air Force. It contains some movingly dramatic scenes and some splendid stage effects. Whether these scenes and these effects cohere into an effective dramatic exploration of the theme Wesker set himself is another question. Sometimes one feels that at times Wesker gets too involved in his own plays and the total pattern of meaning is sacrificed to what might be called a brilliant piece of self-indulgence. For all the moral and social criticism in his plays. Wesker is not a doctrinaire playwright. His plays offer no obvious solutions. But they are the kind of plays that are intended to set us thinking about solutions, in the same way that those of Bertolt Brecht are. *Chips with Everything*, indeed, shows the influence of Brecht—for good so far as Wesker's mastery of the art of the theatre is concerned, more dubiously in its handling of ideas through characters. It is indicative of the richness and variety of mid-century drama that its influences range from Ionesco to Brecht.

It is difficult, in the late 1960's, to see these dramatists and the movement of which they are a part in perspective. But if it is a disadvantage to be living and judging while they are in their heyday and still promise more than they have performed, the advantage of being a contemporary is that one can testify to the excitement their plays aroused on their first performance and to the fact that, whatever posterity's verdict will be, it seems clear to any observer in the 1960's that the drama is now the liveliest of the English literary forms. More interesting things have been happening recently in drama than in poetry or the novel.

CHAPTER TWENTY-EIGHT

Twentieth-Century Poetry

THE MOST STRIKING FACT in twentieth-century English literary history is the revolution in poetic taste and practice which resulted in the rejection of the view of poetry represented by Palgrave's *Golden Treasury* (first published in 1864 and used as a school textbook in Britain well into the 1930's) in favor of one which saw poetry as at the same time more symbolist and more cerebral. This revolution was an Anglo-American achievement. T. S. Eliot (1888–1965), who settled in England before the First World War while still a young man and afterward exchanged his American for British citizenship, and Ezra Pound, the literary gadfly whose stay in England in 1912 stung so many poets and critics into new activity, were in large measure its leaders, but much of the theoretical ammunition was supplied by T. E. Hulme who, before his death in the war in 1917, had contributed to the *New Age* and other periodicals a number of essays in which he declared war not only on what he considered to be the Romantic view of life and of art but also on "the Weltanschauung ... of all philosophy since the Renaissance." Hulme wanted discipline, precision, "the exact curve of the thing," "dry hardness," classicism. "I object even to the best of the romantics," he wrote in his essay "Romanticism and Classicism." "I object still more to the receptive attitude. I object to the sloppiness which doesn't consider that a poem is a poem unless it is moaning or whining about something or other." Hulme produced a collocation of classicism, the "religious" attitude, abstract or geometrical art, belief in original sin, hard, clear, and precise images, the medieval viewpoint, discipline, and authoritarianism in politics on the good side of the ledger against romanticism, humanism, naturalistic art, belief in man's unlimited potentialities, the emotional and soft, the Renaissance attitude, self-expression, and democracy on the bad side. Few of those in the new movement accepted the complete balance sheet as Hulme prepared it (Eliot came nearest to doing so), but many were influenced by his insistence on hardness and clarity and his war on self-expression as a literary ideal. The Imagist movement, deriving from Hulme and Pound (who soon lost interest) and others, demanded clear and precise images, elimination of every word "that did not contribute to the presentation," and a rhythm freed from the artificial demands of metrical regularity.

The French Symbolists had taken a similar view of metrical regularity, and it was their invention of *vers libre* that was adopted by the Imagists. The Symbolists wanted to be precise in order to be properly suggestive; precision, individuality, the "exact curve of the thing" and maximum symbolic projection of meaning were seen as going together. But Imagism even with this symbolist extension was only a brief stopping place for the new poetic movement. The turn away from the Tennysonian elegiac mode with its lingering enjoyment of self-pity to the more complex and intellectual poems of Donne, the insistence that intellect and emotion should work together in poetry and that one should seek to recover the "unified sensibility" of the metaphysical poets which had been lost to English poetry since the latter part of the seventeenth century, the repudiation of personality and assertion of the objective demands of art over those of self-expression ("the more perfect the artist, the more completely separate in him will be the man who suffers and the mind which creates," wrote Eliot in 1917), the proclamation of the absolute difference "between art and the event"—all this is seen in Eliot's criticism as it can be seen working in his poetry. "The poet has, not a 'personality' to express, but a particular medium, which is only a medium and not a personality, in which impressions and experiences combine in peculiar and unexpected ways. . . . If you compare several representative passages of the greatest poetry you see how great is the variety of types of combination, and also how completely any semi-ethical criterion of 'sublimity' misses the mark. . . . Poetry is not a turning loose of emotion, but an escape from emotion; it is not the expression of personality, but an escape from personality." The quotations are all from Eliot's essay "Tradition and the Individual Talent" (1917), one of the most influential critical essays of the century. It was in many respects the manifesto of the new poetic theory and practice.

The poet was no longer the sweet singer whose function was to render in mellifluous verse and an imagery drawn with great selectivity from the world of Nature a self-indulged and personal emotion; he was the explorer of experience who used language in order to build up rich patterns of meaning which, however impressive their immediate impact, required repeated close examination before they

communicated themselves fully to the reader. A core of burning paradox was preferred to a gloss of surface beauty. It was not the function
of poetry to pander to the languid dreams of a pampered sensibility,
or display the poet's emotional problems in artfully cadenced vowel
sounds. Complex, allusive, using abrupt contrasts and shifting
countersuggestions to help unfold the meaning, eliminating all con-
junctive phrases or overt statements that might indicate the relation
of one scene or situation to another, depending entirely on "the music
of ideas," on the pattern of symbolic suggestion set up as the poem
moves, Eliot's long poem *The Waste Land* (1922), pruned by Pound
before publication of every unnecessary explanatory phrase or merely
"poetic" description, was the first major example of the new poetry,
and it remains a water-shed in both English and American literary
history.

There was not, however, a complete vacuum between, say,
Swinburne and the Pound-Eliot revolution, nor was there simply a
decadent cultivation of an overblown Tennysonian rose garden. The
so-called Georgian poets of the early twentieth century often showed
skill and originality, and even interest in technical experiment. But it
was inevitable that in retrospect they should appear timid and conventional, for although such poets as Gordon Bottomley, Lascelles
Abercrombie, Harold Monro, and (most of all and in very different
ways) Walter de la Mare and Edward Thomas displayed at their
best both individuality and strength, the fact remains that each was
content to delimit or modify the poetic inheritance of the nineteenth
century rather than seek a radically new (or radically old) approach.
De la Mare took the romantic imagination into its last and subtlest
refinement, but that achievement, brilliant though it was, pointed
out no new paths to younger poets. Wilfred Owen, who was killed
in the First World War, showed a rapidly maturing exploratory
poetic mind, and his technical experiments and attitude influenced
poets of the 1930's, but neither he nor Isaac Rosenberg, another
casualty of that war, lived to fulfill their exciting promise. The difference between those who sought or accepted poetic revolution and
those who, however experimental or advanced they thought themselves, worked within the accepted limits of poetry remained absolute, and can be illustrated by the work of John Masefield (1878–
1967), whose *Salt Water Ballads* (1902) caused considerable fuss
because of the self-conscious realism of the language (as had Kipling's
Barrack-Room Ballads, which influenced him) and who combined the
influence of Chaucer and Crabbe to produce narrative verse about
ordinary life. But Masefield's early readers grossly overestimated the
degree to which the introduction of a few swearwords revolutionized

the art of poetry, and it is clear today that he belongs to the end, not to the beginning, of a tradition. Masefield's most interesting work was his long narrative poems influenced both by Chaucer and Crabbe. *The Everlasting Mercy* (1912), the story of a ruffianly poacher who reforms, *Dauber* (1913), about a would-be artist serving as an ordinary seaman, and *Reynard the Fox*, a spirited account of a hunt in cantering couplets, are the best of these.

A different kind of conservatism was represented by Robert Bridges (1844–1930), an elegantly craftsmanlike poet with considerable metrical skill. Possessed of a sensitively idealizing mind, yet interested in the sciences (he was trained as a doctor) as well as in music and in language, he produced some finely chiselled lyrics and in *The Testament of Beauty* (1929), written in "loose Alexandrines," achieved qualified success in a form the Victorians had rarely been able to manage, the long philosophical poem. In spite of its date, *The Testament of Beauty* may be regarded as the last significant English poem in the Victorian tradition. Bridges' metrical experiments were not radical, as were Hopkins', and his interest in language was in favor of "purity" rather than new kinds of excitement. In Bridges' poetry the Victorian Muse makes its last formal appearance, appropriately enough as a scholar and a gentleman.

The publication by Bridges of Gerard Manley Hopkins's poems in 1918, long after Hopkins' death, was another significant factor in developing the new poetic style. Hopkins' experiments with words and rhythms, his attempts to force language to a more direct and explosive conveyance of meaning than the usual nineteenth-century modes allowed, the intense individuality of his poems and their air of being shaped to contain unique experience, and perhaps most of all the way the meanings of his words and phrases did not work outward to the building up of a generalized emotion, but inward, to build up a complex pattern of meaning within the poem—all this attracted the admiring attention of the younger poets. Eliot admired but was not radically influenced; he had already gone too far along his own road. But the poets who began to write in the late 1920's and 1930's saw both Hopkins and Eliot as their masters, as well as the metaphysicals, the Jacobean dramatists (whose poetic idiom had influenced Eliot), the French Symbolists and ironists, Wilfred Owen, John Skelton, with his rough, jogging meter, and the popular singers of the English music hall.

That the metaphysical poets and the English music hall should both figure among the influences on modern poetry reflects the emphasis on irony, on the development of simultaneous meanings, on the deliberate counterpointing of the colloquial and the formal, that are part of the modern poet's refusal of solemnity. The reintroduction of wit into serious poetry not only meant the revival of the pun as a serious poetic device, after its banishment from all but comic poetry for over two centuries, but also the realization that truly serious art transcends the vulgar and the everyday by including it, not by rejecting it. The narrowing of attitude to a feverish insistence on the importance and high seriousness of what is treated, the treatment of the poet himself as the single-minded hero of his poems, came to be regarded as a characteristic romantic error, making the poet vulnerable to parody and constricting the exploratory range of the imagination. Love between the sexes, for example, treated in a spirit of Platonic elevation by Shelley, is more likely to be seen by the modern poet as both physical and spiritual, both comic and profound, both ridiculous and splendid, and he will seek for devices to convey both attitudes simultaneously. One of the reasons why Shelley has been the chief whipping boy of modern anti-romantic criticism has been because he makes himself the naïve hero of his own poems and never insures himself, as it were, against the operation of the comic spirit. It is only by including the comic spirit, the modern poet would maintain, that its mocking element can be exorcized from serious poetry. "Ambivalence" thus becomes a favorite critical term, and paradox a quality considered a criterion of good poetry. Critical techniques—though this is more true of American than of British criticism—are developed from a consideration of the revived symbolist-metaphysical tradition, and not only poems but also novels and other forms of literary art are considered and judged in this way. Such a procedure is referred to Eliot's theory of dissociation of sensibility and the necessity of a unified sensibility (intellect and emotion working together, with thoughts operating as emotions and vice versa, as Eliot said that they did in the poems of Donne) for its justification.

The career of William Butler Yeats (1865–1939) epitomizes the history of English poetry in his lifetime. He began under the influence of Spenser, Shelley, Rossetti, and the esthetic movement of the late nineteenth century; at the Rhymers' Club in London he met with Lionel Johnson, Ernest Dowson, Richard Le Gallienne, and others, and together they cursed "Grey Truth" and sought beauty. But Yeats was Irish, and Irish influences were also working on him—the Irish national movement in Dublin and popular Irish folklore and folk speech he found in Sligo where he used to go to visit his grandparents. London brought him into touch with the younger English poets; Dublin introduced him to Irish literary nationalism, to Standish O'Grady's florid narrative of the Irish heroic age, to George Sigerson's translations of older Gaelic poetry, and Douglas Hyde's translations of Gaelic folk songs into "that dialect which gets from Gaelic its syntax and keeps its still partly Tudor vocabulary" as well as to more purely political currents of thought; and Sligo kept him in touch with the folk imagination as it still worked in the Irish peasantry. Yeats hated Victorian science, and he felt that it had made belief in orthodox Christianity impossible, so he continually sought for a new religion, at first an esthetic religion, "almost an infallible church of poetic tradition, of a fardel of stories, and of personages, and of emotions, inseparable from their first expression, passed on from generation to generation by poets and painters with some help from philosophers and theologians." His reading of Blake combined with other impulses to encourage his mystical interest, and soon he was seeking truth and order in every kind of unorthodox speculation, from theosophy to neo-Platonism. Eventually Yeats made contact with what has been called the tradition of heterodox mysticism, which has had a long history in Europe, and has an agreed set of symbols found in neo-Platonism, Cabalism, Rosicrucianism, theosophy, and other systems which Yeats explored with relish. But all the time he kept one foot in Ireland; he had an anchor in the physical realities and folk imagination of the Irish countryside and country people as well as in the more sophisticated Irish activities of the Dublin nationalists. The dreamy and exotic poetry of his earliest phase was punctuated by simple poems in the Irish folk tradition; Sligo kept both the London and Dublin elements in Yeats under some control.

It was not long before the exoticism of Yeats's earliest poetry gave way to a quieter handling of folk and fairy themes deriving from his deep sense of a basic dichotomy in the universe. The imagery in these poems is arranged in pairs of contrasts: man and Nature, the human world and the fairy world, the domestic and the adventurous, the transient and the eternal, are paired against each other. Madness (as in "The Madness of King Goll") is seen as the inability to keep to one's own side of the barrier, while in such a poem as "The Stolen Child" a sense of the precariousness of all human existence is conveyed by presenting the call of the wild and strange away from the drab and familiar; but as the poem progresses the call of the wild becomes more sinister and the familiar (once it is lost) more appealing. In his collection *The Rose* (1893) Yeats tried to combine a neo-Platonic view of eternal ideas—of beauty, love, courage, and so on—existing in a transcendent realm and manifesting themselves through history in individual characters and actions, with themes from Irish heroic history and legend. The Rose itself is the idea of intellectual beauty, which Yeats sees as suffering with man:

Red Rose, proud Rose, sad Rose of all my days!
Come near me, while I sing the ancient ways:
Cuchulain battling with the bitter tide;
The Druid, grey, wood-nurtured, quiet-eyed,
Who cast round Fergus dreams, and ruin untold;. . .

Already the poetry is much more concentrated than his earliest work, and has that combination of dignity and magic, achieved partly by the rhythms, partly by the assured use of imagery, which was to become characteristic of Yeats's greatest poems. "The Rose of the World" is one of the finest poems of this phase: Yeats here uses both classical and Celtic mythology in a context of neo-Platonic thought:

Who dreamed that beauty passes like a dream?
For these red lips, with all their mournful pride,
Mournful that no new wonder may betide,
Troy passed away in one high funeral gleam,
And Usna's children died.

In *The Wind Among the Reeds* (1899) the influence of Blake and of the various mystical speculations he had been indulging in is very much in evidence. He expressed his poetic objective at this time in an eloquent essay: "Who can keep always to the little pathway between speech and silence, where one meets none but discreet revelations? And surely, at whatever risk, we must cry out that imagination is always seeking to remake the world according to the impulses and the patterns in that great Mind, and that great Memory?" The great Memory is an almost Jungian concept of a universal or racial memory which guarantees the meanings and intelligibility of symbols. In addition to the influence of Boehme and Swedenborg, that of Mallarmé, Verlaine, Villiers de l'Isle Adam, and Maeterlinck can also now be seen working in Yeats's poetry. His poetry is now tenuously symbolic, very different from the lush romantic descriptions of his earliest poetry as well as from the tapestry quality of many of the poems of *The Rose*.

In *In the Seven Woods* (1904) Yeats experiments with more colloquial and flexible rhythms and tries to work threads from ordinary life into the texture of his poetry. "Adam's Curse" shows the beginning of a species of discursive, reminiscent kind of poetry, apparently casual in movement but actually perfectly wrought and organized, which Yeats was to develop later with such brilliance in poems like "Among Schoolchildren," "A Prayer for my Daughter," and "The Tower." In 1906, Yeats looked back on his earliest poetry and wrote: "Without knowing it I had come to care for nothing but impersonal thrown upon it by the events of life." He concluded significantly: "We should ascend out of common interests, the thoughts of the beauty. . . . Presently I found that I entered into myself and pictured myself and not some essence when I was not seeking beauty at all, but merely to lighten the mind of some burden of love or bitterness newspapers, of the marketplace, of men of science, but only so far as we can carry the normal, passionate, reasoning self, the personality as a whole." It is this attempt to carry "the normal, passionate, reasoning self, the personality as a whole," into his poetry that effects the first major change in his style and was to bring him to closer touch with the Pound-Eliot movement. The short, almost epigrammatic poem, "The Old Men Admiring Themselves in the Water," shows a new hardness and irony. *The Green Helmet and Other Poems* (1910) continues this development, and includes, in "No Second Troy," Yeats's most powerful blending so far of mythological material, ironic contemporary passion, epigrammatic expression, and glowing verse. His association with the Abbey Theatre at this time brought him very much down to earth; wrestling with practical problems of finance and production gave a controlled bitterness to his verse:

> The fascination of what's difficult
> Has dried the sap out of my veins, and rent
> Spontaneous joy and natural content
> Out of my heart . . .

> My curse on plays
> That have to be set up in fifty ways,
> On the day's war with every knave and dolt,
> Theatre business, management of men.

Responsibilities (1914) shows this new astringency further developed. By this time Yeats had come to know Pound, who had urged on him the importance of squeezing out excess words. The note of epigrammatic scorn is sounded strongly in "To a Wealthy Man Who Promised a Second Subscription to the Dublin Municipal Gallery if it were Proved the People Wanted Pictures," in the splendidly powerful "September 1913," in "To a Shade," one of the finest of all his "middle" poems, and elsewhere. It is now that Yeats shows himself more and more the enemy of the bourgeois, of "our old Paudeen in his shop," the Philistine materialists who ruled the commercial life of Dublin and put every obstacle in the way of the development of a true Irish art and literature. "To a Shade" is only one of many poems directed against them. More and more Yeats came to see in the country-house ideal, the ideal of a life lived with quiet courtesy and ritual in aristocratic leisure, the pattern of adequate living, the Platonic dance of life rendered in contemporary terms. This is seen even more clearly in *The Wild Swans at Coole* (1919) and *Michael Robartes and the Dancer* (1921), volumes which combine magical symbolism with ironic realism. "A Prayer for my Daughter," in the latter volume, is one of the finest expressions of Yeats's view of the country-house ideal and its relation to the dance of life:

> And may her bridegroom bring her to a house
> Where all's accustomed, ceremonious;
> For arrogance and hatred are the wares
> Peddled in the thoroughfares.
> How but in custom and in ceremony
> Are innocence and beauty born?
> Ceremony's a name for the rich horn,
> And custom for the spreading laurel tree.

Yeats wanted to go either above or below the middle classes to see examples of the good life, to either the life of aristocratic grace and ritual, or to the fool or beggar outside the conventions of bourgeois society and able by his own wild gleams to make contact with imaginative reality. For what he was searching for was a way of transcending the dichotomies, "all those antinomies of night and day," that had haunted him from his youth; some third element in which the opposites were fused. The cosmic dance united all opposites:

> Labour is blossoming or dancing where
> The body is not bruised to pleasure soul,
> Nor beauty born out of its own despair,
> Nor blear-eyed wisdom out of midnight oil.
> O chestnut-tree, great-rooted blossomer,
> Are you the leaf, the blossom or the bole?
> O body swayed to music. O brightening glance,
> How can we know the dancer from the dance?

The development of Yeats's complex magical view of history and personality in *A Vision*, a work of prose exposition published first in 1925, and again in revised and expanded form in 1937, cannot be ignored in any detailed study of his poetry, but in his greatest poems the keys provided there are not really necessary, though sometimes other keys, from the neo-Platonic tradition or the general tradition of heterodox mysticism, are helpful in pinpointing the ground meaning of certain symbols. Yeats dealt with words magically, not in any vague romantic sense of the term, but literally; his poetry of ritual and gesture is a poetry in which words are made to act magically, transcending their literal meaning to explore through the most precise symbolism a whole world of reality behind the common world known by sensation.

In *The Tower* (1928) and *The Winding Stair* (1933) the genius of the mature Yeats is seen in all its glory, and he emerges as a realist-symbolist-metaphysical poet, both ironist and magician, with poetic rhythms both ritualist and colloquial, and a gift of phrase that is unequalled in modern English poetry. The two Byzantium poems, "Sailing to Byzantium" and "Byzantium," distill their meaning into a quintessence, haunting the mind and probing the emotions as no English poet had done since the seventeenth century. The theme of both poems is the attempt to escape from old age and decay by escaping altogether from the world of biological change into the timeless world of art, symbolized by Byzantium. Images of breeding, growth, change, and death (for the first involves all the others) give way in "Sailing to Byzantium" to images of a world of artifacts, "of hammered gold and gold enamelling." But the sense of loss is there; the golden bough may be changeless, but it is not the real tree. In "Byzantium" the poet subdues the flesh in the spirit, the world of nature is left behind for the "glory of changeless metal," but even as the poet is astride the symbolic dolphin that carries him above the seething tide of human passion, that passion floods back: art is, after all, nourished by the very world of growth and change, of begetting and dying, that it wants to leave behind in its search for permanence; the spirit is based on the mire and blood it seeks to repudiate:

> Astraddle on the dolphin's mire and blood,
> Spirit after spirit! The smithies break the flood,
> The golden smithies of the Emperor!
> Marbles of the dancing floor
> Break bitter furies of complexity,
> Those images that yet
> Fresh images beget,
> That dolphin-torn, that gong-tormented sea.

"Byzantium" turns out to be a poem not only about life and death but also about the balance sheet of art, the relation between permanence and change, what is gained and lost by moving from life to art: it is essentially the theme of Keats's "Ode on a Grecian Urn."

Yeats's last poems show him experimenting with ballad forms, new kinds of magical and symbolic expression, new combinations of fierce realism and ritual gesture. The strangely quiet "Long-Legged Fly," with its cunning use of the refrain—Yeats experimented throughout his career with uses of the refrain, often with brilliant results—is one of the masterpieces of his final poems. Other themes, satirical, political, autobiographical, show a controlled gaiety which is the mark of the last phase of Yeats's writing. His view of life as something to be acted out with ritual dignity whatever befalls is here expressed in a number of ways, as in that strangely powerful poem, "Lapis Lazuli":

> All perform their tragic play,
> There struts Hamlet, there is Lear,
> That's Ophelia, that Cordelia;
> Yet they, should the last scene be there,
> If worthy their prominent part in the play,
> Do not break up their lines to weep.
> They know that Hamlet and Lear are gay;
> Gaiety transfiguring all that dread.

Life is given meaning by style; the controlled gesture is the last word in meaning:

> Cast a cold eye
> On life, on death.
> Horseman, pass by!

Yeats was without doubt the most remarkable poetic genius in English of his time, and one of the great English poets. He absorbed all his age had to offer him. Yet he did so wholly in his own way. If his career illustrates the history of English poetry in his lifetime, that is not because he is ever like any other poet of his day, for, except in his earliest phase, he never is. His voice is always his own. It is haunting and magical and fascinating and sometimes terrible.

Eliot's career is more easily charted, for, though he has had more influence than Yeats and his work both as poet and critic marks much more distinctly a major shift in poetic taste and poetic practice, he has not Yeats's range and diversity. *Prufrock and Other Observations* (1917) contains the two dramatic monologues that remain two of his finest poems, "The Love Song of J. Alfred Prufrock" and "Portrait of a Lady." The repudiation of conventionally "poetic" imagery, the organizing of symbolic images, incidents, fragments of conversation or of memory without any explanatory links that would lower the pressure of meaning, the arresting of attention by imagistic shock or emotional anticlimax, the purging of self-pity by irony as well as the complete suppression of the poet's own personality and his appearance only through the *persona* of his invented character—all this adds up to a new poetic style for English poetry. There are simpler poems in this collection, more imagist in technique; but in these monologues Eliot gave imagism a dialectic as well as a symbolist dimension and a tone of intellectual irony. He learned from Laforgue as well as from Rimbaud and Verlaine and from the Jacobean dramatists as well as from Donne. In *Poems* (1920) the irony is more evident. "Burbank with a Baedeker: Bleistein with a Cigar," "Sweeney Erect," and other poems achieve ironic comment on the decadence or corruption or emptiness of modern civilization by juxtaposing without comment, or any sort of overt causal linking, images from the present and from the past. This is done so cunningly that the result is not simple contrast between present decadence and past glory; the suggestion emerges that the two are perhaps one, and the past itself becomes tainted by its modern parallels. (This is a device Eliot uses with considerable force in *The Waste Land*, as for example in the Elizabeth and Leicester reference.) "Gerontion," the longest poem in the 1920 volume, uses an elaboration of the "Prufrock" technique to project a symbolic picture of the desiccation of modern civilization.

The Waste Land is the most sustained and complex use of this technique. Taking as its underlying pattern the grail myth as interpreted by Jessie Weston, Sir James Frazer, and others, and weaving the themes of barrenness, decay and death, and the quest for life and resurrection which he found in these anthropological sources with the Christian story and with Buddhist and other oriental analogies, and incorporating into the poem both examples and symbols of the failure of modern civilization—scenes of desolation, moral squalor, and social emptiness—which are in turn symbolically related to the anthropological and religious themes, Eliot endeavoured to project a complete view of civilization, of human history and human failure, and of the perennial quest for salvation. No modern poem has received so much comment and explication. It requires it, for in spite of brilliant and memorable passages, the structure and total pattern of the work, as well as the significance of many references and incidents, are not intelligible without outside information about what Eliot was trying to do. The whole problem of obscurity in modern poetry was raised in its most acute form by the publication of this poem. That the modern poet, acutely aware of the complexities and contradictions of the civilization in which he lives, aware too of the fragmentation of his audience so that he can no longer count on any common body of knowledge in the light of which he can confidently use myth and symbol, is forced by the conditions of his time to create or re-create his own myths and to draw on his own perhaps highly unusual reading for reference and allusion, is a commonplace. It is one thing, however, to explain why any poet of integrity and originality must, in certain circumstances, be in some degree obscure; it is another to see that obscurity as beneficial rather than harmful. The obscurity of Hopkins, as we have seen, had for its purpose the prevention of the escape of premature meanings and the keeping of the whole meaning in suspense until the total poem "exploded" for the reader. Eliot's obscurity is of a different kind, as he indicated by his rather perfunctory and perhaps ironically intended notes. It arises from his use of material known only to him, from associations operating in his own mind as a result of odd reading which he cannot count on sharing with any considerable body of readers, and from the introduction of, for example, Sanskrit words (which conclude the poem) for whose meaning we have to depend entirely on his assurance. Though much can be got from the poem by reading it without any external aids whatever—for the obscurity, while it exists, has been exaggerated and an attentive and sensitive reading will yield the general pattern of meaning as well as some brilliantly rendered symbolic suggestions—there is a fair amount which awaits the exegete. The test here is whether, having read the experts, we can read back what they tell us into the poem and find it flower into something compellingly significant. It may be that for certain kinds of poetry in our civilization we must be content to make use of external aid for full understanding, just as most modern readers need such aid in order to read, for example, *Paradise Lost*. The difference is that Milton utilized a common set of references, biblical, classical, and other, while the modern poet, who knows there is no such common set available, has to construct his own if he wants to go beyond a certain level of poetic communication. On the whole, *The Waste Land* does open up as poetry if we come to it with the explanations of the explicators, but there are passages that do not, such as the conclusion, which remains an incoherent collection of phrases and quotations, while the Sanskrit blessing at the end ("Shantih shantih shantih") has no poetic force because we cannot read back Eliot's explanation into the words with any conviction: for all we know, the words might mean anything at all, or any other unknown words might have the meaning Eliot says they have. It is the comprehensive aim of *The Waste Land* which makes necessary dependence on a synthetic myth. Obscurity resulting from the "music of ideas," the obscurity involved in leaving out causal connections and in operating by symbolic projection instead of propositional statement, is another matter. This demands no explicator, but a careful reading. The obscurity of "Prufrock" is of this latter kind, a kind that has become a permanent feature of modern poetry.

Ash Wednesday (1930) is the first of Eliot's long religious poems, in which he draws on Christian liturgical literature, Catholic symbols, and Catholic poets such as Dante to provide the underlying pattern of symbolic reference. The style anticipates that of the *Four Quartets* in its chastened movement, its quiet incantatory flow, its cunningly woven repetitions and variations. Without the surface brilliance of "Prufrock" and "Portrait of a Lady," *Ash Wednesday* has its own controlled power and—if one may use a term not popular among post-Eliot critics—subtle charm. The *Ariel Poems* (1927-30) shows a similar quietness combined with the irony of "Prufrock," and the result, in "Journey of the Magi" especially, is a poetic style of intriguing concentration. "Marina" has this style without the irony, but the subject admits only the minimum of irony, and the poem achieves with moving effectiveness a sense of redemptive peace. The *Four Quartets* ("East Coker," 1940; "Burnt Norton," first published in the collected volume of 1936 and separately in 1941; "The Dry Salvages," 1941; "Little Gidding," 1942) treat with an almost mystical intensity of the search for the "still centre," the quest for spiritual peace and assurance, which may lead through the dark night of the soul. Using material from St. John of the Cross and from other Christian sources, and anchoring each poem in a local scene which gives a concreteness to the imagery and a point of reference from which the symbolic suggestions can move out and to which they can return, Eliot builds up his series of poems of spiritual exploration. He sometimes falls into flatness when he seeks quietness, and his desire to counterpoint the ordinary and the mystical sometimes leads him to step out of the poem and talk about it with a curious deadness, but in spite of such passages *Four Quartets* represent an impressive achievement, perhaps the best religious poetry of its time.

Yet Eliot's poetry lacks scope and sympathy. In spite of his immense technical skill, and in spite of his variation of styles from "Prufrock" to the *Four Quartets*, his range and interests are limited, and he has none of the deep imaginative sympathy with the human condition which the greatest poets have had. He is impatient with imperfection, and tends to see nothing interesting between Apeneck Sweeney on the one hand and the saint and martyr on the other. His introduction into English poetry of wit and irony, his renovation of the English poetic dialect, and his restoration of intelligence to poetry were all necessary and salutary achievements; Eliot's work both as poet and critic will remain of the utmost significance for the literary historian. It looks as though the revolution he led is to be permanent. The next generation was to strive, sometimes crudely and only occasionally successfully, to remove those deficiencies of human sympathy that are so striking in Eliot's poetic personality. W. H. Auden—who, like every poet of his generation, learned much from Eliot—could write in such a poem as "Lay your sleeping head, my love, /Human on my faithless arm" a moving answer to the superior contempt that so dismissed the "young man carbuncular" and his unfortunate typist in *The Waste Land*. Eliot remains a great minor poet and a major historical influence.

The poets of the 1930's faced a world of economic depression, not only of spiritual desiccation, and they turned from contemplation of the symbolic waste land to the portrayal and diagnosis of a literal one. Freud and Marx were brought in to assist the diagnosis, which was expressed in a style incorporating influences we have already noted—Eliot, Hopkins, Owen, Skelton, and the music hall. It is in the context of such influences that W. H. Auden (born 1907) first broke on the English poetic scene. Auden's early poems are examinations of the contemporary English situation in a tone combining the farcical and the tragic. His *Poems* (1930), explore a variety of new and provocative ways of illustrating the futility of modern English middle-class existence. In cadences that fell with a disturbing new sound on the English ear—deriving sometimes from the poets cited above, sometimes from contemporary colloquial speech, sometimes even from Anglo-Saxon poetry—he assaulted prejudices and conformities with a rhetorical gaiety and a wit which often hovered on the brink of the irresponsible. Here, as in all his early poems, Auden is sometimes uncertain of his audience, speaking as a "we" against a "they" when neither are clearly defined, and constructing private myths and parables and symbols which intermingle oddly sometimes with the vigorous colloquial wit of his language. This produces a certain lurching in and out of obscurity in, for example, *The Orators* (1932) and even in his verse play *The Dance of Death* (1933), in spite of its simplicity of diction and symbolism. *Look Stranger* (1936; entitled *On This Island* in America) marks the maturing of Auden's first phase. Here he has disciplined his wit and ordered his previously darting movements from himself to society, from private to public, from Freud to Marx, from present to past, into a richly thoughtful verse in which history penetrates the present and personal feeling confronts the confusions of the modern world if not with a crystal-clear purpose at least with poise.

Auden then moved to the United States and gradually became less concerned with the social problems of the modern western world and more involved in a personal and religious solution to contemporary ills. There had always been an element of personal questing for a psychological or religious 'healer' in Auden. It now moves in a new direction, producing first characteristically quiet-spoken poems of almost quizzical reflection (as in "Musée des Beaux Arts," in *Another Time*, 1940), then ambitious, discursive, argumentative and highly diversified clusters of poems such as those in *For the Time Being* (1944). Now a professed Christian, Auden had a more stable base from which to contemplate the contemporary world, but in fact, though his Christianity is recognizable in many of the poems, his always intensely personal use of imagery and his irrepressible passion for being witty or ironical at the expense of conventional or popular attitudes kept his later poetry almost as volatile in its changing stances as his earlier. Auden was always a great wit poet, and sometimes his wit moved over into clowning, of a most skilful sort. "Under Which Lyre," the Phi Beta Kappa poem he wrote for Harvard in 1946, is both witty and funny, and at the same time captures with great precision the mood of intellectual America just after the war. Other poems of this period are reflective, gnomic, or descriptive. He developed a use of topographical imagery very different from the wasteland urban imagery of his early poems, sometimes related to the landscape of his native Yorkshire and profoundly symbolic of human types and attitudes. "In Praise of Limestone" (in *Nones*, 1951) is one of the finest of these. In diction, in rhythms, in attitudes towards the reader, Auden has always shown himself inventive and exploratory. His skill, his exuberant craftsmanship, his ability to make arresting verse out of an informal observation or a chatty confession, combine to make him one of the most continuously interesting of modern poets. If nevertheless many readers are left with a feeling of slight disappointment, it is because the excitement aroused by the early Auden was so great, his early promise so manifest, that his achievement, though considerable, is not quite what had been looked for. The immensely skilled verse chat of many of the poems in *About the House* (1966) are not what one expects of a distinguished poet in absolute control of his medium. There is something both engaging and disappointing in Auden's clinging to the status of minor poet. The accent remains quietly colloquial, unfussed. His poem in memory of Louis MacNeice is moving by its very chattiness: but who else would end an elegy on a friend and fellow-poet like this?

> you won't think me imposing if
> I ask you to stay at my elbow
> until cocktail time: dear Shade, for your elegy
> I should have been able to manage
> something more like you than this egocentric monologue,
> but accept it for friendship's sake.

Louis MacNeice (1907–63) is a poet less immediately exciting than Auden and it was not until after his death that he was at all widely recognized as, after Auden, probably the best of those who first broke on the English poetic scene in the 1930's. MacNeice was less politically involved than Auden, Spender or Day Lewis, all of whom were, in the 1930's associated with the left-wing diagnosis of the social and economic ills of the time. A lucid, orderly, undoctrinaire poet, MacNeice cultivated a dry yet highly personal observation of the world around him. In *Autumn Journal* (1938) he showed a freely moving discursive style admirably suited to the mixture of topographical description and personal reflection that winds through the twenty-four linked poems that make up the book. He expects no revolution, yearns for no Utopia:

> Not that I would rather be a peasant; the Happy Peasant
>   Like the Noble Savage is a myth;
> I do not envy the self-possession of an elm-tree
>   Nor the aplomb of a granite monolith.
> All that I would like to be is human, having a share
>   In a civilized, articulate and well-adjusted
> Community where the mind is given its due
>   But the body is not distrusted.

Like Auden, MacNeice sometimes uses the rhythms of popular song, but in general his technique is less exhibitionist than Auden's, his art more subdued, his wit quieter. *Holes in the Sky* (1948) showed him capable of producing admirably constructed short lyrics as well as the longer, more discursive type of poem. His posthumous *Collected Poems* of 1966 revealed a poet with an intensely personal sensitivity to scenes and objects and the ability to relate this to the ironies and sadnesses of daily life, to the place of memory in colouring experience, to the satisfactions afforded by transient pleasures. His poetry has not the cultural intensity of Eliot's or Auden's compulsive extravagances, though he could flash out in moments of wild Celtic gaiety or sudden grief. On the whole it is the subdued, controlled poetry of a man who knows the world and does not expect too much. And what he sees is not Eliot's waste land but something more human, more immediate, and in the last analysis sadder:

>   elbow to elbow
> Inside the roadhouse drinks are raised
> And downed, and downed, the pawns and drains
> Are blocked, are choked, the move is nil,
> The lounge is, like the carpark, full,
> The tulips also feel the chill
> And tilting leeward do no more

Than mimic a bishop's move, the square
Ahead remains ahead, their petals
Will merely fall and choke the drains
Which will be all; the month remains
False animation of failed levitation,
The move is time's, the loss is ours.

(Another Cold May 1962)

Cecil Day Lewis (born 1904) began as a belated Georgian but soon moved to a conspicuously "modern" verse, strongly left-wing in attitude and conspicuously contemporary in vocabulary. In the early 1930's he was much under Auden's influence. His later poetry is more personal, less doctrinaire, content to record with accomplished fluency his own emotional history or to document events and perceptions with a certain rhetorical ease that is sometimes mere facility. Stephen Spender (born 1909) was also in the 1930's much under Auden's influence, but eventually he developed his own kind of compassionate lyricism whose autobiographical earnestness, innocent of Auden's technical virtuosity or MacNeice's subdued ironic sadness, nevertheless succeeds more often than might be expected in finding the proper cadence and imagery for the effective embodiment of a mood or a moral. In Spender we always feel that the justification of the poem is not its status as an artifact but the experience which lies behind it and which it exists in order to communicate. His own response to human emotional need and to the fleeting gesture of appeal or frustration was often able to prompt him to the phrase that captured it. In this sense he is the most "romantic" of the poets who started out in the 1930's. Yet he plays down the rhetoric and, at his best, is able to harness a post-Eliot vocabulary to an emotional directness (innocence, perhaps) in a way that few poets of his generation were able to do.

Robert Graves (born 1895), an older poet who had to wait until the 1950's before his stature was realized, remained untouched by the Eliot revolution, which was one reason for the slowness of his climb to fame. Graves drew on an older English tradition, giving it new strength and meaning by adapting and modifying it to suit his own highly idiosyncratic personality. John Skelton, Robert Herrick, Andrew Marvell and Thomas Hardy are among the few English poets whom Graves recognizes as in the authentic tradition; he also accepts certain kinds of folk poetry and certain Celtic bards. Beginning as a more or less conventional Georgian, Graves eventually developed his own kind of quizzical, familiar, wryly humorous kind of poetry which moves between trance-like intensity and a teasing colloquialness. Freed by the success of his best-selling account of his experiences as a soldier in the First World War (*Goodbye to All That*, 1929) to settle in Majorca and live as an independent writer, he culti-vated his allegiance to what he called the White Goddess, the great inspirer of myth and poetry, with a wilful disregard of contemporary poetic fashion. He wrote novels and miscellaneous prose for a living, including some brilliantly imagined historical novels of which the first *I, Claudius* and its sequel *Claudius the God* (both 1934) remain the best. In *The White Goddess* (1948) he produced a characteristi-cally wayward "historical grammar of poetic myth" in which he drew on his own considerable but eccentric mythological and anthropo-logical scholarship in order to construct a theory of myth and poetry, air his own poetic preferences and prejudices, and attack currently fashionable literary practices and attitudes. His poetry, which at one extreme has affinities with Hardy's and at another to that of E. E. Cummings, is sometimes epigrammatic, sometimes mischievous, sometimes simply tripping like a nursery-rhyme, sometimes drily ironical. But the tone is always his own, the utterance honest, the mood and sentiment clearly wrung from experience directly con-fronted. The directness is sometimes startling:

> Any honest housewife could sort them out,
> Having a nose for fish, an eye for apples.
> Is it any mystery who are the sound,
> And who the rotten? Never, by her lights.

Sometimes deadpan abstract statement is accompanied by an imagery that gives it a special kind of resonance:

> The climate of thought has seldom been described.
> It is no terror of Caucasian frost,
> Nor yet that brooding Hindu heat
> For which a loin-rag and a dish of rice
> Suffice until the pestilent monsoon.
> But, without winter, blood would run too thin;
> Or, without summer, fires would burn too long.
> In thought the seasons run concurrently.

The wisdom is often sardonic but not tragic. Children on the beach "fearlessly rush in" to the water. But

> The horny boatman, who has seen whales
> And flying fishes, who has sailed as far
> As Demerara and the Ivory Coast,
> Will warn them, when they crowd to hear his tales,
> That every ocean smells alike of tar.

He can mock his own scholarship. Zeus was once overheard complaining loudly to Hera about the weather. The short poem concludes:

> A scholiast explains his warm rejoinder,
>   Which sounds too man-like for Olympic use,
> By noting that the snake-tailed Chthonian winds
>   Were answerable to Fate alone, not Zeus.

Sometimes he addresses children:

> You learned Lear's *Nonsense Rhymes* by heart, not rote;
>   You learned Pope's *Iliad* by rote, not heart;
> These terms should be distinguished if you quote
>   My verses, children—keep them poles apart—
> And call the man a liar who says I wrote
>   All that I wrote in love, for love of art.

(This little poem illuminates a great deal about Graves: it is significant that for him Lear, not Pope, is the true poet.)

His later poems centre largely on problems of human relations, on love between the sexes, on the paradoxes of marriage. He has continued unflinchingly to go his own way, repudiating alike "the ornate academic Victorian tradition and the more recent but no less artificial Franco-American modernism." His highly individual idiom achieves its most significant purpose: Graves's poems demand attention, they cannot be merely accepted and classified. The arresting human voice is always there. In the late 1960's there is a good case for considering him the finest living English poet.

Edwin Muir (1887–1959) is another poet who stands very much alone. He, too, was interested in history, in myth, in time, but his interest was different from Graves', deriving partly from his childhood in the Orkney Islands and partly from an almost mystical temperament which sought continually to arrest memories and objects into timeless symbols. Biblical and classical story haunt his imagination and mingle with the Scottish landscape and themes from Scottish history. Adam, Abraham, Moses take their place with Oedipus, Odysseus, and the Trojan heroes in his imagination. The language is not colloquial, but Muir manages to subdue unusual words to the rapt quietness of his tone:

> He left us there, went up to Pisgah hill,
> And saw the holiday land, the sabbath land,
> The mild prophetic beasts, millenial herds,
> The sacred lintel, over-arching trees,

> The vineyards glittering on the southern slopes,
> And in the midst the shining vein of water,
> The river turning, turning towards its home.
> Promised to us . . . .
>
> (Moses)

Muir was much concerned with dreams; he was a visionary poet who sought by steadiness of contemplation to reach to the timeless reality of things. He was fascinated by the myth of the Garden of Eden and by the time-bound reality to which man was doomed after the Fall. One of his finest poems is called "Adam's Dream," describing Adam's first dream after the Fall. Or he imagines the future, as in "The Return":

> I see myself sometimes, an old old man
> Who has walked so long with time as time's true servant,
> That he's grown strange to me—who was once my self—
> Almost as strange as time, and yet familiar
> With old man's staff and legendary cloak,
> For see, it is I, it is I . . . .

He sees himself walking back to the house of his own life in a scene where everything calls him back and "not a room but is /My own, beloved and longed for." He draws near,

> And yet I cannot enter, for all within
> Rises before me there, rises against me,
> A sweet and terrible labyrinth of longing,
> So that I turn aside and take the road
> That always, early or late, runs on before.

Muir's range is limited, but within it he produced poetry of great power and purity.

Edith Sitwell (1887–1964), an exact contemporary of Muir's, produced poetry of a modernity very different from anything written by Muir or indeed by Eliot. Her characteristic poetry of the 1920's, notably that included in *Façade* (1922), used words as counters with which to build up brightly colored patterns. "Patterns in sound" she called her poems, "virtuoso exercises of an extreme difficulty." Many were brilliant if brittle productions, sometimes very amusing, often needing to be read aloud (as Miss Sitwell used to do herself) to achieve the proper effect. Moving between symbolism and nonsense verse, these poems illustrated the difficulties involved in considering words as elements in sound patterns; for often the effect of the pattern depended on the suggestions evoked by the meaning of the words and never were the words in fact totally empty of meaning, used merely as sound, for when they were used as though they were, the result was often a rather charming nonsense verse, both the charm and the nonsense depending on the semantic values of the words used. In *Gold Coast Customs* Miss Sitwell used her special rhythmic effects and her patterning of vowels and consonants not for the purpose of constructing playful patterns but to achieve sinister suggestions of corruption and doom. After this her poetry becomes steadily more emotionally committed and her technique, though still carrying something over from her early experiments, more like that of late nineteenth-century poets. Her much admired "Still Falls the Rain" (on the air-raids of 1940), with its traditional crucifixion imagery and its quotation from the end of Marlowe's *Doctor Faustus*, now appears histrionic and melodramatic. Training in "patterns of sound" was clearly not the best way to learn how to embody real passion in cogent yet disciplined language.

It was Edith Sitwell who first hailed the genius of Dylan Thomas (1914–53), and one can understand why: the verbal excitement of Thomas's early poetry appealed to her lively sense of word-magic. Thomas first appeared, to readers now trained to regard Eliot's dry gentlemanliness as the approved poetic stance, to be a prophet of wild new romanticism, challenging the cerebral orderliness of the fashionable poetry of the time. His breathless and daring imagery, with its skulls, maggots, hangmen, wombs, ghosts and thighs, his mingling of biblical and Freudian imagery, of the elemental world of nature in the raw with the feverish internal world of human desires, human secrets, human longings and regrets, his compound adjectives ("sea-sucked," "man-melted," "tide-tongued," "man-iron," "altarwise")—all this suggested a great liberating verbal energy, with echoes of such earlier romantic extravagants as Beddoes. An American critic reflected this feeling exactly when he wrote that "Thomas discovered poetry on his hand like blood, and screamed aloud." In fact, however, though some of Thomas's poetry of the 1930's was clotted with over-excited imagery, a closer look at his poems revealed not only that they were constructed with enormous care and the images were most carefully related to each other and to the unfolding meaning, but also that these images were put at the service of a number of clearly conceived themes—the relation between man and his natural environment, the problem of identity in view of the perpetual changes wrought by time, the relation of the living to the dead and of both to seasonal change in nature.

> The force that through the green fuse drives the flower
> Drives my green age; that blasts the roots of trees
> Is my destroyer.

The natural processes that linked past with present and man with nature gave him comfort:

> This bread I break was once the oat,
> This wine upon a foreign tree
> Plunged in its fruit;
> Man in the day or wind at night
> Laid the crops low, broke the grape's joy . . . .
>
> This flesh you break, this blood you let
> Make desolation in the vein,
> Were oat and grape
> Born of the sensual root and sap;
> My wine you drink, my bread you snap.

As Thomas developed, and his imagery became more disciplined, the theme of the unity of all life and of life and death as part of a continuing process in which the whole world of nature was involved, became steadily more discernible. So did the ritual and sacramental element in his poetry. "After the Funeral" (1938), an elegy on an aunt in which he sees the sad shabbiness of her life and environment transfigured by love, is a triumph of compact emotional suggestion, every image having its place in building up the transition from mourning to comfort. Many of his poems of the 1940's are more open-worked than his earlier productions, and sometimes possess a rhythmic fluidity that sweeps on the meaning with fine effect. "Poem in October," for example, begins:

> It was my thirtieth year to heaven
> Woke to my hearing from harbour and neighbour wood
> And the mussel pooled and the heron
> Priested shore
> The morning beckon
> With water praying and call of seagull and rook
> And the knock of sailing boats on the net webbed wall
> Myself to set foot
> That second
> In the still sleeping town and set forth.

Here the compound adjectives ("Mussel pooled," "heron priested") and the sacramental suggestions ("priested," "praying") are carefully placed in the run of the stanza and the uneven line-lengths give a rocking motion that helps to involve the reader emotionally in the poem. *Deaths and Entrances* (1946) and *Collected Poems* (1953) show clearly that Thomas was capable of finely disciplined effects in both language and movement, and that, in spite of a tendency to overdo favourite images and to confuse poetic gesturing with poetic achievement, he was not a shouting madman but, at his best, a highly craftsmanlike poet. His popular adulation followed by his early death evoked a reaction, and the charge of empty verbal posturing was brought against him by some of the younger poets of the mid-1950's who were seeking a new chastity of diction and economy of effect. But though Thomas's reputation is not as high now as it was in the few years immediately before his death, his place is secure—not as the romantic whirling dervish he was once thought to be, but as a thoughtful, indeed a cerebral, poet who sought to put new drive and passion into the language of English poetry and who in his brief life left a handful of poems that will be read and remembered outside the classroom and the critic's study.

Another poet whose popularity (for very different reasons) runs far beyond the normal audience for poetry is John Betjeman (born 1906), who uses unpretentiously traditional verse forms to pinpoint, with an odd mixture of nostalgia and ironic criticism, details of the life of the English bourgeoisie before the Second World War. Betjeman's rhythms are often almost jog-trot ("Rumbling under blackened girders, Midland, bound for Cricklewood, /Puffed its sulphur to the sunset where that Land of Laundries stood."). But he captures the sights, sounds, and evocative qualities of the suburbia of the 1930's with absolute precision. And not only suburbia—seaside towns and other holiday resorts of the bourgeoisie, rustic scenes of boating and courting, Victorian churches with their human echoes, all figure amid the furniture of Betjeman's sad-comic poems. The sadness is real; life was really like that in the recent past, and the fact that we remember it as like that means that we are growing older. Betjeman's verse is adroit and skilful, his subjects expertly chosen for his purpose. He has invented a new kind of popular poetry, far from unsophisticated yet not in the least difficult or complex, which appeals to the English national fondness for nostalgia. It may be that when the generation to whom Betjeman's kind of nostalgia is a bitter-sweet reminder of oncoming old age has died away, his poems will lose some of their appeal. They depend on shared knowledge and shared memory for their effect. But that effect is still, in the late 1960's, potent and widespread. Betjeman's feat, whatever the future destiny of his poetry, has been a remarkable one.

Meanwhile, Scottish poetry had been having a twentieth-century renaissance of its own. The sentimentalities of post-Burns Scottish poetry, the stereotyping of Scottish characters and situations in a cosily idealized rustic environment, had proceeded apace throughout the nineteenth century. Corroding nostalgia became increasingly the vice of Scottish literature, both prose and poetry. One of the aims of the Scottish renaissance of the twentieth century was to create a more astringent literature that really confronted experience as it was found in modern Scotland. To do this, poets had to get behind the precarious balance represented by Burns's achievement to the poets of the Golden Age of the fifteenth century, when Scots was a full-blooded literary language and Scottish literature was both fully national and fully European. Not Burns but William Dunbar was the literary hero of this movement, and the slogan "Back to Dunbar" began to be heard more and more among Scottish poets after the First World War.

The founder and by far the greatest figure in this movement was Hugh MacDiarmid (pen-name of Christopher Murray Grieve, born 1892), without question the finest Scottish poet since Burns. MacDiarmid's early poetry is written in a Scots language that he deliberately synthesized from his own native Border dialect, words from other regions of Scotland, and (most notably) words no longer in use which he culled from the poetry of Dunbar and other late medieval Scottish poets. The result was, surprisingly, a lyric poetry of wonderful verbal delicacy, combining precise observation of natural objects with tense mystical clarity of vision. *Sangschaw* (1925) and *Pennywheep* (1926) contain some of his best poems in this mode. *A Drunk Man Looks at the Thistle* (1936), perhaps MacDiarmid's masterpiece, is a long poem made up of a number of related lyrics and passages of descriptive and reflective poetry. Using the speaker's drunkenness as a means of removing his inhibitions and getting him into that visionary state in which he can see into the very soul of Scotland and diagnose her modern predicament, MacDiarmid alternates between lyricism, savage satire, comic irony, philosophic reflection, and personal confession. The drunkenness is a liberating device, rather as the dream in medieval dream-allegory or the journey in Dante.

In MacDiarmid's later poetry he largely dropped Scots and wrote in standard English, sometimes in English with such a wide-ranging vocabulary (culled sometimes from technical dictionaries) and so different in tone and movement from anything being written in England, that it almost becomes a language of its own. This highly personal use of language does not mean, however, that MacDiarmid was out of the mainstream of modern European literature. On the contrary: from the beginning he self-consciously associated himself and his work with European avant-garde movements, and side by side with his Scottish nationalism there was an active internationalism which manifested itself not only in his physical visiting of a great number of foreign countries (including Russia and China) but also in his incorporating into his poems quotations from and references to innumerable foreign writers. MacDiarmid's political attitude, which emerges often in his poems and especially in his *Hymns to Lenin* (1931–35), is a mixture, at first sight puzzling, of Communism, Scottish Nationalism, and internationalism. As a diagnostician of Scotland's ills and a prophet and preacher against the "establishment" he not only combines these apparently conflicting attitudes but uses them, separately or together, to attack complacency, provinciality, stuffiness, respectability, wherever he can find them. He is a sworn fighter against what he has called in his autobiography (*Lucky Poet*, 1934) "the whole gang of high muckymucks, famous fatheads, old wives of both sexes, stuffed shirts, hollow men with headpieces stuffed with straw, bird-wits, lookers-under-beds, trained seals, creeping Jesuses, Scots Wha Ha'vers, village idiots, policemen, leaders of white-mouse factions and noted connoisseurs of bread and butter, glorified gangsters, and what Billy Phelps calls Medlar Novelists (the medlar being a fruit that becomes rotten before it is ripe), Commercial Calvinists, makers of 'noises like a turnip,' and all the touts and toadies and lickspittles of the English Ascendancy, and their infernal women-folk, and all their skunkoil skullduggery."

The inconsistency and violence of MacDiarmid's thought was bound up with his drive toward realizing his almost mystical vision of a people redeemed from falsity and perpetual second-handness. His poetry defies classification; it ranges from the beautifully articulated early Scots lyrics where reality is penetrated to its inexpressible core with an extraordinary combination of tenderness and violence to the later long discursive pieces in English with their long Whitman-like catalogues covering virtually the whole world of modern knowledge. There is nothing in English or Scottish poetry like those remarkable lyrics that make up the sequence "Au Clair de la Lune" in *Sangschaw*, or like the powerfully phrased mixture of natural observation, grotesquerie, and mysticism in "Ex Vermibus" in the same volume. He can move from the cosmic to the intimate, from religious to domestic imagery, from eternity (a favorite word) to the kitchen sink or the farmyard dunghill or the slum streets of Glasgow. His poems seem to grow out of the language yet at the same time seem to be the compelled utterance of an intense personal vision. Some of his later poems, very different in style, read in parts like doggerel; but in their context they can be seen as part of the whole sweep of MacDiarmid's response to experience.

All of MacDiarmid's poetry is about Scotland, but then for him

Scotland is more than a particular country with a particular destiny and particular woes and problems. It is a focussing point for the universe, or (looking at the matter another way) a mode of knowing. MacDiarmid associates his Scottish nationalism with every kind of self-realization, with the precise individuality of natural objects, with the distinctiveness of languages, the characteristics of peoples, the *trueness* of things. (In this he resembles Hopkins, with his insistence on the *haecceitas* or "thisness" of things.) He can say

> Mine is the antipathy of the internationalist to the nationalist,
> The cosmopolitan to the Englishman,

seeing his difference from the English as the difference between a man who takes the whole world for his province and the man who is content to live amid second-hand and unrealized gestures of national complacency. At the same time he can write

> The rose of all the world is not for me.
> I want for my part
> Only the little white rose of Scotland
> That smells sharp and sweet—and breaks the heart.

(It was Yeats, in his early romantic phase, who had written of the rose of all the world.) There is a link between these apparent contradictions, and it is to be found in MacDiarmid's "nominalism" (in the medieval sense), his belief that universals or abstracts are mere names and reality consists in concrete particulars. Thus MacDiarmid's nationalism is part of his internationalism, his use of Scots a justification of the use of any language if it is used with full integrity, his descriptions of fishing flies, domestic utensils or moonlight equally symbolic of reality.

MacDiarmid was the luminary round which many lesser stars of the Scottish renaissance clustered. Some wrote in Scots ("Lallans" as it became fashionable to call it) and some in English. In spite of MacDiarmid's brilliant use of a synthetic Scots in his early lyrics and of some wholly successful poems in Scots written by his followers (e.g. Sydney Goodsir Smith), it is doubtful whether he established it as a viable medium for modern Scottish poetry. But he raised the whole question of the texture of a national culture and the relation of language to that texture. He made writers in Scotland aware of themselves in a new way. And he himself achieved international recognition as a great Scottish poet to an extent that Burns never achieved in his lifetime and in a manner that makes Burns's international popularity seem facile.

Of poetry in England in the 1950's and 1960's it is difficult yet to talk with the historian's perspective. But one can note a reaction against the verbal excitement of Dylan Thomas that began before Thomas's death and provides a characteristic note for the 1950's. The young poets of the 1950's were suspicious of systems and of grandiose formulations of the poet's role; they were suspicious also of language that was not quiet and lucid. In his anthology of new poetry entitled *New Lines* (1956), Robert Conquest remarked of the poetry of the fifties: "It submits to no great systems of theoretical constructs nor agglomerations of unconscious commands. It is free from both mystical and logical compulsions and—like modern philosophy—is empirical in its attitude to all that comes. This reverence for the real person or event is, indeed, a part of the general intellectual ambience (in so far as it is not blind or retrogressive) of our time. . . . On the more technical side, though of course related to all this, we see refusal to abandon a rational structure and comprehensible language, even when the verse is most highly charged with sensuous or emotional intent." The new poets are seen as having in common "little more than a negative determination to avoid bad principles." This is not the trumpeting of a new movement; it suggests a recipe for good minor poetry. And indeed the last two decades in England have produced a considerable amount of good minor poetry—intelligent, good-mannered, sensitive, restrained, concerned at all costs to avoid the shrill and the hysterical, anxious for the freshness and purity of the English language. The poets of *New Lines—II* (1963) show similar characteristics.

The poems of Thom Gunn (*The Sense of Movement*, 1957; *My Sad Captains*, 1961) illustrate how the new insistence on exactness of image and movement can produce something more than agreeable verse craftsmanship. Reminiscent sometimes of Graves, sometimes of Muir, sometimes of the American Yvor Winters, Gunn's poems have a special kind of modest and honest individuality which make them, if not continuously exciting, at least always engaging. "Human Condition" opens

> Now it is fog, I walk
> Contained within my coat;
> No castle more cut off
> By reason of its moat:
> Only the sentry's cough,
> The mercenaries' talk.
>
> The street lamps, visible,
> Drop no light on the ground,

> But press beams painfully
> In a yard of fog around.
> I am condemned to be
> An individual.

And it concludes:

> Much is unknowable.
> No problem shall be faced
> Until the problem is:
> I, born to fog, to waste,
> Walk through hypothesis,
> An individual.

There is a considerable amount of abstract language here, but it is solidly rooted in an apprehension and in a situation. And the movement of the verse—as the title of his first volume shows, movement is a prime concern of Gunn's—is always carefully controlled, subtly varied, linked on the one hand to a fairly traditional metrical scheme and on the other to the shifting needs of the poem's emotional pattern. Gunn is not afraid of rhyme, and some of his poems appear at first glance as much more traditional than any serious modern poetry since the 1930's. But the movement is not really the regular metrical pattern of earlier English poetry, nor is his use of rhyme at all conventional. Witness the opening of "Rastignac at 45":

> Here he is of course. It was his best
> trick always: when we glance again toward
> The shadow we see it has consist-
> ed of him all along, lean and bored.

But Gunn's poems are carefully constructed wholes, and suffer from partial quotation. The *rightness* of his images and the appropriateness of the studied casualness of tone only emerge when we come to the end and see where the poem has all along been moving to.

The other young poet who began in the fifties and who is worth selecting from the large number of candidates for inclusion in this concluding section is Ted Hughes (*The Hawk in the Rain*, 1957; *Lupercal*, 1960). Hughes's imagery is richer and more sensuous than Gunn's: sometimes there is even a suggestion of the American Wallace Stevens crossed with Dylan Thomas:

> In a cage of wire-ribs
> The size of a man's head, the macaw bristles in a staring
> Combustion, suffers the stoking devils of his eyes.
> In the old lady's parlour, where an aspidistra succumbs
> To the musk of faded velvet, he hangs as in clear flames,

Like a torturer's iron instrument preparing
With dense slow shudderings of greens, yellows, blues,
Crimsoning into the barbs:

But this is not characteristic, even though it indicates an element of brash humor in Hughes's imagery that is often arresting and refreshing. His poems show an inventiveness, a joy in the exercise of his art, that exist side by side with—and indeed are put at the service of—a compassionate curiosity. Sometimes he adopts the quiet, off-hand posture that Gunn manages so well, but when he does so (as in "The Hag") the subject of the poem demands a more rapid opening out, is more immediately evocative, than a typical subject of Gunn's. Sometimes a phrase suggests Muir quite vividly, as in the opening of "Bayonet Charge"—"Suddenly he awoke and was running." In his later work the control is firmer, the more riotous aspects of his imagery are subdued, and we have the poetry of chastened purity called for in the 1950's deepened and enriched by a powerful and humane imagination so as to develop into something more, as in the opening of "Relic":

I found this jawbone at the sea's edge:
There, crabs, dogfish, broken by the breakers or tossed
To flap for half an hour and turn to a crust
Continue the beginning. The deeps are cold:
In that darkness camaraderie does not hold:
Nothing touches but, clutching, devours. And the jaws,
Before they are satisfied or their stretched purpose
Slacken, go down jaws; go gnawn bare. Jaws
Eat and are finished and the jawbone comes to the beach:
This is the sea's achievement; with shells,
Vertebrae, claws, carapaces, skulls.

To a critic writing in the late sixties it appears as though Gunn and Hughes are poets worth singling out for real (if so far limited) achievement as well as for promise. But it must be emphasized that there is no dominating figure in English poetry at this time. And there are more accomplished minor poets writing than it is possible to discuss in a work of this scope.

CHAPTER TWENTY-NINE

The Twentieth-Century Novel

THE ENGLISH NOVEL, as we have seen, was essentially bourgeois in its origins, and throughout the eighteenth and nineteenth centuries it was solidly anchored in a social world. The fact of social class was not only taken for granted but even depended on by English novelists; it provided humor and atmosphere and local color as well as motivation for self-advancement. The heroine of Richardson's *Pamela* was a servant girl who married into the squirearchy; and though this fairy-tale pattern was not a common one in English fiction, it simply exaggerated a feature that *was* common, namely, patterning of the plot in terms of gain or loss of social status or fortune. Even Hardy in *Tess* projected his meaning through such public social symbols. Fortune, status, and marital position were all important for the Victorian as for the eighteenth-century novel. The novelist's world was an assured one, however much he might criticize or wish to reform it. The view of what was significant in human affairs on which he based his selection of events to constitute the plot was a view shared with his readers; he never had the problem of wondering whether what was significant in his view was also significant in that of his readers. His standard of significance was public and agreed; whatever was important in a character's fictional life was registered by public symbols as social, financial, or institutional change. This presentation by the novelist of his world as a wholly objective world determined in large manner his technique; he could display his world like a showman or, with a "two-travellers-might-have-been-seen" type of opening, deploy characters and events beneath the reviewing stand on which he stood with the reader in the confident knowledge that everything of significance that was to happen to them would be externally visible.

The loss of the confident sense of a common world, of a public view of what was significant in human action, which was reflected in the move toward private association in poetry, had an effect on both the themes and the technique of fiction. "To believe that your impressions hold good for others," wrote Virginia Woolf of Jane Austen, "is to be released from the cramp and confinement of personality." Mrs. Woolf wrote this almost in envy, for she was herself bound by the cramp and confinement of personality; her sense of the significant was intensely personal and individual, depending on subtle shifts of mood and feeling. "What is meant by reality?" she once asked and replied: "It would seem to be something very erratic, very undependable—now to be found in a dusty road, now in a scrap of newspaper in the street, now in a daffodil in the sun. It lights up a group in a room and stamps some casual saying. . . ." This is related to James Joyce's view of the "epiphany," the sudden realization that some quite ordinary incident or situation or object encountered in daily experience has an intense symbolic meaning. The construction of a plot pattern based on such subtle and private interpretations of the significant in human affairs would necessarily take the novel out of the public arena of value in which it had hitherto moved. The novelist would then either have the problem of making convincing to the reader, while he reads, his (the novelist's) own principle of selection and sense of significance, which might involve various kinds of technical innovations and subtleties, some of them imported from lyrical poetry (which is what Virginia Woolf did); or of presenting a world which did not depend on any single criterion of significance at all but in which everything interpenetrated everything else and the same event or character became important or trivial as the author's view and way of presentation kept shifting (James Joyce was almost alone in adopting this method).

New concepts of time, influenced by or at least akin to William James's view of the "specious present" which does not really exist but which represents the continuous flow of the "already" into the "not yet," of retrospect into anticipation, and Henri Bergson's concept of durée, of time as flow and duration rather than as a series of points moving chronologically forward, also influenced the twentieth-century novelist, particularly in his handling of plot structure. If time could not be properly conceived of as a series of moments moving forward in a steady progress, then the traditional conception of plot, which generally involved taking the hero through a sequence of testing circumstances in chronological order, would cease to satisfy. Further, new psychological ideas emphasized the multiplicity of consciousness, the simultaneous coexistence of several levels of consciousness and subconsciousness in which past experience was retained and by whose retention the whole of personality was colored and determined. Marcel Proust in France had explored ways of presenting the past as contained in the present, and more and more the new concept of time came together with the new concept of consciousness to develop a new view of character. The truth about a character is the sum of his whole emotional experience, and that sum is always there, pervading and indeed constituting his consciousness. It is not therefore necessary to take a character through a series of testing circumstances to reveal the whole human truth about him; the proper exploration of his consciousness at any given moment or in a very short space of time (say a single day) could reveal all his history and all his potentialities. For on this view a man *is* his history; nothing is lost, and his reaction to every new event is conditioned by the sum of his reactions to all earlier events. Thus retrospect is of the very stuff of present consciousness, and need not be formally introduced by set pieces of retrospect or by reported memory introduced by some such phrase as "this reminded him of ... " or "he recalled that ... " Development depthwise rather than lengthwise becomes the logical technique.

The novel had been moving toward a greater increase in psychological subtlety, or at least in the increase of the apparatus for psychological diagnosis, for some time. Henry James in particular had brought a new precision and complexity into the description of states of mind. But it was not until the 1920's that the full impact of the three factors just discussed—the apparent collapse of a public standard of significance, new notions of time, and new notions of consciousness—made itself felt on the technique and the themes of fiction. The isolation of the individual consciousness steadily became the most important psychological fact in a world from which public value seemed to have departed and where every individual was seen to be the prisoner of his unique stream of consciousness. Our response to every new event is conditioned by our private past: Mrs. Dalloway in Virginia Woolf's novel of that name opens her front door to go out into the London streets and as she does so is aware with one part of her mind of a similar feeling on opening the French window onto the lawn in the house she had lived in as a girl. The gestures we make to other people are bound to be in some degree misread, for other people will read them from the other side, from *their* side, and will not see them as they appear to us, who projected them out of our isolated consciousness. The difference between the private stream of consciousness and the public gesture is emphasized again and again in Joyce's *Ulysses* (1922) where we see the true state of Stephen's or Bloom's consciousness side by side with the quite different public conversation they become involved in; the two are wrought and presented together, thus stressing the inevitable loneliness of men. If the characteristic theme of the eighteenth- and nineteenth-century novel was the relation between gentility and morality, that of the twentieth century is the relation between loneliness and love. How is love possible when we are all, whether we know it or not, the prisoners of our private selves? How is even communication possible? To those who raised this question in this way, society as a whole seemed to provide simply a collection of empty gestures and institutions which had no real meaning and could provide no real basis for communication between individuals. As E. M. Forster put it, the "great society" is always the enemy; only the "little society," the intimate group of real friends who have somehow managed to break down the walls of individuality that separate them, is worth anything —or is really possible as a true society. The great society becomes a contradiction in terms. To D. H. Lawrence (1885–1930), the mystical awareness of the core of otherness in the other person is the basis of a true sex relationship—not Whitmanesque merging, which he thought disgusting even if it were possible. To Joseph Conrad (1857–1924), the testing time comes when a man finds himself in a situation where the normal public codes which he has hitherto professed do not work, are not relevant or even real, and he either finds strength and recovery out of self-knowledge and loneliness, or goes down to destruction in the heart of darkness. (There is also for Conrad a third way: if a character is sufficiently unimaginative not to realize that he is in a radically new and challenging situation, and goes on doggedly applying the conventional code, like Captain M'Whirr in *Typhoon*, he may with luck win through—not to new knowledge, of which such a character is incapable, but to survival.) Where Conrad took up public themes, as in *Nostromo* (1904), it was to write a political novel very different from the Disraelian political novel: Conrad explores the various ways in which politics and economics threaten the integrity of character and corrupt personal relationships, often without the knowledge of those who are threatened and corrupted. The violent external action is less important than the subtle movements in character which illustrate the difficulties, if not indeed the impossibility, of adequately reconciling the social and the individual, political and economic efficiency on the one hand and personal integrity on the other. *Nostromo* is not a story of surrender to temptation under particular circumstances; it is—among other things —a brilliant symbolic rendering of the inevitable fate of political man, and as man is in one part of his nature a political animal, this means of the inevitable fate of man.

Conrad was a deeply pessimistic novelist, but full recognition of this was delayed by Conrad's own comments on his novels and stories, which are not always to be trusted: he often describes them as deriving from a simpler ethical impulse than they clearly do. Sometimes he talks as though the straightforward virtues of the sailor—fidelity, loyalty, endurance—provide the key to his moral vision; at other times he may use such high-falutin abstractions as his definition of a work of art "a single-minded attempt to render the highest kind of justice to the visible universe, by bringing to light the truth, manifold and one, underlying its every aspect." This definition comes from the Preface to *The Nigger of the Narcissus* (1897), his first important novel, and certainly neither a straightforward presentation of the moral effectiveness of the sailor's code nor simply a rendering of the truth of the visible universe. It is a novel that probes the necessary corruption of any kind of human society. James Wait, the dying negro sailor, puts a curse on the ship by arousing in the crew feelings of sympathy which are nevertheless at bottom feelings of self-interest. "The latent egotism of tenderness to suffering," wrote Conrad, "appeared in the developing anxiety not to see him die." Wait's effect on the crew of the *Narcissus* is to test the validity of the ship's company as a microcosm of a valid society. "He was demoralizing. Through him we were becoming highly humanized, tender, complex, excessively decadent: we understood the subtlety of his fear, sympathised with all his repulsions, shrinkings, evasions, delusions—as though we had been over-civilized and rotten, and without any knowledge of the meaning of life." The old sailor Singleton, the only one of the crew to be indifferent to Wait and his illness, becomes a heroic, almost Christ-like figure when he steers the ship in a storm ("In front of his erect figure only the two arms moved crosswise with a swift and sudden readiness, to check or urge again the rapid stir of circling spokes"). But on debarkation he joins the society of ordinary men and is immediately seen by the clerk who pays him off as a dirty old man.

Society is necessary, yet inevitably corrupting: this is a theme which Conrad explores again and again. It is the theme of *Nostromo*, in many ways the most remarkable of all his novels, in which he shows how "material interests" corrupt human relations yet at the same time the attempt to escape from such interests into solitude results in destruction. Up to a point *Nostromo* can be read as a reformer's novel, a novel pointing out the evils of economic exploitation of a young nation by a powerful and established capitalist country; but when all the threads of this complex novel come together and we see the total pattern, it becomes clear that Conrad is not protesting against anything, only illustrating a permanent aspect of the human condition. All alternatives to what he presents as corrupting are in fact worse. Conrad was a conservative for the same reason that Dr. Johnson was—he did not believe that there was any way out of the human predicament, and therefore saw political reform as folly. In *Heart of Darkness* he portrays the evils of nineteenth century colonialism in Africa with extraordinary vividness, yet the Congo he portrays, like that recently portrayed by Graham Greene, is a Congo of the mind. Idealism corrupts, and loneliness can force a man into horrified awareness of his identity with his own moral opposite, "the secret sharer." How do we come to terms with "the secret sharer," the enemy we are forced to recognize as ourself? This is another characteristic Conrad theme—it explains, incidentally, the final crisis of *Lord Jim*. *Under Western Eyes*—a novel whose universality of implication Conrad deliberately disguises by suggesting that it is a strange Russian story incredible to Westerners—tells the desperate tale of a lonely Russian student who is forced by circumstances into a more ultimate loneliness, to mingle with a band of conspirators out-wardly as one of them but in reality (though against his will) a police spy. He is adored by the sister of a dead conspirator whom in fact he had been forced by circumstances into betraying but the girl believes that Razumov had really been her brother's devoted friend and leader. It is a study of loneliness and society as equally untenable, of the ultimate in false positions, from which the only escape is self-destruction. Razumov had tried to keep himself uncommitted, but he was trapped into commitment by his very neutrality and that commitment in turn is seen as radically false, involving a lie in the soul. Society is necessary but corrupting; solitude is inevitable but it destroys. We can trace this theme again and again in Conrad. If he never avowed this degree of pessimism in his Prefaces, it is because he wanted to hide from his readers, and perhaps even from himself, the real implication of his own insights. How far Conrad's interest in the relation between loneliness and the demands of society derives from his own history as a Pole who became first a British merchant seaman and then an English novelist it is difficult to tell precisely. But it is significant that his pessimism has a different quality from that of any of the other pessimistic or stoical or sceptical writer of the late nineteenth and early twentieth century.

Of course not all twentieth-century novelists reflected the changes just described. The lively, inquiring mind of H. G. Wells (1866–1946) produced fables of all kinds inquiring into the prospects for mankind and the problems of his day as he saw them, as well as some exciting science fiction and—his best literary work—a group of novels dealing with immense gusto with lower middle-class English life, notably *Kipps* (1905) and *The History of Mr. Polly* (1910). Wells, who was sometimes an artist in spite of himself but who, as his correspondence with Henry James reveals, had little sense of artistic form and no awareness of the significance for fiction of new concepts of time and consciousness, was essentially a Baconian and a Victorian, and his best novels are really good Victorian minor fiction. Similarly, John Galsworthy (1867–1933) remained unaware of the novel as anything more than a social documentary. His Forsyte novels, of which *The Man of Property* (1906) is the best and which were published together as *The Forsyte Saga* in 1922, document an era with perceptiveness and intelligence, but his art remains a surface one; he never quite succeeded in rendering the life he knew fully in the texture of his novels, and it is when he tries to be most profoundly symbolic (as in the portrait of Irene) that he is least successful. His humanity and social observation exceeded his creative and imaginative powers as a literary artist. Arnold Bennett (1867–1931) was another documentary novelist unmoved by the contemporary problems we have discussed. His best novel, *The Old Wives' Tale* (1908), deploys an extended plot in such a way as to enable him to present with considerable vividness aspects of English and French social life, behavior, and history in the nineteenth century; and in some of his other novels, notably *Riceyman Steps* (1923), he shows skill in rendering local atmosphere. But these three novelists were for Virginia Woolf "materialists"; they dealt with the material surface of social life and did not come to grips with what she considered the realities of human consciousness, so difficult to capture but so essential to capture if the truth is to be told.

E. M. Forster published the last of his five novels, *A Passage to India*, in 1924, when he was forty-five, and in a long life produced no more fiction. The fact is significant. Forster had one theme—human relationships—and when he had exhausted it on fiction he wrote no more novels. But well after the Second World War Forster retained his symbolic significance as the embodiment of a special and valuable kind of English liberal imagination that both pinpoints a historical moment and stands for something permanently valuable. For while he is the great spokesman for an idea of human behavior and a concern with human relationships which were characteristic of certain circles at Cambridge in the early years of the twentieth century, he is also the inheritor of a nineteenth-century tradition of high-minded religious benevolence—and he is a literary artist with a strong sense of esthetic form. His novels reflect these three aspects of his life and character.

Forster's second novel, *The Longest Journey* (1907), explores different kinds of life and of deadness in human relationships while at the

THE TWENTIETH-CENTURY NOVEL

same time satirizing the narrow, unimaginative conformity of the English public school and the dangers and distortions implied in the English notion of respectability. It is still a young man's novel; eager, committed, not afraid of melodramatic contrivances or loaded characterizations. But it has freshness and a certain intellectual gaiety. *A Room with a View* (1908) explores the nature of love as felt by the English middle classes and sets against the frozen English heart the passionate, if often irresponsible and cruel, Italian. (Italy had been used as a liberating agent, too, in Forster's first novel, *Where Angels Fear to Tread.*) *Howards End* (1910) explores the relation between inward feeling and outward behavior; it is a novel of considerable structural and psychological complexity. Impressive as it is, there are certain evasions and obliquities in its handling of the social and sexual themes which it develops, and one feels that Forster drew back before the implications of some of his own insights. The novel does not push its knowledge hard enough, but instead resolves situations in esthetically tidy but humanly dubious gestures. *A Passage to India* (1924) is Forster's masterpiece; here he takes the relations between the English and the Indians in the early 1920's as a background against which to conduct the most searching and complex of all his explorations of the possibilities and the limitations, the promises and the pitfalls, of human relationships. Forster as the liberal humanist on the side of Indian independence is also Forster the connoisseur of human littleness and absurdity. Neither English nor Indians are spared: there is a kind of comic mysticism mitigating the tragic undertones in the novel. Obviously the difficulties of genuine human contact can be projected on a large scale when one side consists of English and the other of Indians. But this is not a novel that preaches integration or even toleration. The kinds of contact which are made between English and Indian are odd and inexplicable. Indeed, there are symbolic moments and incidents in the novel which make one wonder whether Forster was not deliberately covering his tracks—refusing to push his insights. All of Forster's novels are unsatisfactory in one way or another. But the satisfactions they provide are nevertheless substantial. They illustrate the English liberal imagination at its best—humane, intellectually honest, and modest. It is because the humanity and the honesty sometimes interfere with each other—we want the cultivated mind, which needs moneyed leisure, but our social conscience leads us to want to abolish moneyed leisure—that Forster in the end fell silent.

Virginia Woolf (1882–1941) produced in *Mrs. Dalloway* (1925) and *To the Lighthouse* (1927) two of the finest treatments of the problem of loneliness and love which so haunted her. The former novel opens

with the heroine planning to give a party; parties bring people together—but do they really bring people together or is one lonelier
still in a crowd? As she moves about London shopping, every encounter she has produces a response colored by the whole texture of
her earlier experience, so that as we follow her stream of consciousness
we learn all of her previous history, or all that matters. The events
of Mrs. Dalloway's day, artfully organized so as to project in a host
of different ways the nature of this question of the possibilities of
communication, are counterpointed against the events in the day of
Mr. and Mrs. Septimus Warren Smith, whom she never meets, but
with whom she has a symbolic relationship, which is emphasized
when the specialist who treated Smith comes to her party that evening and, in telling of Smith's suicide, produces in her a feeling of
identification with the poor man. Septimus Warren Smith goes mad
because (as a result of his experiences in the First World War) he has
lost all sense of contact with other people at all, is driven into the
isolated emptiness of himself, and is dragged back by representatives
of crude conventionality who imagine that by imposing their artificial social norms on him they can restore his sense of communication. The pattern of the novel is woven with extreme delicacy, and
the various elements from Mrs. Dalloway's past brought into the
present through a variety of persuasive devices. The prose itself is
carefully cadenced and at times almost poetic, though never rhetorical. The highly individual sense of significance which provides the
basis for the plot pattern is conveyed through style and imagery,
through the suggestiveness and cunning of the language.

In *To the Lighthouse* Virginia Woolf takes a group of characters on
holiday on an island in the Hebrides and uses the setting—very
different from the teeming London of *Mrs. Dalloway*—to help her
to arrange the characters into symbolic relations with each other
and to the landscape. Time is almost as much a character here as it
is in Shakespeare's *The Winter's Tale*. In the first section of the novel
we see Mr. and Mrs. Ramsay, their children and their guests on
holiday on the island one late September day a few years before the
First World War. In the second section we get an impressionable
evocation of the passage of time over the next few years, while
the house stands empty, Mrs. Ramsay dies, one of the Ramsay sons
is killed in the War, a Ramsay daughter dies in childbirth. In the
third and final section we see the remnant of the Ramsay family
revisiting their house on the island some ten years later, with some
of the same guests and the book closes with Lily Briscoe, a guest
on both visits, completing a picture she had begun on the first
visit, being enabled to complete it by the vision which finally comes

to her and lets her see for a moment in their proper relation the true significance of the dead Mrs. Ramsay, of the whole Ramsay family, and of the physical scene before her. At the same moment Mr. Ramsay and two of his children finally reach the lighthouse, a visit to which had to be put off in the earlier visit because of bad weather. A fluid and sensitive prose helps Virginia Woolf to build up as the novel moves a fine pattern of symbolic relations and moral and psychological problems are if not exactly explored at least suggested and evoked. The novel combines strength with delicacy and is a remarkable achievement.

That there was a robust side to Virginia Woolf's genius, as there was to her character, is shown by *Orlando*, which might be called a symbolic biography of the author's friend Victoria Sackville-West, with the hero, Orlando, acting out the history and background of the Sackville-West family from Elizabethan times to the present, and changing sex in the process. It is a lively and humorous work, a *jeu d'esprit*, containing a considerable number of private jokes. It is also a literary work of great virtuosity. *The Waves* (1931) is the most stylized of Virginia Woolf's novels, based on the carefully organized impressions of a limited number of characters, each of whom presents those impressions in a series of monologues. Some critics feel that this sort of stylization is peculiarly appropriate to Virginia Woolf's genius and consider *The Waves* her finest work. But it lacks the flexibility and subtle movement of *Mrs. Dalloway* and *To the Lighthouse* and the prose is (surprisingly in this author) occasionally turgid. *The Years* (1937) is more conventional in technique but *Between the Acts* (1941) is the most "poetic" of all Virginia Woolf's novels and represents her final attempt to find an adequate form for her subtle and fleeting insights. There is an effective interweaving of lyrical and narrative devices. Yet the novel has no real ending: "life," Mrs. Woolf had written in 1919, "is not a series of gig-lamps symmetrically arranged; but a luminous halo, a semi-transparent envelope surrounding us from the beginning of consciousness to the end." There is a paradox here, for art requires pattern, and if experience lacks pattern how should it be rendered in art? In her best novels Virginia Woolf managed to resolve the paradox and use pattern in such a way as to suggest its opposite, the "semi-transparent envelope."

James Joyce (1882–1941) faced the implications of the loss of a world of public values in a very different way. His attitude was complicated by the fact that he early adopted the view, developed in the late nineteenth century, of the alienation of the artist. The artist had to be outside all conventions, all normal society, and this not only because those conventions and that society as Joyce found them in

Dublin represented a "paralysis," a dead set of gestures having no meaning in terms of genuine human experience, but because the artist must be outside society in order to be objective, and he must be objective if he is to adopt the peculiar microcosmic view which was the way Joyce solved the modern problem. For, instead of using quasi-poetic techniques persuasive to the reader while he reads, Joyce sought a method of presenting a limited tract of time and space as microcosm, as a small-scale model of human life, to which all attitudes were possible, depending on your point of view. The artist's function was thus not to render his own personal viewpoint, but to take all points of view and to construct in his fictional world an enormous interrelating, punning, kaleidoscopic verbal universe which, it might almost be said, presents everything as also everything else. Joyce began, in the collection of short stories he called *Dubliners* (1914), with carefully etched pictures of Dublin life which were meticulously realistic in detail and atmosphere and at the same time were so organized that each detail became symbolic and each story had a symbolic relation to the other stories, the whole constituting not only (as he claimed) a picture of "the centre of the paralysis" but a projection of the basic crises of human experience and the archetypal rituals with which men confront them. In *A Portrait of the Artist as a Young Man* (1916) he transmuted autobiography into objective fiction and organized his account of a potential novelist from infancy to the moment when he realized that art implies exile in such a way as to emphasize at every point the connection between the artist's objective, comprehensive, microcosmic vision and his inevitable alienation. Stephen Dedalus, the hero, is at the beginning of the novel firmly anchored in his family and in the institutions of his country. They continue to put forth claims on him throughout the period of his growing up. But when he realizes at last that his destiny is to be free of all these claims—it is a brilliantly rendered moment in the novel—he has to learn to escape from them, to cultivate the terrible neutrality of the artist. Like the Greek Daedalus who made the labyrinth for King Minos and afterward made wings to enable him to escape across the sea from the tyrannous king, Stephen Dedalus seeks to escape from the labyrinth of Dublin life and claims. Stephen was the first Christian martyr, Daedalus the first craftsman; in giving his hero the name of Stephen Dedalus, Joyce was emphasizing his view of the artist as outcast.

Ulysses is the work of the exiled artist re-creating at a distance but with total knowledge the life he has escaped from. In its rendering of events of one day in Dublin (16th June 1904), Joyce achieves a realistic surface so brilliant, so convincing in its life and color and movement, that the book can be enjoyed merely for its superficial vitality. But its true vitality goes much deeper. Joyce expands the action of *Ulysses* into microcosm, he makes his account of the adventures of Leopold Bloom, the unsuccessful advertisement canvasser, Stephen Dedalus, would-be artist a few years after we left him in the *Portrait*, and others, into a symbolic picture of all history and all experience. He does this by providing overtones of meaning for every literal action, by the deft use of allusion and suggestion, references to the other arts, and by the use of devices, such as the viceregal procession in the tenth episode, for the simultaneous presentation of different streams of action that are happening at the same time. The seedy and unheroic Bloom is a true hero; not only is he the *homme moyen sensuel*, humane, inquiring, but always inexpert, always the layman; he is also the Ulysses of Homer, who in turn was husband of Penelope, lover of Calypso, wanderer and home-lover, brave warrior and cunning schemer. Bloom, too, an Irish Jew, is both of Dublin and not of Dublin, both a member of his community and an exile; his humane curiosity shows him as the Baconian scientist, concerned with "the relief of man's estate," while his relative lack of formal education and the streak of vulgarity in him shows him as simultaneously the antiscientist, the prey of popular half-truths. He is the complete man, now hero and now fool, and in the devastatingly complete presentation of his consciousness in the course of the day during which we see him, Joyce not only shows all of him, including his whole past (for his whole past is contained in the texture of his present consciousness), but also shows him as everybody else. All points of view are applicable; the same man is hero and fool depending on how you look at him. *Ulysses* is the comedy of multiple identity. To the question: "What is significant in human experience?" Joyce seems to answer: "Nothing, and everything. It all depends on how you look at it. I shall present a picture of a slice of life so organized that you will see this: I, as the objective artist standing outside all human commitments, will be able to show all of human history contained in my one carefully patterned set of events, for the significant is also the insignificant, the trivial is the heroic, and the familiar the exotic, and vice versa: it is a matter of point of view, and the artist has all points of view because he has no point of view." It is a daring and at the same time supremely logical view of art; no one else pursued the logic as far as Joyce did.

Joyce pursued it even further in *Finnegans Wake* (1939). In *Ulysses* he had displayed his brilliant linguistic ingenuity in the use of puns and portmanteau words in order to indicate relationships and identities and simultaneities. In *Finnegans Wake* he develops this to the point where the work becomes a vast, complex, and multiple pun, each word helping to build up several threads of meaning, which interweave and combine in a highly complex manner in order to make the trivial events narrated in a popular Irish ballad contain everything— absolutely everything—that can be said about human history and psychology. It is an astonishing and in its way a highly comic work, but one feels that the law of diminishing returns begins to apply here, and wonders whether the years of careful explication (this is no exaggeration) required to bring out the different levels of meaning are really worth the effort. One feels that what Joyce was really after was one, final infinitely reverberating pun which would say in a single fantastically multiple word everything that can possibly be said about man from every point of view simultaneously.

Joyce founded no school; he developed an esthetic theory and practice as far as it would go; there was no further road that way. The inheritance of the great experimental age of the English novel —the age which produced Conrad, Lawrence, Woolf, and Joyce— seemed in the end to be little more than a greater degree of subtlety in handling character, a greater flexibility in dealing with time, a compression of expository techniques. Delicacy of psychological perception had been developing in many ways and was being encouraged in many different quarters. There were the very different examples of Proust and James; there were also the delicately wrought short stories of Katherine Mansfield (1890–1923). But a permanent increase in the sensibility of English novelists seemed a small legacy from the heroic age of experiment.

D. H. Lawrence also created a new kind of novel, though very different from Joyce's, and his legacy, too, proved less available than might have been expected. *Sons and Lovers* (1913) deals with ties connecting mother and son with an emotional precision and a clarity of compelling detail that derive in part from the autobiographical nature of the novel; it is a striking achievement, though technically it shows nothing new. The theme involves an exploration of family relationships of a sort in which Lawrence always retained a passionate interest. Ties of blood and calls from the outside, the different ways in which maternal and filial love can operate and the stultifying or liberating effects of such love, the conflicting claims of protectiveness and self-realization—these are characteristic Lawrentian preoccupations. In *Sons and Lovers* the background conflict is that between the hero's working-class father and his refined middle-class mother. The rift between the father, with his coarse vitality, and the mother, with her genteel pretensions, grows even wider, and the mother turns to her sons for the emotional fulfilment denied her by her husband. The resulting pressures on the hero are charted with brilliant particularization of incident and situation. The claims of sexual love then assert themselves and the tensions mount. The novel ends with the mother's death and a sort of liberation for the hero.

In *Sons and Lovers* the mother is treated with great tenderness in spite of Lawrence's clear acknowledgement of the effect of her love on her son's masculinity. But more and more the genteel culture for which the mother stood—as Lawrence's mother did—came to represent death for Lawrence. In much of his later work, especially in some of his short stories, the deadening restrictiveness of middle-class conventions are challenged by forces of liberation often represented by an outsider—a peasant, a gipsy, a working man, a primitive of some kind, someone freed by circumstance or personal effort from the distorting or mechanizing world that Lawrence saw in modern industrial society. Lawrence was not however, a social reformer, at least not in any normal sense. His main interest was always human relationships, the problem of reconciling full self-realization with true love of another.

The Rainbow (1915) and *Women in Love* (1920) show Lawrence really extending the scope of the novel, though not by means of any immediately obvious innovations in technique. In these novels (originally conceived as a single novel to be called *The Sisters*) Lawrence takes three generations and, probing both vertically and horizontally, explores with great power and subtlety all the basic human relationships—between man and his environment, the relationship between the generations, the relationship between man and woman, the relationship between instinct and intellect, and, above all, the proper basis for the marriage relationship as he conceived it. This sort of novel had nothing to do with the chronicle novel then becoming popular throughout Europe. It was rather, in F. R. Leavis's phrase, a "dramatic poem" in which a passionate imagination, working through a prose sometimes incantatory in its poetic movement, selected and presented the smallest incident for its suggestive and symbolic power. The high poetic symbolism goes side by side with an acute surface realism, a sharp sense of time and place, and brilliant topographical detail.

Lawrence drew so intently on his autobiography, on the passions and convictions that the circumstances of his own life had developed in him, that sometimes personal feeling spills over and the story is spoiled by an excess of emotion, by a spluttering outburst of hate or a murky, overwrought, highly throbbing symbolism that suggests hysteria rather than artistic control. This was the penalty he paid for his kind of insight, which was intimately bound up with his own needs and activities. *Aaron's Rod* (1922) draws heavily on Lawrence's own experience in Italy and elsewhere and on his relationship with his German-born wife. In spite of brilliant individual passages the novel fails to convince as a sustained work because the basic motivating forces which operate on the principal characters are projected directly from Lawrence's own life without being made convincing or even intelligible to the reader in terms of the novel. Problems of moral and political leadership as well as the question of which partner should dominate in marriage (arising directly out of his own stormy yet deeply committed relationship with his wife) were now much on his mind. They are seen, too, in *Kangaroo* (1923), set in Australia and containing moments of brilliant insight into Australian society and psychology together with passages transcribed straight out of his disputes with his wife, and in *The Plumed Serpent* (1926), set in Mexico, an unsatisfactory novel with its willed atavism and compulsive anti-feminism. With *Lady Chatterley's Lover* (1928) Lawrence returned to the central theme of his earlier novels—the possibilities of adequate human relationships in modern civilization —but in a story whose symbolic action is so crude and whose basic structure is so mechanical that it is a great pity that, because of its frankness about sex, it remains the only one of his novels that most people read.

Much of Lawrence's writing reveals his deep sense of English provincial life in which—in spite of all his wanderings abroad—his sensibility was really deeply rooted, much as George Eliot's was. This sense of intimacy with the English scene is found in *Women in Love* and, together with his deep understanding of provincial middle-class and working-class patterns of thought and feeling and the relation between them, in many of the short stories. *Fanny and Annie, Daughters of the Vicar, The Horse-Dealer's Daughter, The Fox, The Christening*, and *Tickets Please* are some of the stories that reveal this deep Englishness of Lawrence. Lawrence is less likely to fall into passages of murk or hysteria in his short stories because he has less space in which to maneuver and therefore works with more concentration. But the short stories are no less disturbing than the novels: Lawrence's aim is to project character and incident in such a way as force on the reader a radically new apprehension of the meaning of human personality and human relationships. And the assault is frontal, not through the slow and complex accumulation of moving moments whose total effect might in retrospect seem to be challenging. In this respect he is more like Blake than any other English writer. Like Blake, he is a great but flawed writer who can exasperate as well as enchant.

A determinedly modern novelist who nevertheless stands some-what apart from the great practitioners of the modern novel is Ford Madox Ford (1873–1939). Ford's masterpiece was his tetralogy begin-ning with *Some Do Not* (1924) and ending with *The Last Post* (1928), published in one volume in 1950 as *Parade's End*. The other of his numerous novels to survive is *The Good Soldier* (1915). Ford has always been a critic's novelist rather than a novel-reader's. The reason for this lies partly in the weight of theory which seems to underlie his craftsmanship. He was an avowed "impressionist" in fiction and his characteristic aim was a subtle and muted rendering of an "Affair," by which he meant a complex of psychological and social pressures, responses and inter-relationships without any artificially clear-cut ending but nevertheless constituting a distinct and even an inevitable pattern. He liked to filter the action of his novels through the consciousness of an observer, a narrator, or a central character in a way partly reminiscent of the "stream of consciousness" technique and partly suggestive of Joyce's concept of the "epiphany" or Virginia Woolf's view of reality as an evanescent personal intuition. He talked a lot about the theory of the novel, learning much from Flaubert and James and both teaching and learning from Conrad.

Few critics have been able to make up their minds whether *The Good Soldier* is a great novel or just a supremely accomplished one. It is a triumph of method, with everything beautifully "rendered" in characteristic Fordian manner. It shows, too—as *Parade's End* also shows—that acute diagnosis of the inter-relationship of personal and public maladies that was such an important part of Ford's view of the modern world, but it lacks vitality somehow. *Parade's End*, with its brilliant inter-relating of private maladjustment and public cata-strophe, gave a new dimension to war fiction. These are novels about civilization, with the moral projected through the carefully deployed "Affair." Yet to many readers Tietjens (the hero) himself seems—for all the quite extraordinary brilliance of the technique with which he is projected—a completely theoretical character, an English Tory gentleman that never was on sea or land, a totally incredible and pre-posterous person.

Ford is in his way a distinguished novelist, yet there is a certain lack of conviction in some significant aspects of his best novels. He is the last of the important English novelists for whom technique came first. It was this primacy of technique, in a much more than Jamesian sense, that leads to a certain bloodlessness, a certain domi-nance of manipulation over human insight, in much of his fiction. Some critics list him with Lawrence and Joyce as one of the great innovators in the English novel of the twentieth century. But he was not essentially an innovator, rather an inheritor from Flaubert and James whose vision never quite rose to the level of his technical equipment.

Wyndham Lewis (1884–1957) also stands apart from his contemporaries, but in a different way and for different reasons. He set himself firmly in opposition to the novelists' surrender to the flux of experience and the call of the unconscious—to everything, that is, represented by the work of Joyce and Lawrence and Virginia Woolf —and advocated "conceptual quality, hard exact outline, grand architectural proportion." Edwin Muir called him "the antidote to the other writers of his generation, the hair of the dog that bit Lawrence and Joyce." But he was not simply a negative force. Though his powerful satirical novel attacking the cultural values of the avant-garde of his time, *The Apes of God* (1930), had as the immediate object of its satire contemporary personalities and literary fashions, the very savagery of the attack gives the work an almost Rabelaisian energy that proclaims its own values. Lewis was also a painter with a painter's eye for striking colours and a sharp sense of planes, edges and shapes; these qualities can be seen in his prose, with its bright visualization and tightly controlled movement. Lewis's right-wing contempt for all kinds of "softness" in modern life and letters links him in some degree with T. E. Hulme, with Ezra Pound (with whom he edited the periodical *Blast* in 1914–15) and with T. S. Eliot (who wrote the introduction to the 1960 edition of Lewis's verse satire *One Way Song*, first published in 1933). Lewis's most striking achievement is *The Childermass* (1928) and its sequels *Monstre Gai* (1955) and *Malign Fiesta* (1955). *The Childermass* is set in a waste land outside heaven, where the 'emigrant mass' of humanity awaits examination by the Bailiff. The hallucinatory atmosphere, the grotesquerie, the power of the narrative, the ritualistic and symbolic overtones of meaning, together make this novel sequence something unique in modern English literature. Lewis's most important critical work is *Time and Western Man* (1927) where he attacks the "time philosophies" of Henri Bergson and of many modern novelists as well as the fashionable worship of the unconscious. In general it can be said that Lewis stood for intellect and order, for conscious control by the writer himself, against the Lawrentian dark gods and the Joycean attitude to both language and consciousness. But in his critical work and in his fiction he voiced a great protest against the dominant cultural trends of his time.

In the late 1930's, under the more immediate threat of war, fascism, and social catastrophe, a number of English novelists turned away from the new themes described above to write social diagnoses or moral or political fables. Though this was a temporary fashion, it marked a break in the steady advance of the themes and techniques which were handled so brilliantly in the 1920's and early 1930's, and it helped to ensure that when young novelists, emerging after the smoke of the Second World War had cleared away, set themselves to writing novels, they already saw the giants of the period between the two world wars as removed from them both in time and in literary interests.

Standing apart from the ephemeral social novelists of the 1930's but responding to the same environment George Orwell (pseudonym of Eric Blair, 1903–1950) refused to jump on any band-wagon and with an almost obsessive clarity documented the realities of social and political life of his time. His autobiographical works, *Down and Out in London and Paris* (1935), *The Road to Wigan Pier* (1937) and *Homage to Catalonia* (1951), cut through the sentimentalities of fashionable left-wing reporting by stressing uncomfortable truths ignored by left as well as by right. There is an almost masochistic honesty in his work, as indeed there was in his life, for he insisted on living with the ills he exposed before exposing them. The same temperament can be discerned in his novels. *Keep the Aspidistra Flying* (1936), written with the quietly colloquial precision of style that marks all his writing, is a grim story of attempted escape from the rat-race of striving for material success. The hero ends in a trap and enjoying it: the novel is almost an ironic reversal of H. G. Wells's *Mr. Polly*. *Animal Farm* (1945), by far his best-known work and his best, is a political allegory anchored in a savagely accurate command of the details of the way in which successful revolution betrays the idealists who worked for it. By making the characters animals, Orwell gives a Swiftian dimension to his merciless account of the progressive take-over by the sadistic, the corrupt and the self-interested. He was of course thinking of Russia under Stalin but he was also making a more universally applicable point concerning revolutions, the people who make them and the people who take control once they are made. Orwell's sense of the vulnerability of the left to betrayal by its opposite which uses all the left's own terms grew steadily. *1984* (1949), an anti-Utopia picturing in self-torturing detail the destruction of all human values in a future society which exists simply to stamp out individuality and to maintain the machinery for stamping it out in devilishly perfect condition, yet which uses the language of the conventional left, is a sick man's nightmare. The nightmare is all the more terrible because this society is shown as developing out of a socialist and not a fascist society. He felt that the larger totalitarian extinction of all humane feeling might arise from *anywhere*, and indeed was more likely to arise from the very quarter where it was least expected. Orwell was himself a Socialist, but at the same time he despised the platitudes and self-deceiving slogans and generalities of all existing parties on the left. This compulsive honesty is seen also in his essays, where again and again he cut through generations of accepted judgements or ways of thinking by relating his subject directly to the personally realized facts of human experience.

There were of course novelists writing after the war who had also written before the war. Some of these handled in their own way themes and attitudes developed in the great age of experiment and expansion. Ivy Compton-Burnett (born 1892) continued to produce her characteristic novels in which the elegant surface of the dialogue (and her novels are built up entirely out of dialogue) is in deliberate contrast to the nightmarish reality of mutual destructiveness and selfishness that is revealed by the plot—a variation of the modern theme of the inevitable disparity between social gesture and private reality. The titles of her novels suggest the restricted domestic atmosphere within which the counterpointing of horror and gentility is developed; *Brothers and Sisters* (1929), *Daughters and Sons* (1937), *Parents and Children* (1941), *Mother and Son* (1955), *A Father and his Fate* (1957). L. P. Hartley's (born 1895) *The Go-between* (1953), the story of a child's misinterpretations of the signs sent out by the adult world, is his most explicit of a number of novels—including *Eustace and Hilda* (1947)—which deal in one way or another with the interaction of public and private worlds and the difficulties or the impossibility of sharing sensibility. Elizabeth Bowen (born 1899), whose best work is probably still her novels written in the 1930's (notably *The House in Paris*, 1935, and *The Death of the Heart*, 1938) continued to explore the tragic implications of the incommunicability of individual sensibility within the context of the novel of manners. Henry Green (pseudonym of Henry Yorke, born 1905) continued his series of strangely visionary social novels, with such oddly characteristic titles as *Living* (1929), *Loving* (1945), *Back* (1946), and *Concluding* (1948), in which a curious and impressive quality of cultivated innocence evokes that momentary sense of revelation in looking at ordinary things that James Joyce had striven to record in what he called his "epiphanies." And Joyce Cary (1888–1957), who from the beginning had striven to inject an almost Dickensian robustness into the delicate sensitivities and evanescent moral subtleties of modern fiction, continued into the 1950's to write novels which attempted to restore some of the traditional energies of characterization and variety to the English novel. *The Horse's Mouth* (1944) is the most full-blooded of his novels.

As well as the great theme of the relation between loneliness and love, the novelists of the inter-war period had also explored another very modern problem—the relation between knowledge and value. The brilliant early novels of Aldous Huxley (1894–1963), written in the 1920's—notably *Point Counter Point* (1928)—explored with self-lacerating mockery the ways in which a scientific understanding of causation seemed to have destroyed all possibility of belief in ethical or other norms. If no man is a hero to his valet, it is also true that no man can be a hero to his psycho-analyst; knowledge of psychological process seems to destroy the possibilities of heroism. Further, if modern technological development succeeds in creating a world in which every individual will be so perfectly adapted to his environment that no moral effort will ever be necessary and no sense of loss or frustration will ever be felt, then the possibilities of moral effort will disappear and with them the traditional moral virtues and the traditional ways of judging personality. This theme, wittily explored in *Brave New World* (1932), is part of the larger theme of the possibilities of heroism in the modern world that has been steadily growing in importance in English fiction.

The earlier novels of Evelyn Waugh (1903–1967) brilliantly explored the possibilities of the hero as fool, reversing the traditional English view, as old at least as Henry Fielding, that ignorance of the wicked world, innocence, virtue and heroism go together. This produced an extremely sophisticated and cruelly ironical kind of comedy, which is seen in *Decline and Fall* (1928), *A Handful of Dust* (1934), and *Put Out More Flags* (1942). Waugh continued after the war—especially in the trilogy beginning with *Men at Arms* (1952)—to play variations on the same theme, but with an increasing romantic nostalgia for a lost gentlemanly code which, oddly enough, he identifies with English Catholicism (*Brideshead Revisited*, 1945). The worldly and the knowing prosper, while the innocent make fools of themselves and are victimized. The bitter awareness of the paradox of innocence (it goes back, in English literature, at least to Milton's *Paradise Lost*) is curiously distorted in some of Waugh's later novels by this association of gentlemanliness with religion. But he remains the wittiest novelist of his generation—not verbally witty like Wilde, but witty in his inventiveness of character and incident.

Roman Catholicism also comes into the novels of Graham Greene (born 1904), a tough writer of sophisticated adventure stories (which he calls "entertainments") who in his more serious novels explores the disparities between human decency and theological virtue, between moral intention and irreligious act, so as to shatter the complacency of those religious readers who had always thought that good intentions on the humanist level were somehow related to divinely approved human behavior. This is another kind of probing into the nature and possibilities of heroism, made explicitly in *The Power and the Glory* (1940), implicitly in *The Heart of the Matter* (1948), and with deliberate provocativeness in *The Quiet American* (1955). The psychological and moral tensions set up in Greene's novels are explored with both vigor and subtlety. His irony, which often seems to be at the expense of the values the novel seeks to promote, arises not only from his profound sense of paradox in human affairs but also from his refusal to be content with easy or obvious answers. His Catholicism is of a very personal kind.

With the establishment in Britain of the Welfare State and the emergence of a generation of younger writers into a world lacking the appalling social problems of the 1930's but lacking also the sense of something to fight for, the social novel, which just before the war had become more and more "committed" and even propagandist, takes over from the pre-war satirical novelists such as Huxley and Waugh the theme of the impossibility of heroism in the modern world. In a society of "I'm all right Jack," a society of *nouveaux riches* and complacent provinciality, the sensitive young man looks back to the promise of a world of high culture (symbolized by Oxford dons talking wittily over their port as the firelight flickers on the college silver), which never was and never will be his world, with a sense of having been cheated. We have seen the effect of this on the drama of the fifties; it can be seen to a lesser degree in the novel. We suddenly begin to see in English fiction the beer-drinking provincial student, schoolmaster or university lecturer, surrounded by a philistine affluent society which is utterly indifferent to the job he is doing and implicitly denies the value which such a job stands for, mocking his own cultural pretensions, deriding his own earlier symbols of high culture, and settling for the role of clown or cynic or shrugging compromiser. Kingsley Amis's *Lucky Jim* (1954) first dealt with this theme, and while there have not been a great many novels with exactly the same theme, the nature of the response to the relatively few that did employ it in the fifties and sixties made it clear that it was a theme which touched the new generation closely. This theme, and the attitude which led to its being developed, are related to the larger problem of the possibilities of heroism in modern life and art. The characteristic novelist's attitude here is not anger (the phrase "angry young men," once applied to such writers as John Osborne, Kingsley Amis and a number of others, was quite inaccurate) but partly self-pity, partly masochism, partly concern.

A more old-fashioned treatment of a modern theme is found in John Braine's *Room at the Top* (1957), less interesting as a novel than as a cultural symptom. The hero, anxious to rise above his working-class origins to become a flourishing member of the affluent society whose conspicuous consumption he cannot help envying, destroys the integrity of his personal relationships and corrupts himself in the process, in order to achieve his goal. (This is not an uncommon late Victorian theme.) But he is aware of his self-corruption, and is tortured by it at the same time as he profits by it: this is very far from Lucky Jim, the hero as clown. More interesting as a novel is Alan Sillitoe's *Saturday Night and Sunday Morning* (1958), which shares with many novels of the fifties an acuteness and a particularity of social observation that make us think sometimes of the social documentaries of the 1930's. But there is greater technical sophistication and greater subtlety here than in the social realism of the thirties. Sillitoe's novel has no trace of masochism or clowning: it is a shrewd, realistic, compassionate, intensely rendered account of a few days in the life of an industrial worker during which not only particular emotional and sexual complications are shown but the whole quality of living and feeling involved in this kind of life is presented, with no moral comment either implicit or explicit. His story, *The Loneliness of the Long-Distance Runner* (1959), concentrates on a particular case of social alienation, and here there are moral overtones. The hero, who comes from a desperately "under-privileged" working-class family, is in profound rebellion against all the forces of order and respectability which he hates and despises. But he has his own kind of integrity, manifested when he wilfully loses the race which the governor of the prison in which he is confined wants him to win and for winning which the governor has promised him lenient treatment. The world, he believes, is divided into those in power and those who have to accept domination by those in power. To pretend that there is not a natural antagonism between these two (as the governor implicitly pretends) is, in the hero's view, dishonest. So he deliberately loses the race he could win and which the governor wants him to win. "I say, I won't budge, I won't go for that last hundred yards, if I have to sit down cross-legged on the grass and have the governor and his chinless wonders pick me up and carry me there, which is against their rules so you can bet they'd never do it. . . . No, I'll show him what honesty means if it's the last thing I do, though I'm sure he'll never understand because if he and all them like him did it'd mean they'd be on my side which is impossible." There is perhaps a touch of sentimentality in this projection of the integrity of the outcast, but Sillitoe's treatment of the theme shows a sensitivity to that need for re-defining moral standards which became ever more clamant in the fifties and sixties.

Anthony Powell's (born 1905) elaborate novel sequence, *The Music of Time*, begun before the war and continued into the 1950's, presents a very English kind of ironic social comedy whose ingenuity and sublety derive from a pattern of human inter-relationships belonging fundamentally to an older world—much older than that of Amis and Sillitoe, and even older than that of Virginia Woolf. Sophisticated social comedy written for readers on the inside, as it were, is no new tradition in English fiction, though this is not to deny Powell's brilliant originality. On the inside in a very different way is C. P. Snow (born 1905), whose novels about patterns of power and policy-making in universities and ministries involve human relationships in a much blunter manner: Snow's intelligence is both institutional and humane, and he tries to compensate for lack of delicacy of response to the human situation by a determined compassion which is engaging if not always artistically viable. He is perhaps the Galsworthy of the mid-century.

Social satire of a kind quite different from that of either Powell or Amis is found in the earlier work of Angus Wilson (born 1913). Like Graham Greene, he probes the vulnerabilities of the liberal humanist position, but not from any theological standpoint; rather, from the standpoint of a shrewd ironic wisdom that knows too much about people to be fooled. With irony goes understanding, especially in his later novels (e.g., *The Middle Age of Mrs. Eliot*, 1958), and there is clearly a tension in much of Wilson's work between his satirical aim and his psychological awareness. Understanding brings compassion, in spite of the author (the paradox is most clearly seen, perhaps, in *Hemlock and After*, 1952). If certain kinds of knowledge makes heroism impossible, it becomes for the same reason impossible to believe in villainy. Wilson has learned from Dickens as well as from nineteenth-century French novelists; yet his sensibility is sharply and unmistakeably mid-twentieth-century. His is the irony of the man who has lived through the passionate hopes and fears of the 1930's to arrive after the war at a mood in which disillusion is only prevented by lowering one's sights and moderating one's expect-ations of one's fellow men; at the same time, one's ironic awareness of the disparity between the ideal and reality and of the pathetic contradictions in which the human personality can get involved is unabated, and curiosity about the human animal in the contempor-ary world livelier than ever.

So one might have said of Wilson, looking at his work at the end of the 1950s. But the publication of *The Old Men at the Zoo* in 1961 brought a quite new aspect of Wilson to view. On the surface a political satire, with a four-fold movement suggestive of the four books of *Gulliver's Travels* (and there are other parallels with Swift), this novel is set in the early 1970's during a period which sees at least one war and one liberation. The old men of the title are the administrators of the London Zoo, but clearly the management of animals is meant to be seen as illuminating the management of people—indeed, the link between animals and people is made in all sorts of ways. All the anxieties, psychological and social as well as political, of Wilson's age, are projected in this novel, whose plot has complex symbolic reverberations which are intended to reach out and illuminate the moral, psychological and socio-political problems of our time. It is an interesting experiment in what for Wilson is a new form, and it is not managed as skilfully as some of his earlier novels and short stories. But it shows a gifted novelist in mid-career still developing.

A more violent and more deeply disturbed novelist is William Golding (born 1911), whose concern with evil is not civilized, as it is in Angus Wilson, by irony and by chastened expectation, but remains at a level of almost mythic intensity. *Lord of the Flies* (1954) is probably the most powerful English novel written since the war. It is the story, told with meticulous realism and at the same time with a visionary clarity that shows up everything as symbolic, of a group of small children wrecked on a desert island degenerating into a society based on fear, violence and tyranny. Most of Golding's later novels show this same visionary intensity and show him also groping for a form that will contain this kind of tortured moral vision. None of them is wholly satisfactory, but they are all of immense interest and show a remarkable talent. Golding is a man haunted by his own sense of human inadequacy who, disregarding all novelistic traditions available to him, is conducting a bold search for the kind of novel which will contain his own vision of man.

Golding is a symbolic novelist, and sometimes has trouble with his symbols. The novelist today, partly as a result of the immense amount of critical work done on the novel, much of it pointing to the symbolic implications of particular aspects of particular works, is more self-conscious about symbols than he has ever been. Iris Murdoch (born 1919), a professional philosopher, has produced a group of novels whose intellectual brilliance and structural ingenuity are often marred by a fussy symbolic pattern which suggests that she is searching for ways of embodying her philosophical insights in an adequate fictional form. Some have seen her novels as too neatly diagrammatic, as, in the words of one critic, "a rigged geometry of token events and straw-characterization." Yet if there is this geometrical element in her novels, it is also true that there is a deliberate incompleteness in their resolution. "Since reality is incomplete, art must not be too much afraid of incompleteness," she wrote in 1961. "Literature must always represent a battle between real people and images; and what is required now is a much stronger and more complex conception of the former." The French philosopher and novelist Jean-Paul Sartre (on whom she wrote a book in 1953) was an influence here, and she was influenced by Sartre's view that "at the heart of the esthetic imperative we discern the moral imperative." Miss Murdoch is at bottom a moralist. The philosophical problem of how we know other minds—a problem which has been of especial concern to English philosophers—she tries to solve by acting out encounters in her novels. The novel is concerned, she maintained, with "people's treatment of each other," and the involved patterns of confrontation into which she throws her characters are designed to explore problems of knowledge of self and others, sincerity, love, and the making sense of the chaos of daily feelings and happenings. From her first novel *Under the Net* (1954) to her most ambitious so far, *The Red and the Green* (1965), she has presented the reader with a rich and even bizarre surface of action in which a certain intellectual gaiety only partly disguises the underlying moral seriousness. The most fantastic of her novels, *A Severed Head* (1961), is constructed like a set of Chinese boxes and we never really get to the centre. To some extent this is true of all her work. But Miss Murdoch's inventiveness and her sharp intelligence combine to make even the most preposterous of her novels a fruitful challenge to the reader who is willing to ponder what he reads. The novels in themselves do not, indeed, carry the whole burden of meaning: to some extent they are pointers leading the alert reader to reflection and surprised reconsideration. She seeks the reader's co-operation in a far different sense from the way it is sought by Joyce in *Finnegans Wake*—not in construing but in reflecting. These are a philosopher's novels.

The highly individual voice of Muriel Spark reminds us once again of the difficulties (and the uselessness) of classification when dealing with the novels of the 1950's and 1960's. Her disturbingly cold wit is combined with a kind of inspired lunacy both in the projection of character and in the choice of physical detail. *The Ballad of Peckham Rye* (1960) shows very clearly Miss Spark's combination of aloof wit and bizarre imagination. *The Prime of Miss Jean Brodie* (1961) finely illustrates her uncanny brilliance in the selection of the right detail: this is a school story with a difference, about a group of girls at an Edinburgh school and their brilliant, frustrated and hence (surprisingly) fascist teacher. *The Mandelbaum Gate* (1965), by far her most ambitious novel so far, is set in contemporary Jerusalem and makes significant symbolic capital out of Arab-Israeli division. Complexly organized and presented with immense sophistication this novel by its very nature makes the largest claims. The wit, the sheer cleverness, the adroitness in handling the narrative, are undeniable. The human vision, in spite of religious overtones, is less fully realized. It remains to be seen whether Miss Spark will be able to bring her remarkable intellectual apparatus and her personal religious beliefs fully to the service of the projection and illumination of human reality.

The fact that the great experiments and advances of the earlier years of the century, associated with such names as Joseph Conrad, James Joyce and D. H. Lawrence, have not been continued in the last twenty years and more sometimes gives rise to lugubrious prophecies of the imminent death of the novel in England. But no art form can be continuously in a state of experiment. The present age, so far as technique is concerned, is one of consolidation; so far as subject matter is concerned, we find in part the continuation of the themes of the thirties (loneliness and love; the possibilities of heroism; knowledge and value); in part the puzzled confrontation of the latest phase of English social history; in part the seeking after ways of implementing a new moral vision—and only the last of these suggests any degree of technical experiment. But any such summing up as this is bound to be inadequate. It ignores not only the vast number of competent conventional novels written largely or wholly for entertainment, but also many remarkable individual novelists who may not illustrate a trend or who are so far removed from any trend that they are to be mentioned only as oddities, anachronisms or lonely geniuses exempt from all generalizations. In the last group is a much older novelist, John Cowper Powys, who, though born in 1872, went on writing right into the late 1950's. His masterpiece, A *Glastonbury Romance*, appeared in 1933, but it belonged to its period no more than it does to the present. Powys's massive mythic imagination is positively clairvoyant in its effects of combined magic, myth and realism. His concern is to get back to the archetypal, and he uses antique symbols (for example, the Grail myth) with a conviction and a sense of personal winning-through to wisdom that is positively overpowering. Some tribute must be paid to him in a survey of this kind. He reminds us that the life of art cannot always be charted in neat patterns.

"Outsiders" are not confined to members of the older generation continuing to write after the war. Perhaps the most determined outsider among the novelists of the 1950's is Lawrence Durrell (born

1912), the four novels of whose *Alexandria Quartet* (1957–1960), tell-ing over from several different points of view a complicated story of love, politics and perversion set in the exotic atmosphere of pre-war and war-time Alexandria, are unusual both for the deliberate virtu-osity of their technique and the exhibitionist waywardness of their subject matter. Sensuality, cruelty and intrigue in a society of sweet-smelling decadence provide an unexpected kind of color to the modern English novel, and even if the recurring flashes of would-be gnomic wisdom, the reiterated epigrams which turn out to have much less meaning than they first appear to have, give an air of bogus profundity to Durrell's Alexandrian novels, they were welcomed for the original and even exciting way in which they enlivened the English literary scene. Except in the drama, the English literary scene in the late sixties, with its conscientious and intelligent but rarely adventurous practitioners, is in need of enlivening. But it is a mistake to close a history of literature with a generalization. Liter-ature goes on, and only a rash man would care to predict what lies in wait even in the immediate future.

Index

Aaron's Rod, 1166
Abbot, The, 835
Abercrombie, Lascelles, 1124
"Abou ben Adhem," 933
About the House, 1137
Absalom and Achitophel, 563–67, 568–69
"Abt Vogler," 1005
Acts and Monuments, 462, 476
Acts of Andrew and Matthew, 18
Adam Bede, 1067–69
"Adam's Curse," 1128
"Adam's Dream," 1142
Adams, Thomas, 499
Addison, Joseph, 459, 503, 554, 555, 593–
    98, 607, 632, 636, 638, 662, 700,
    786, 788, 791, 807, 859, 1095, 1098
Address of the Soul to the Body, 6
"Address to the Deil," 819, 822–23
"Address to the Unco Guid," 825
Admirable Crichton, The, 1108
"Adonais," 912
Advancement of Learning, The, 392, 485,
    486–87
Adventures of Harry Richmond, The,
    1073
Adventures of Ulysses, The, 937
Ælfric, 28–29, 34, 41, 47
Aeneid, 52, 91, 94, 158, 518, 520, 574,
    584
Aeschylus, 45, 672
Aesop, 510, 573
"After the Funeral," 1144
"Afterwards," 1036
Age of Reason, The, 803
"Ah! Sunflower," 868
Aidan, 6
Ainsworth, W. H., 1085
Akenside, Mark, 663–64, 787, 857
Alaham, 203
Alamanni, Luigi, 155
Alarm against Usurers, 478
"Alastor," 907, 908
Albery, James, 1102
Albion's England, 346
Alchemist, The, 316, 317, 318, 544
Alcuin, 29

Aldhelm, 29
Alexander, Sir William, 530
"Alexander's Feast," 578–79
Alexandria Quartet, 1178
Alfred, king of Wessex, 24–27, 37, 44
Alice's Adventures in Wonderland, 1086
"Alley, The," 665
All Fools, 324
All for Love, 287, 552, 581
"All for the Cause," 1025
All's Well that Ends Well, 288, 291, 292
Alma, or The Progress of the Mind, 646
Almond for a Parrot, An, 464
Alphonsus, King of Aragon, 230
Alton Locke, 1084
Amazing Marriage, The, 1073
Amelia, 726–27
America, 871
American Discourses, 982
Amis, Kingsley, 1113, 1172, 1174
"Among Schoolchildren," 1128
Amoretti, 177–78
Anacreon, 378
Analogy of Religion, The, 770
Anatomy of Absurdity, The, 478
Anatomy of Abuses, The, 478
Anatomy of Melancholy, The, 494, 734
"Anatomy of the World, An," 366
Ancient and Modern Scots Songs, 814
"Ancient Mariner, The," 877, 878, 889,
    892–98
Ancren Riwle, 48
"And do they so?" 375
"Andrea del Sarto," 1005
Andreas, 6, 17, 18
Andrewes, Lancelot, 497–98
Androcles and the Lion, 1107
Angel in the House, The, 1025–26
Anglo-Norman Chronicle, The, 112
Anglo-Saxon Chronicle, The, 21, 22, 27,
    32, 47
Animadversions upon the Remonstrant's
    Defence, 417, 418
Animal Farm, 911, 1169
Anna St. Ives, 803
Annals of the Parish, 854

1179

Colloquy (Ælfric), 29
Colman, George. 1097
Colonel Jack, 600
"Come live with me and be my love,"
    378
Comedy of Errors, The, 248
Comical Revenge, The, 541
Common Sense, 803
"Common Singing-Men in Cathedral
    Churches, The," 502
Commonweal, The, 1025
Communist Manifesto, 985
"Complaint of Henry Duke of Bucking-
    ham," 162
Complaint of Rosamund, The, 347
Complaint of Scotland, The, 506, 532
*Complaint or Night Thoughts, The; see
    Night Thoughts*
"Complaint to the King," 515
Complaints, 175, 176
Complaynt of Schir David Lyndsay, The,
    521
Compleat Angler, The, 500
Compton-Burnett, Ivy, 1170
Comus, 234, 403, 404, 405–12
"Concerning Geffray Teste Noire," 1022–
    23
Concluding, 1170
Conduct of the Allies, The, 607
Confessio Amantis, 122, 297
Confessions of a Young Man, 1090
Confessions of an English Opium-Eater,
    940
Confessions of Harry Lorrequer, The,
    1085
Confidential Clerk, The, 1111–12
Congreve, William, 540, 541, 542, 544,
    545–47, 548, 552, 578, 589, 623,
    637, 701, 1094, 1096
Coningsby, 1084
Conquest, Robert, 1148
Conquest of Granada, The, 550, 551,
    581
Conrad, Joseph, 1155–57, 1164, 1167,
    1177
Conscious Lovers, The, 1096
*Considerations touching the likeliest
    means to remove Hirelings out of
    the Church,* 430
Consolation of Philosophy, The, 25–26
*Conspiracy and Tragedy of Charles,
    Duke of Byron,* 324
Constable, Henry, 195
Contes moraux, 738
"Convergence of the Twain, The," 1034
Cook's Tale, The, 112
"Cooper's Hill," 555–56, 625, 654
Copernicus, 147

Copland, Robert, 135
Corbet, Richard, 383
"Corinna's Going a-Maying," 378
Coriolanus, 164, 280, 294–96
"Corn rigs are bonie," 819
Corneille, Pierre, 550
"Coronet for his Mistress Philosophy,
    A," 360
Corsair, The, 925
"Cotter's Saturday Night, The," 816,
    820, 824
Count of Narbonne, The, 1101
Countess Cathleen, The, 1109
Country Wife, The, 539, 542–44
Court of Sapience, The, 131–32
Courtier, The, 465, 472
Coverdale, Miles, 468–70
Cowley, Abraham, 360, 384, 557, 578,
    589, 596–97, 787, 788, 789, 791,
    936
Cowper, William, 663, 692–97, 857, 889,
    891, 936
Coxe, William, 876
Crabbe, George, 694, 697–99, 1124, 1125
Craft of Deyng, The, 532
Craig, Alexander, 204
Cranford, 1083–84
Cranmer, Thomas, 469, 471
Crashaw, Richard, 357, 371–73, 1026
Critic, The, 1089
Critical Review, The, 729, 796
Crockett, S. R., 854
Croke, Richard, 145
Croker, John W., 948
Crotchet Castle, 943
Crown of Wild Olive, The, 969, 971
Crowne, John, 549, 551, 701
Crucible, The, 1119
Crusaders, The, 1102
"Cry of the Children, The," 1008
Cuckoo and the Nightingale, The, 128
Culex, 175
Culture and Anarchy, 973–77
Culture and Environment, 973
Cumberland, Richard, 1096–97
Cummings, E. E., 1140
Cura Pastoralis, 24, 25
Curl, Edmund, 642
Curse of Kehama, The, 903
Cursor Mundi, 43
Cyder, 659
Cymbeline, 294, 296, 298–99
Cynewulf, 16–18, 19
Cynthia, 200
Cynthia's Revels, 314
"Cyriack, this three year's day these
    eyes," 434

Is He Popenjoy? 1083
Isabella; or the Pot of Basil, 917
Isle of Man, The, 585
It is Never Too Late to Mend, 1083
"It was upon a Lammas night," 819
Italian, The, 742
Ivanhoe, 835

Jack of Newbury, 481
James I, king of Scotland, 96, 507–9, 524
James V, king of Scotland, 521, 524, 526
James VI, king of Scotland (later James I of England), 527, 528, 529
James, G. P. R., 1085
James, Henry, 1074, 1088, 1153, 1154, 1158, 1164, 1167, 1168
James, William, 1153
Jane Eyre, 1065
Jane Shore, 1099
Jean de Meun, 82–83, 90, 135
Jefferies, Richard, 1087
Jeffrey, Francis, 830
"Jenny," 1020
"Jenny kissed me," 934
Jenyns, Soame, 768, 769
Jephson, Robert, 1101
Jerusalem, 871
Jew of Malta, The, 244, 255
"Jinny the Just," 646
Jocasta, 161, 223, 224
"John come kiss me now," 78, 525
John Inglesant, 1087
John Milton's Defence of Himself against Alexander More, 429
John of Trevisa, 36–37
Johnson, James, 814, 827
Johnson, Lionel, 1041, 1126
Johnson, Samuel, 250, 360, 384, 555, 556, 558, 561, 580, 589, 596, 598, 604, 654, 655, 656, 662, 675, 677, 678, 679, 684–89, 695, 697, 698, 739, 769, 770, 772, 774–94, 795, 796, 797, 807, 856, 859, 867, 941, 948, 956, 1060, 1099, 1157
"Jolly Beggars, The," 826
Jonathan Wild, 726, 729
Jones, Henry A., 1102
Jones, Inigo, 310, 321
Jonson, Ben, 121, 193, 309–22, 323, 325, 326, 339, 340, 350, 351, 357, 359, 377, 379, 380, 381, 382, 383, 384, 407, 530, 540–41, 543, 546, 553, 556, 561, 578, 581, 638, 1096
Jorrocks' Jaunts and Jollities, 1085
Joscelyn, John, 475
Joseph Andrews, 713–18, 723

Joseph of Arimathie, 59
Journal (Wesley), 662
Journal of a Tour to the Hebrides, 795
Journal of a Voyage to Lisbon, 727
Journal of the Plague Year, 600
Journal to Stella, 611
"Journey of the Magi," 1135
Journey to London, 547
Joyce, James, 49, 167, 246, 376, 479, 1153, 1154, 1161–64, 1167, 1168, 1170, 1176, 1177
Jubilate Agno, 690
Juda, Leo, 468
Judas, 78
Jude the Obscure, 1080–82
Judith, 6, 19
Julia Benson, 739
Julia de Roubigné, 739
"Julian and Maddalo," 905
Juliana, 6, 17
Julie, ou la nouvelle Héloise, 738
Julius Caesar, 265, 266–67, 282, 283, 294, 295
Jungle Book, The, 1091
Junius, 804
Junius Manuscript, 6, 14
Juno and the Paycock, 1111
Justice, 1109
"Justing and Debait up at the Drum," 527
Juvenal, 311, 319, 349, 569

Kangaroo, 1166
Kant, Immanuel, 940, 942
Keats, John, 193, 323, 577, 741, 853, 857, 860, 861, 878, 893, 912, 913–22, 933, 934, 997, 998, 1017, 1021, 1042, 1131
Keep the Aspidistra Flying, 1169
Kenelm Chillingly, 1085
Kenilworth, 835
Kennedy, Walter, 516
Kidnapped, 1089
"Kilmeny," 830
Kim, 1091
King, Henry, 384
King and No King, A, 337
King Hart, 518
King Horn, 63–64
King Johan, 219
King John, 250, 263–64
King Lear, 223, 258, 276–80, 281, 283, 287, 288, 296, 299, 785
Kingis Quair, The, 96, 507–9
Kinglake, A. W., 1086
"King's Birthday in Edinburgh, The," 816
King's Tragedy, The, 1020

Overbury, Sir Thomas, 501–2
Ovid, 52, 55, 91, 161, 206, 254, 307, 347, 360, 460, 465, 574, 581, 582, 633, 729
Ovid's Banquet of Sense, 360
Owen, Wilfred, 1124, 1125, 1136
Owl and the Nightingale, The, 45, 70
Oxford, R. Harley, Earl of, 599, 636
Oxford and Cambridge Magazine, The, 1018
"Ozymandias," 913

Paine, Thomas, 801, 802–3, 850
Painter, William, 206, 291, 465
"Palace of Art, The," 999
Palace of Pleasure, The, 206, 291, 465
"Palamon and Arcite," 575
Paley, William, 774
Palgrave, F. T., 993, 1122
Palice of Honour, The, 517
Pamela, 602, 701–5, 711, 712, 724, 1152
Pandion and Amphigenia, 701
Pandosto, or The Triumph of Time, 299, 480, 481
Paracelsus, 1002
Parade's End, 1167
Paradise Lost, 80, 183, 187, 236, 266, 304, 392, 395, 407, 412, 431, 434–49, 450, 453, 456, 577, 597, 791, 946, 1134, 1171
Paradise of Dainty Devices, The, 149, 159, 161
Paradise Regained, 392, 431, 446, 449–54
Paradiso, 94, 119
Pardoner's Tale, The, 69, 110, 115–16, 462
Parents and Children, 1170
Paris, Matthew, 38
Parisina, 926
Parker, Matthew, Archbishop, 474, 475
Parliament of Fowls, The, 96–99, 178
Parnell, Thomas, 607
Parson's Prologue and Tale, The, 110, 119–20
Parthenissa, 701
Parthenophe and Parthenophil, 195
Parish Register, The, 698
Passage to India, A, 1158, 1159
Passionate Pilgrim, The, 203
Passionate Shepherd, The, 351
"Passionate Shepherd to his Love, The," 205
"Passions, The," 672–73
Past and Present, 957
Pastime of Pleasure, The, 133–35
Paston Letters, 459
Pastoral Care, 24, 25

Pastorals (Philips), 649
Pastorals (Pope), 621, 647
Pastorals (Virgil), 574
"Past ruined Ilion Helen lies," 932
Pater, Walter, 973, 986–90
Patience, 46, 84
Patience (Gilbert and Sullivan), 1103
Patmore, Coventry, 1025–26
Patriot for Me, A, 1115
Pauline, 1002, 1006
"Paying Calls," 1035, 1038
Peacock, Thomas Love, 914, 942–43
Pearl, 46, 83–84
"Peblis to the Play," 524
Pecock, Reginald, 459
Peel, Sir Robert, 951
Peele, George, 203, 227, 228–29, 350
Pelham, 1084
Pendennis, 1061–62, 1063
Pennywheep, 1146
Pepys, Samuel, 537, 557, 588–89
Percy, Thomas, Bishop, 88, 814, 831, 859
Percy, William, 204
Peregrine Pickle, 728–29
Peri Bathous: or, the Art of sinking in Poetry, 640
Pericles, 296–98, 299, 302
Persian Eclogues, 671
Persuasion, 745, 761–65
Pervigilium Veneris, 988
"Peter Bell," 881, 884
Peter Grimes, 699
Peter Plymley's Letters, 944
"Peterloo Massacre," 906
Peter's Letters to his Kinsfolk, 853
Petite Palace of Pettie his Pleasures, 465
"Petition of the Gray Horse, Auld Dunbar," 515
Petrarch, 90, 114, 150, 151, 152, 157, 167, 171, 178, 195, 417, 530
Petronius, 315, 729
Pettie, George, 465
Phaedrus, 182
Pharsalia, 91
Philaster, 335–37
Philip Sparrow, 137–38
Philips, Ambrose, 639, 641, 648
Philips, John, 658–59
Phillis, 195
"Philomela," 1009
Philosophical Enquiry into the Origin of our Ideas of the Sublime and the Beautiful, A, 798
Philosophical Transactions, 556
Philostratus, 358
Phineas Finn, 1083
Phoenissae, 161

Young, Thomas, 391, 395, 416
"Young Gentleman of the University, A,"
  502
"Young Raw Preacher, A," 502

Ywain, ou le Chevalier au Lion, 57
Ywain and Gawain, 57, 59

Zwingli, Ulrich, 468